exploring
MOTION GRAPHICS

Rebecca Gallagher
Andrea Moore Paldy

THOMSON
DELMAR LEARNING™

Australia Canada Mexico Singapore Spain United Kingdom United States

THOMSON
DELMAR LEARNING

Exploring Motion Graphics

Rebecca Gallagher and Andrea Moore Paldy

Vice President, Technology and Trades ABU:
David Garza

Director of Learning Solutions:
Sandy Clark

Senior Acquisitions Editor:
James Gish

Managing Editor:
Larry Main

Product Manager:
Jaimie Weiss

Marketing Director:
Deborah S. Yarnell

Marketing Manager:
Penelope Crosby

Production Director:
Patty Stephan

Production Manager:
Andrew Crouth

Content Project Manager:
Benj Gleeksman

Editorial Assistant:
Niamh Matthews

Cover Design:
Chris Navetta

DVD Author:
Mark Ezovski

Printed in Canada
1 2 3 4 5 TC 08 07 06

For more information contact Thomson Delmar Learning
Executive Woods
5 Maxwell Drive, PO Box 8007,
Clifton Park, NY 12065-8007
Or find us on the World Wide Web at
www.delmarlearning.com

Library of Congress Cataloging-in-Publication Data:
Gallagher, Rebecca.
Exploring motion graphics / Rebecca Gallagher and Andrea Moore-Paldy.
p. cm.
Includes index.
ISBN 1-4180-1421-4
1. Computer animation. I. Moore-Paldy, Andrea. II. Title.
TR897.7.G33 2006
006.6'96--dc22
2006021183

ISBN: 1-4180-1421-4

NOTICE TO THE READER

table of contents

preface

INTENDED AUDIENCE

Exploring Motion Graphics is for anyone who is interested in the design process of motion graphics. Whether you are beginning your studies in motion graphics, or you have considerable experience using software for motion graphics creation, this book provides a comprehensive breakdown of graphic design components and discusses how to use them to create effective and communicative motion graphics. *Exploring Motion Graphics* also presents a historical context within which to study emerging design styles while also developing your own signature look.

This book is intended for students in two- and four-year college and graduate level programs. In particular, it is geared toward students in the areas of digital media and visual communications, who are familiar with design but not with moving text, and toward film students, who are familiar with the moving image but who have no background in design. This book can also benefit the professional designer or filmmaker whose specialty is not motion graphics, but who wants an introduction to the field.

EMERGING TRENDS

As advanced technologies for mobile interactive devices are introduced in the United States, designers will be allowed more freedoms with the development and execution of motion graphics created specifically for that medium. Better technologies mean not only more stylish consumer electronics with bigger screens and more colors but also faster downloads, more memory, and increased media-sharing capabilities. Many countries around the world, specifically in Asia, already use advanced technology, allowing users to interact with each other in new and different ways. For example, some phones use the caller's favorite song as the ring tone on the phone of the person receiving the call. Motion graphics could soon be implemented in this manner as well; a user creates a personalized motion graphic greeting that plays on the receiver's phone when the call is made.

BACKGROUND OF THIS TEXT

As chairs of the Digital Media and Digital Filmmaking and Multimedia programs at the Katharine Gibbs School in New York, we were both met with the challenge of finding appropriate textbooks to teach our students about the aesthetics of motion graphics. We found that there were not a lot of books about motion graphics, and in particular, there were not a lot of books about the *design* of motion graphics. Most books focused on software acquisition, and we wanted a book that focused more on the creative process. It was then that we decided to write this book.

Not only do traditional media such as movies and television continue to have a strong presence in our daily lives but the Internet along with the growing trend of digital convergence (which we discuss in Chapter 12, Interactive Interfaces) is indicative of the growing importance of digital media in our society. With individuals more dependent on portable devices such as PDAs and cell phones to download information from the Internet and to "stay connected," and films, TV shows, and video games as popular as ever, there is a growing need for people to design for these media. *Exploring Motion Graphics* addresses that need by looking at and analyzing design in these particular industries.

Information in the book was gathered from many sources including books on design and film history, as well as articles from trade magazines and periodicals that stay abreast of current trends, research papers, and, of course, one-on-one interviews with design professionals in various fields.

Because our focus is on design aesthetics, we have written a book that is non-software specific. The design concepts covered in this book are applicable, regardless of the software used in the classroom. We have chosen to include a few tutorials that walk students through processes in specific software as more advanced exercise options. Even so, we assume that students have little or no prior background in design or motion graphics.

TEXTBOOK ORGANIZATION

The recurring theme throughout the book is how style dictates how one uses the basic elements of design. The exploration of style and its representation of theme and identity leads to the discussion of how to achieve the premiere task of motion graphics, communicating a specific message to an intended audience.

We have divided the book into two parts: the first section gives an overview and history of motion graphics design, while also defining the elements of motion graphics design and discussing their roles in determining style. Case studies in chapters three, four, five, and six highlight successfully applied design and production techniques discussed in each chapter. The second half of the book focuses on the different media—film and video, television, web, DVDs, video games, and interactive devices—in which motion graphics appear. We organized the book in this way so that readers could first grasp an understanding of the design fundamentals before seeing how they are applied by professionals in specific media.

Section 1: Design Methodologies for Motion Graphics

The concept of motion graphics and its importance in modern society is defined in Chapter 1. Since the goal of motion graphics is to communicate, this chapter discusses the ways in which they communicate—information, branding, education, entertainment—as well as the media through which they communicate—television, movies, digital billboards, websites, video games, and handheld devices. Finally, the chapter addresses why we as a society respond to motion graphics.

In order to break out of the box and experiment with technique for optimal results, one must understand the history of the medium. Chapter 2 links pivotal events in the development of moving pictures, special effects and animation, and the emergence of title design.

Chapter 3 looks at the process of pre-production in motion graphics design. From the first meetings with clients, to brainstorming sessions, to rough sketches and storyboards, this chapter focuses on the importance of getting to know the audience and incorporating the client's identity into a communicative motion graphics design.

One of the fundamentals of motion graphics is typography. Chapter 4 covers the basics of type, offering a fundamental understanding of how we read and use type for communication. This will be reinforced by examples of typical mistakes that beginners make.

Color is an integral element of motion graphics. Chapter 5 will introduce the fundamentals of color with discussions on theory and usage.

Each designer develops his or her own style over time. Chapter 6 introduces beginners to the theory and practice of elements of style, particularly how they apply to motion graphics. It also explores how sound can be incorporated to achieve a unique sense of style.

Section 2: Motion Graphics Applied to Different Fields

Chapters 7 through 11 provide practical examples of the design theories introduced in previous chapters. Each chapter will be devoted to a particular medium with discussions on the specific technical considerations for that medium.

Chapter 7 focuses on how motion graphics are used in film and video. Interviews with filmmaker Henry Ferrini and title designer Jeffrey Sproul discuss the audience and technical considerations that factor into their choices when designing film and video titles.

The focus of Chapter 8 is how motion graphics have been used in television. Interviews with motion graphics designers Roger White and Bill Byrne discuss the audience and technical considerations that factor into their design choices, as well as how working with clients influences their work.

Chapter 9 focuses on motion graphics for the World Wide Web. Interviews with art directors Carlos Pisco and Carlos Lema highlight the process of collaborating with a design team as well as working around the technical challenges of designing for the Internet.

Chapter 10 focuses on the role of motion graphics in DVD interface design. Interviews with Mark Ezovski, Darton Simons, and Nick Balda discuss the technical and navigation considerations that come into play when designing for this relatively new medium.

Chapter 11 focuses on motion graphics in video game design. Interviews with game designers Luis Cataldi and Prithvi Virasinghe discuss the importance of catering to the audience, while balancing their wants against technical constraints when creating motion graphics for video games.

Chapter 12 focuses on motion graphics in interactive interface design, while exploring the trend in media convergence. Interviews with designers Robert Hall and Jung Yi Sin highlight the importance of innovation and solid design in creating devices that audiences can easily navigate.

Key terms are boldface throughout the book, and we provide readers with a glossary of definitions at the end of the book for convenient reference.

Exploring Motion Graphics also comes with a DVD that features work from the professionals highlighted in Chapters 7 through 12 along with their on-camera interviews. In addition, samples of student work demonstrate successful use of motion graphics.

SPECIAL FEATURES

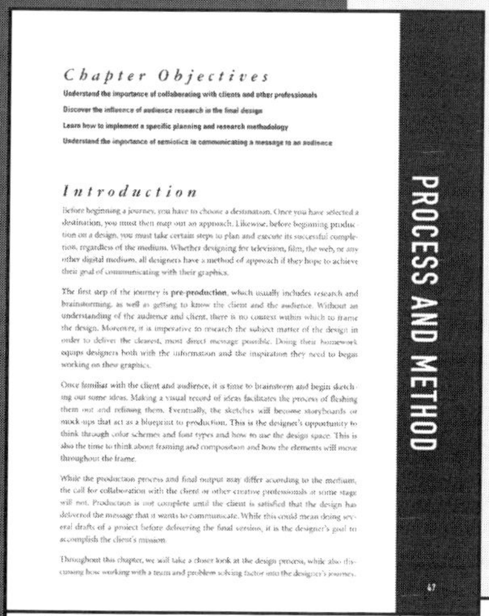

▶ Objectives

Learning objectives start off each chapter. They describe the competencies the reader should achieve upon understanding the chapter material.

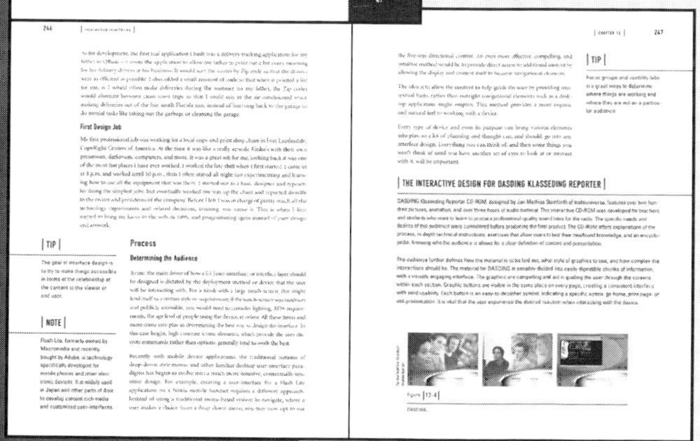

▶ Tips and Sidebars

Tips provide special hints, practical techniques, and information to the reader. Sidebars offer additional information on specific topics.

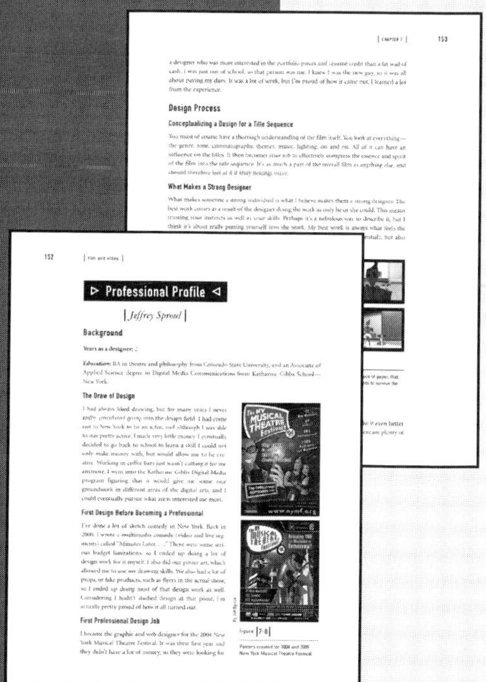

▶ Professional Profiles

These profiles, located throughout the book, allow the reader to learn from the example of successful designers in the field.

▶ Case Studies

Case studies follow several motion graphics projects focusing on specific design issues related to those covered in the chapter.

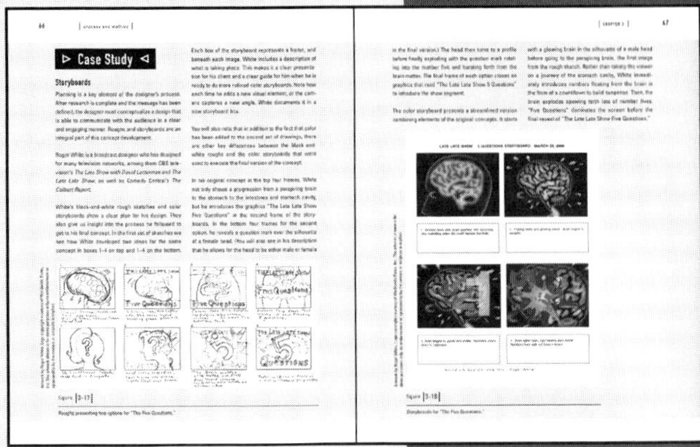

▶ Review Questions and Exercises

Review Questions and Exercises are located at the end of each chapter and allow readers to assess their understanding of the chapter. Exercises are intended to reinforce chapter material through practical application.

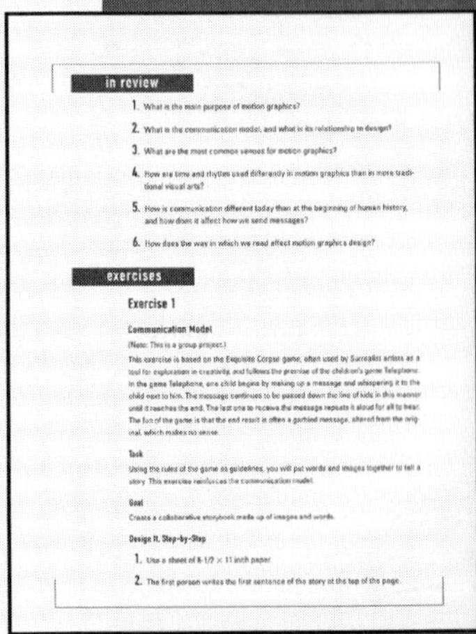

in review

1. What is the main purpose of motion graphics?
2. What is the communication model, and what is its relationship to design?
3. What are the most common venues for motion graphics?
4. How are time and rhythm used differently in motion graphics than in more traditional visual arts?
5. How is communication different today than at the beginning of human history, and how does it affect how we send messages?
6. How does the way in which we read affect motion graphics design?

exercises

Exercise 1

Communication Model

(Note: This is a group project.)

This exercise is based on the Exquisite Corpse game, often used by Surrealist artists as a tool for exploration in creativity, and follows the premise of the children's game Telephone. In the game Telephone, one child begins by making up a message and whispering it to the child next to him. The message continues to be passed down the line of kids in this manner until it reaches the end. The last one to receive the message repeats it aloud for all to hear. The fun of the game is that the end result is often a garbled message, altered from the original, which makes no sense.

Task

Using the rules of the game as guidelines, you will put words and images together to tell a story. This exercise reinforces the communication model.

Goal

Create a collaborative storybook made up of images and words.

Design It, Step-by-Step

1. Use a sheet of 8-1/2 × 11 inch paper.
2. The first person writes the first sentence of the story at the top of the page.

E.RESOURCE

This guide on CD was developed to assist instructors in planning and implementing their instructional programs. It includes sample syllabi for using this book in either an eleven- or fifteen-week semester. It also provides chapter review questions and answers, exercises, PowerPoint slides highlighting the main topics, and additional instructor resources.

Order # 1-4180-1422-2

ABOUT THE AUTHORS

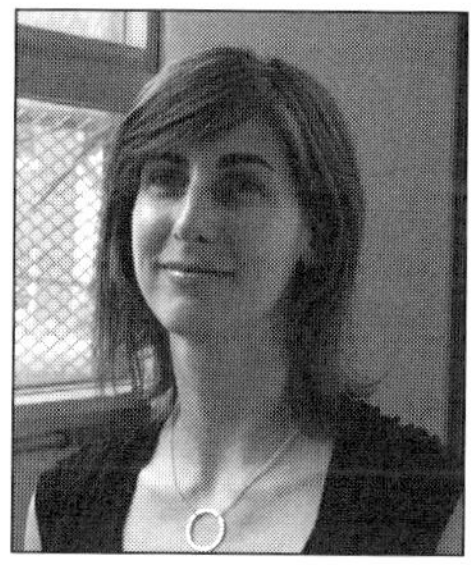

Rebecca Gallagher is currently an adjunct instructor at Touro College in New York City and a freelance web designer. As former Chair of Digital Media Communications at Katharine Gibbs School, she was an integral part of curriculum development for the design department and taught classes on the principles and theories of motion graphics and typography. Ms. Gallagher has also worked in the graphic design and web design divisions of such world-renowned companies as TV Guide Online and Associated Press. She received her MFA in Fine Art Photography from the State University of New York at New Paltz.

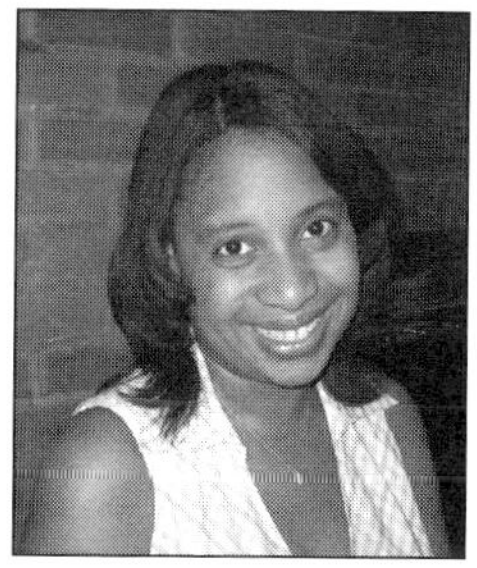

Andrea Moore Paldy is a screenwriter who has had articles published in the St. Petersburg Times and Flavour Magazine. Formerly Chair of the Digital Filmmaking and Multimedia program at the Katharine Gibbs School, she continues to teach classes in screenwriting, directing, and career development at Gibbs. She is also part of the teaching staff of NBC/Universal's "Bravo on the Set," a digital filmmaking boot camp for high school students across the country. She received a BA cum laude in French and English history and literature from Harvard University and an MFA in Film from Columbia University.

ACKNOWLEDGMENTS

There are a number of people without whom this book would not have been possible.

Our greatest thanks go to the designers who not only share their work in the pages of this book but also their wisdom: Henry Ferrini, Jeffrey Sproul, Roger White, Bill Byrne, Carlos Pisco, Carlos Lema, Mark Ezovski, Darton Simons, Nick Balda, Luis Cataldi, Prithvi Virasinghe, Robert Hall, and Jung Yi Sin.

Thank you also to all of the designers and artists who submitted their work, making this text a beautifully illustrated guide for anyone who wants to learn motion graphics design.

We would like to thank Nancy Miller at the University of Pennsylvania Archives, Dr. Loren Winters and Ed McBride at the North Carolina School of Science and Mathematics, Ippolita Passigli from the Artists Rights Society, Roni Lubliner at Universal Studios, Megan Forbes at The Museum of Moving Images, and Barbara Swift at The Weather Channel for their assistance in helping us acquire images that helped illuminate the text.

Special thanks go to Mark for his unending support and inspiration. – R.G.

Special thanks to Dave for his partnership and wisdom, Mommy and Daddy for cheering and believing, and Benjamin for his impeccable timing! – A.M.P.

And thank you to everyone at Thomson who helped guide us through our first book: Jim Gish, Jaimie Weiss, Nicole Stagg, Benj Gleeksman, and Niamh Matthews.

Thomson Delmar Learning and the authors would also like to thank the following reviewers for their valuable suggestions and expertise:

MARC HESS, Multimedia Department, The College of Westchester, White Plains, New York

JEFF MARTINI, Digital Film & Multimedia Department, Katharine Gibbs School, New York, New York

THOR METZINGER, Visual Effects & Motion Graphics, Digital Media Production, The Art Institute of Colorado, Denver, Colorado

LINDA RZOSKA, Center for New Media, Kalamazoo Valley Community College, Kalamazoo, Michigan

—Rebecca Gallagher and Andrea Moore Paldy
2006

QUESTIONS AND FEEDBACK

Thomson Delmar Learning and the authors welcome your questions and feedback. If you have suggestions that you think others would benefit from, please let us know, and we will try to include them in the next edition.

To send us your questions and/or feedback, you can contact the publisher at:
Thomson Delmar Learning
Executive Woods
5 Maxwell Drive
Clifton Park, NY 12065
Attn: Media Arts & Design Team
800-998-7498

Or the authors at:
rebecca@fatlittlebird.com

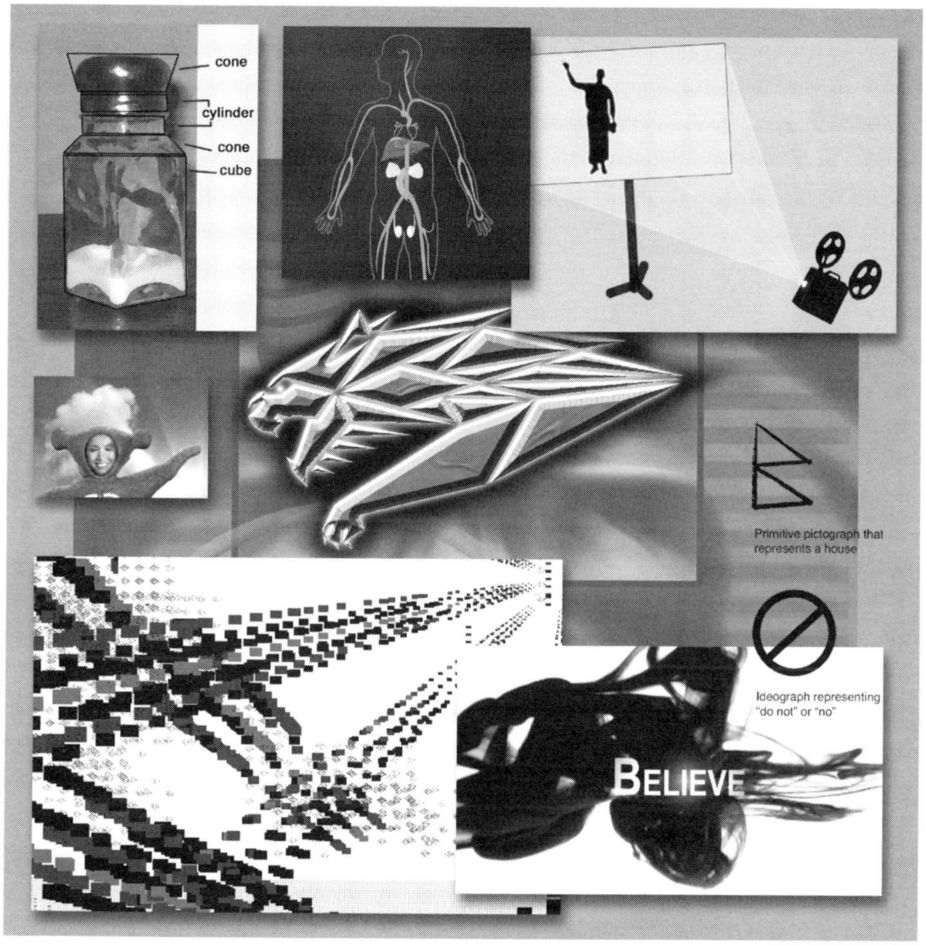
cone
cylinder
cone
cube
Primitive pictograph that represents a house
Ideograph representing "do not" or "no"
BELIEVE

SECTION 1

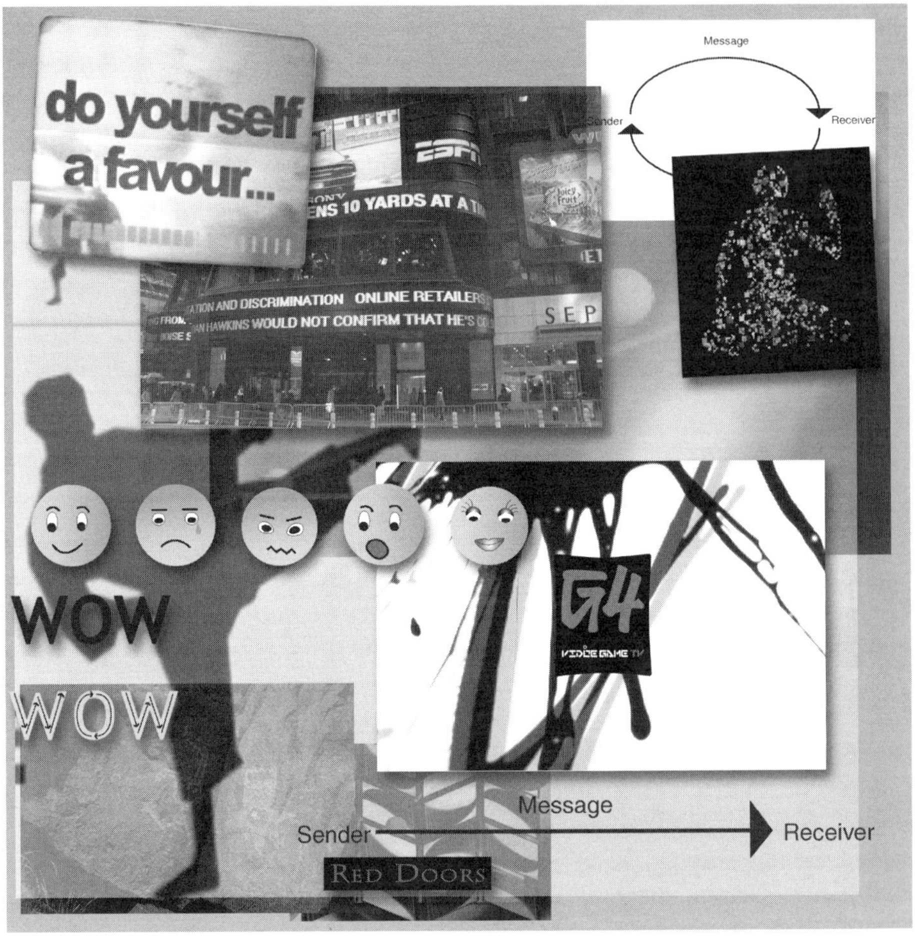

Message
Sender
Receiver
do yourself
a favour...
ENS 10 YARDS AT A
ATION AND DISCRIMINATION ONLINE RETAILERS
HAWKINS WOULD NOT CONFIRM THAT HE'S
SEP
WOW
WOW
G4
Message
Sender
Receiver
RED DOORS

CHAPTER

1

THE ART OF MOTION GRAPHICS

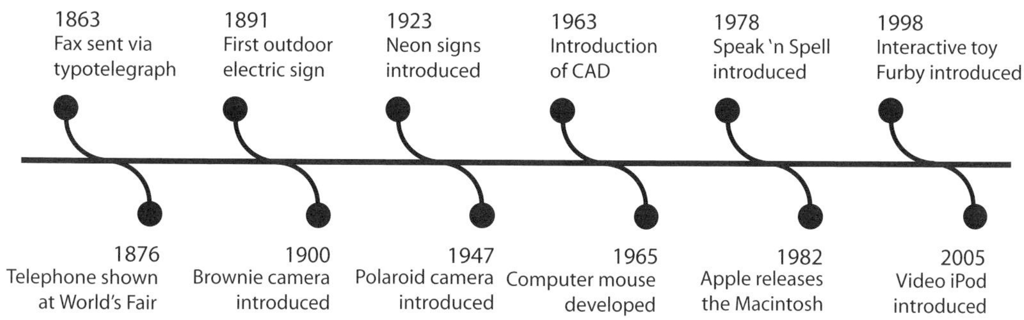

Chapter Objectives

Learn the key role of motion graphics and why they are a particularly effective form of communication

Explore what makes motion graphics stand apart from more traditional art forms

Recognize the role of the audience in determining the design of motion graphics

Understand the nature of human communications, how we process information, and how this knowledge can be used to design successful, communicative motion graphics

Introduction

The art of motion graphics is as dynamic as its name implies. It gives life to inanimate words and images, encoding them with a message for an intended audience. Motion graphics are text, graphics, or a combination of both that move in time and space and use rhythm and movement to communicate.

Motion graphics, whether imparting important information or simply entertaining us, crop up in all aspects of daily life—on home entertainment systems, computers, communication devices, informational kiosks or billboards, and office systems. They are used on television and in movies to introduce or help define the story. Over time, motion graphics have evolved to become a particularly sophisticated form of communication and entertainment that is almost always present.

COMMUNICATION MODEL

Human beings communicate at various levels, ranging from a person's inner dialogue to interaction with another person to interaction within a group to, ultimately, mass communication among a society.

Communication has two basic components: a sender and a receiver. The sender is the one with the initial message. The intent of the sender is to get it to the receiver, who will hear or see the message and successfully interpret the content. This model applies to both animate and inanimate objects. People communicate with words, animals with sounds, and computers with bytes, but in each of these scenarios a sender and a receiver are required. This sender-to-receiver scenario is a basic **communication model**.

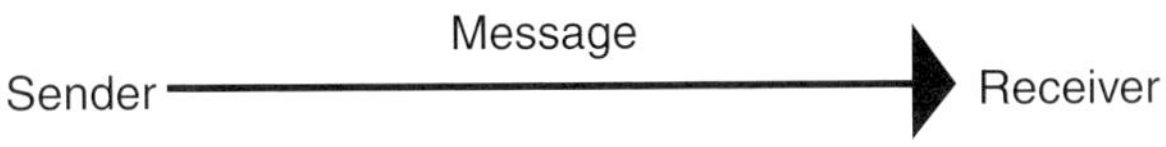

figure |1-1|

A communication model with a message from sender to receiver.

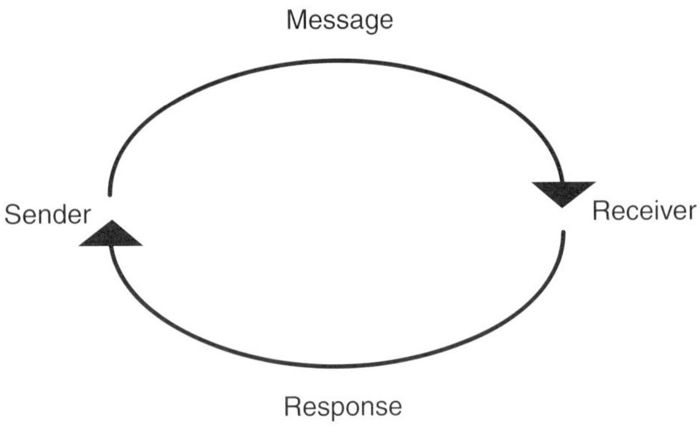

figure |1-2|

A communication model with a message from sender to receiver, followed by a response that is sent back to the sender.

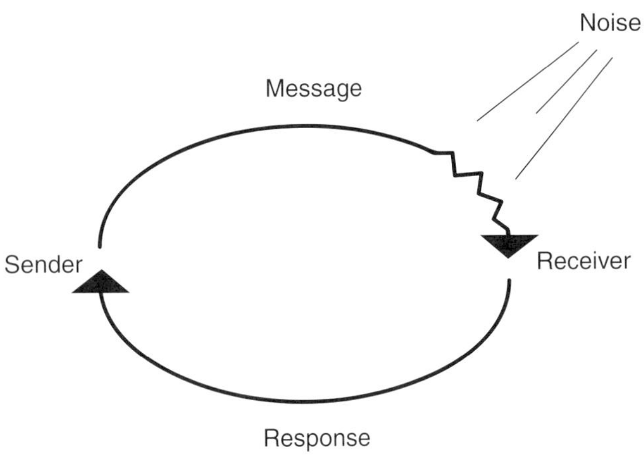

figure |1-3|

A communication model with a message from sender to receiver, garbled by noise, followed by a response that is sent back to the sender.

Rarely is a message sent and received without a response to the initial message. You might get a response from another person or from an interactive device, such as a server on the World Wide Web. A response from the receiver complicates the communication model and creates a circular mode of communication. One example of this is a conversation between two people. One person starts the conversation with the initial message, and the other hears it, determines the appropriate response, then sends back that response to the sender. This goes around as such until either the sender or the receiver decides to end the conversation.

The communication model can also be applied to television shows like *American Idol* where the viewer is asked to call in to vote for his favorite singer. How the audience votes determines who will appear on the show the following week. This example follows the basic communication model with sender, receiver, message, and response.

This model can now be expanded to include interference, or **noise**. We all experience interruptions throughout the day that impede our sending or receiving a message. An example of interference can be seen in the *American Idol* scenario. If the viewer sits down to watch the show but misses one of the performances because the telephone rings, then part of the message is missed and the response is limited to only a portion of the information sent.

There could also be interference because of a lack of understanding about what the sender is trying to communicate in the message. Both types of interference, or noise, can be roadblocks to a successful design.

WHY COMMUNICATE WITH MOTION GRAPHICS?

Because time is valuable we have become a society of multitaskers, engaging in several activities at once. Movies, television, video games, and digital billboards, in particular, reflect this fast-paced aspect of society in the way in which they are edited, jumping from one image to the next.

This style of using rapidly moving images and type, with quick transitions and layered with textures interwoven with popular music, is a very popular design format. We live in a world of multiplicities and learn to put our energies into many projects. Often this does not allow for us to take in 100 percent of the information from each task or project. Motion graphics appeal to our sense of urgency by giving us the most relevant information, delivered in snippets, allowing us to absorb the information we think important and saving us from processing superfluous text and visuals in the message.

By Jan Mathias Steinforth (mateuniverse)

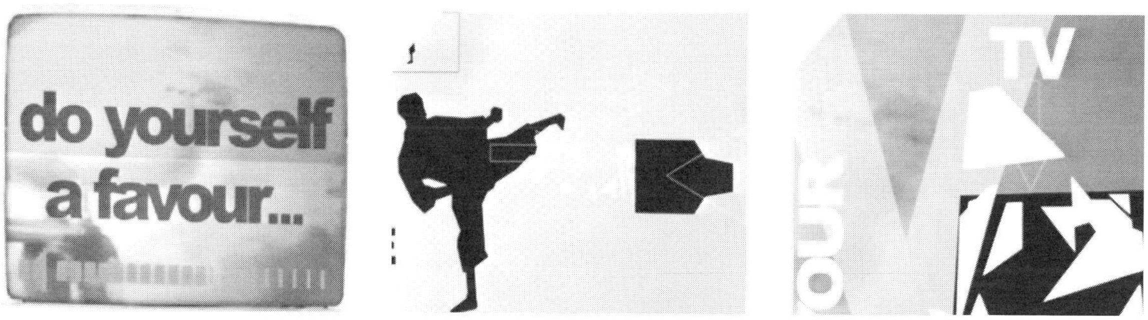

figure |1-4|

Smash TV is a video commentary that uses layered images that consist of type, graphics, and silhouettes and is an example of the style made popular by early music videos.

Information

In today's age we can get up-to-the-minute information at the touch of a button. With the use of motion graphics, we are able to get a large amount of information into a small space in a shorter period of time. Take the morning news as an example. We can listen to the anchorperson while reading about the traffic conditions as they scroll across the bottom of the television screen. The scrolling text and animated icons are a very simple use of motion graphics to convey information.

Branding

Although the formal concept of branding is a modern idea, the practice of branding, or creating a visual association that ties a product and company together, has been around since the first communities developed. Clans, tribes, or other communities branded themselves with designs that identified their origin. These designs were used on coats of arms or on pieces of clothing. Today motion graphics are used regularly in advertising in all media—television, the World Wide Web, handheld devices, and digital billboards—to enhance the visibility of a product. The use of motion graphics in these scenarios is to either sell a new product or reinforce the brand of an existing product.

EARLY BRANDING CAMPAIGNS

Branding, as a formal concept, began in the late nineteenth century. In 1898 the newly formed National Biscuit Company, now known as Nabisco, introduced the Uneeda biscuit. The National Biscuit Company had a good deal of competition, so it developed a consumer product that would stand out. During this time biscuits (crackers) were not packaged, but sold out of large barrels. The consumer would simply fill his own brown paper bag with whatever was in stock. The young company initiated a marketing campaign that capitalized on the product name, Uneeda biscuit, suggesting that "you need a biscuit." They reinforced this brand in the stores by marking the shipping barrels carrying the crackers with a branding iron specifying the name.

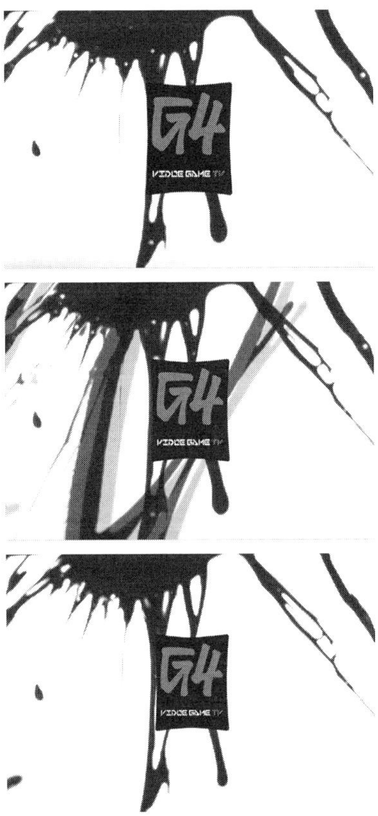

By Dorian J. Compo/Designer/www.rekonstrukt.com

figure | 1-5 |

Motion graphics are used as a tool for branding, as seen in this G4 video game TV promo.

One example of branding that is used to reinforce a product name probably happens every time you turn on your cell phone. When you turn it on, a motion graphic with the cell phone brand logo fills the screen or marches across it and reinforces the brand identity of the phone in your hand. Television stations have also begun using motion graphics to reinforce the station's identity. The clearest example of this on television is the station logo that appears on screen as a simple way to remind the audience what station it is watching.

The idea of displaying the TV station logo was taken from radio stations, required by the Federal Communications Commission (FCC) to announce their call signs during broadcast to inform their listeners—or remind them—what station they were listening to. On old television sets the channel number often appeared on the dial or LCD screen, so viewers always knew which channel they were tuned to. On televisions now, the channel number is not visible anywhere, and with so many channels to watch, it is easy to forget which station you are tuned to. Television stations needed a way to reinforce their identity with the viewers. The station logo you see placed in the lower quadrant of the screen is referred to as a **bug**.

The larger, full-screen version of the bug, known as the **station ID**, is shown between shows and during commercial breaks. A station ID serves the same purpose as a bug but commands our undivided attention. Whereas the bug takes up a small amount of screen space and is displayed in the background while the larger picture—the television show—plays, the station ID takes up the whole screen and acts as a commercial to sell the station as a product, or commodity.

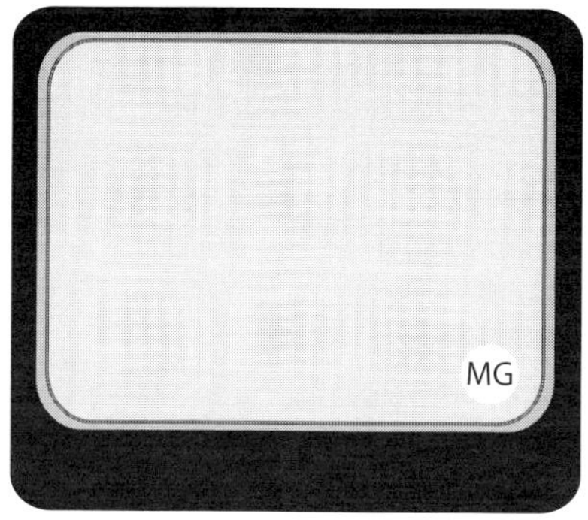

figure 1-6

A bug is a television station logo placed in a lower quadrant of the screen, used to remind viewers what channel they are currently watching.

Education

Motion graphics incorporate words, color, graphics, and sound and are a wonderful tool for teaching new information. They are often directed to a younger audience and reflect the aesthetic children have developed over years of playing video games, watching television and movies, and using computers. Shows like the long-running *Sesame Street* series or *Blues Clues* have demonstrated the successful implementation of motion graphics for educational purposes, used to teach children to read, compute, and visualize problems. This technique is also used in the ever-expanding field of interactive toys and books. Not only does this approach work for younger audiences,

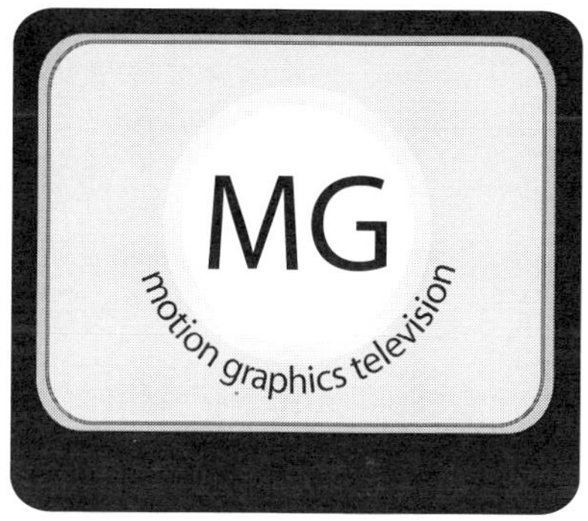

figure 1-7

A station ID is the television station logo used in a motion graphic to advertise the station.

By Sharon Gorman, Production Director; Kevin Mackett, Project Lead and Lead Programmer; Clint Forrester, Lead Designer and Animator; Jason Robinson, Programmer; Ben Kirby, Assistant Art Designer; Thomas Lon Owen, Ph.D., Content Expert/Instructional Designer/ Narrator, Professor of Biological Sciences, Northern Arizona University

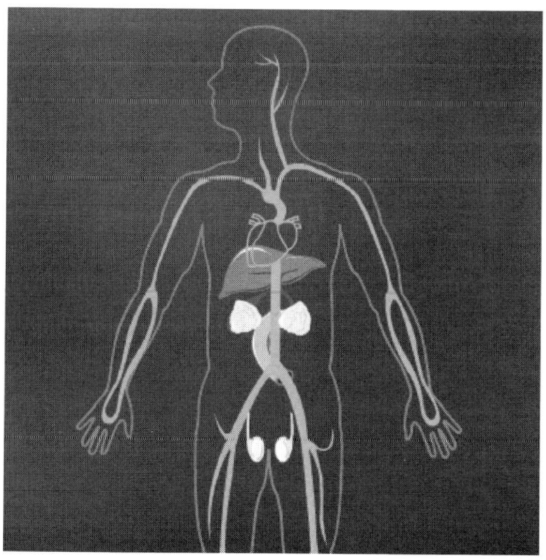

figure 1-8

Motion graphics are a wonderful tool for educational instruction as seen in this example, Bio 320 Lipo Protein Transport interactive learning module.

but it has been successfully used to teach adults as well. The technique of incorporating elements of motion graphics is often used to teach adults a second language, pairing visuals that represent the word, the typed word on the screen, and a voice-over saying the word. Using an approach that is visually familiar makes it easier to absorb the information. Motion graphics are also particularly helpful in teaching science and anatomy, taking examples out of the static realm and allowing the viewer to see movements of the body and organs, which provides for a fuller understanding of the material.

Entertainment

One of the first things you are likely to do when setting up a new digital device is to select your screen graphics. The display you choose reflects your personality and taste. We are a visual society and respond to what we see around us, so we spend a good deal of time seeking out just the right graphics, colors, and pictures that both appeal to us and reflect who we are. Often the most popular screensavers and desktops reflect current popular cultural trends. When *The Matrix*, a movie about humans trapped in a world run by machines, was released in 1998, it was an immediate phenomenon that captured people's imaginations about the world of science fiction. With the particular application of stop-action, which creates the illusion of freezing time, the movie introduced elements that had not before been seen in film. One of the most memorable scenes is when a bullet, and the air around it, freezes in mid-air. The release of the movie spurred the development of designs that reflected the art of the film and could be applied to other digital devices, such as a screensaver with green colored bits of computer data rapidly scrolling vertically down the screen, mimicking the visuals of the movie.

Small animated graphics attached to e-mails or web posts, called **emoticons**, are another creative use of motion graphics for the sake of entertainment. Emoticons are the two- or three-dimensional faces that are embedded in an e-mail or web post, often used to support the message's overall mood, or emotion.

figure |1-9|

Emoticons are used to support the overall mood or emotion of an e-mail, post, or instant message.

If you send an e-mail to a friend and write something sarcastic, you may choose an emoticon that winks to express that you are joking. **Avatars**, also called **blinkies**, are colorful, blinking messages and are another entertainment motion graphic. They are used as personal signatures on e-mails and on chat boards. While emoticons are used to support the emotion of the message, blinkies are used to reinforce personal style.

MOTION GRAPHICS MEDIA

Motion graphics are used with devices we handle every day, such as cell phones and computers. They have become an integrated visual element of our daily lives, so much so that we do not recognize them as anything new or out of the ordinary. This can make it that much more difficult for advertisers to get the attention of the consumer. Throughout history, the seller has always looked for new, exciting ways to command the attention of consumers and to get them to buy a product or service. As competition grew every business had to look for ways to increase its livelihood. To do this then, as they all do now, advertisers had to come up with innovative ways to convince consumers that they absolutely needed the products advertised.

Neon signs are an early form of motion graphics used to entice consumers. These designs used colorful tubes of light to create informational graphics. As the individual tubes of light turned on and off, they created an illusion of movement. We can refer to these early, pre-computer age designs as analog motion graphics since they were dependent on the physical form of the tubes and not on the binary data of computers, nor were they confined to the screen of a device.

Television

Television is an excellent medium for motion graphics, which appear in commercials, station IDs, television shows, news broadcasts, and sports events. They may be used as a branding tool in a commercial or station ID, as an informational tool on the news or sports broadcast, or purely for entertainment as on a TV show. The pressure to squeeze in as much paid advertising as possible during commercial breaks has given birth to a form of graphics called the **snype**.

The snype is the graphic that appears near the bottom of your television screen to inform you what show is coming up next. Because stations do not have enough time to advertise their own shows during commercial breaks, and because viewers are prone to change channels during commercials, they use another show's airtime to list coming attractions, in the hopes of enticing viewers to stay tuned.

A contemporary trend for many television commercials, especially pharmaceutical products, is to use motion graphics to display the product name, information, and tagline. We also see consistent use of motion graphics on the evening news and news magazine shows to introduce each separate news segment within the larger program. Finally, we must not forget the opening title sequences to our favorite TV shows.

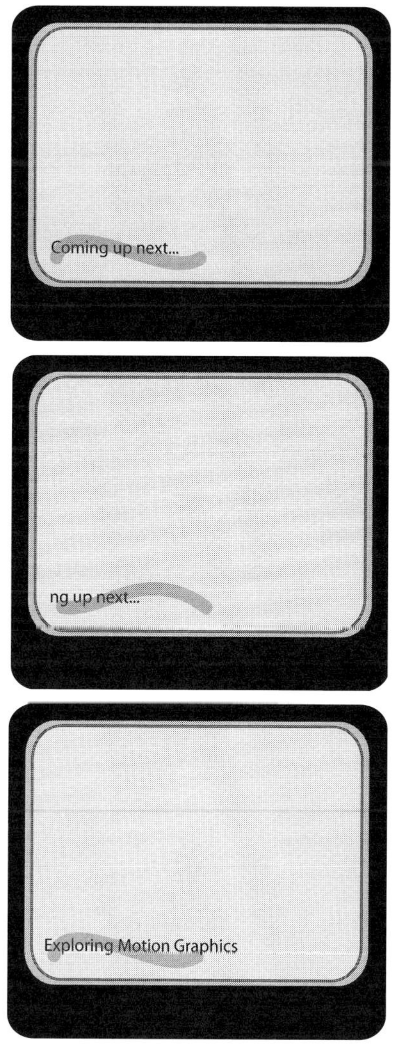

figure | 1-10 |

A snype uses graphics and type to advertise another show that will air later that night. It appears in the lower part of the television screen while another show is on the air.

Movies

Similar to the opening titles of our favorite TV shows are the opening titles to movies. Though not all films necessarily begin with a full title sequence, at the very least they begin with the studio's production logo—another example of motion graphics—and the title of the film.

Whether simple or elaborate, the opening title sequence builds anticipation and excitement, preparing the audience for the world it is about to enter. The graphics for the opening of *The Matrix* are reminiscent of the DOS computer interface and are consistent with the movie's theme. They therefore are successful at setting the mood for the film.

Just as movie titles build anticipation, movie trailers are also designed to entice an audience and do so with the assistance of motion graphics. The graphics for the trailer of Steven Spielberg's *War of the Worlds* adaptation give the audience a taste of what the movie will be. A sense of fear and foreboding is communicated as each block letter is revealed, accompanied by the clang of metal. Eventually, they spell out the words "WAR OF THE WORLDS."

Other movies may use a title sequence to introduce the characters of the story. This is done by overlaying credits with an introductory scene from the movie, showing a character, or characters, in action, and engaging with the storyline.

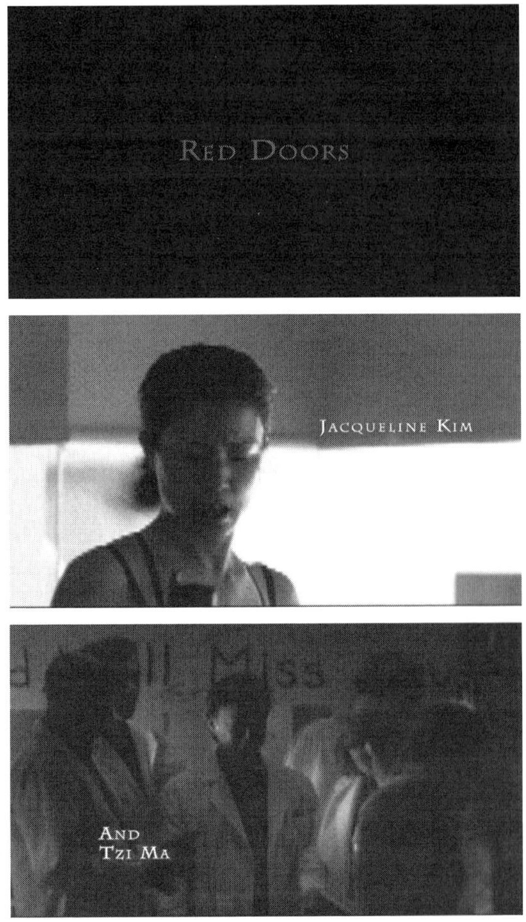

Courtesy Red Doors

figure |1-11|

This title sequence introduces the main character while relaying information with the credits.

Digital Billboards

With the emergence of digital billboards, advertisements can be shown on buildings, at stadiums, on tops of taxi cabs, at subway entrances, and even in subway systems so that they can catch their audience as people go to work or run errands.

Another advantage to digital billboard systems is, of course, the fact that content can be changed quickly and easily, ensuring that a large variety of material can be displayed and that breaking news can be added as needed. Some digital billboards use color and some are made only of lights on a black background. The advantage, nevertheless, is that they can be located almost anywhere, both to advertise and to provide important information. A prominent example is the messages that appear on the video screens at sporting events.

Websites

The interactive quality of the Internet makes websites stand out from the other media in which motion graphics appear. We can actually respond to the graphics on a website by clicking on a link, instigating a reaction from the website that opens a new page. Graphics on a website often serve as a guide to the user by visually mapping out different methods of interaction.

Advertisements have also found their way to the web. Web advertisements, using type, graphics, photographs, and sound, often try to lure the user from one site to the next. While surfing the Internet, pop-up advertisements, additional windows that open in the browser, continue to open in an attempt to convince the buyer to purchase a new product.

Video Games

Video games are played on computers, television consoles, cell phones, and personal gaming devices. Each device has different design concerns, with consideration given not only to the motion graphics but also how the player will interact with the game device. Game graphics support the narrative with graphic visuals designed to enhance the background environment and as text that informs the player of the directions and any additional storyline information.

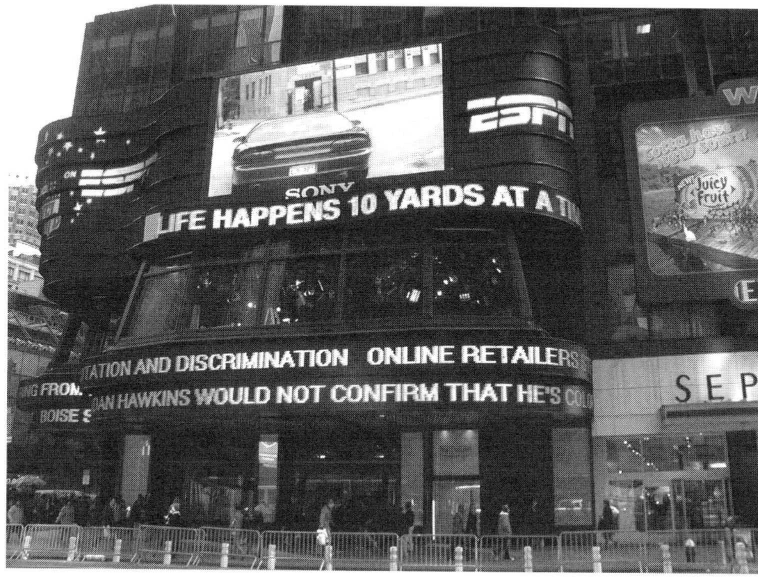

figure |1-12|

Motion graphics used on billboards can relay a large amount of information in a short amount of time and in a small space.

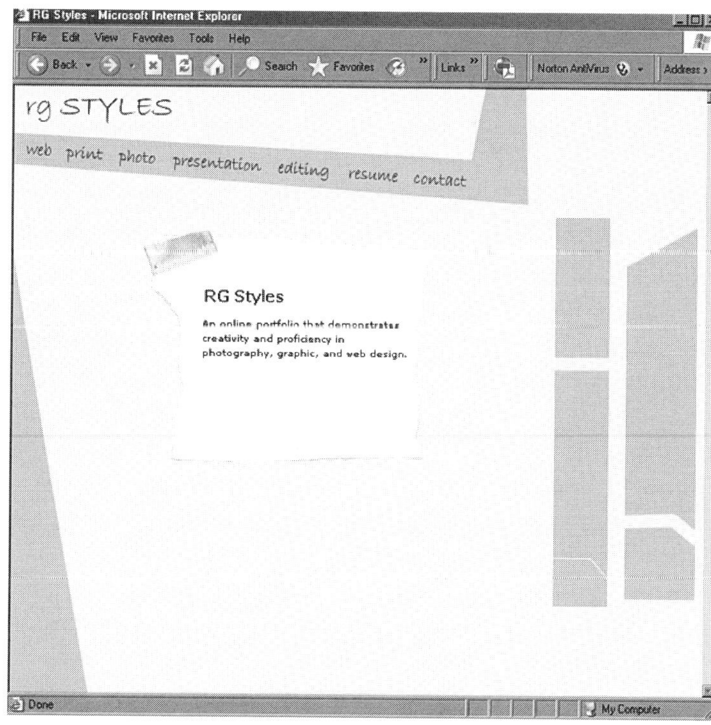

figure |1-13|

Motion graphics used on a website can enhance the visual appeal and offer more information to the viewer.

Handheld Devices

The range of electronic handheld devices has greatly expanded over the last few years. Handhelds include portable MP3 players, digital organizers, cell phones, and many combinations of the three. This opens up a new venue for the exploration and design of motion graphics. This medium lends itself to getting our individual attention as we are intimately engaged with the device when in use. The benefit of creating motion graphics for handheld devices is also that since it is completely mobile, the information can be carried at all times. Once information is downloaded onto the device, it can be retrieved at any time from any location.

WHY SOCIETY RESPONDS TO MOTION GRAPHICS

Originally, with drawings, paintings, and then photography, people saw static images. The only time people viewed information in motion was at the theater. Otherwise, stories were created with multiple single images that could be viewed in either a linear or nonlinear fashion. With the invention of motion pictures in the 1890s, television as we know it in the 1950s, and the World Wide Web in the 1990s, we have changed our methods of looking at and understanding information. The advent of digital technology has brought us back to looking at information in a nonlinear fashion. Whether it is an advertisement for the latest fashion trend or the corner restaurant, or a traffic sign, we are constantly being stimulated visually and called upon to process the information. With the way we live in society today, it is no wonder that we respond to all of the colorful, fast-moving images that we see. We respond to images that grab our attention and are quite adept at filtering out unwanted information that may be boring or unnecessary.

BASIC DESIGN ELEMENTS

Basic design elements are the first things every designer needs to study. Putting all of these elements together successfully is what makes a design great. Each element needs to be considered for how it works individually as well as how it works as part of the larger collective whole.

As the designer, you need to use the elements of design to create a visually stimulating piece. Once viewers are stimulated by the visuals, they will take the time to read the text, and you will have communicated your message. If the information is presented in a visually interesting manner, we will most likely take the time to look at it, catalog the information, and remember the message. How you use basic design elements will greatly influence the success or failure of the work.

We can divide the elements that make up graphics into the standard building blocks of design—type, color, shape, and line—and combine them with the most basic technical elements of film—composition and framing, sound and editing. These basic elements of design provide a visual constant in the ever-evolving field of motion graphics. All of these elements will be discussed in more detail later in the book.

Motion graphics is an interesting hybrid; both a visual art that calls upon the basic elements of design as used in traditional forms of art and design, and also a digital art that requires the use of technology. Motion graphics are a supporting element to the larger art, the film itself, the television show, or the video game; but when used for an advertisement on a billboard, television, or handheld device, they stand alone.

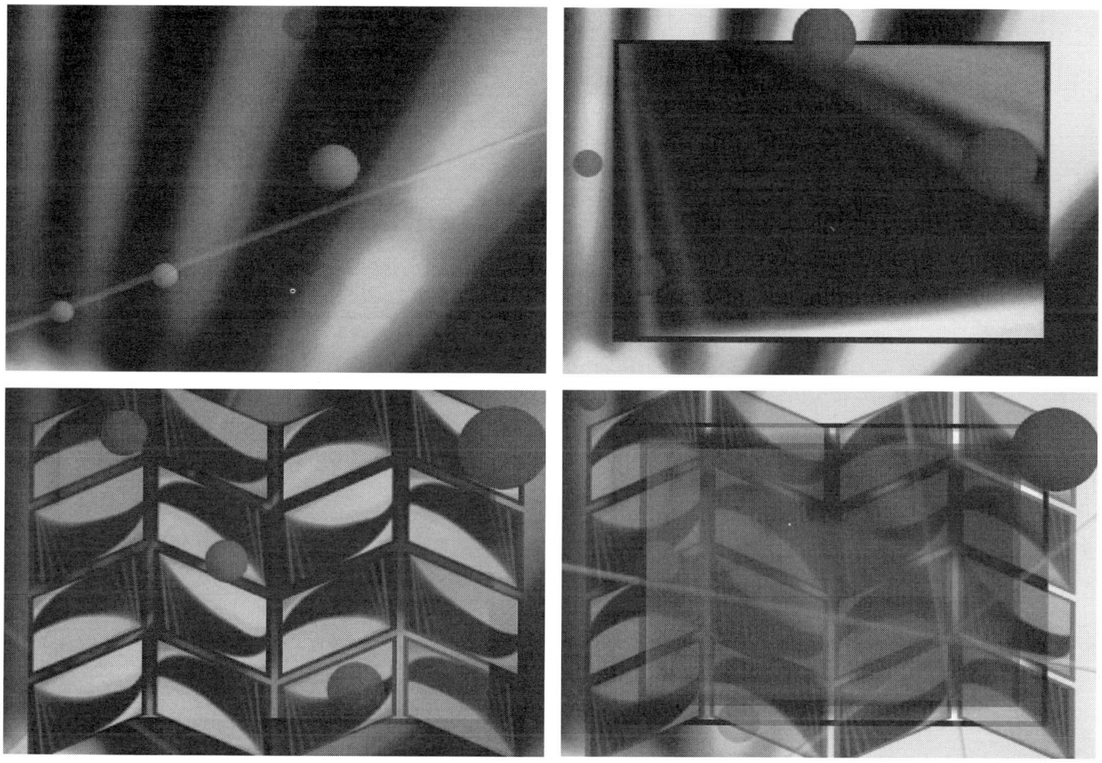

figure |1-14|

Using color, shape, and line, the designer creates a visually intriguing piece that grabs, and holds, the viewer's attention.

Visual Organization

Visual organization is one of the fundamentals of design. It refers to the manner in which objects are placed on the screen and how they interact with each other and the edges of the screen. The material needs to be organized in a way that makes it easy for the audience to take in all of the information. It needs to be presented clearly and in the right order to successfully tell the story or sell the message. If you do not organize your visuals in a manner that your audience can understand, you will fail to deliver the message.

Time and Rhythm

Everything we do can be broken into distinct sets of minutes and hours; a typical day's schedule is based on half-hour increments. We are used to watching certain media set in a specified time frame. Commercials last anywhere from fifteen to sixty seconds. A weekly television show is on for thirty or sixty minutes. A television special is on for two hours. A movie lasts for approximately one and a half hours. A typical song plays for approximately three minutes.

Static visual art exists in three dimensions—space, time, and dimension (length, width, height)—for as long as it is physically available to the viewer. Motion graphics exist in space, time, and dimension, as well, with the ability to move up and down on the y-axis, left and right on the x-axis, and in and out on the z-axis. All this movement takes place within a structured amount of time, which is considered a fourth dimension. Its existence is transient, just as, in traditional art forms, music, a movie, or a dance performance exists only in the time that it occurs.

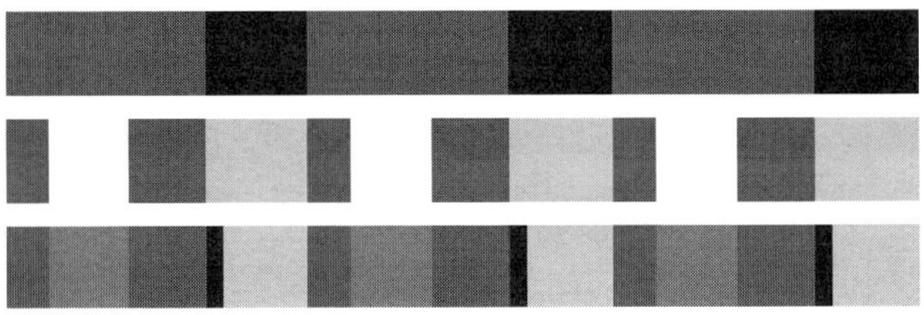

figure |1-15|

Although made up of the same shapes and shades of the same color, by changing the order, each row represents a different visual rhythm.

Rhythm is not a term applied only to music, dance, or any other art in motion. A painting or the sentences in a book impart their own rhythm to the viewer. Rhythm affects how our eyes move across a painting, taking in the details, or the way we hear the words of the novel we are reading in our heads. This notion of rhythm is also applied to motion graphics and is recognized in the movements of type and images and the accompanying audio.

Creation

When creating an imaginary or virtual world, we want to draw our audience in so that it believes that everything happening within that space is real. The minute that the designer includes something unnatural within that world, the audience is thrown out of its willing suspension of disbelief, and once that happens, it cannot really be restored.

When we watch the opening title sequence of a film, not only does it build excitement, but it prepares us for the world we are about to enter. It defines the tone, the style, and sometimes even the theme. In essence, it is part of the **mise-en-scène** of the film. Translated literally, mise-en-scène means *put on the stage*; however, for designing purposes it can mean anything on the screen that helps an audience understand the story or the message the designer is trying to convey. To wit, it means everything on the screen. Are there people on screen, and what are they wearing? What are they saying? What color is the type? What kind of type? Does the type move? Is there music? What kind of music? While these are quite a few questions to ask yourself, they underscore the point that everything that appears on your website, in your title sequence, or on an electronic billboard must be in service of the message you are conveying.

The first step in creating is to develop a plan of action. Before turning on the computer, you should sketch your ideas. When dealing with motion graphics, designers make a **storyboard** and use this as a guide while the design is created digitally.

It will be important to organize your information in a way that will be understood visually. Remember that a motion graphics design is a digital pictorial element given to properties of time, space, and dimension, all of which can be changed and modified over a set length of time. With motion graphics, viewers do not have the same control over viewing the design as they would when viewing print design.

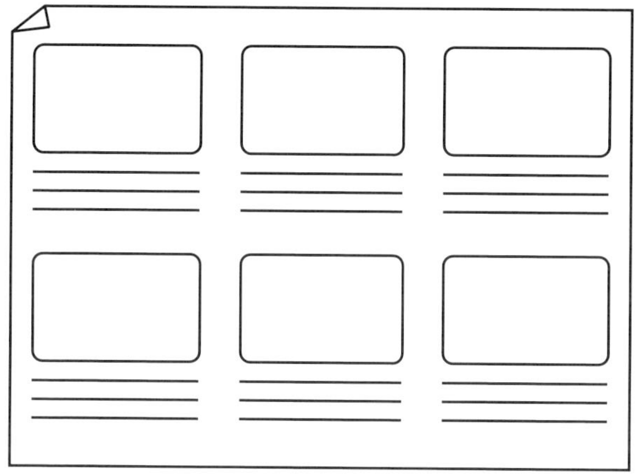

figure |1-16|

Motion graphics designers use a storyboard, such as this one, to sketch out ideas for their design.

ART AND DESIGN AS COMMUNICATION

Since the beginning of time, human beings have used graphics as a form of communication and as a way of sharing information. The earliest known example is the famous cave paintings from Lascaux, France. There are examples of this kind of design across the globe.

The people of the American Southwest used the rock faces to carve pictures, called petroglyphs, which detailed their lives and their surroundings. Many early cultures used this form of communication. As nomadic people traveled from one location to another, they used symbols to indicate particulars about their surroundings, such as an abundance or lack of food sources or to mark where a community member died or was born. Through the use of shared images and shared associations for those images, humans have been able to pass messages long before paper and pen.

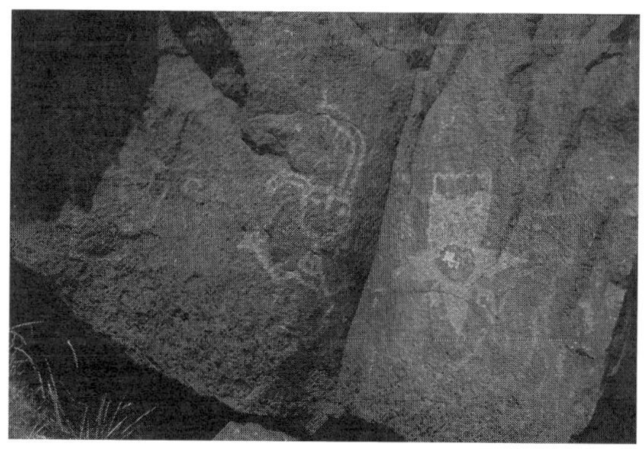

figure |1-17|

Humankind has always been compelled to communicate. Some of the earliest forms of communication were petroglyphs, such as these found in Petroglyph National Monument, Albuquerque, New Mexico.

Humans still seek to share their stories in the digital age, despite the fact that we may be communicating with each other across greater distances and across different cultures. Though we speak different languages, this does not stop us from wanting to share experiences. It does mean that, unlike caves, instead of leaving messages in one place to be found, messages are broadcast and distributed so we have to utilize symbols and images that have meaning to all people with whom we want to communicate.

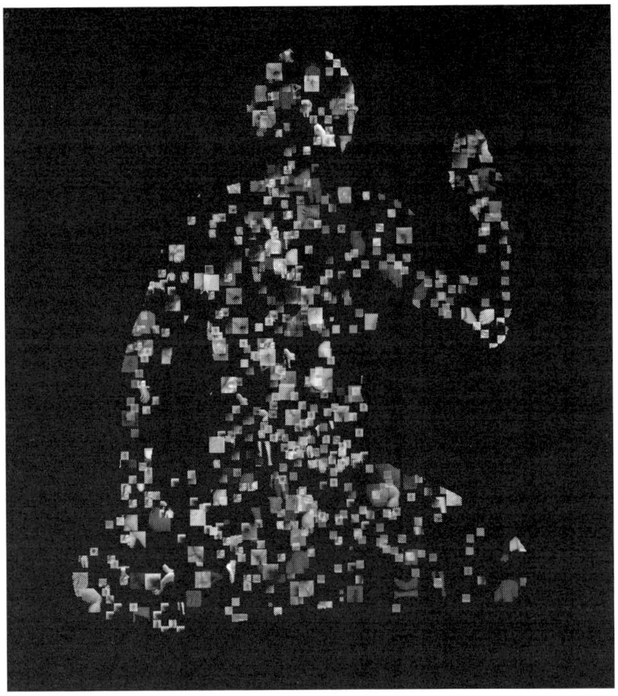

By Bovey Lee

figure | 1-18 |

This motion graphic, *Meander*, is intended for viewing by an audience comfortable with interpreting art.

Your Audience

While most visual art and design are meant to speak to many people at once, it does not engage in an actual dialogue between the artist and the audience. The audience is not predetermined, nor is any potential outcome analyzed. Motion graphics, however, are most often used to send a specific message, so designers must tailor their messages to a particular group of anonymous receivers. To do this, the designer must know his audience—at least in broad strokes.

Choosing the Medium Based on Your Audience

There are many considerations when choosing a medium for your design. In some cases you will simply be told by your client what medium to use, but if you are given the choice, there are certain things to take into account. If you know your audience is technically savvy, for instance, you have more options, such as developing an interactive website. If, on the other hand, you know they are not "techies," you will want to make sure that your message is not reliant on the audience's technical know-how.

In most cases your message should dictate the best medium for the job. If you are sending a message about an accident that is causing delays on the highway, your medium should be a digital billboard that drivers can read before they get to the congested area and hopefully avoid the problem. The message about this delay will not be effectively communicated if delivered via website, where it will not be easily accessible when most needed.

How We Process Information

We process information best through internalization. We often internalize through interaction and discussion. As we interact, whether with another person or digital device, we watch for visual cues as a guide when processing information. Every message is encoded with cues specific to the successful interpretation of that message. Think about the last interaction you had with a friend. If he smiled at you when you walked up to him, you could take that as an indicator that he was happy and in a good mood, but if he looked down at the ground as you approached, you may have taken that as an indication that he was sad or having a bad day. These cues help you to decide what to do or say as you approach your friend. How we process visual cues helps us better understand the information at hand. Regardless of how the information is presented to us, whether sent from another individual, a computer, or other digital messenger, we rely on these cues to help us deconstruct the information and interpret the message.

When we listen to an individual speak, it is relatively easy to tell if he is happy or angry or tired from the inflection in his voice or the gestures he uses. In writing, we still use conventional methods to emphasize certain components of the message by **bolding** or underlining words, or we use ellipses [. . .] to show that we have trailed off from our initial thoughts. With so much communication happening through a digital messenger, we have come up with new devices to encode the message to make sure our intended meaning is understood. We use a smiley face [:)] in e-mails to signify that we are joking, or a sad face [:(] to signify that we are pouting. These new visual cues have slowly become an integrated part of our cultural language and part of mainstream communication. However, if they were presented to someone who does not use e-mail or instant messenger, the code, and therefore meaning of the message, would not be fully understood. In order for them to properly decode the message, they must have the shared cultural experience of using the computer for communication. Without this shared experience, it is likely that they will not even recognize the keyboard characters as an abstract representation of a smiley face, but only a colon and a closing parenthesis. As a designer it is your job to understand what visual cues, or codes, to put in the message so it will successfully be processed based on the shared cultural experience. This absence of cultural understanding of the visual cues is noise that interferes with the successful understanding of the message.

How We Read

We all have an innate way in which we read information. In Western culture we read from left to right, top to bottom. The human eye naturally scans back and forth to process any new information. When first learning to put letters together to make words, we read phonetically, sounding out each word. As we become more adept at reading, we learn to read visually. We learn to see shapes of letters that make up words that we recognize.

Knowing that words are read visually, by shape and not by sounding them out letter-by-letter, is important to remember when designing motion graphics because it allows designers to take more liberties with moving type. It gives the designer freedom to work with depth, front to back, and not just left to right and top to bottom.

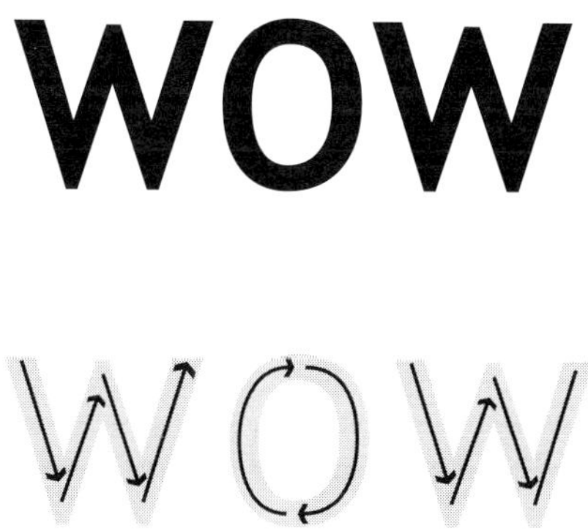

figure 1-19

This visual shows how each letter is individually scanned before seeing the word, then deciphering the meaning.

SUMMARY

Motion graphics are both a source of entertainment and a method of delivering information. To be a successful motion graphics designer, you must study the communication model to anticipate potential problems with interference that could prevent the message from reaching the viewer. It is also necessary to understand the audience and the medium on which the graphics will be viewed. The considerations for designing motion graphics differ for different media: television, movies, video games, websites, billboards, and portable devices. The graphic on a cell phone's LCD screen will have a much different impact on the viewer than a graphic on a digital billboard in Times Square because the environment and relationship between the viewer and delivery system are different in each case. With research and planning, proper implementation of the tools of design, and appropriate choice of the medium, an emotional response will be elicited from audiences and will convince them of the validity of the message, and they will remember the communication.

in review

1. What is the main purpose of motion graphics?
2. What is the communication model, and what is its relationship to design?
3. What are the most common venues for motion graphics?
4. How are time and rhythm used differently in motion graphics than in more traditional visual arts?
5. How is communication different today than at the beginning of human history, and how does it affect how we send messages?
6. How does the way in which we read affect motion graphics design?

exercises

Exercise 1

Communication Model

(Note: This is a group project.)

This exercise is based on the Exquisite Corpse game, often used by Surrealist artists as a tool for exploration in creativity, and follows the premise of the children's game Telephone. In the game Telephone, one child begins by making up a message and whispering it to the child next to him. The message continues to be passed down the line of kids in this manner until it reaches the end. The last one to receive the message repeats it aloud for all to hear. The fun of the game is that the end result is often a garbled message, altered from the original, which makes no sense.

Task

Using the rules of the game as guidelines, you will put words and images together to tell a story. This exercise reinforces the communication model.

Goal

Create a collaborative storybook made up of images and words.

Design It, Step-by-Step

1. Use a sheet of 8-1/2 × 11 inch paper.
2. The first person writes the first sentence of the story at the top of the page.

3. Pass the paper to the person to the right.
4. The second person writes a sentence that somehow connects to the first sentence, then folds the paper down so only the second sentence is visible.
5. Pass the paper to the person to the right.
6. The third person writes a sentence that somehow connects to the second sentence, then folds the paper down so only the third sentence is visible.
7. Pass the paper to the person to the right.
8. Continue until everyone in the group has written a sentence. The first person should then get to read the last sentence.
9. Number the sentences in order, then make a copy of the paper with the complete story.
10. Cut the paper apart by sentence.
11. Pass out the sentences, one to each person in the group. The first person gets the second sentence, the second person gets the third sentence, and so on. Go around the room in this manner until everyone has one sentence.
12. Each person creates a graphic for the selected sentence. The design for the graphic should illustrate the content of the sentence he was given while reflecting what he thinks the story is about based also on the sentences he read and wrote.
13. Put all of the graphics together, with the corresponding sentences, in the order of the original story, up on the wall or in book or slide show format.

Exercise 2

Medium as Message

This exercise will reinforce the importance of choosing the right medium for your message.

Task

Research the use of motion graphics as a branding tool used in the digital medium. Find five examples of motion graphics used on cell phones, billboards, or websites. Document where you see the graphics, what medium is used, and what the brand is.

Goal

Bring in examples and discuss the findings.

Research It

Answer the following questions:

1. In what type of environment are you viewing the motion graphic?
2. Is it presented as an ad, selling a specific product, or is it just reinforcing the brand identity?
3. Was the information presented in a clear manner?
4. Did you find it informative?
5. Did you find it entertaining?

Exercise 3

Motion Graphics on Television

This exercise will reinforce the different uses of a bug, station ID, and snype.

Task

Find five examples of bugs, snypes, and station IDs on television. Document what television stations they are aired on, what time of day or night they appear, and in what context.

Goal

Bring in examples and discuss the findings.

Research It

Answer the following questions:

1. Did the design represent the attitude of the television station?
2. How were motion graphics applied in the design?
3. Did the graphic help to clarify what television station you were tuned into or what television show you were watching?
4. Was the snype or bug distracting during the viewing of the show, or did you find it informative?

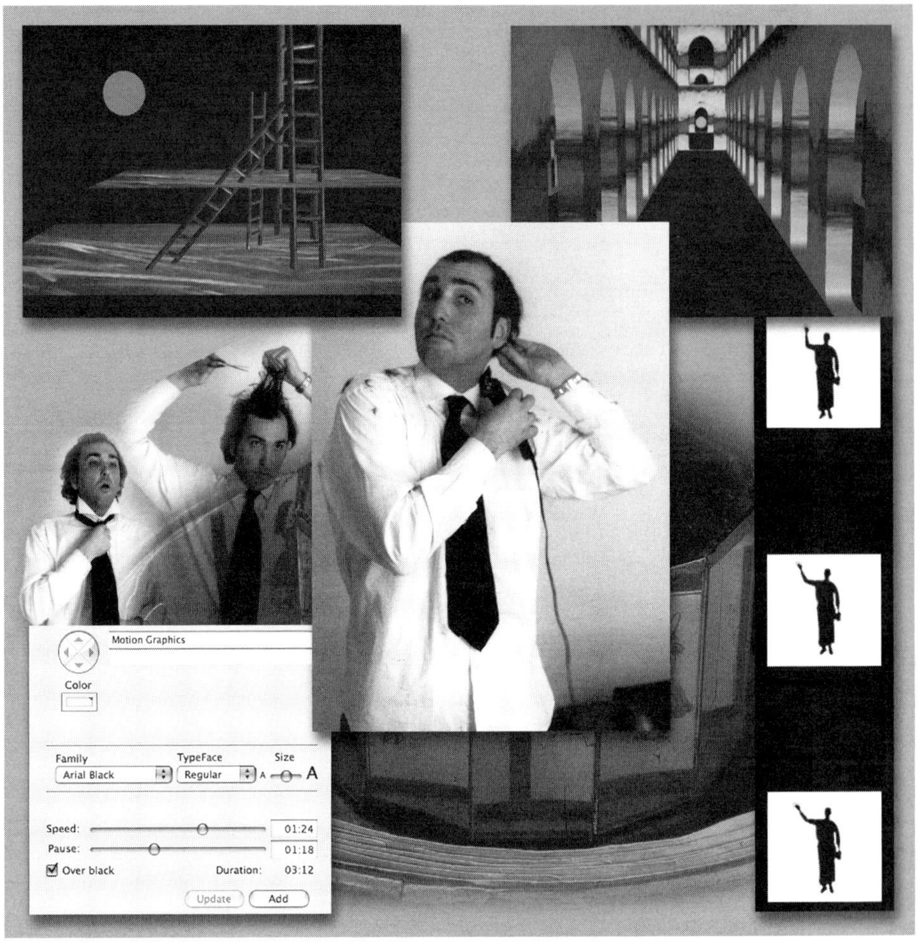
Motion Graphics
Color
Family
TypeFace
Size
Arial Black
Regular
Speed:
01:24
Pause:
01:18
Over black
Duration:
03:12
Update
Add

CHAPTER 2

THE EVOLUTION OF A MODERN MEDIUM

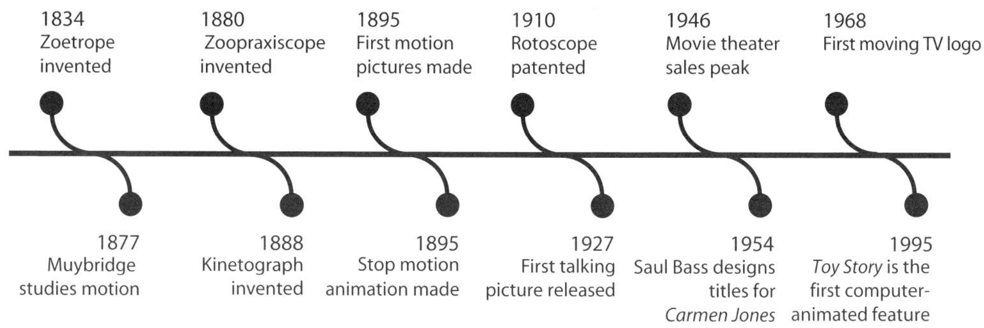

Chapter Objectives

Understand the influence of cinema history and title design on motion graphics

Gain insight into the illusion of motion and how it is created

Develop an appreciation for the influences of early special effects and animation on motion graphics

Acknowledge the groundbreaking motion graphics design before computers and recognize the advances that have occurred with computers

Introduction

Artists are inspired by the world around them. They are inspired by art, by poetry, and by culture. Impressionist painter Edgar Degas, for example, based much of his art on the study and representation of ballet. A filmmaker becomes a better filmmaker not only by watching films but also by attending art museums, viewing paintings, and studying composition and perspective. Romantic composer Bedrich Smetana's famous tone poem, *The Moldau*, was inspired by the natural world surrounding him and his impressions of the Moldau River flowing through the countryside of Bohemia. An artist is aware and prepared for the fact that inspiration may strike at any moment, from any source. Part of being an artist is opening oneself up to the world, allowing it to fill the spirit with new ideas.

While a designer looks to the surrounding world as a muse, she is also influenced by technology and the message that stands before her. A designer will also consider the work that has preceded her and how it has successfully communicated with an audience.

Style refers both to the ways in which a particular design is unique and also how its elements may conform to a larger stylistic movement. In order to understand style, one must have some understanding of where design has been and where it is going. An appreciation for the history of motion graphics and the cultural and technological advances that inspired its evolution will allow a designer to draw on the medium's past to enhance her own creativity.

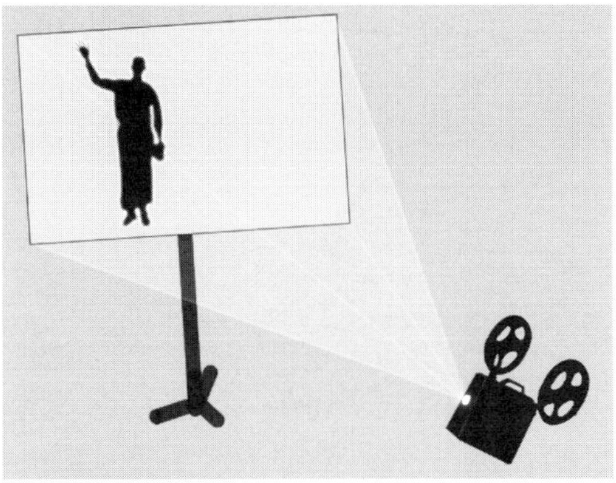

figure |2-1|

Persistence of vision: Scholars believed that a series of still images were stored on the retina, and this was why humans perceived motion.

PERCEPTION OF MOVING IMAGES

For decades film scholars taught **persistence of vision** as the phenomenon that allowed an audience to see, or believe it was seeing, still images in motion. It brought movement to animated drawings and still frames of a film and explained how a stop-motion animator could breathe life into a clay figurine. Scholars defined persistence of vision as the result of the eye's tendency to hold a memory of an image on the retina a moment after the image had disappeared. They believed it fused the separate still images in the mind so that it appeared as though they were connected and moving. However, if this were true, the images would actually build up on top of each other in a blur, rather than give the appearance of progressive action.

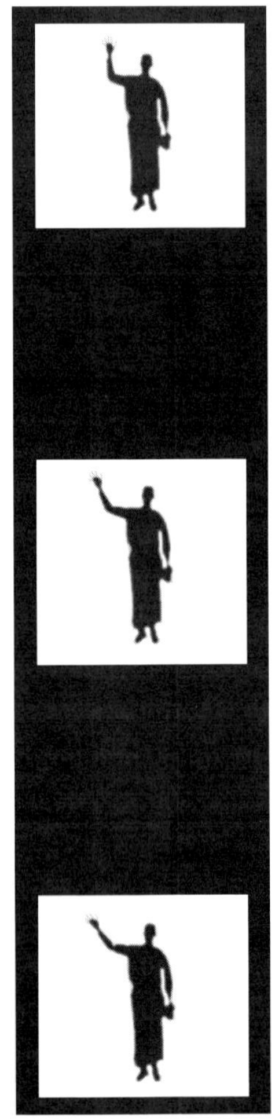

figure |2-2|

Flicker fusion explains how separate beams of light are perceived as one continuous beam.

While studies are still being conducted to better understand how the brain sees moving images, scholars now seem to agree upon two theories: **flicker fusion** and **apparent motion**. These theories work in conjunction with one another to explain how we perceive movement on a screen. Flicker fusion occurs when the eye perceives separate static images as one constant image, while apparent motion occurs when we "see" movement in those continuous images.

Discussions about film, video, or computer graphics sometimes focus on **frames**, the smallest component of the overall image. We also discuss **frame rates** because these are the rates at which a new static image is presented per second. Film runs at twenty-four frames per second, meaning that twenty-four different static images, separated by darkness, comprise one second of viewing. Video runs at thirty frames per second. Although the light that allows us to see each frame is not constant (this is a result of darkness between frames), once the rate at which the light occurs reaches a certain threshold—twenty-four frames per second—our brain processes the light as being one steady stream of light. This is flicker fusion in action. And while the technology is different for video and computer graphics, the concept of flicker fusion applies to both, because our persistence of vision in both media is dependent upon the rapid succession of static images and our brain processing the images as one continuous image.

Yet flicker fusion alone does not explain how an audience can see moving images, for while it allows the audience to perceive a constant image, it does not explain how an audience sees *motion* in that image. An audience sees motion because of apparent motion, which occurs when the brain assumes that a different positioning of an image indicates movement. In other words, a series of images appear to be in motion if, although similar, they have slight variations in position. A neon sign is a simplistic example of this principle. It appears to be animated because when the lights change positions our brains interpret this as movement. Flicker fusion and apparent motion are processes that occur as a result of the brain's active interpretation of what is received, whereas the theory of persistence of vision is based upon the brain being a passive recipient of information.

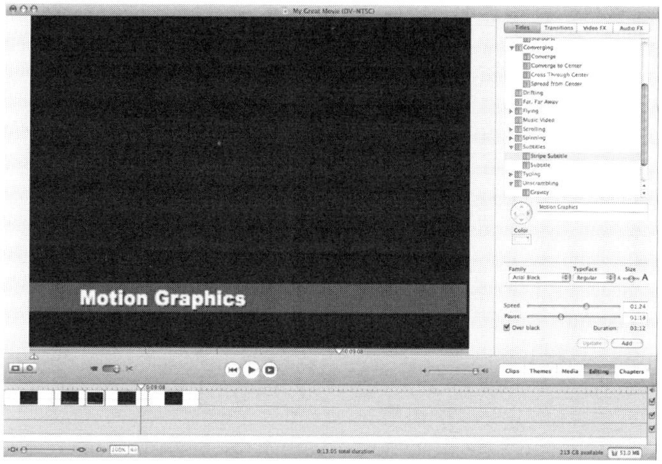

figure |2-3|

A frame is the smallest component of a film. Twenty-four frames make up a single second of film.

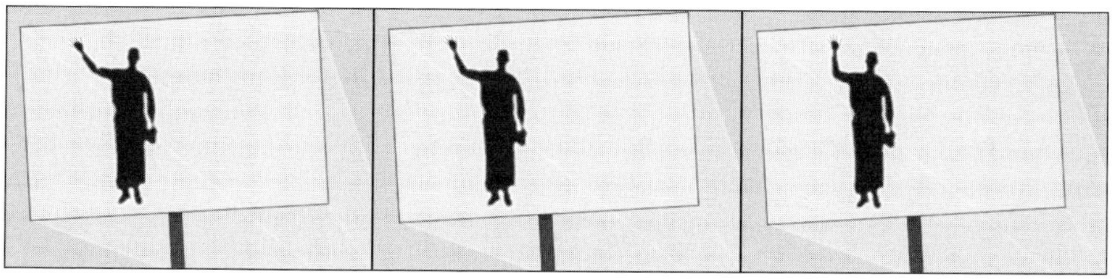

figure |2-4|

Apparent motion explains how we see movement in a series of still images

Optical Toys

Long before cinema, human beings were interested in creating the illusion of motion. Physicists attempted to create motion with inventions such as the thaumatrope in the 1820s and the phenakistoscope and zoetrope in the 1830s.

While each new invention improved on the previous one, they all shared certain constants. For example, each was adorned with a progression of still images, each slightly different from the next, that when spun would give the appearance that the

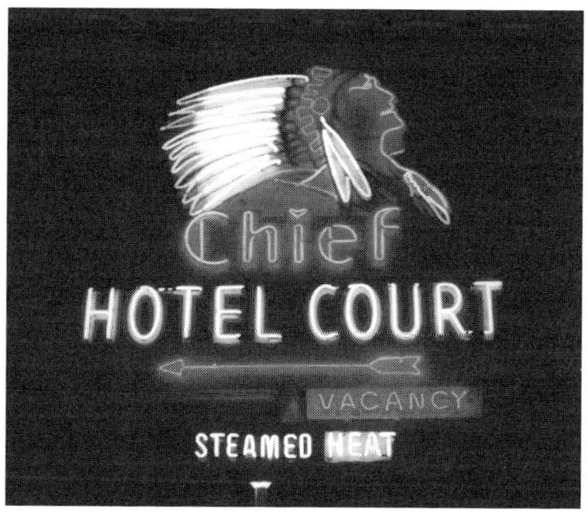

By Mark Ezovski Productions/Diabolical Brain

figure |2-5|

The lights on a neon sign may change position, making it appear as though movement is taking place.

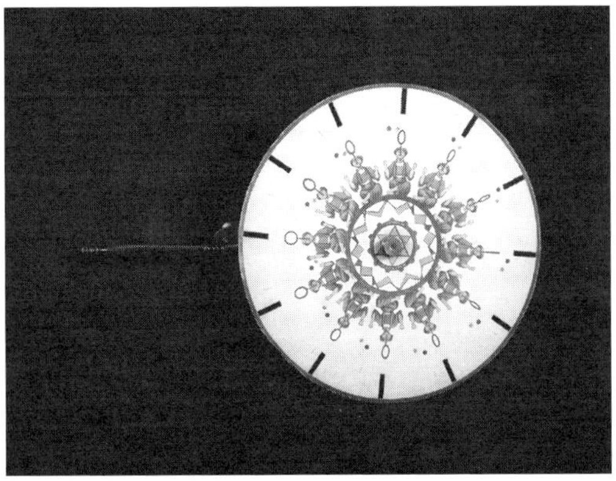

figure |2-6|

Phenakistoscope

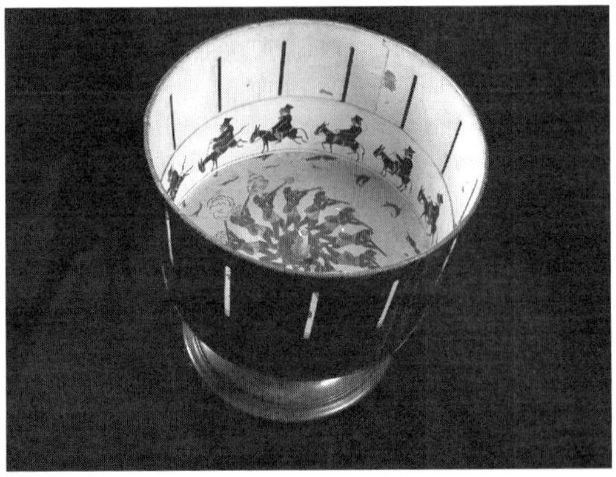

figure |2-7|

Zoetrope

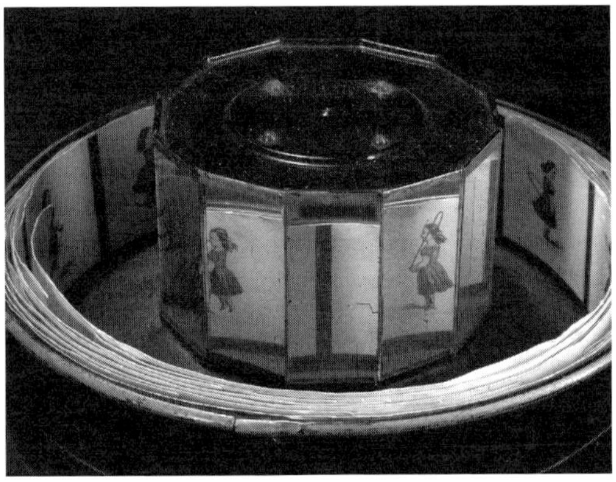

figure |2-8|

Praxinoscope

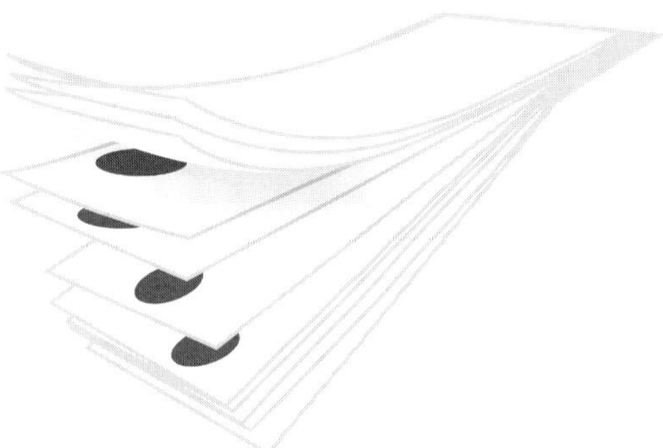

figure |2-9|

Flipbook

images were in motion. Finally, the praxinoscope actually reflected the "moving images" on a mirror that sat stationary while a rotating drum with still images circled it, thus solving the problem of image distortion that occurred in the zoetrope.

Flipbooks

Flipbooks achieved popularity in the nineteenth century. Like early optical toys, the flipbook consisted of a single image on each page that was slightly different from the one preceding it. Flipping through the pages quickly animated the images, giving them the appearance of moving. Flipbooks contained images of popular pastimes as well as scenes from daily life. The principle was the same as that of the optical toys: the individual images appeared to be in motion both because of the speed at which they were viewed and because of the slight variations in appearance of the images.

CAPTURING MOTION ON FILM

In his book *American Cinema/American Culture* John Belton notes the importance of certain nineteenth century inventions that changed human-kind's perception of time and space, while also allowing us to record our world in new ways. Along with the continued fascination with moving images, people started to look for new ways to preserve important life events for future enjoyment. The invention of the phonograph resulted in recorded sound, and with the camera came recorded images. In addition to those accomplishments, people looked for ways to communicate in real time over long distances, first through code with the telegraph and later by voice with the telephone. By the close of the century, forward thinkers looked for ways to record moving images as well.

The invention of photography in the 1820s was an enormous step toward an ability to capture moving images on film. In particular, the work of photographer Eadweard Muybridge and physiologist Étienne-Jules Marey in the late 1870s helped move us closer to motion pictures. In an attempt to settle a dispute about the physical placement of horses' hooves while they galloped, Muybridge set up a series of cameras around a racetrack. Attached to the cameras were wires that were activated when the horse's hooves snapped them while running past. A series of photographs resulted that separated the horse's gallop into very detailed, specific movements, or into frames.

Muybridge made his greatest contribution to the science behind moving pictures when he created the zoopraxinoscope (1880), a projector that could show up to 200 image stills in rapid succession. By breaking down motion and then reconstructing it during the projection, Muybridge's zoopraxinoscope was a direct precursor to the concept of early cinema.

Marey created a camera that captured twelve images per second, first on a round disk of film and then later on a flexible film for use with a special camera he invented. This new film allowed Marey to capture more images and, consequently, separate movement into a greater series of frames. Next, with Eastman Kodak's invention of celluloid, flexible film allowed for the capture of even more images and longer periods of movement. Marey

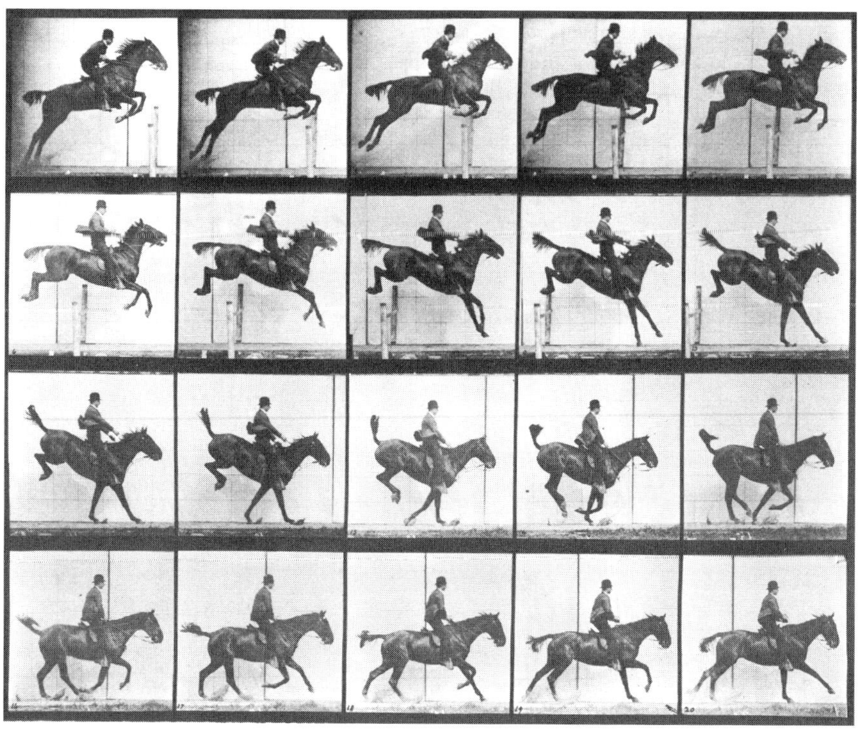

From the collections of the University of Pennsylvania Archives

figure 2-10

Muybridge's photography breaks the horse's gallop into frames that isolate each movement.

continued to improve film camera technology. With the addition of the "cross gear" on his 1888 camera, he was able to control the film's movement through the camera so that each frame would advance for exposure.[1]

Marey provided the groundwork from which other inventors, including Thomas Edison and his assistant W. K. L. Dickson, as well as Auguste and Louis Lumière, would develop their first motion picture cameras. In 1891 Edison and Dickson invented the kinetograph camera. This camera shot moving images on Eastman Kodak film. The images were then played back on the **kinetoscope** and viewers watched through a peephole at the top of the device. The Lumière brothers, however, went a step further and invented a camera that also acted as a projector. They created the first motion picture projector and opened the world of film viewing to a mass audience.

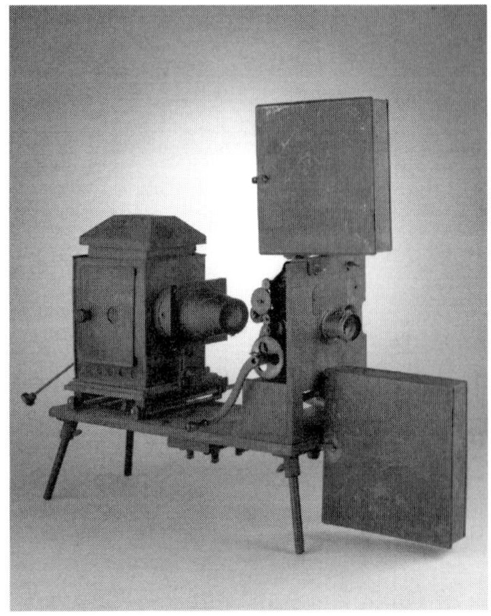

figure |2-11|

Spectators could view Edison's films through a peephole in his kinetoscope.

PRIMITIVE COMPOSITION

The first films were usually recordings of vaudeville, theater performances, carnival acts, or daily street scenes. They were composed of a single shot, or camera set-up, and therefore required no editing. Since filmmakers did not have multiple camera angles from which to choose, they designed their composition to capture all of the action within a single frame. While panning (camera movement from side to side) occurred in some early documentaries, it did not gain widespread use in narrative films until around 1903. Since the camera always acts as narrator, particularly in early films at a time when people were not accustomed to watching them, audiences needed guidance in understanding the story. It was necessary to frame the action so that the audience could not miss it.

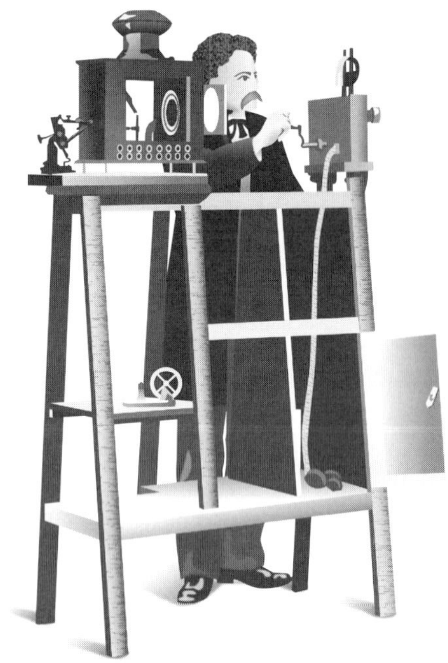

figure |2-12|

The Lumière brothers invented the first film projector.

1 David Bordwell and Kristin Thompson, *Film Art: An Introduction* (New York: McGraw Hill, 2004), 465.

As film stories became more complex, and filmmakers sought to engage a more sophisticated audience, the way that the camera told the story had to evolve with the spectators. Around 1908, films had more varied camera angles, both high and low (1911), in addition to more variation in the composition of the shots.[2] We first start to see close-ups at this time, giving us more access to the main characters and to their minds. This technique gave actors a chance to provide more subtle performances. Though their performances may still seem exaggerated by today's acting standards, these changes in framing allowed for performances that were less like theater performances, and more subtle, tailored for the screen. Around 1912 D. W. Griffith became known for using various camera angles to help convey the internal state of his characters and for encouraging actors to give more natural and realistic performances.

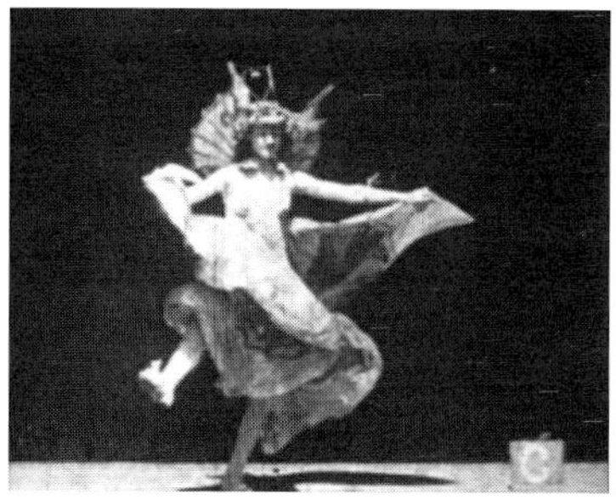

figure |2-13|

Serpentine Dance captures the dancer's performance from a single angle.

With German impressionism in the 1920s, actors continued to fine-tune their performances, and the camera continued to become a more sophisticated narrator. The use of a moving camera became more widespread, allowing for more extensive tracking shots, which either followed alongside the action or dollied in to a scene, literally pulling the audience into the action.

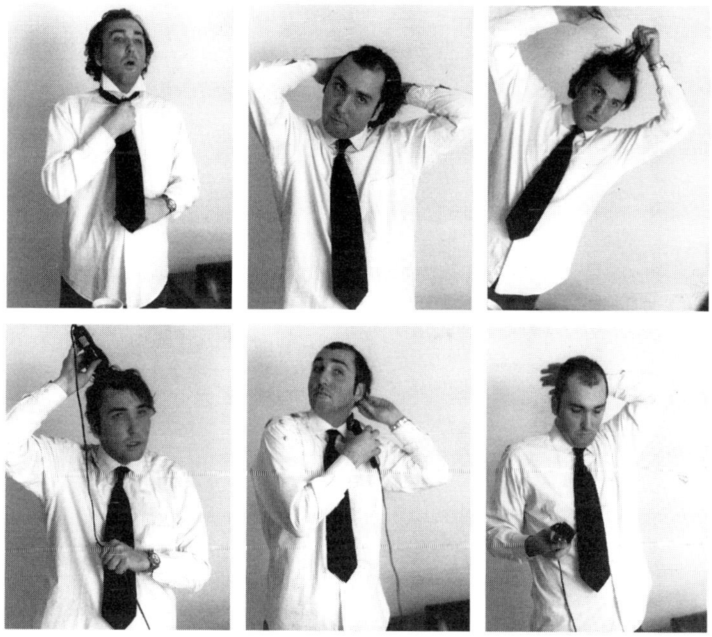

"Hair Cut Loop," Animated Gif, Genco Gulan, 2000

figure |2-14|

Each frame in this sequence uses different angles.

TITLE CARDS

Though the camera served as a narrator in early films, there was, of course, no recorded sound. In the earliest single-shot films, **title cards** informed the audience of the name of the movie they were watching. As film stories became more complex and composed of more than one shot or more than one scene, title cards began to serve as narration. Not until 1908–1909, however, did intertitles with dialogue become more common in films. Particularly in American-made films, the dialogue helped to move the narrative along and began to replace

2 Barry Salt, *Film Style and Technology: History and Analysis* (London, UK: Starword, 1992), 85.

cards composed only of prose. Though simple white text on black cards, they served the same purpose as modern graphics in that their job was to deliver a message. In their case, of course, it was to deliver the message of specific characters and to drive the cinematic story forward.

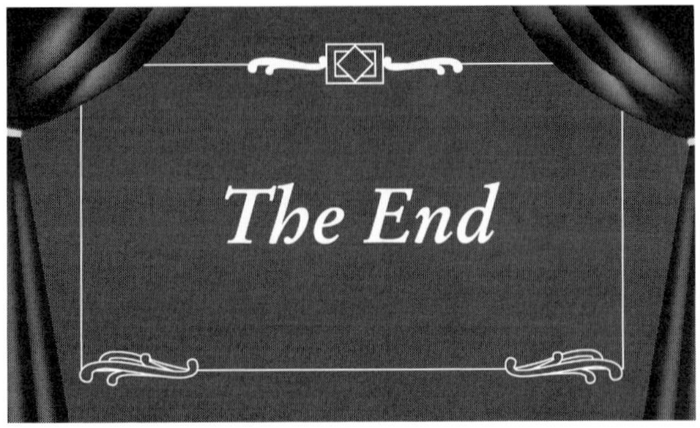

figure |2-15|

Art titles were a very early form of title design.

Art titles are title cards with illustrations on them. As early as 1915, title cards were designed with simple drawings that coincided thematically with the subject of the film. D. W. Griffith, a prolific director best known for his appallingly racist, yet groundbreaking epic *The Birth of a Nation*, designed special title cards for his films that contained simple graphics of D. W. Griffith at the top of each card almost like personalized stationery. The art titles and Griffith's title cards are both examples of early title design and, in the case of the latter, a clear example of using the graphic as a branding tool.

With the advent of synchronized sound in 1927, intertitles were no longer vital to an audience's understanding of a film. Certainly, there were films that relied upon an opening title card to set the stage of the film, or the intertitle superimposed over an image to tell the audience where or when a story was taking place, but the intertitle as it had appeared in the 1910s and 1920s was no more. Throughout the decades, titles typed or drawn and superimposed over various backgrounds became the norm to introduce the film and its players. While the type style varied from film to film, titles were static and acted as a separate entity from the actual film. In fact, it is rumored that when *The Man with the Golden Arm* (title design by Saul Bass) was released in 1955, there were actually notes telling film projectionists to open the curtains *before* the titles, because up until then, the film did not really start until after the credits were finished.[3]

FILM TITLE DESIGN

The opening sequence of *Metropolis*, a silent German science fiction film of the late 1920s, is an early example of title design. It used animation to make the word *Metropolis* emerge from a sunrise over a city as a shiny, glowing example of the futuristic utopia the audience is about to view in the film. Early in the story, a downward scrolling intertitle that reads "Deep below the earth's surface lay the workers' city" mimics the image of workers on an elevator going underground and further underscores workers' oppression beneath the city.

3 "Saul Bass," Designmuseum.org.

This was, however, the exception rather than the rule, and the design of opening title sequences did not begin to evolve in leaps and bounds until the 1950s when Saul Bass came onto the scene.

Saul Bass's first titles were for the Harry Belafonte and Dorothy Dandridge film *Carmen Jones* in 1954. What made his designs stand out from those before him was the way in which they were both abstract, yet thematically linked to the films they introduced. His opening for *Pyscho*, for instance, uses lines that dart across the screen in time to urgent, jabbing music to reveal type that is fractured. Critics liken the breaks in the type to the split in the psychotic Norman Bates character. With designs for other Hitchcock films like *Vertigo* and *North by Northwest*, Bass showed that the opening sequence was actually a part of the film. It was an introduction that set the mood and ushered the audience into the world of the film it was about to see. At the same time, Bass respected the role of the credits as an opening that was not to overshadow the main event—the film itself. Throughout his career Bass designed titles for Otto Preminger, Stanley Kubrick, Martin Scorsese, and John Singleton, among other directors. He also designed the recognizable logos for companies such as AT&T, Quaker, Minolta, and United Airlines.

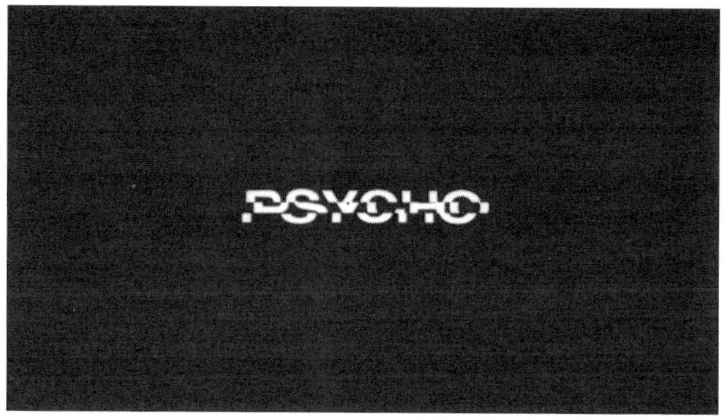

figure 2-16

Saul Bass designed the titles for *Psycho* (1960).

Pablo Ferro, who coupled hand-drawn titles over fighter planes being refueled in flight for *Dr. Strangelove*, also left his mark on title design. With a career as impressive as Bass's, Ferro continues to influence the face of opening sequences. His most recent contribution was as a consultant on the film *Napoleon Dynamite*. Since the film chronicled the days of an eccentric high school student, Napoleon Dynamite, the opening titles set the tone perfectly by featuring handwritten graphics—the penmanship was remarkably reminiscent of an adolescent's—on notebooks, pencils, and other school supplies, as well as scrawled on cafeteria foods with condiments like mustard.

Maurice Binder was also a pioneer in title design. He is best known for his sexy female silhouettes that characterized the James Bond openings of the 1960s, 1970s, and 1980s and whose style has been honored in recent Bond films.

All three of these designers were important in their time, and their work has continued to inspire the work of today's designers. The opening of *Catch Me If You Can* (2003), designed by Olivier Kuntzel and Florence Deygas, is reminiscent of Bass's early style. A marriage of traditional animation with digital technology, this opening sequence reinforced the film's 1960s setting with its retro style. The opening sequence is an animated chase that mirrors the main characters' pursuit in the film. What makes the sequence stand out is not so much that it is animated, but that it is done in the style of movies and commercials of the 1960s so that it successfully draws the audience into that time period before the first shot of the film.

STOP-MOTION CAMERA AND EARLY SPECIAL EFFECTS

According to Barry Salt, author of *Film Style and Film Technology*, Thomas Edison used the effect of **stop-motion camera** in 1895 in *The Execution of Mary, Queen of Scots*. However, it is Georges Méliès, a French film director whose roots were in the theater, who is better known for his use of trick photography in his early films. In his film *Trip to the Moon*, moon people disappear into clouds of dust when hit by an earth scientist's umbrella. He was able to create this illusion with stop-motion camera, which is the technique of stopping the camera, removing an element from the frame, and replacing it with another. By the same token, stop-motion camera can also make something suddenly appear in the frame by stopping the camera and adding an object. Television shows like *Bewitched* and *I Dream of Jeannie* in the 1960s exploited the technique much to the pleasure and amusement of their audiences.

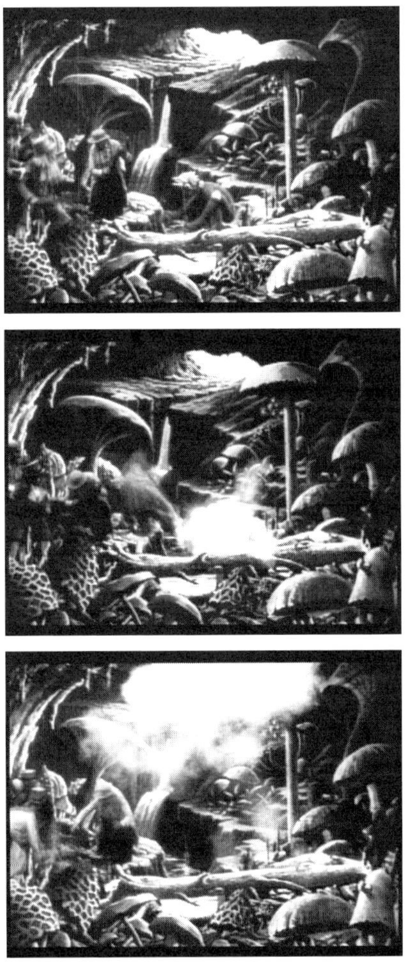

figure |2-17|

In *Trip to the Moon* (1902), Georges Méliès uses stop-motion camera techniques to make moon people disappear.

Another effect, employed by Méliès and other directors as early as the late 1890s, was superimposition, the process of having images on top of one another. This effect could be created either through double printing or exposing the film more than once in a camera. Masks, black cloths placed over part of the lens to cover up part of the image filmed, were being used as early as the turn of the twentieth century. The use of masks could create the sensation of viewing the action through binoculars or a keyhole, as per the point of view of a particular character. These effects continued to evolve throughout the years. Though technology helps to make these effects more manageable, filmmakers' goals have likewise become more ambitious, thus making these effects sometimes as time-consuming and labor intensive as they were in the days before innovations. Today these basic effects can be created with most editing and motion graphics software and are therefore created during post-production rather than production.

STOP-MOTION ANIMATION

Pixilation, the animation of objects by adjusting their position frame by frame, is an early form of animation. In their book *Film History: An Introduction*, Kristin Thompson and husband David Bordwell discuss films such as *Le Théâtre de Petit Bob* (1906) and

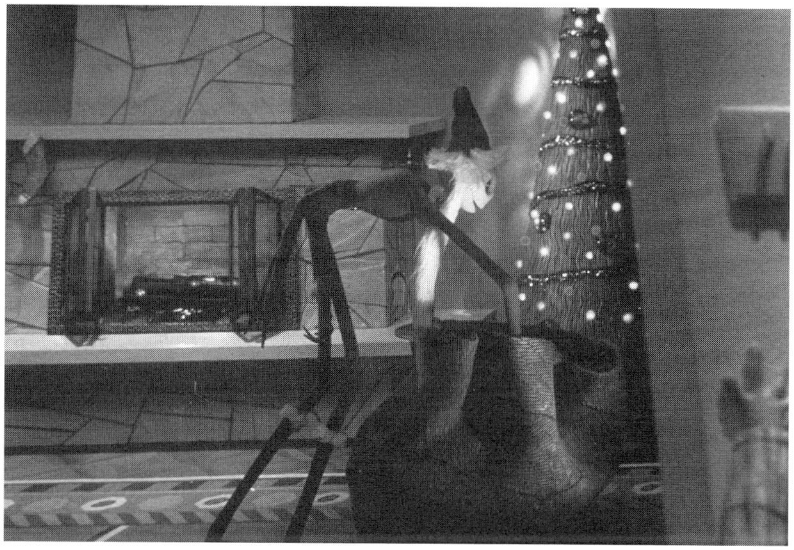

figure |2-18|

Tim Burton's *The Nightmare Before Christmas* was created using stop-motion animation.

The Haunted Hotel (1907), which used **stop-motion animation** to bring toys to life in the former and to make kitchens perform their assigned duties in the latter. Even as technology further developed, these early methods were used on a larger scale in Ray Harryhausen productions like *Clash of the Titans*, *Jason and the Argonauts*, and the *Sinbad* movies, which boasted ferocious, mythic monsters. Harryhausen, who said in a 2004 *Entertainment Weekly* interview that he was inspired by the gorilla in the original *King Kong* (1933), went on to create amazing battles between live-action actors and miniature models. He would do the painstaking work of manipulating the models of sea monsters, serpents of Medusa's hair, or skeleton monsters inch-by-inch by hand as action was captured a single frame at a time. And although the effects of today are mostly the result of computer programs and computer-generated imaging (CGI), stop-motion animation was the technique used in Tim Burton's films *The Nightmare Before Christmas* (1993) and *The Corpse Bride* (2005), as well as in the 2005 Academy Award winning film *Wallace and Gromit in The Curse of the Were-Rabbit*. Harryhausen's work also laid the foundation for George Lucas's *Star Wars* effects, Steven Spielberg's dinosaurs in *Jurassic Park*, and the various creatures and battles of Peter Jackson's *Lord of the Rings* and *King Kong* (2005) remake.

TRADITIONAL ANIMATION

Motion graphics have naturally been influenced by animation, and in fact, they are indelibly linked since animation, both traditional and digital, is often employed in creating motion graphics. Today animation is most often associated with children's entertainment, or at the very least, shows like *The Simpsons* or *South Park*, which depict fictional worlds of the absurd. By contrast, there is Japanese anime, which is geared toward more mature audiences and is also narrative in nature as it depicts worlds of fantasy or science fiction. But lest we forget the role of animation in advertising, a glance at television commercial archives of the 1950s and 1960s will remind us that animation has its place in branding and mass communication just as motion graphics do. Thus, a discussion of the background of motion graphics would not be complete without touching upon the history of animation.

While animation existed in some form from the beginning of film, 1906 marked the beginning of animation within the structure of the film industry. Stuart Blackton, a founder of the early American film company Vitagraph, created *Humorous Phases of Funny Faces* by shooting the stages of his chalk-drawn faces frame by frame so that the faces appear in the film little by little. At the end of the film when the faces are complete, they all roll their eyes.

Single-frame filming was made possible when a camera was calibrated to expose only one frame with the turn of the crank instead of eight. The first examples of this appear to be in Edwin Porter's films *How Jones Lost His Roll* and the *Whole Dam Family and the Dam Dog*. In these films letters are made to form words by moving into position with each frame.

The development of the **cel** marked the beginning of a new era in animation. The cel is a sheet of clear celluloid that contains a drawing. The use of sheets of celluloid in 1910 changed the way animators worked. Rather than having to redraw a background each time they redrew a character to show the character's movement, they were able to layer cels with images of the background, midground, and foreground. In other words, they could place different images of a particular character on top of the static background. This process of layering completely different images that are not actually in the same location to create the appearance of them being in the same location is called **compositing**. This method saved time and work because it limited the number of times a background had to be redrawn. Multiple layers of cels, the peg system, was developed. To this day cels from early Disney films like *Snow White* and *Fantasia*, as well as from more recent Disney films like *The Little Mermaid* and *Aladdin*, are worth thousands of dollars.

In 1915 Max and Dave Fleischer patented the rotoscope, a device that allowed them to project a live-action film and trace around the live-action characters. When they drew the characters on cels, one frame at a time, they were able to capture all of the characters' movements. The results were animated characters that had the freedom of movement of live-action characters. In 1919, using the rotoscope technology, the Fleischer brothers released a series of cartoons, *Out of the Inkwell*, featuring Koko the Clown as well as the Mutt and Jeff cartoons. Their most enduring creations, however, are probably Popeye and Betty Boop. **Rotoscoping** is still used today and is particularly useful in combining animated footage with live action. Richard Linklater's *Waking Life* (2001) is a recent animated feature utilizing the rotoscope technique.

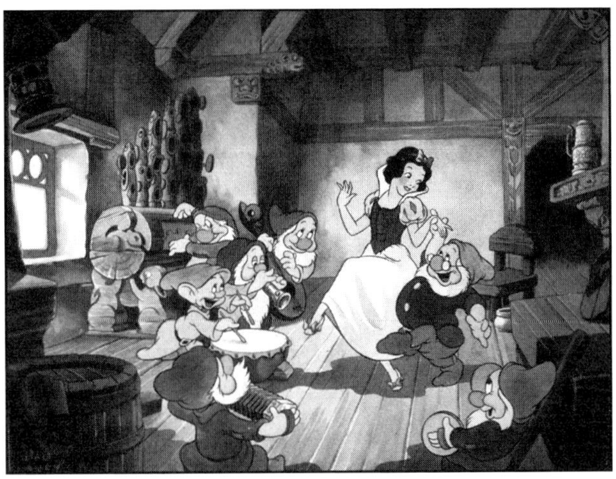

Getty Images Entertainment

figure | 2-19 |

A scene from Disney Studios' *Snow White and the Seven Dwarfs* (1937).

The 1920s saw a rise in independent animation studios, the most well known being Disney and his mascot, Mickey Mouse. At that time the practice was for head animators to draw the key frames, or the starting and ending positions of the characters. The drawing of the in-between positions, a monotonously difficult job, was handled by the key assistants. Other artists then traced the drawings onto cels and yet another set of artists painted them before they were photographed by the cinematographer, frame by frame. In the 1930s the Disney studios invented the process of photocopying penciled drawings onto celluloid. This was less expensive and time-consuming than artists having to hand-ink the drawings, though many animators continued hand-inking through the late 1950s. Traditional animation had filled a niche in entertainment, with Disney commanding the theatrical animation market and studios like Warner Brothers and Hanna-Barbera joining them in the 1930s. With television came a new outlet for animated fare both as children's entertainment and in advertising.

As technology has continued to evolve, so has traditional animation. Animation has not only become a staple of Saturday morning children's programming, or garnered enough of a presence to warrant its own network—The Cartoon Network—but with the success of *The Simpsons*, *South Park*, and even MTV's *Beavis and Butthead*, it has also made it to prime time with animated sit-coms like *Family Guy* and the *Boondocks*.

With more powerful computers and advanced software, traditional animation has become less traditional when it comes to feature-length animated films. In 1995 Pixar Studios teamed with Disney to release *Toy Story*, the first feature film fully animated using computer 3-D software. Dreamworks Studios followed their lead with the release of *Antz* in 1998. In 2002 Fox threw its hat into the 3-D animation ring with *Ice Age*. Since then, computer-animated films have been successfully received by both critics and audiences alike, thus revolutionizing the look and process of theatrically released animated films in the United States.

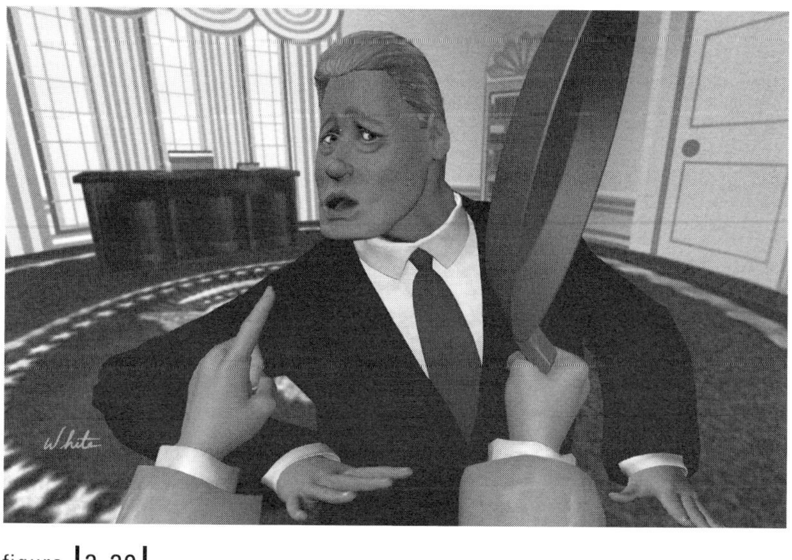

Artwork by Roger White

figure | 2-20 |

3-D computer animation.

| PIXAR AND DISNEY STUDIOS: THE NEXT GOLDEN AGE? |

Pixar, which was purchased by current CEO Steve Jobs for $10 million in 1986, was originally the computer graphics and special effects department of LucasFilms. The animators at the small company aspired to do more than special effects. They wanted to be storytellers. In the ten years to come, they would create award-winning shorts and 3-D commercials, while laying the groundwork for their foray into feature filmmaking. In 1991 Pixar formed an alliance with Disney in which they would develop, produce, and distribute up to three feature-length animated films. *Toy Story* was the first fruit of the union, and with each film to come, the successes would be greater. They would all receive Academy Award nominations, and some—*Monsters, Inc.*, *Finding Nemo*, and *The Incredibles*—would actually take home Oscars. They would also go on to break box office records and DVD and VHS sales records. It only stood to reason that Disney, which was having its own problems—declining attendance at its parks, disappointing box office performances, the ousting of its CEO—would want to hold on to its golden goose.

After reaching the height of its success with *The Lion King* (1994), Disney had begun to see a decline in the theatrical performance of its traditionally animated films. Disney had been distributing Pixar's films since its first hit, *Toy Story*, and decided to make the union more binding in January 2006. With $7.4 billion in hand, Disney purchased Pixar, making it an official member of the Disney family. At the time of the merger, Disney had not only just shut down one of its traditional animation studios in Orlando, Florida, but was also settling into the reign of a new CEO, Robert Iger. With the purchase of Pixar, the oldest animation studio was going to get a breath of new life. John Lasseter, longtime creative head at Pixar, would become head of the Disney animation department.

Disney's stock remained stable after the merger, showing that most analysts viewed the expensive merger as a positive play for the future of Disney. The key is whether Disney can incorporate the culture that has made Pixar a success into its model. If so, then perhaps it will be able to revive its own animation departments and return to the successes of its past. Moreover, the merging of one of the biggest media companies with a company that has a direct tie to one of the biggest technology companies, Apple, can only open the door to greater media convergence. Soon after the merger, in fact, Disney-owned ABC licensed episodes of its most popular television shows to Apple's iTunes for download to Apple's iPod.

This union of a member of the old guard to this generation's *wunderkind* could very well give dawn to the next golden age of animation, as well as new and innovative media.

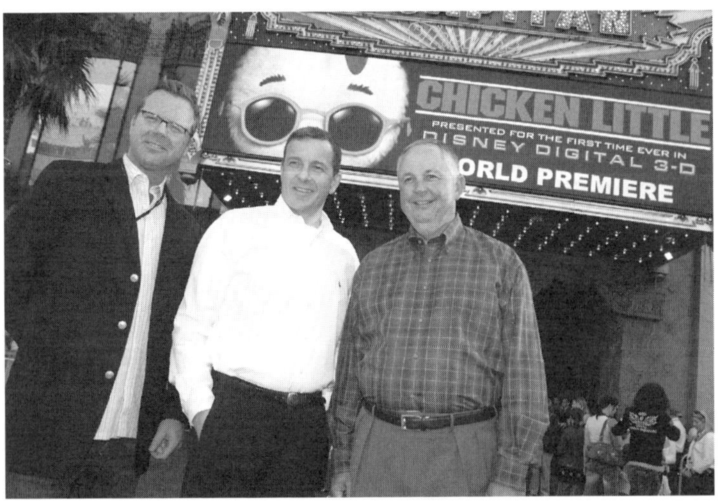

Getty Images Entertainment

figure |2-21|

Robert Iger (center) at the premiere of Disney's *Chicken Little*.

EXPERIMENTAL ANIMATION

Outside of the standard broadcast industry and studio system there are a host of fine artists who used animation as their medium, and in so doing have also had an impact on modern graphic designers.

By the 1920s experimental and avant-garde films appeared on the scene. Taking their inspiration from the writers and painters of the era, filmmakers were influenced by the various movements that directed the art world. Abstract art, Cubism, Dadaism, and Surrealism, in particular, found their way into the film world and more notably into animation. Oskar Fischinger, for example, allowed films to inspire his paintings and then reflect back upon his animation. He and other experimental animators after him took advantage of the lack of physical boundaries presented by animation and used the medium as a way to explore and exploit color, sound, and movement.

Fischinger's ideas about choreographing animated images to music even found their way into mainstream animation by Disney. Although Fischinger did not find his experience working with Disney Studios satisfying—he felt that it was a factory that did not encourage artistry to flourish—his sketches inspired the opening Bach fugue sequence of *Fantasia*, and he animated the fairy's magic wand in *Pinocchio*. Fischinger continued to work on his own experimental films after requesting leave of his Disney contract. Such works as *Motion Painting #1* were marked by his linking of images to sound—music, in particular—and by the vibrancy of his color choices. As a result, his work has had a lasting effect on animation and eventually on the motion graphics that came after.

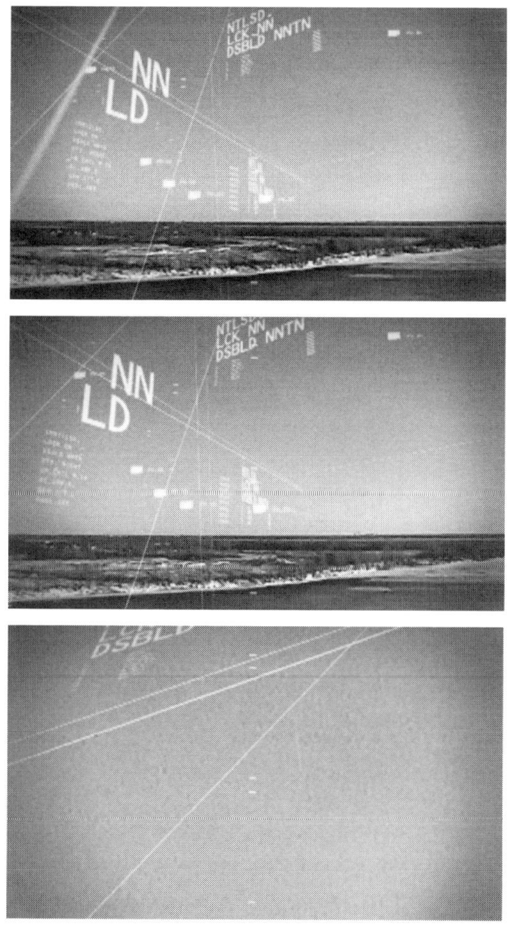

By Patrick Doan

figure |2-22|

This computer animation exploits negative and positive space, just as Fernand Léger had done using traditional animation techniques.

Jules Engel, a renowned abstract painter and filmmaker, also made a direct contribution to traditional animation, having worked on Disney's *Bambi* and designing the choreography for the *Nutcracker* sequences in *Fantasia*. His paintings and films were characterized by his interest in all styles of dance, color, and movement, and his artistic talents extended to documentaries as well as sculpture.

Works by artists such as Fernand Léger, who did *Ballet Mechanic* in 1924, were an example of how animation could be used to create abstract cinema. Hans Richter, a Dadaist, used the film screen as a canvas on which he could experiment with music and time through the manipulation of images throughout screen space in his films *Rhythm 21* and *Rhythm 23*. Today we see this influence in commercials and station IDs that feature moving shapes and lines. In his later work, Richter combined live-action footage with animation to create surreal effects.

Len Lye, an American experimental filmmaker, used a **direct-on-film** technique for some of his work. He would paint, scratch, and stencil images directly onto the celluloid film. His film *Color Box* (1935) was the result of painting on film. This technique of scratching was later adopted by Kyle Cooper to create the disturbing, yet groundbreaking title sequence for the 1995 film *Se7en*. Burning and rubbing the film can also produce dramatic artistic and thematic effects without a camera.

Experimental filmmakers and animators were instrumental in opening the minds of commercial artists, as well as audiences, to viewing animation in new ways. In particular, many techniques and styles once seen as experimental, such as compositing and morphing (a transition in which the features of one image transform into the next), were the ones artists chose to explore in more depth as computer animation became more prevalent. Today much of what we see on a daily basis is a result of the experiments conducted by forward-thinking, experimental artists. Even the modern music video, Dr. William Moritz, longtime professor of film and animation history at California Institute of the Arts, pointed out, is a contemporary adaptation of a form introduced by experimental filmmakers.

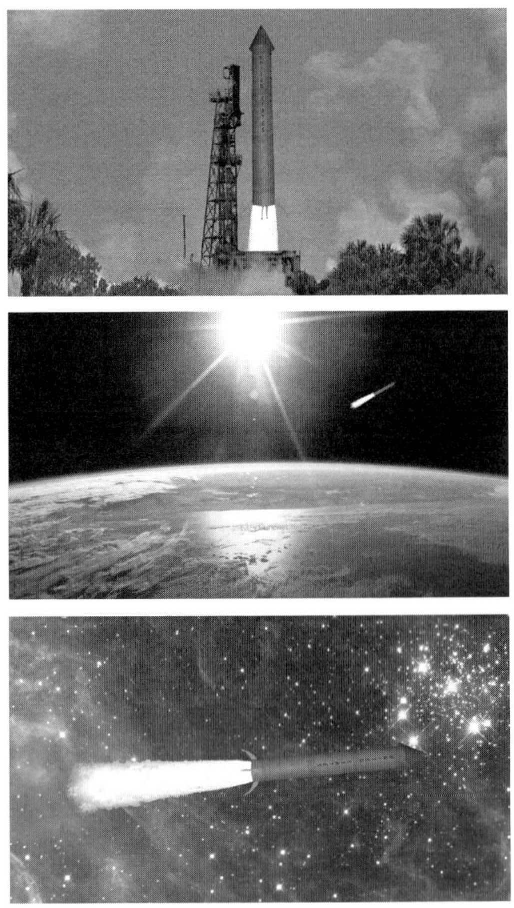

Art and animation by Dave Gordon. Some background photos courtesy of NASA

figure | 2-23 |

Experimental animation, *Faster, Better, Cheaper*, using compositing with photographs of everyday objects and the solar system.

| EXPERIMENTAL FILM TECHNIQUES |

The **pinboard**, or **pinscreen**, style of animation was created by married couple Alexander Alexeieff and Claire Parker. They pushed and pulled pins at various lengths into a screen creating varying shades of blacks, whites, and grays with strong textural qualities. The haunting results can be seen in their films *Night on Bald Mountain* (1933) and *The Nose* (1963).

The **collage** technique of animation combines photographs, drawings, and textures into a single frame to create a single image. Stan Brakhage in his 1963 film *Mothlight* made a collage of moth wings, flower petals, and glass by compressing them between two film strips and then photographing them.[4]

Sand animation is the manipulation of different colored sands under a film camera. Animation occurs with the use of stop-motion camera techniques.

Not all **computer animation** is experimental, especially when one considers that computers are an integral part of producing today's mainstream animations. However, the concept of using computers in animation in the 1960s was an experiment because animation, up until that point, had been a manual process, whether it was painting cels, painting directly onto the film, or manipulating pins on a pinboard.

In 1964 John Stehura used algorithms to create his film *Cybernetik 5.3*, an abstract manipulation of three-dimensional images, shapes, and colors. What is particularly remarkable is that he used a punch card computer that lacked a screen. This meant that he could not see what he was creating as he worked. When he finished programming the algorithms into the computer, he took the tapes, output from the computer, and transferred the information to a digital film recorder to create the final film (Faber and Walters 20).

Ed Emshwiller's film *Sunstone* (1979) had a very different look from *Cybernetik 5.3*, though it too was animated on a computer. Emshwiller's film showed that the computer could be used to create a more traditional look, though the film itself was still rather abstract. He used two different approaches in this piece. The first was by using color map cycling, which entails moving colors over static images to create the illusion of movement. The second method was stop-motion animation. Emshwiller was able to create 3-D images before 3-D computer software had been invented (Faber and Walters 26).

Even as computers have become an invaluable tool in creating commercial 3-D animation, they continue to be instruments for modern experimental pieces as well. Yoichiro Kawaguchi, a contemporary animator from Japan, has successfully used the computer to create his award-winning experimental films and to create software based on growth algorithms to complete his innovative artwork (Faber and Walters 36).

---

4 Liz Faber and Helen Walters, *Animation Unlimited: Innovative Short Films Since 1940* (London, UK: Laurence King Publishing, 2003), 18.

THE COMPUTER AGE

John Whitney was a composer, a filmmaker, and an inventor. The bridge between traditional animation and computer animation and digital graphics was built when John Whitney took leftover anti-aircraft hardware used to plot missile trajectories and built an analog computer that could plot graphics instead. Not only could he create graphics without drawing them, but he was able to manipulate the movement of these graphics. Seeing the possibilities for the entertainment industry, he founded Motion Graphics, Inc., in 1960 and hired his company out to do work in advertising and commercial titling. In addition to doing opening titles for *The Bob Hope Show* and *The Dinah Shore Show*, he also worked with Saul Bass on the opening sequence of *Vertigo*.

Named an artist-in-residence at IBM from 1966 to 1968, he moved from working on analog systems to the early digital computers. It should be said that it was not just his technical contribution to the evolution of motion graphics that is important but also his stylistic contribution. As an experimental filmmaker and composer, his work up until the time of his death in 1995 focused on the harmony between image and sound. This approach to animation along with his contributions to motion graphics helped propel the art of title and logo design forward.

TELEVISION

While television shows were still being shot on film near the end of the 1960s, videotape technology became available. With the advent of videotape technology, along with the addition of analog computers, the look of the network ID continued to evolve. Harry Marks of ABC was the first to design the moving logo and added depth to the television station ID with his "ABC movie of the week" logo in 1968. The look was accomplished with the slit-scan camera, a technique conceived by Douglas Trumbell and used in the stargate sequence of Stanley Kubrick's *2001*. Backlit artwork moved behind a large black slit that limited the view of the camera. As artwork passed behind the slit for each exposure, the camera, mounted on tracks, would slowly move toward the slit. The resulting effect was streaks that added another dimension to the text. Incidentally, John Whitney had also devised a way to achieve the slit-scan effect, but his proposal to create it for the film *2001* was turned down.

As the technology for computers became smaller and more refined, it also became more accessible to consumers. In the 1980s both IBM and Apple unleashed personal computers on the public, making it possible for people to have computers in their home. In 1984 Apple's Macintosh was born. The early 1980s was also the time that Pacific Data Images (PDI) began developing computer software to produce television graphics. In addition to producing computer generated graphics for *Entertainment Tonight*, ABC 1984 Olympic promotions, and commercials for familiar products like Pillsbury and Crest, it also worked with the then up-and-coming network MTV to produce a innovative look that influenced all of broadcast design. The late 1980s also saw the beginnings of 3-D television graphics in commercials and on-air promotions.

Within the last fifteen years, graphics have continued to grow more sophisticated as PDI introduced morphing, in commercials. Three-dimensional characters have become more commonplace—so much so, in fact, that they are the main characters on many children's shows. Dreamworks purchased PDI in 2004 and has since produced computer-generated films *Shrek II*, *Madagascar*, and *Over the Hedge*.

As people have grown to rely and interact more with the Internet in the past ten years, the style of graphics used in the entertainment arenas have also found their way onto websites and web banners. Following the same vein, we can also see how the movement in the past ten years toward 3-D animation in children's entertainment and advertisements has resulted in video games that boast realistic 3-D images that are capable of life-like maneuvers and activities.

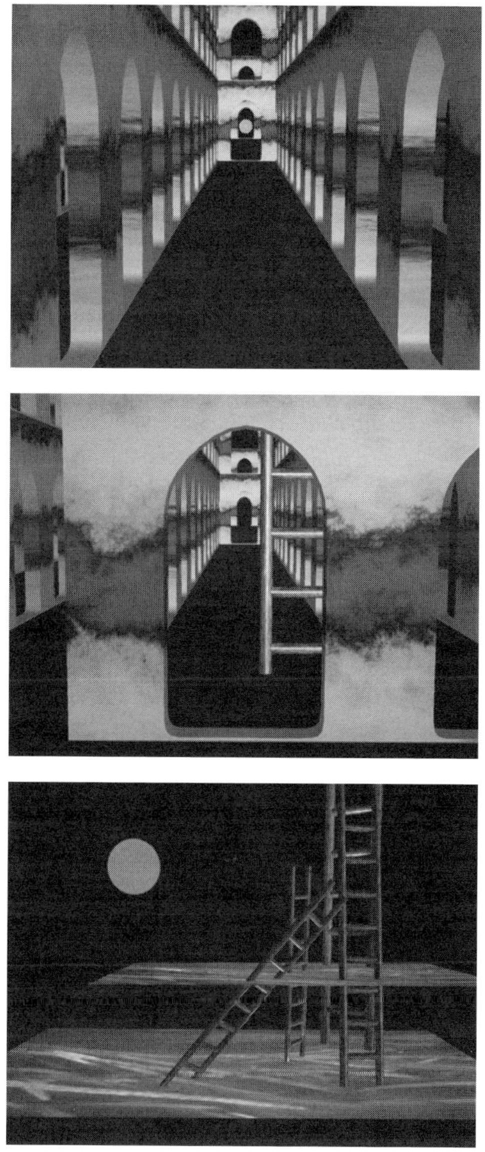

By Cecily McKeown

figure |2-24|

Modern computer animation, *Conclusion #17*.

SUMMARY

Visual storytellers have come a long way since the days when people were trying to figure out how to capture motion on film. Without the steps that led inventors from photography to early film, we would not understand how the illusion of motion is created. With the discovery of film came a need for crafts such as cinematography, editing, and set design. However, even with such visual cues, images were not always enough to deliver the message. Communicative graphics were also necessary. With the growth of technology, the art and innovations of film graphics were passed on to new media as they emerged. We have seen throughout this chapter how motion graphics techniques from film and animation eventually made their way to television.

In an attempt to create the illusion of motion, inventors developed optical toys such as the zoetrope and flipbooks. At the end of the nineteenth century, advances in photography set the foundation for Thomas Edison and the Lumière brothers to invent motion picture cameras. Sophisticated storytelling in early films required title cards for narration. Though intertitles were no longer needed when sound came to film, opening titles, which introduced the film and its players, remained. Film techniques and trends were a strong influence on animation, both traditional and experimental, and eventually both served as inspiration for television graphics. Computers have contributed to the art of title design by facilitating the designer's move to the realm of three-dimensional graphics in film, television, the Internet, and other emerging media.

in review

1. What are flicker fusion and apparent motion?
2. What was Eadweard Muybridge's contribution to film?
3. What was the difference between Thomas Edison's kinetoscope and the Lumière brothers' camera?
4. What was the purpose of title cards in early films?
5. Who was Saul Bass and what was his contribution to modern cinema?
6. Describe the stop-motion camera technique and how it differs from stop-motion animation.
7. Why was the cel a valuable invention for animators?
8. How has experimental film influenced modern motion graphics?
9. Who was John Whitney?
10. What impact have computers, in particular personal computers, had on motion graphics?

exercises

Exercise 1

Flipbook

This exercise will reinforce the basic principles of animation and allow for collaboration.

Task

(Note: A partner is required for this exercise.)

You and a partner are going to explore the illusion of motion by creating your own flipbook. One of you will go through the motions of cutting a piece of paper with a pair of scissors, while the other will capture the action with a still camera.

Goal

Construct a flipbook that illustrates the basic principles of animation.

Design It

1. Decide who will be the photographer and who will cut the paper.
2. Set the camera on a tripod so that the frame is consistent. Look through the viewfinder to make sure you are happy with your frame.
3. The person cutting the paper should practice making very gradual hand movements with the scissors. Remember, for the flipbook to work, each successive image needs to be almost identical to the one before it. There should be only a slight variation in the position of the hand and scissors.
4. If you are using a camera that allows you to take multiple pictures in a row, it will not be necessary for the person cutting the paper to make slow, deliberate moves. Instead, cut the paper in real time, while the photographer shoots as many exposures as the camera will allow until the action is complete.
5. When both parties are ready, begin the photo session. The photographer should snap at least twenty frames of action.
6. Print the photographs and leave the same amount of white margin above each photograph. You can cut off the rest of the margins.
7. Arrange the pictures in order with the last shot at the top of the pile.
8. Punch holes through the margin at the top of the pictures and bind them with brass fasteners.
9. Starting with the top image, slowly flip through the photographs one by one.
10. Begin to increase the speed at which you flip through the book.
11. Notice how the faster you flip through the book, the more it appears as if the pictures are moving and the paper is being cut!

Exercise 2

Trends in Title Design

This exercise reinforces the principles of title design.

Task

Choose two different films from the same genre but from different time periods, like a teenage comedy from the 1980s and one from the 1990s. Watch the opening titles of each and then compare and contrast the style of each of the openings.

Goal

Document your findings, with examples, and present them to the class.

Research It

1. How are the two films similar? How are they different?
2. Which do you prefer? Why?
3. How does each of the titles reflect the genre of the film?
4. How do the films reflect upon the trends of title design at the time they were released?
5. How do the title designs relate to the theme of the film?
6. Are the titles timeless or do they date themselves?
7. Do the later titles reference the style of the earlier titles?

Exercise 3

Title Cards

This exercise allows you to develop the dialogue and design for title cards of a silent movie, reinforcing the important role they played during the era of silent films.

Task

Choose a scene from a television show or film. Watch the footage without sound. Create your own dialogue and write it down.

Goal

Create title cards with your own dialogue to go along with the silent version of the footage. This exercise could be done on paper or on the computer.

Design It

Since you want your cards to match seamlessly with the footage, you may want to ask yourself some questions to help you determine a style that will work:

1. What is the genre of the scene?
2. What is the director's shooting style?

3. Are the colors vibrant, muted, or monochromatic?

4. What is the tone of the scene? Is it funny? Serious? Melodramatic?

5. Does the production look high-budget or low-budget?

6. Is the film's overall look unique or generic? Simple or ornate?

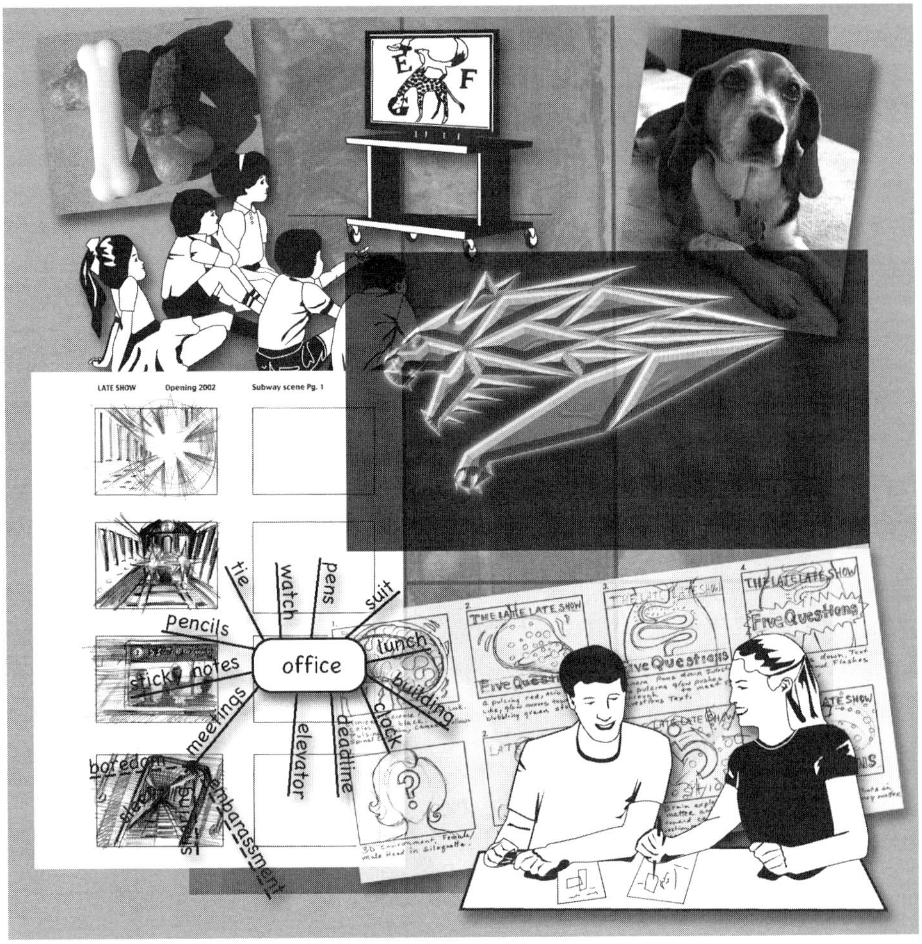
LATE SHOW Opening 2002 Subway scene Pg. 1
office
tie
watch
pens
suit
pencils
lunch
sticky notes
building
meetings
clock
elevator
deadline
boredom
embarassment
THE LATE LATE SHOW
Five Questions

CHAPTER 3

Chapter Objectives

Understand the importance of collaborating with clients and other professionals

Discover the influence of audience research in the final design

Learn how to implement a specific planning and research methodology

Understand the importance of semiotics in communicating a message to an audience

Introduction

Before beginning a journey, you have to choose a destination. Once you have selected a destination, you must then map out an approach. Likewise, before beginning production on a design, you must take certain steps to plan and execute its successful completion, regardless of the medium. Whether designing for television, film, the web, or any other digital medium, all designers have a method of approach if they hope to achieve their goal of communicating with their graphics.

The first step of the journey is **pre-production**, which usually includes research and brainstorming, as well as getting to know the client and the audience. Without an understanding of the audience and client, there is no context within which to frame the design. Moreover, it is imperative to research the subject matter of the design in order to deliver the clearest, most direct message possible. Doing their homework equips designers both with the information and the inspiration they need to begin working on their graphics.

Once familiar with the client and audience, it is time to brainstorm and begin sketching out some ideas. Making a visual record of ideas facilitates the process of fleshing them out and refining them. Eventually, the sketches will become storyboards or mock-ups that act as a blueprint to production. This is the designer's opportunity to think through color schemes and font types and how to use the design space. This is also the time to think about framing and composition and how the elements will move throughout the frame.

While the production process and final output may differ according to the medium, the call for collaboration with the client or other creative professionals at some stage will not. Production is not complete until the client is satisfied that the design has delivered the message that it wants to communicate. While this could mean doing several drafts of a project before delivering the final version, it is the designer's goal to accomplish the client's mission.

Throughout this chapter, we will take a closer look at the design process, while also discussing how working with a team and problem solving factor into the designer's journey.

WORKING WITH OTHER PROFESSIONALS ON A TEAM

Unlike school assignments or personal projects, designing for a client requires working with other people who make up a team. Before a designer can even think of designing a project, a meeting with the client must take place. This allows the designer the chance to incorporate the client's ideas, needs, and goals into the creative vision. Ultimately, the project is not a representation of the designer's vision so much as the designer's rendition of the client's vision.

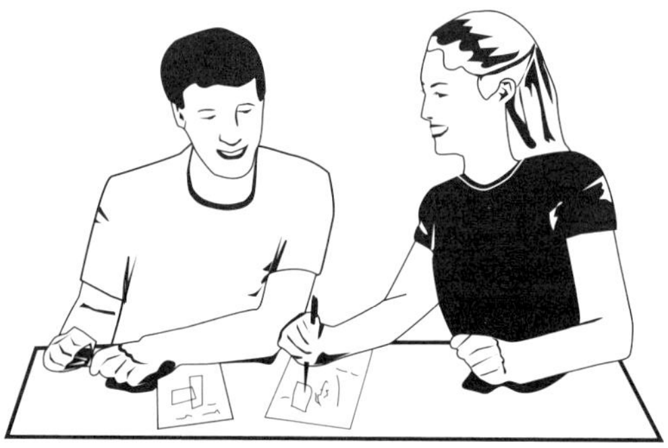

figure |3-1|

Collaboration between designer and client is an important part of the design process.

Because a designer is working with other people who have their own deadlines to meet, the designer must strive to complete his part of the job on schedule. Companies want to work with designers who are dependable and meet deadlines. And while they may value the designer for his talent, they will value the designer even more for his ability to work well with the people on the team.

Depending on the budget and the scale of the project, designers may either execute their own designs, or they might act as art director overseeing someone else who brings the design to fruition. Either way, there is usually a director (for television or film) or an art director (for ad agencies, the Internet, and handheld devices) who sees that all of the creative pieces come together into a coherent vision.

CONCEPT AND DEVELOPMENT

Even before the first meeting with the client, the designer should become familiar with the client's image and current branding strategy. Good sources for such information, besides the client, of course, are the Internet and back issues of trade magazines. The client will probably be happy to provide additional press materials from the company archives. With a strong sense of the company's history, along with its current goals and desires, the designer can begin the next phase of research before conceptualizing the design.

Once the designer and client meet, it is time to define the mission. What is the message? How will the designer or design team go about communicating it? By asking these questions, the project can be broken down into parts to be investigated and researched. The results of the research should give way to ideas of how to approach the mission and then communicate the message.

RESEARCH

Motion graphic designers often break their research process into two stages: the field of study and the project focus.

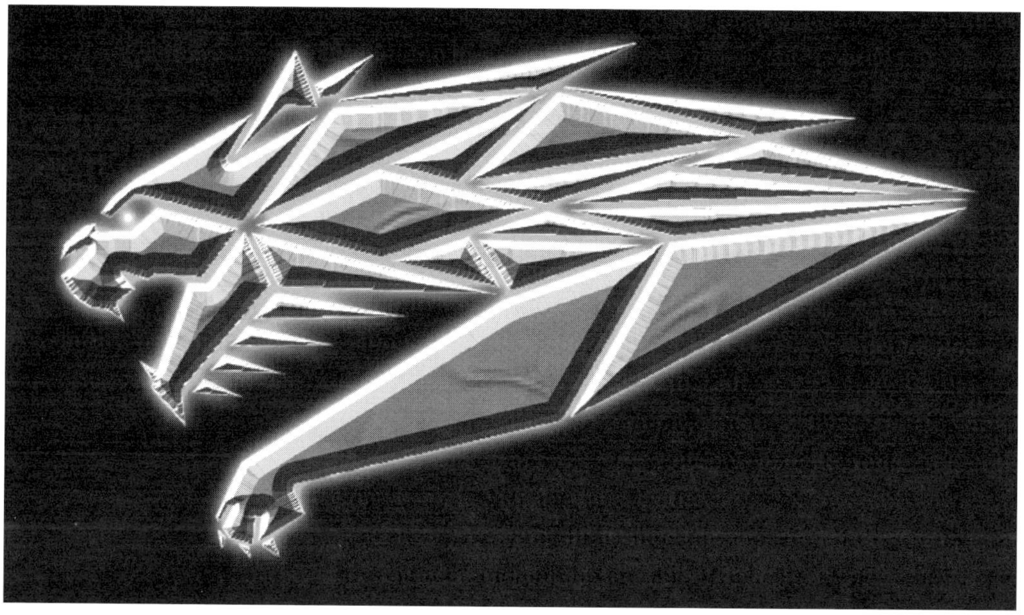

figure |3-2|

This production logo represents the image that Lionheart Films wants to cultivate.

The Field of Study

The field of study refers to the perimeters within which the project falls. The designer and client must decide upon the general goal of the project along with its audience. This is also a good time for the client (internal or external) and designer to make sure that they are on the same page concerning budget and expectations. Both parties should have a realistic understanding of the cost of the project and its relation to what the designer can reasonably produce within the desired time frame. This is also when to set a timetable for the delivery of materials from both the client and the designer.

In order to move forward with the process, it is imperative that the designer understands both the audience and the medium for the message. This means the designer should be aware of competing messages and the success that these competitors have experienced with this audience. As the client has probably performed its own market research and studies of the audience and its response to the product or service, the designer will likely see what approaches have been successful or have failed with this audience. While striving to be original, the designer will also want to communicate using symbols and images that mean something to this audience.

Audience

Audience is one of the most important factors for designers to consider if they are to communicate effectively. In order to interact, two parties must have a shared language, and though it certainly helps if they speak the same tongue, language goes beyond what is verbal. Language

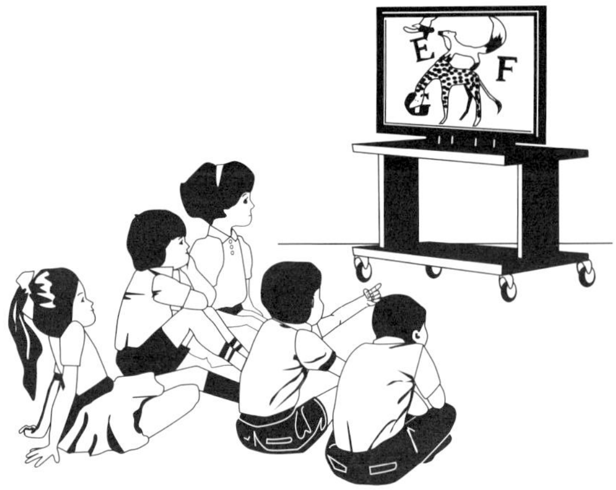

figure |3-3|

Children tend to respond to pictures, simple illustrations, and bright graphics.

includes visual and cultural associations, as well as idioms and slang.

For instance, communicating with an audience that does not read, such as young children, or a group of tourists who do not speak English, will certainly affect the choices of images and graphics a designer uses to deliver a message. Simple, colorful graphic illustrations and pictures will greatly appeal to children and enable a clear connection with them as audience. This approach will not be as successful with the tourists because they will not want to be viewed as incapable children, so another style of visual communication will need to be created.

Understanding an audience's social and cultural values is just as critical as being able to use words and images to which it can relate. In order to understand the audience's personality and demographics, the designer and client should first ask the right questions.

The first questions to ask are general ones about day-to-day lifestyle. This is a sample list of questions to present to potential audience members:

1. What is your gender? [Male or Female]
2. What is your age range? [18–25 26–35 36–45]
3. What is your income bracket? [< $50,000 $50,000–$75,000 > $75,000]
4. What is your professional occupation?
5. What is your race?
6. What is your cultural or religious affiliation?
7. Are you married or single?
8. Do you live in a suburban or urban environment?
9. Do you own a car?
10. Do you rent or own your own home?

These questions will provide insight into the overall personalities and general interactions of audience members over the course of a day. Based on their answers certain assumptions can be made about their preferences and desires. Based on answers to questions about their gender, age, and cultural or religious affiliations, we are given some insight into their choice of style and aesthetics. Based on their responses to questions about where they live and work, we can determine the best placement for the message, and based on their answers regarding their finances, we are clued in to whether they have disposable income to spend on the product or service for sale. With this information you can make a general determination as to what medium to use for your message or how to break down the information in the message. Once you have made some general determinations, you can move on to more specific questions that will help determine the aesthetic of the design.

The potential list of questions is endless, but here are a few suggestions:

- What are your hobbies?
- What is your preferred mode of daily transportation?
- How many times a year do you go on vacation?
- What do you do in your leisure time?
- How many hours a week do you work, on average?
- Do you consider yourself to be technically proficient?
- How often do you use the Internet?
- How do you prefer to receive information: via e-mail, television, or the Internet?

Medium as Message

When clients dictate the medium for a design, they do so because through their internal research they have determined that particular medium to be the best way to reach that particular audience. It is a designer's job to develop a visual concept that will best utilize the strengths of the medium, communicate the message without interference, and engage the viewer.

Marshall McLuhan's famous statement, "The medium is the message," is true insofar as the person responding to the message is aware of the medium and may already have certain expectations of that medium. We expect technology to act in a certain way; cell phone buttons allow us to dial a number or retrieve information, using a joystick with a video game allows us to manipulate characters on the screen, and by selecting the "play movie" button on a DVD interface we will be able to view the movie. Such expectations help the viewer to retrieve the message as intended. Changes to the medium that go against these expectations can hinder the retrieval and change the effect of the message. Moreover, the inability to use or understand a particular medium can interfere with the audience's ability to get the message that it is meant to deliver. A faulty DVD interface, for example, could hinder the viewers' ability to use the menu and find the proper chapter to be viewed.

When the medium reaches a level of transparency, or state in which the audience does not even notice the medium, it is less likely to interfere with the message. When the Internet was just catching on to mainstream society, checking e-mail posed problems for many new users, thus making them as aware of the e-mail interface as they were of the message they were trying to

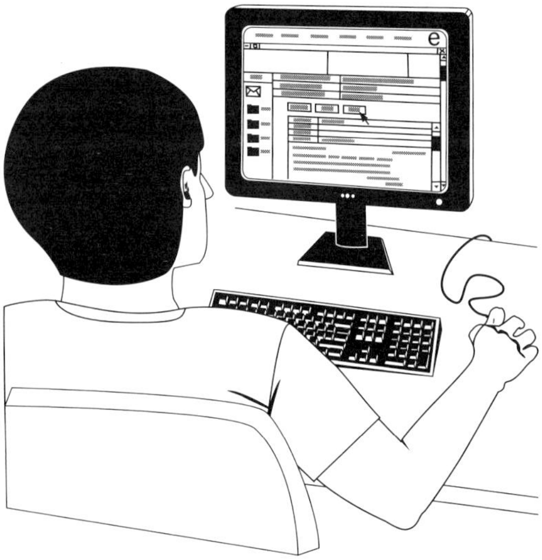

figure |3-4|

People are so accustomed to checking e-mail that the Internet is almost transparent.

retrieve. Ten years later, people are so accustomed to e-mail and the Internet that it is becoming more transparent. Transparency, in fact, is the goal of a filmmaker who wants the viewer to be so drawn into the film that he forgets that he is watching a film and instead believes he is inside the imaginary world depicted on screen.

The Project Focus

The project focus, as discussed by Ian Noble and Russel Bestley in their book *Visual Research: An Introduction to Research Methodologies in Graphic Design* is more specific than the field of study. Having become more familiar with the audience and the context of the project, the designer can be more specific about determining the message to the audience. There are two research models for this stage of information gathering. The first is context definition, which focuses on continuing to familiarize oneself with the field of study, while the second, context experimentation, focuses on just that—experimentation.

Whereas context definition gathers information through reports and other secondary sources, context experimentation will actually test different designs and concepts on a target audience. In web, game, and interface design this is also referred to as usability study and testing. This approach requires that the designer and client come to a decision earlier in the process about what they believe their message to be. The results of these numerous experiments can have the power to change the focus of the project should they appear to be unsuccessful with the audience. A proper analysis of what makes the communications successful or unsuccessful is key, and some critical components to investigate would be the images and language used in the failed messages. Linguists, those who study words, and the field of semiotics play an important role in this investigation.

Semiotics

Semiotics is the study of signs and their relationship to the actual objects or things they represent. It looks at language and asks the question of whether a word or image can represent the object it names and how effectively it can do so. This is particularly relevant to design since a designer uses language and images to represent real-world concepts and to evoke a genuine, emotional response from an audience. If the designer does not use images that have a meaning to the audience, then the audience will have no understanding of the designer's communication.

Linguist Ferdinand de Saussure (1857–1913), credited as the father of semiotics, developed a model to examine how meaning is determined. Saussure applied his model only to the study of language and did not include material objects or images. He developed a two-part model to study signs, **signifier** and **signified**. In Saussure's model the **sign** is the word as written, the signifier is the spoken word that refers to a concept, and the concept is the signified.

Charles Pierce, a contemporary of Saussure, expanded upon Saussure's model to include objects. He used a three-part model to define the sign, the thing itself. Rather than focusing solely on the structure of language, he divided signs into visual categories: **icon**, **symbol**, and **index**.

The icon most closely resembles the sign. It contains recognizable features of the sign, making the relationship between the signifier and the signified easy to identify. An icon could be a photograph, a drawing, or some other form of imitation. A sound that is spoken like the sound itself, referred to as onomatopoeic, is also an icon. "Woof" as a spoken word may act as an icon for a dog because the sound a dog makes when it barks sounds the same.

The relationship of the symbol to the sign and signified must be learned, as it is arbitrary like language. We know that the word *dog* represents an actual "dog" not because there is any inherent relationship between the word and the animal, but because we learn the word and the object it represents. Say the word "dog" to someone who does not speak English, and the word has no meaning to him; he will be unable to summon an image of a dog in his head or point to a dog on the street without understanding the inherent relationship between the word and object or idea. A chew toy may be a symbol of a dog.

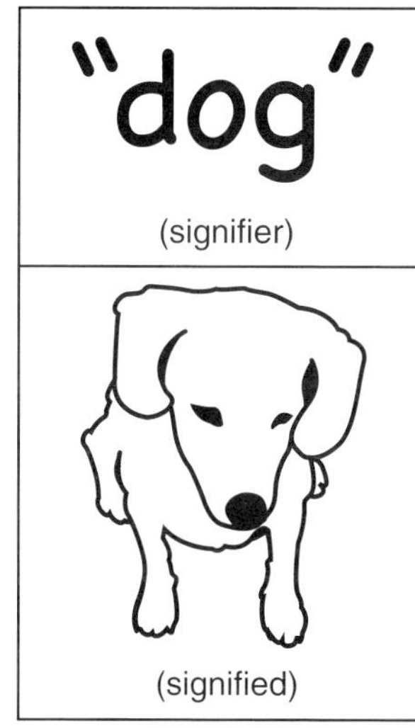

figure |3-5|

The signifier and the signified according to Saussure's model. The sign is the written word *dog*, and the signifier is the spoken word "dog." The resulting visualization, or signified, is an image of a dog.

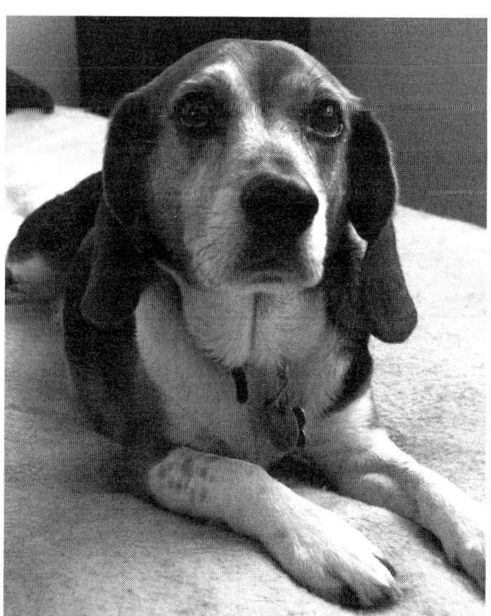

figure |3-6|

This photograph of the dog, the icon, most closely resembles the actual dog.

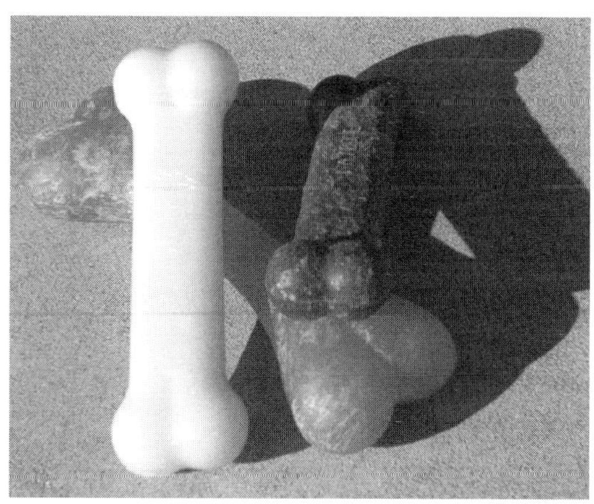

figure |3-7|

These dog bones are symbols of the dog.

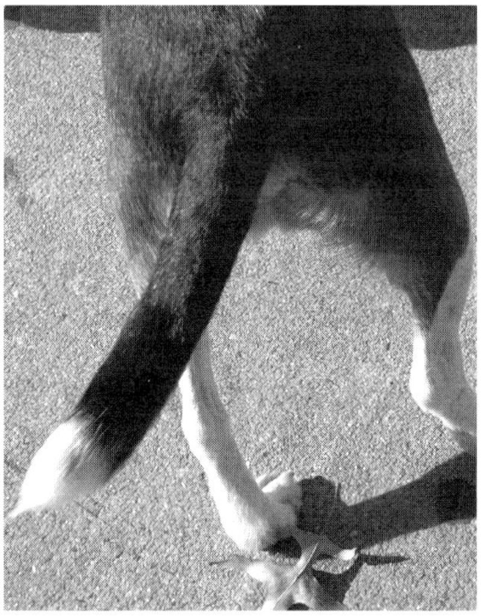

figure | 3-8 |

The wagging tail, a universally understood, physical manifestation of a happy dog, is the index for the dog.

The index is a signifier that does not resemble the signified per se, but represents the physical manifestation of the signified. For example, the ringing of a telephone indicates that someone is calling to speak, or a signature can represent a person and his consent to an agreement. A wagging tail is an index of a dog.

Roland Barthes (1915–1980) took semiotics even further than Saussure and Pierce and included the study of language in all of its forms, visual and verbal. He considered gestures, music, objects, and other aspects of culture to be at the very least "systems of signification," Daniel Chandler explains in *Semiotics for Beginners*. Like Barthes, many semiologists apply semiotics to art and literature as a way of decoding and analyzing their textual meanings. It is for this reason that a general understanding of semiotics is important to the designer, who is trying to communicate visually with an audience. The designer needs to be aware of the power of certain images and their cultural associations.

Research Methodology

Research methodology refers to the manner in which the designer will conduct and analyze research and ultimately how the research results will be synthesized into a design. The methodology is the designer's plan of action for acquiring information through experimentation and audience feedback, which will ultimately help the designer to create a successful, communicative design.

The Internet is among the many valuable resources for gathering information, as long as information is gleaned only from official websites where facts are checked and verified. Additionally, search engines such as EBSCOhost and LexisNexis, accessible through many libraries, can provide numerous articles on various topics. Research into specific design trends and design history can also be useful, depending on the direction of the particular project.

In addition to factual information and meetings with the client, designers are guided by their personal inspiration as well. They are always acutely aware of what is taking place in the world of design. Designers who have been in the business for years continue to read design magazines regularly and deconstruct designs that they encounter in their daily lives. They are constantly gathering information, tearing out pages from magazines, taking notes, and picking up objects that will inspire a future design.

BRAINSTORMING

Once research is complete, the designer is ready to brainstorm concepts for the design. The first step in brainstorming is defining the "problem" or message to be delivered. Since the research stage already heeded this information, the designer may either sit alone or with the client or other members of a creative team to begin a brainstorm session.

The concept of group brainstorming was invented by advertising executive Alex Osborn in 1941. Participants should adhere to several rules of brainstorming:

- Participants do not criticize each other's ideas
- Numerous ideas are generated
- People build upon each other's ideas
- Unorthodox and outrageous ideas are encouraged

| TIP |

Even when brainstorming alone, ideas should be allowed to flow without self-censoring.

The first rule is particularly important because brainstorming can only be successful if the people involved feel comfortable sharing ideas with one another without fearing judgment or embarrassment.

The more ideas that are generated, the more the group has to work with. Once the obvious list of ideas is exhausted, participants have to dig deeper to come up with less common, more innovative ones. For this to be successful, participants should record the fruits of the brainstorming session either on a large board for all to read or on a sheet of paper for later review.

One of the values of group brainstorming is that several people concentrating on the problem at once gives many more ideas than could be generated by a single person working alone. Moreover, if people are encouraged to piggyback on other people's ideas, they are able to use them as a springboard to either a more thoroughly developed idea or a whole new concept. In a brainstorm session no one person can take ownership of the final idea because it truly is a collaborative process and the result of the group's hard work.

Finally, because the group has created an environment in which people are comfortable sharing ideas, the last rule of brainstorming encourages the participants to think outside of the box. It is from these unusual ideas that a creative team can really hit on something original and develop a gem of a design concept.

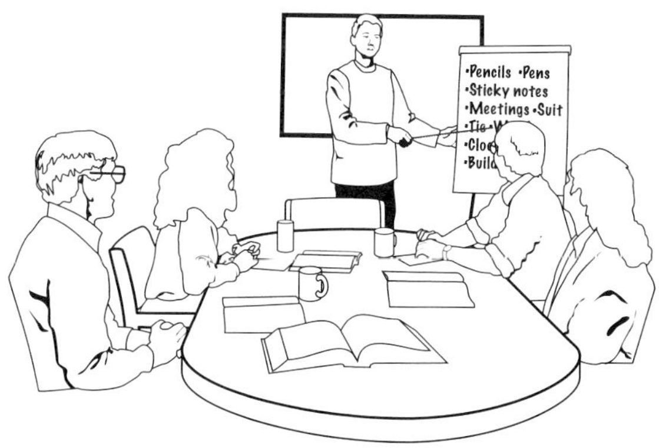

figure | 3-9 |

Brainstorming is most effective when a comfortable sharing environment is established.

Word Association

A common brainstorming technique is **word association**, making a list of words that spring to mind in association with a particular concept. For example, if a client wants an ad for its office products, a brainstorm session might result in the following list:

- Pencils
- Pens
- Sticky notes
- Meetings
- Suit
- Tie
- Watch
- Clock
- Building
- Elevator
- Deadline

The list for office products could be one of many that the team creates. They could create other lists starting from different points. For instance, instead of the obvious work items, they could list things associated with a vacation from work or items at home or at school.

The group could then take these lists and generate more words and concepts in association to the ones already listed, or they could begin to focus the list back to the original problem at hand. What is the message to be delivered, and how can those words or concepts be enlisted to help deliver the message? If this list is not substantial enough to answer those questions, the group needs to continue generating words or perhaps move on to another type of brainstorming called **webbing**.

Webbing

Webbing is making links between words and concepts and can bear further fruit as the team begins to branch off from the original list or make connections between items already on the list.

Using the previous list, one might link "meetings" to "boredom." "Boredom" could then be linked to "sleep." "Sleep" could be linked to "snoring," which would certainly be linked to "embarrassment" when it takes place in a meeting. Once a chain of words ceases to bear ideas, the team can work with other words on the list or continue to free associate to generate more words.

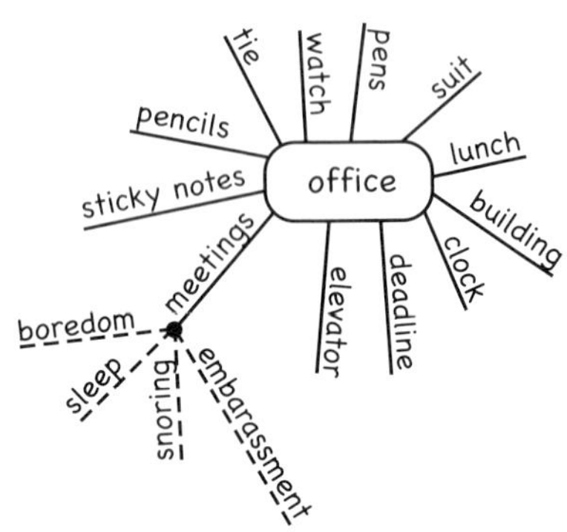

figure 3-10

Webbing is making connections between words.

As with the results of word association, the results of the brainstorming session must be refocused to answer the original question of communicating with a specific audience. The team should agree upon the ideas that can best accomplish the mission at hand and then begin to refine those ideas. Full-fledged

| EFFECTIVE BRAINSTORMING |

Leigh Thompson, a professor at Northwestern University's Kellogg School of Management, found that brainstorming had become less effective in part due to "social loafing, conformity [and] production-blocking." Thompson suggested in her report that brainstorming could be more efficient if the teams were more diverse in their members and if they used analogies to encourage more original ideation. She also postulated that brainstorm sessions would be more successful with trained facilitators to keep the group focused and to keep a written record of the ideas generated.

SOURCE: Eugene Sadler-Smith, "Maximizing the Benefits of Brainstorming," *People Management*, October 23, 2003.

design concepts or marketing campaigns should be the final outcome of this process. At the end of the session, the group can select two or three concepts for the designer to work with.

FORM VERSUS FUNCTION

At the end of the brainstorming stage, the designer must take the ideas generated and begin to synthesize them into a design that delivers the message the client wants to communicate. It is at this point that form and function may come into play.

What does "form versus function" mean? Is each mutually exclusive? Balancing between the artistic aesthetic and functionality can be a challenge for designers who do not want one element to get in the way of the other. Even so, reaching the balance between form and function is not unattainable. In fact, the wedding of the two elements often results in a more communicative design.

The Bauhaus School

The **Bauhaus** School, founded by the architect Walter Gropius in 1919 in Weimer, Germany, sought to find the union between form and function. The mission of the school was to bring art (form) and craft (function) together in the age of modernity. Rather than separate fine art from the crafting of buildings, furniture, and other industrial products, the two would come together resulting in products that were aesthetically pleasing, useful, and relatively easy to manufacture with the emerging technology of the day. In particular, Bauhaus style was applied to architecture and was the driving force behind the metal and glass skyscrapers of the twentieth century.

Laszlo Moholy-Nagy was a teacher at the Bauhaus before leaving Germany to take over a new art school in Chicago (The Art Institute of Illinois). His light sculptures are a classic example of Bauhaus principles, for the sculptures are works of art that also serve a function. The director of an experimental film, *The ABC of Sound*, he also specialized in photography and typography and was instrumental in seeing that the Bauhaus included a curriculum in graphic design.

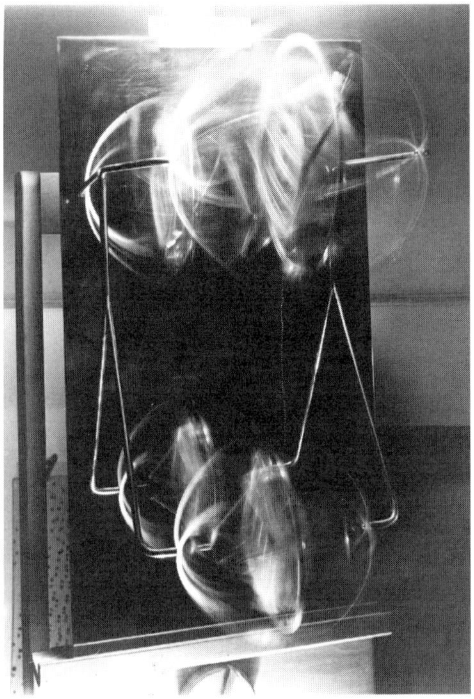

figure |3-11|

Moholy-Nagy light sculpture represents the principles of the Bauhaus movement.

Form and Function in Modern Design

Even today the principles of the Bauhaus School are evident in the proliferation of handheld devices meant to make our lives easier. Cell phones continue to get smaller, while also being capable of surfing the web, playing music, and taking photographs—all of this while still serving their original function of allowing us to communicate on the run. MP3 players, which serve as personal organizers and music playing devices, also play videos, store photographs, and act as a hard drive. While highly functional, their design is modern and sleek, coming in sophisticated black, white, or pleasant pastel casings.

In the same way that portable devices make our lives easier, graphics that help us navigate a website or give us additional facts in a commercial or television program are effective both by adhering to an artistic aesthetic and by giving us needed information.

It is the principle of form and function that inspires designers to make sure that their design choices are in service of their messages, while seeing that they are also aesthetically sound. This is part of the challenge of design, made even more complicated at times by technology. Because advanced software enables a designer to do so much more than before and because it makes many tasks very easy, it can be tempting to allow the software to dictate design choices. But as engaging as a designer wants the design to be, he will never let it be at the cost of delivering the message, the entire function of the design.

ROUGHS AND THUMBNAILS

The designer is now ready to sketch ideas for the design. As with any project, it takes several drafts to get everything right. This is where roughs and thumbnails come into play. They are often hand-drawn renderings of the design. The idea behind them is to allow the designer to test-drive the plan to see where problems may lurk and solve those problems before presenting them to the client and before actually executing the final project. Many designers carry around a small notebook to sketch ideas and jot down notes as they come.

STORYBOARDS AND MOCK-UPS

Storyboards are more detailed, more polished versions of thumbnail sketches. Now is the time when color is added and more precise drawings are rendered. Like a comic strip, storyboard drawings are laid out in separate boxes in order to show the progression of a design over time.

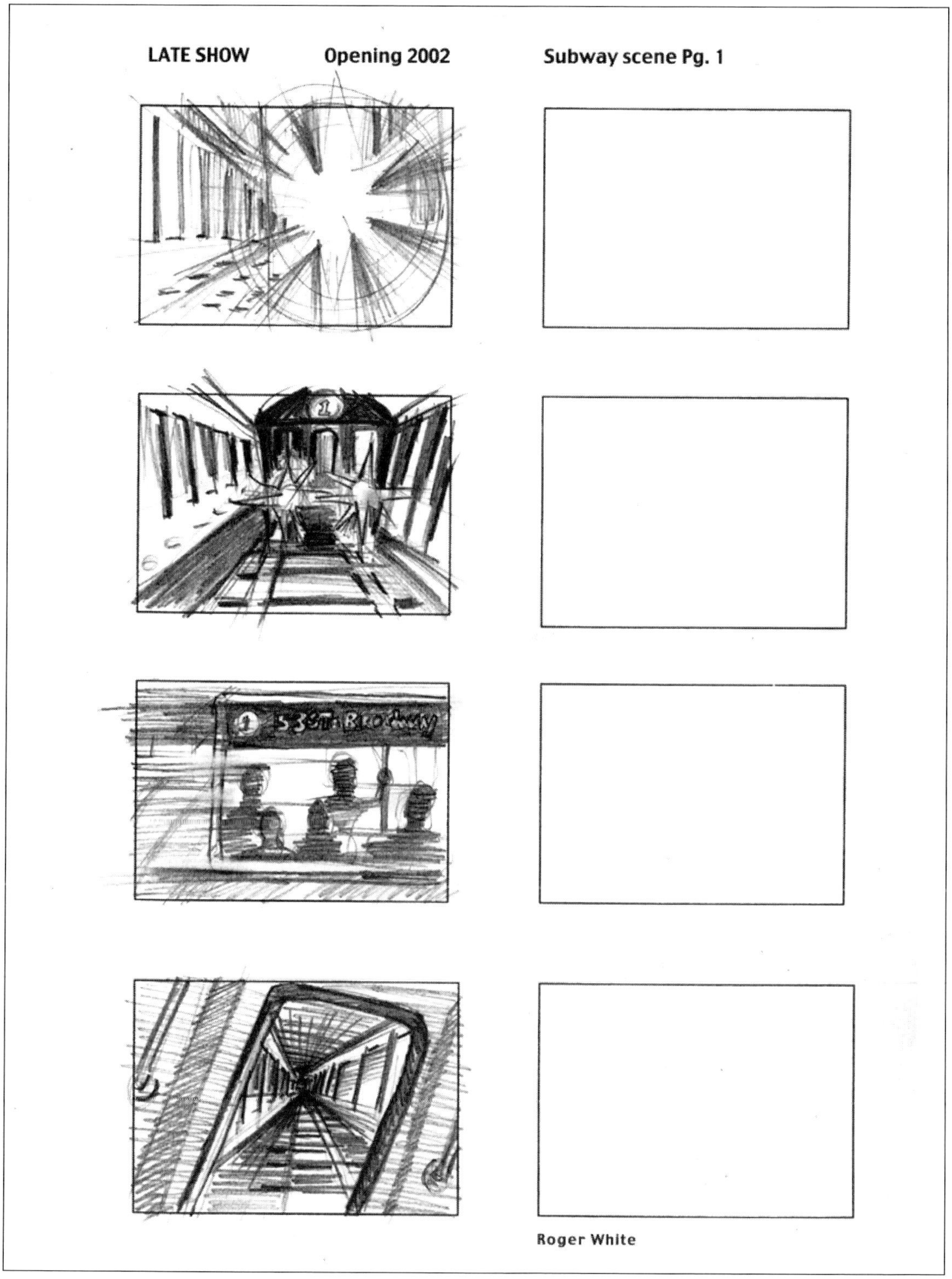

figure 3-12

Storyboards for the opening sequence to *The Late Show with David Letterman*.

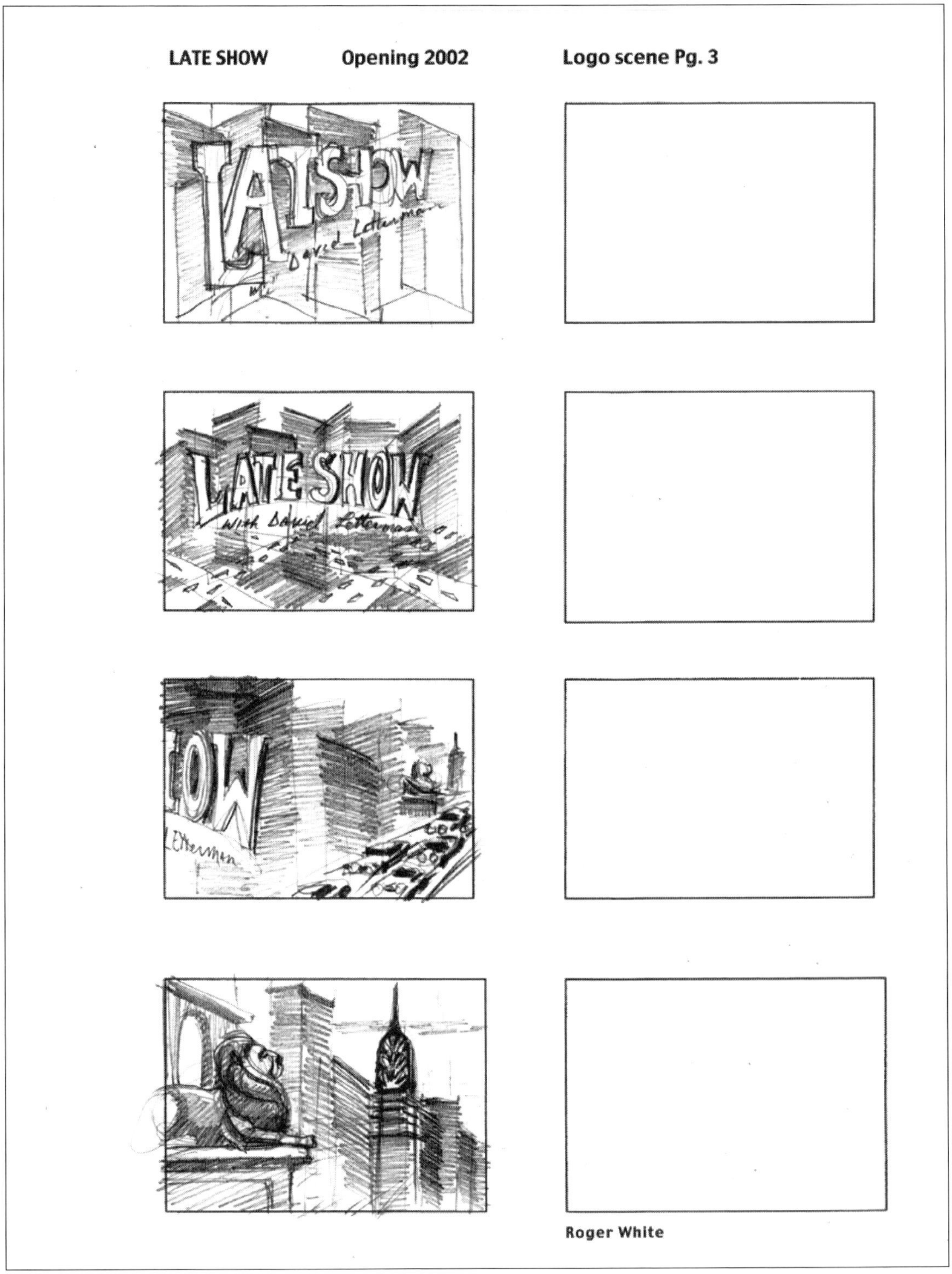

figure |3-12| (continued)

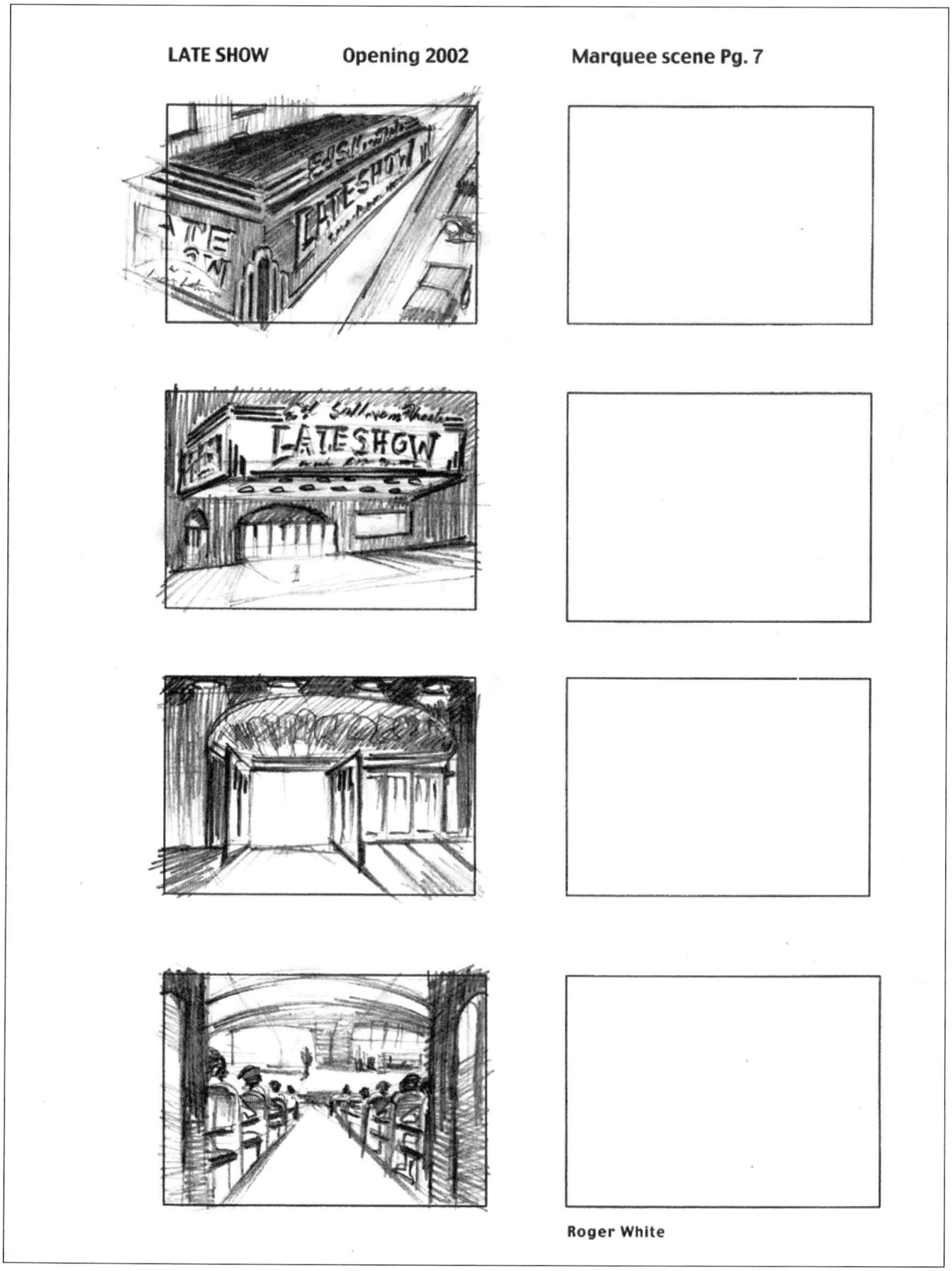

figure |3-12| (continued)

The detail of storyboards can vary according to the length of the project, but they always represent the most important frames of the piece and can also be accompanied by sluglines, which describe point of view, style of movement, direction of motion, and any other details that explain movement within the frame or between frames. Storyboards can be either done by hand or prepared in Illustrator or Photoshop. In the case of web design, a mock-up of the webpage is done in Photoshop. The difference between it and the actual webpage is, of course, that the Photoshop file is inactive and inaccessible to web users.

Designers include the client at the storyboard stage of the process because their main objective at this point is to please the client. A designer should not spend the time and resources to complete the project until he gets approval on the storyboards or mock-ups. The more detailed the storyboards and mock-ups, the better for both the designer and the client.

The Grid

The **grid** is the designer's work canvas. It is composed of imaginary lines that equally divide the design space into squares that pull together and unify the elements of a design. As the designer begins to make choices about the colors, shapes, and fonts, as well as the trajectory of movement for the graphics, they will all fall within the grid, and the grid will hold them together. When determining the composition of a shot, or the composition of a design, the grid is useful because it helps the designer to organize images so that they communicate information both coherently and powerfully.

| DRAWING TIP |

Even if you feel that you lack drawing skills, you should not shy away from putting your ideas down on paper. Storyboards and roughs are extremely important to help you visualize your idea and prepare it for transition to the digital world. They are also often essential when initially discussing your idea with a client. Clients will want to see designs on paper to help them visualize the design concept.

There are four basic geometric shapes inherent in all forms: sphere, cylinder, cube, and cone. Any form can be broken down into these basic shapes and this will aid you in realizing your vision on paper. By using these shapes you can illustrate any object and simply, but clearly, convey your design ideas.

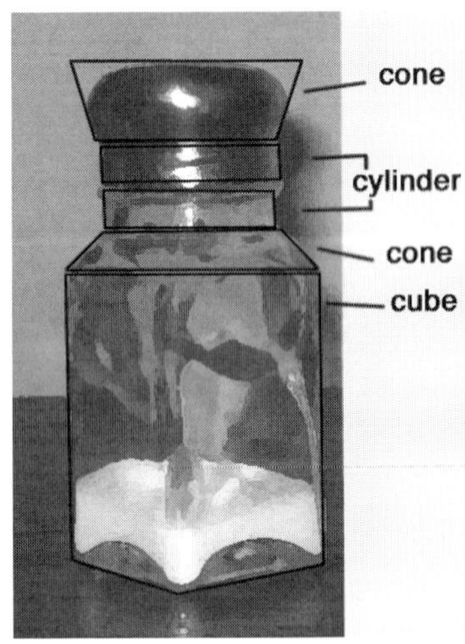

figure |3-13|

Any form can be broken down into one or more of the four basic shapes: sphere, cylinder, cube, or cone.

Once a designer begins to add movement, things become more complicated, and having the grid as a guideline becomes even more helpful. Just as grid lines assist in solving mathematical equations involving diagonals and curves, the design grid can assist with determining the trajectory of moving images.

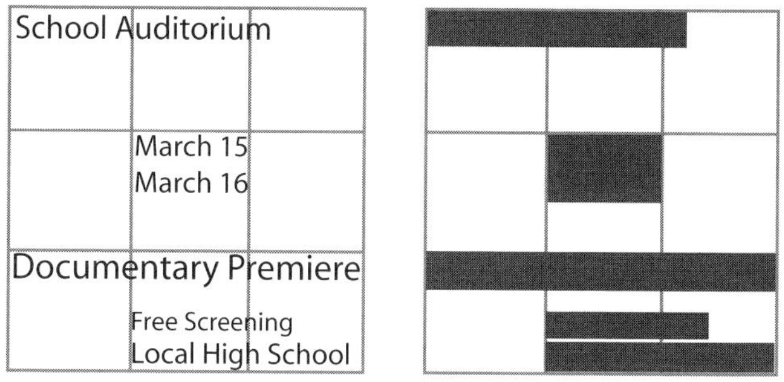

figure |3-14|

The grid organizes design elements within the frame.

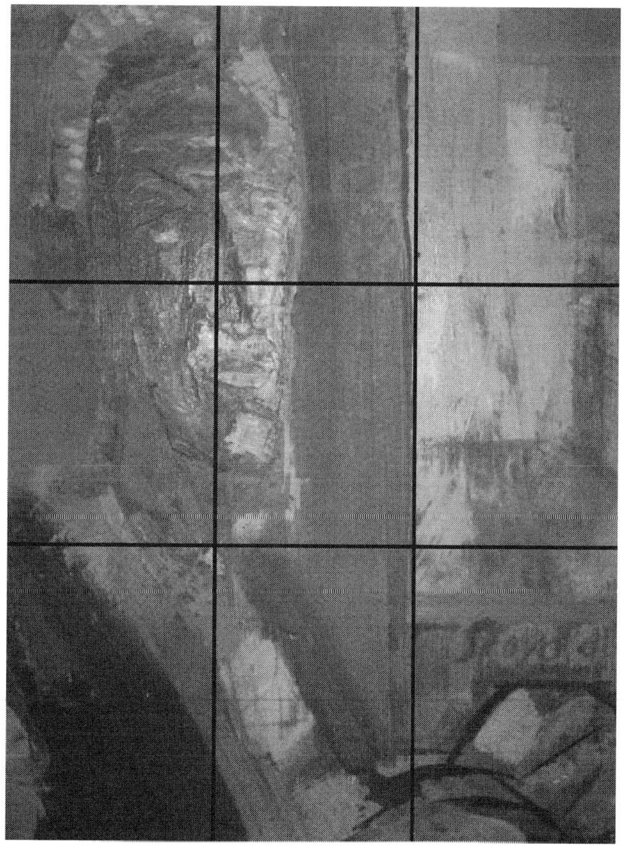

figure |3-15|

The man's face is positioned at the intersection point of the horizontal and vertical grid lines, following the rule of thirds.

The Rule of Thirds

The **rule of thirds**, utilized by photographers, artists, and designers alike, divides the grid into thirds both horizontally and vertically. Application of the rule of thirds allows for the most dynamic placement of the composition's most important elements. Rather than placing them at the center of the composition, they are positioned directly on the intersecting grid lines, either left or right from the center, and nearer to the top or bottom.

PROBLEM SOLVING

Problem solving is among the many tasks of the motion graphics designer. As designers are faced with numerous challenges, both creative and technical, they will have to find creative solutions. A key element of problem solving is anticipating problems before they occur and having contingencies on hand.

Both making sure the design fits within the allotted format and also being able to complete the work on time can be a struggle. In both instances, the designer has to think of a way to either combine elements or omit elements that can save him time in the piece and time in the execution—all without compromising the delivery of the message.

Money can be an issue in relation to supplies or tools needed to complete a particular project. Most motion graphics today are created on computers using software specific for motion graphics. The most high-end software and most powerful computer systems can, of course, get pretty pricey, thus posing a possible challenge to a designer. High-end software or not, there are still software glitches that may require a work-around, or an alternative way of accomplishing the task without the software. A work-around may take more time or require more work, but if it allows the graphics to be effective, it is well worth the effort. Sometimes a work-around solution may call for altering the original effect for one that evokes the same emotional response from the intended audience.

Sometimes we think software can do anything and do not give enough credit to the human imagination. There may come a time when a design entails doing something software cannot do. This situation begs even more creativity of designers for they must then plot out a way to accomplish their plan with the tools that are available to them. These problem-solving skills help a designer to develop as he invents and discovers new ways of communicating. Just as the pioneers before us invented the telephone, motion pictures, and the Internet, the designers of today are taking us to new frontiers.

Designers are manic about saving their work often. They also budget their time wisely, beginning with the initial planning and sketching phase, in anticipation of obstacles, so that they can still make their deadlines.

PRODUCTION

Having made it through the pre-production phases of researching, brainstorming, sketching, and designing, the concept is now ready to be implemented. Regardless of the medium, all designers have to follow the previous steps in order to get to the production stage. In fact, up until the point of production almost all conceptual work, with the possible exception of the storyboards, has been completed without specialized computer software. It is at this point of production that we see the biggest variation in process among the media due to the differences in technology.

Television and Film

Television budgets can vary a great deal, and as a result production can too. With computer hardware and editing and graphics software so much more affordable, it has become more common for smaller companies to have at least one in-house editing and graphics station. In those cases, it is likely, due to economics, that they will have a single editor who is also the motion graphics designer. This person will complete the final edit in a program like Avid or Final Cut and deliver the finished project complete with graphics done in After Effects.

For higher budget projects like agency commercials or television show openings, a designer will complete the storyboards and then oversee the production of the design at a post-production house with highly specialized animation systems like Flame, Flint, or Inferno.

Similarly, in film, if it is a higher budget piece, the designer probably will not be the person executing the design, whereas if it is a lower budget film, the motion graphics designer will likely complete the opening and closing credits on the final film.

Web Design

The size and scope of a website will again impact the size and structure of the design team. A smaller website (one with fewer pages), for example, might have one person design and program the entire site. Meanwhile, a larger website, such as a magazine site that must be updated regularly, would most likely have a team of designers overseen by an art director who ensures consistency in the aesthetic sensibility. The design team would be responsible for selecting photographs and images, as well as designing new pages as the need arises. Depending on the financial resources, the designers may or may not be the ones actually implementing the changes on the website. A separate production team may be responsible for updating the website and adding new functionality, using JavaScript, DHTML, PHP, or ActionScript, which is used only in Flash, to name but a few web programming languages.

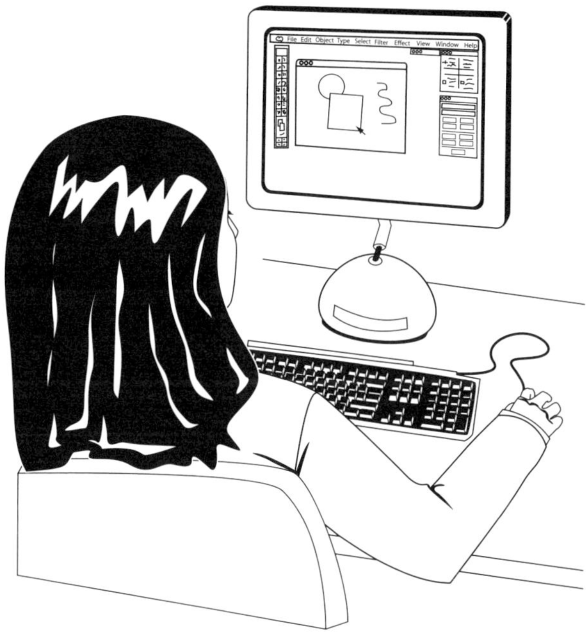

figure |3-16|

Once the designs have been approved by the client, the motion graphics designer begins to execute the project on the computer.

Production on a big budget website, which would not require regular design updates, would follow a slightly different process. Once the designer has completed the mock-up of the design, it would be handed over to the programmers. The designer would act as art director, overseeing the execution of the webpage, but the actual page building and scripting would be left to the programmer.

Video Games

As with the higher end websites, designers for emerging media like video games, personal organizers, and cell phones tend to create a template for programmers to follow and execute. The technology for each medium is so specific that it requires programmers with the expertise in that particular area to execute the design. Video games, for example, are the product of the collaboration of large teams of designers who design very specific elements of the game's environment. While the designers may sketch out the designs and then mock them up on the computer themselves, they must pass their designs on to an animator. The animator is a highly skilled technician trained in the high-end software, Maya and 3ds Max, required for game animation. After the animator has animated the world created by the designers, a programmer builds all of the animations and designs into the world of the game. Programmers for other handheld devices such as cell phones and personal organizers are equally as skilled in breathing life into the designs given to them by a designer.

▷ Case Study ◁

Storyboards

Planning is a key element of the designer's process. After research is complete and the message has been defined, the designer must conceptualize a design that is able to communicate with the audience in a clear and engaging manner. Roughs and storyboards are an integral part of this concept development.

Roger White is a broadcast designer who has designed for many television networks, among them CBS television's *The Late Show with David Letterman* and *The Late Late Show,* as well as Comedy Central's *The Colbert Report.*

White's black-and-white rough sketches and color storyboards show a clear plan for his design. They also give us insight into the process he followed to get to his final concept. In the first set of sketches we see how White developed two ideas for the same concept in boxes 1–4 on top and 1–4 on the bottom. Each box of the storyboard represents a frame, and beneath each image, White includes a description of what is taking place. This makes it a clear presentation for his client and a clear guide for him when he is ready to do more refined color storyboards. Note how each time he adds a new visual element, or the camera captures a new angle, White documents it in a new storyboard box.

You will also note that in addition to the fact that color has been added to the second set of drawings, there are other key differences between the black-and-white roughs and the color storyboards that were used to execute the final version of the concept.

In his original concept in the top four frames, White not only shows a progression from a perspiring brain to the stomach to the intestines and stomach cavity, but he introduces the graphics "The Late Late Show Five Questions" in the second frame of the storyboards. In the bottom four frames for the second option, he reveals a question mark over the silhouette of a female head. (You will also see in his description that he allows for the head to be either male or female

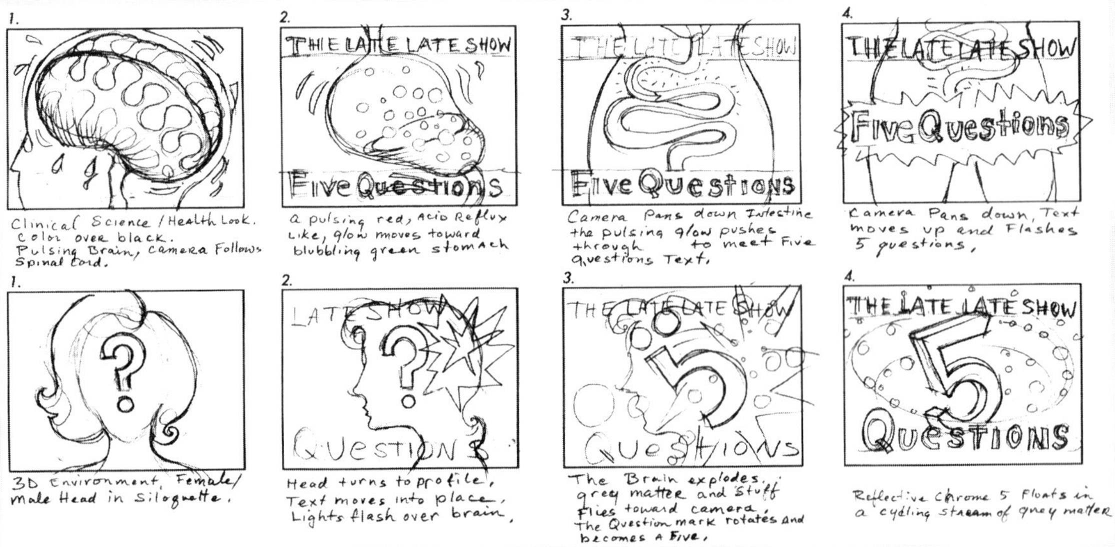

figure |3-17|

Roughs presenting two options for "The Five Questions."

in the final version.) The head then turns to a profile before finally exploding with the question mark rotating into the number five and bursting forth from the brain matter. The final frame of each option closes on graphics that read "The Late Late Show 5 Questions" to introduce the show segment.

The color storyboard presents a streamlined version combining elements of the original concepts. It starts with a glowing brain in the silhouette of a male head before going to the perspiring brain, the first image from the rough sketch. Rather than taking the viewer on a journey of the stomach cavity, White immediately introduces numbers floating from the brain in the form of a countdown to build suspense. Then, the brain explodes spewing forth lots of number fives. "Five Questions" dominates the screen before the final reveal of "The Late Late Show Five Questions."

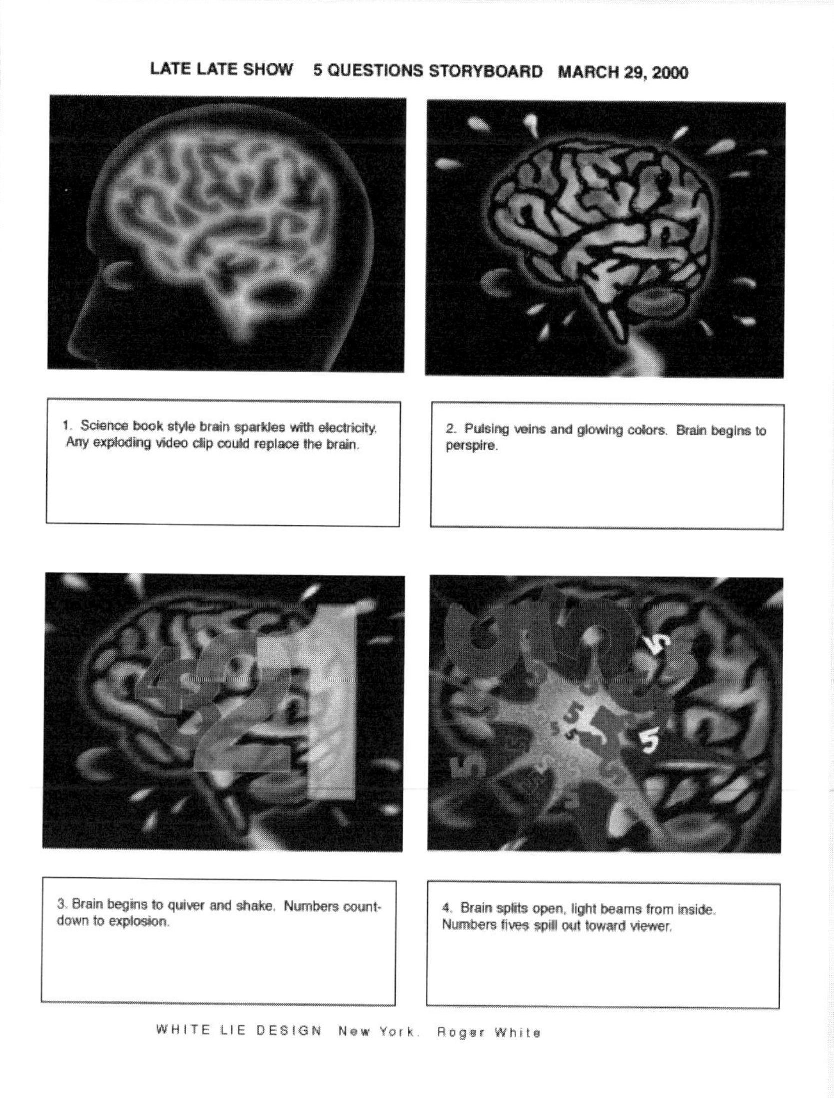

figure 3-18

Storyboards for "The Five Questions."

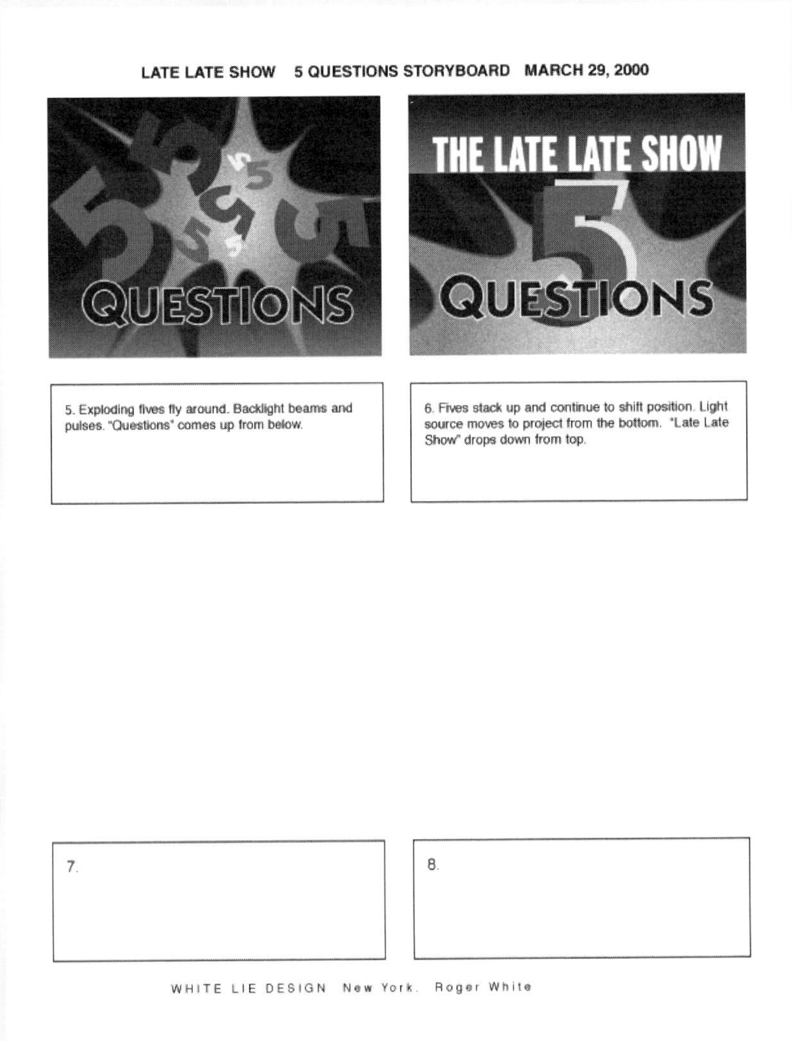

figure | 3-18 | (continued)

Despite the fact that White has taken out a few images between his rough sketches and his storyboard, we cannot help but notice that the basic message is the same. He has simply made it tighter and more cohesive. For instance, he is very specific in his roughs that the brain has a "clinical science/health look" and that it appears over black. When we see it in the first frame of the color storyboard it is described as a "science book style brain" and appears over black as specified in the roughs. And though the "pulsing red, acid reflux like glow" was originally supposed to refer to the stomach and intestines in the sketches, White transfers that idea in the storyboard to the perspiring brain, which has "pulsing veins and glowing colors."

The question mark over the silhouette of the human head image has been dropped, and therefore, a question mark no longer transforms into a floating five as it does in the original bottom sketch. Even so, the message does not suffer, but is actually strengthened because White replaces the question mark with the numbers in the countdown. We attribute the agitated state of the brain to the numbers that are springing forth, and so tension mounts until the brain explodes with a spray of fives.

Though the message has not changed, White's choice not to introduce the graphics "The Late Late Show Five Questions" until the last frame helps to build anticipation in the viewer. Moreover, having a countdown followed by a frame of fives and another frame consisting of a dominant "5 Questions" places the emphasis more on the concept of the Five Questions, rather than on the "Late Late Show" itself.

It is also clearer from the color storyboard with the bright colors and graphics that move out toward the audience that the message is meant to be fun and playful and delivered in jest.

Whether White chose to take out the images he did because of a client's suggestion or issues of screen time, his two sketches show us the value of drawings in helping a designer and client work through an idea. Though the images used to deliver the message evolved, the concept and the message did not change. They simply became more streamlined and stronger as a result of the designer's process.

SUMMARY

Every successful designer follows a methodical approach in order to achieve a design goal. One of the first steps of the process is to get to know the audience for whom the design is intended. Because collaboration is a part of the design process for all media, a designer must stay on schedule. By preparing roughs and storyboards that can be refined with the client, the designer ensures that the design suits the client's needs. If the designer does not complete the final design himself, he will oversee another professional who completes the final graphics. A designer who plans ahead and anticipates problems will have a more successful journey to the completion of the design.

in review

1. Describe the designer/client relationship.
2. What are the two stages of research and how do they help the designer?
3. Why is it important to understand the audience?
4. What is semiotics and why is it important to the field of graphic design?
5. What were the principles of the Bauhaus movement?
6. What is the purpose of roughs and storyboards?
7. What are some examples of problem solving during the design process?
8. What are some of the roles of the designer during production?

exercises

Exercise 1

Brainstorming

(Note: This is a group exercise.)

This exercise is similar to the communications model exercise you completed in Chapter 1. Again, each person will make a contribution to a creative endeavor. Since this is a brainstorming exercise, the goal is for members of the team to use each person's idea in the design of this new device. No idea can be rejected, and each subsequent idea must build from the last.

Task

The group will invent a new digital device that lives up to the Bauhaus principles of being both beautiful and functional. The device should be able to perform basic functions, such as make phone calls, browse the Internet, download music and ring tones, text message, and whatever else you determine appropriate.

Goal

Develop a design for the new device based on a brainstorm session.

Research It

1. Use a sheet of paper from your artist's sketchpad.
2. The first person in the group will draw a device and describe its first function.
3. The next person will draw a new element to the device and describe its function in addition to the first.
4. The third person will draw a third structure and describe its function to the device in addition to the previous two.
5. This process will continue until everyone in the group has contributed a new function that complements all of the previously listed functions.

Exercise 2

Audience Considerations

This exercise will reinforce the importance of audience profiling and how to spot similar characteristics in different audiences. The similar characteristics can be used to shape the design and development of the motion graphic.

Task

Develop profiles for multiple audiences who will use the same website to get their news every day.

Goal

Compile the information and determine how motion graphics could be applied to the website successfully and satisfy different audiences.

Research It

Develop audience profiles for the following audiences:

- Busy professionals
- College students
- Retirees

In addition to the list of audience-related questions suggested earlier, here are some other questions to ask yourself before beginning your designs:

- Are there similarities between any of these groups that would allow you to use similar elements in the templates?
- How much free time does each audience have?

- What kind of news would interest each group?
- What is the reading and education level of each group?
- Would any group be prone to physical ailments that might impair its ability to see or read a computer screen?
- What are the audience's political leanings?

Exercise 3

Storyboards

Sketching what you see on screen, effectively recreating the designer's storyboard, will better enable you to understand the pre-production process.

Task

Create storyboards based on video that has already been shot and edited. Although storyboards are usually created before the execution of the design, you are going to go about the process from the other direction.

Goal

Create complete storyboards that reflect the video footage.

Design It, Step by Step

1. Select fifteen seconds of edited video footage.
2. Watch the video clip all the way through without stopping it.
3. To make a storyboard template, draw six rectangular boxes on an artist's sketchpad. There should be three boxes per row. Make sure you save room below each box for sluglines and captions.
4. Make copies of this template so that you have plenty of boxes available to sketch what you see on screen.
5. With pencil and storyboard template in hand, prepare to watch the video clip again. This time, pause the clip each time a new shot appears so that you can do a rough sketch of the frame.

6. If the framing of the shot remains the same but a new element is introduced, you must sketch that as well. Include a caption describing the introduction of that new element.

7. If dialogue or music accompanies the video, write either the line of dialogue or song lyric as a caption below the sketch it accompanies.

8. Pay close attention to the graphics in the clip, making sure to sketch the graphics' first position in the frame and their ending position in the frame in separate boxes.

9. To demonstrate camera movement such as a track in or out, an up or down tilt, or a side-to-side pan, draw the starting camera position in one box, and then draw the ending camera position in the box next to it. Indicate the direction of the movement with arrows inside the box. Also, describe the camera motion in the sluglines directly below the box.

10. Once you have finished watching the entire clip, you should have a roughly sketched storyboard resembling what you have seen on screen.

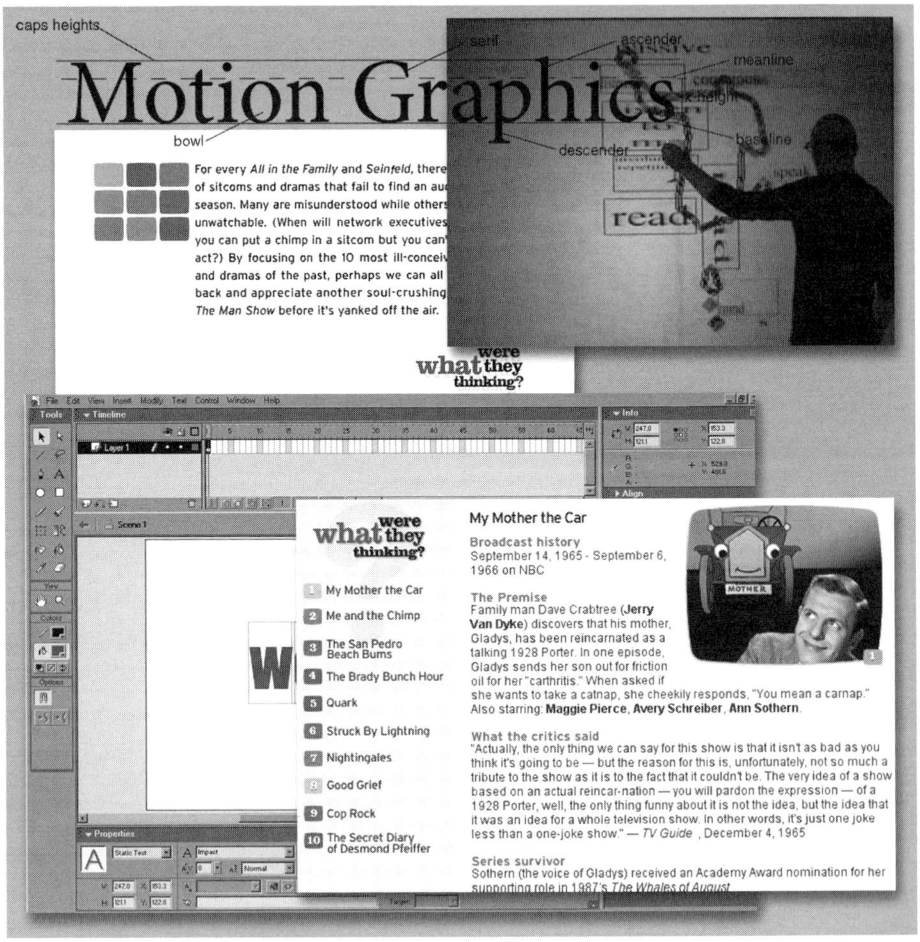
caps heights
serif
ascender
meanline
x height
baseline
descender
bowl
Motion Graphics
read
what were they thinking?
My Mother the Car
Broadcast history
September 14, 1965 - September 6, 1966 on NBC
The Premise
Family man Dave Crabtree (Jerry Van Dyke) discovers that his mother, Gladys, has been reincarnated as a talking 1928 Porter. In one episode, Gladys sends her son out for friction oil for her "carthritis." When asked if she wants to take a catnap, she cheekily responds, "You mean a carnap." Also starring: Maggie Pierce, Avery Schreiber, Ann Sothern.
What the critics said
"Actually, the only thing we can say for this show is that it isn't as bad as you think it's going to be — but the reason for this is, unfortunately, not so much a tribute to the show as it is to the fact that it couldn't be. The very idea of a show based on an actual reincar-nation — you will pardon the expression — of a 1928 Porter, well, the only thing funny about it is not the idea, but the idea that it was an idea for a whole television show. In other words, it's just one joke less than a one-joke show." — TV Guide , December 4, 1965
Series survivor
Sothern (the voice of Gladys) received an Academy Award nomination for her
1 My Mother the Car
2 Me and the Chimp
3 The San Pedro Beach Bums
4 The Brady Bunch Hour
5 Quark
6 Struck By Lightning
7 Nightingales
8 Good Grief
9 Cop Rock
10 The Secret Diary of Desmond Pfeiffer
MOTHER
Timeline
Layer 1
Scene 1
Properties
Static Text
Impact
Info
Align

CHAPTER

4

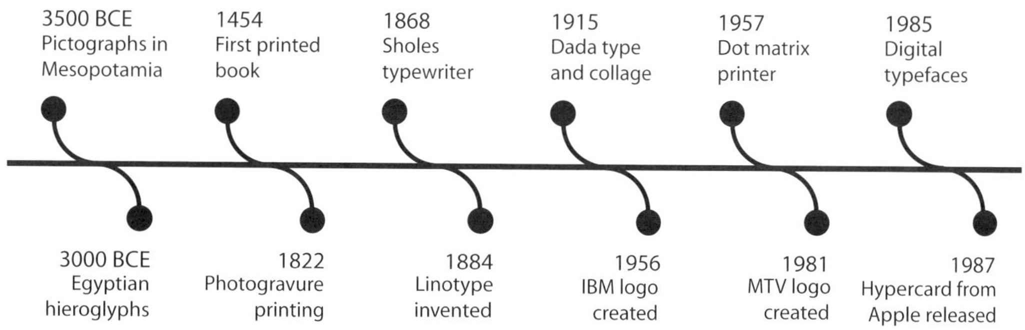

Chapter Objectives

Learn the development and history of typography

Learn the characteristics and vocabulary specific to typography

Understand how we see letters and words

Explore the role of typography in motion graphics

Introduction

The digital design world of motion, sound, and space frees us from the still, silent plane of print design. In the digital world possibilities of typographic design are limitless. Type is released from stasis as we take advantage of the flexibility of the digital medium.

Typography is a regularly used component in motion graphics. Words race across the screen, letters fade in and out of visibility, and a message is communicated. It is not only the meaning of the words that communicates your message to your audience but also the artistic decisions and applied movements and effects. The style in which the letters are treated and the method in which the words are presented reinforce the message behind the communication. Before we study typography in motion graphics, it is important to understand a bit about the origins and history of letters and words themselves.

PICTOGRAPHS AND IDEOGRAPHS

Before there were letters and words, people used pictographs to represent important objects in their communities. A **pictograph** is a simple drawing that represents a specific object or item, such as a bull, mountains, or an arrow.

Pictographs very much limited the scope of the messages that could be communicated nonverbally. Pictographs allowed only for communication about tangible objects, not about abstract thoughts. The simple drawings represented an individual object, and

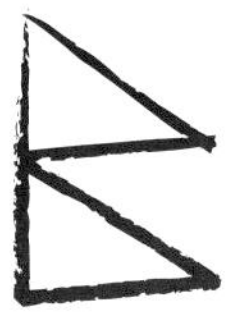

Primitive pictograph that represents a house

Ideograph representing "do not" or "no"

figure |4-1|

A pictograph is a simple line drawing that represents an important object in society. An ideograph is a more complex drawing that signifies an idea or abstract thought.

there was no method of putting multiple signs together to make a new symbol. This made it impossible to record detailed stories, poems, or any other artistic or academic thoughts. Early societies used these pictographs to document locations of food sources, the number of members of the tribe or clan, and other statistical information of vital importance to the group.

Societies developed a yearning to record beliefs, thoughts, dreams, desires, loves, and hates—everything in and about their culture. They needed more complex symbols to communicate abstract ideas, and this led to the development of drawings that represented more than just specific objects. **Ideographs** are simple drawings that represent an idea or abstract thought. A skull and crossbones on a bottle of cleaning fluid is an example of an ideograph. This combination represents the abstract idea of danger. The drawing represents a literal thing, bones, but it also signifies a hazardous item.

ALPHABET

The development of the Western alphabet remained a mystery for quite some time. For many centuries the alphabet was thought too great a thing to have been created by humans, so it was attributed as a gift from God, and every religion had a story of its origin. Explanations and accounts of this divine gift can be found in written discourse well into the eighteenth century. Although these divine explanations continued, rapid growth in both the linguistic and archaeological fields in the seventeenth century opened doors to advanced studies of the history of the alphabet. Scholars began to study the alphabet in more depth, and as people traveled the world and unearthed historic samples, they were able to trace the origins of the modern alphabet.

Since its inception, our twenty-six-letter alphabet has grown to suit the needs of the different societies it has passed through. Phoenicians initially developed the alphabet as a way to communicate with foreign merchants and traders. In order to keep track of goods traded, they needed a universal language to record and share the information. With this simplified method of documenting information, merchants could keep records of the amount of goods bought and sold, sea captains could keep records of ships' manifests, and cities could keep records of ships entering and leaving port.

The symbols (letters) of the alphabet were developed in a manner that was meant to represent the sound of spoken language. The shape of existing pictographs became letters, and the sound of the beginning of the word the pictograph stood for became the sound of the letter. An important symbol that was used often was for "ox." Phoenicians pronounced the word as *aleph*, which is where the sound of the letter *A* comes from. The pictograph for aleph was shaped very similarly to the letter *A*, and this shows the transition of an existing pictograph into a letter of the alphabet. It can be assumed that "aleph" represented such an important object in their culture that it was used as the first letter in the alphabet. The word for *house*, another important word in the culture, was "beth," thus the letter *B* is the second letter in the alphabet. Phoenicians developed the rest of the alphabet in a similar fashion. They deconstructed the sounds of the word. The sound that was uttered at the beginning of a word was separated from the rest of the sound and became the individual letter.

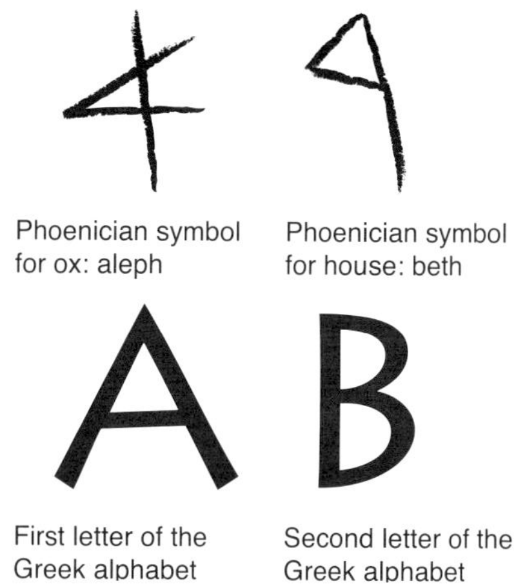

figure 4-2

Pictographs of important objects eventually came to represent letters of the alphabet, and the sounds uttered when pronouncing the words became the sounds of the letters of the alphabet.

Using letters instead of pictographs for writing also simplified communications. The letters could be reused for any word with that sound in it, instead of having a separate pictograph for every object, place, and person in the society. Any word in their language that had the same "A" sound as aleph would use the same letter. As more groups traded with the Phoenicians, the alphabet spread and continued to develop to suit each society's needs.

The Greeks saw the practical usefulness of the Phoenician alphabet but also saw it as a means to archive their knowledge and record their literature, philosophy, poetry, theatrical plays, government documents, and more. They began to collect information for uses beyond record keeping. For the first time a society meticulously and consistently collected and documented their culture and stored it in hopes of aiding and enlightening future civilizations.

The Romans continued to use the alphabet as the Greeks had to record all aspects of their culture and society. They carried it to all corners of their ever-growing empire. As they conquered foreign lands, they used the alphabet to mark their new territory. They put up stone monuments, carving communications into the stone and branding their newly acquired lands. This aided in the spread of the Roman alphabet, the immediate forerunner of the modern alphabet, and Latin spread over the world as the language of learning.

WRITING

Early in human history, written communication was only available or accessible to the upper class. Writing was an art form, and individuals trained for years to perfect this craft. Monks skilled in the art of writing were called scribes. They penned numerous manuscripts using colored dyes and gold leaf on vellum. Scribes handwrote the text in black letter, a style characterized by heavy forms with thick lines. They designed elaborate typographic illustrations and accented the pages with drawings designed to frame the text. Each page is seen as an individual work of art. Before the advent of printing, there was no mass production and dissemination of information. Information could not be easily shared and passed on. Before writing became more popular, stories, traditions, and histories were passed along through oral storytelling.

PRINTING

The advent of printing is a milestone in history and marks the beginning of the mass dissemination of information. At the beginning, though, the sharing of information was limited by the technological constraints of the printing press and the availability or capabilities of the audience. Many people were illiterate, and printing was expensive, so printed materials were only available to the upper class, and were not created for mass consumption. Johannes Gutenberg is credited with the invention of the printing press. Although he was the first to publish a multipage document with the printing press, there is documented evidence that moveable type was first used in Korea circa 1241. They used clay to mold individual squares with raised characters that, after fired, were porous and hard enough to transfer ink to another surface.

The first mechanically printed book, the Bible, was printed by Gutenberg in 1455. He used existing technologies, such as the screw press and metallurgy, and combined them in a new way to create the printing press. This screw press printed one page at a time when a metal plate was pressed down on a piece of paper positioned face down over rows of inked lead blocks with raised letters. He not only had to develop the press, but he had to determine the right consistency for the ink, the right thickness and absorbency for the paper, and create the lead raised letters that were hard enough and porous enough to transfer the ink to the paper. It took much experimentation with the new technology to get it right.

TYPE CHARACTERISTICS

Every letter can be identified and classified based on its characteristics. Typefaces can generally be broken down into two main categories, copy and display. Copy refers to chunks of text. Display refers to a title, headline, banner, or the like. When choosing a typeface for copy, you want it to be easy to read without any extra flourishes that will cause the viewer to have a hard time deciphering the letters. When choosing a typeface for display purposes, you have more freedom to select a face with extreme flourishes or to create your own decorative face with a unique look that will be used for a specific application.

| NOTE |

Both display and copy typefaces may be used in one design. A webpage that uses a display typeface for the title of the page and a copy typeface for other text on the page is one such example.

Legibility and Readability

A typeface needs to be legible and readable to ensure correct communication of your message. **Readability** is the ability to decipher the letters, meaning that the shapes are easily recognizable. With motion graphics, an added concern is that the letters are still recognizable when moving. If the viewer is unable to discern the shapes of the letters and make out what the words say, then the communication fails. **Legibility** is the ability to successfully read the words as they are laid out in the design. The words need to be readable at the appropriate distance. If type in a motion graphic for a digital billboard is too small and the viewer cannot read it from the street, then the communication fails. This is true for any medium. If type on a website is too small and difficult to read, the viewer will click through to another website and again the communication will fail. There are certain characteristics that either help or hinder our reading letters.

Weight

The **weight** of each letter contributes to the readability of your message. Weight refers to the thinness or thickness of the stroke of the individual lines that make up the letter, or character.

Light type on a dark background generally looks thinner than dark type on a light background. To correct for this optical illusion that occurs when using a light typeface against a dark background, you will want to compensate with a heavier weight font that uses thicker strokes. If a character has a very thin weight, it could be very difficult to read due to the lack of contrast and inability to distinguish the edges of the letter. If the weight of the character is too thick, it will be equally hard to read because the edges will blur together, again making the edges indistinguishable.

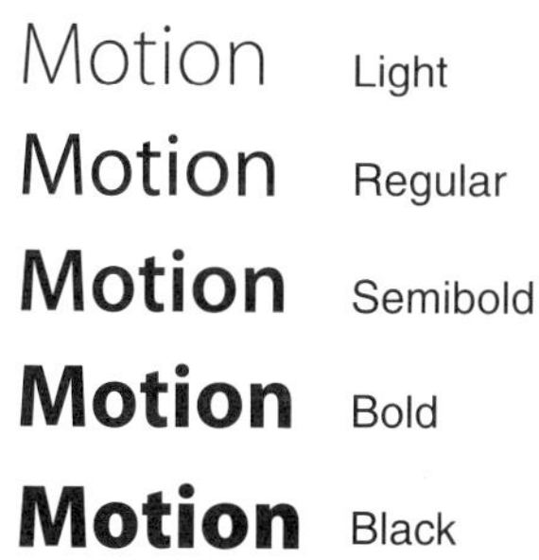

figure |4-3|

The same word in varying weights.

Width

The **width** of a character refers to how narrow or wide each character is; not just the stroke, but the whole letter. Very wide or very narrow, also referred to as condensed, characters may be difficult to read because the edges of the individual characters will blend together, and the contrast between the type and the background will be minimized. Another problem a reader may encounter with characters that are too wide or too narrow is that the character shape may become distorted and therefore difficult to decipher.

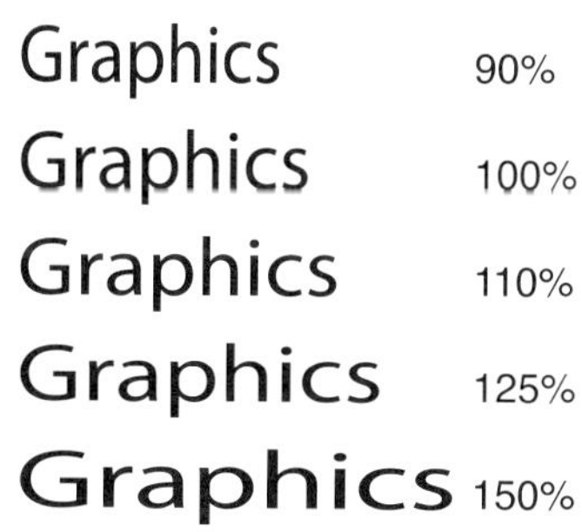

figure |4-4|

The same word in varying widths.

Kerning and Tracking

You can make a number of adjustments to the type to compensate for low legibility or readability. **Kerning** is when you adjust the space between two characters, and **tracking** is when you adjust spacing equally between characters in whole words, sentences, or paragraphs.

If characters are too close together, the edges get blurred, making the words difficult to read. If the characters are too far apart, the viewer will lose track of the visual flow of the characters and will

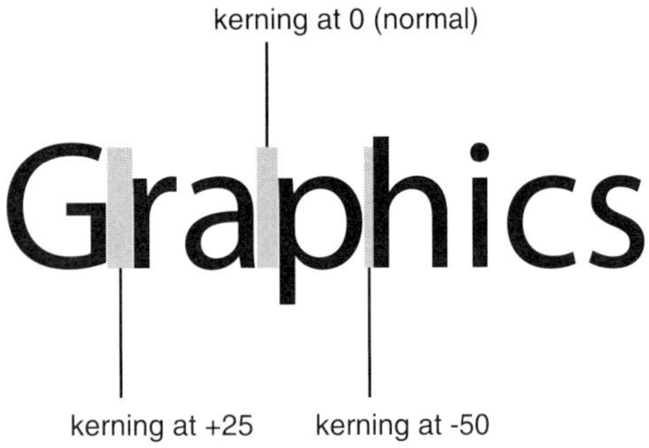

figure |4-5|

A word with varying amounts of kerning applied between letters.

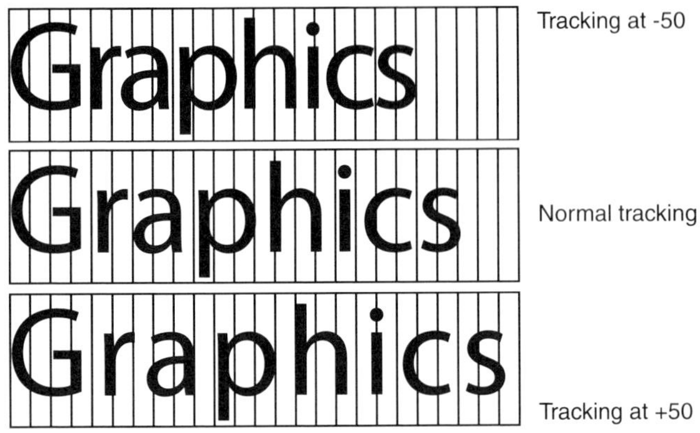

figure |4-6|

The same word with varying amounts of tracking applied.

Motion graphics combine typography, graphics, sound, and motion to illustrate a point and convey a message to an intended audience. It is information packaged in an entertaining, visually dynamic package.

figure |4-7|

A paragraph of text with the same amount of leading applied between each line.

see a word space where there is none between characters. It is important not to interrupt the visual flow of the words and to keep the viewer focused on properly receiving the message.

Leading

Another problem the viewer may face that will make it difficult to read the message is a lack of space, or too much space, between sentences, words, and characters. The spacing between lines of type is referred to as **leading**.

The term *leading* comes from the age of mechanical printing when printers used lead bars in between rows of moveable type to separate the lines of text and add white space to make the document easier to read.

SEEING WORDS

We first learn to read phonetically, putting letters together to make words and sounding out each word. As we become more adept at reading, we learn to read visually. We learn to see shapes of letters that make up words that we recognize.

As we become proficient at reading, we unconsciously follow a certain set of steps. First, we recognize the visual pattern of the letters placed before us and categorize it based on our prior knowledge; then, upon closer inspection, we look at the shape of the word. We categorize what we see based on the shape of the entire word. Finally, we read it, applying meaning to the word. This all happens in an instant, and we do not recognize it as a method of processing the information at hand. With this in mind, let us look at several typeface characteristics that help us to see words.

Serif and Sans Serif Typefaces

While certain characteristics help us to better decipher the letters of each word and read the copy, other characteristics are more for decoration and visual enhancement. In the process of seeing, we decipher letters through recognition of the edges against the background. **Serif** typefaces are often easier to read because of the shape and contrast of the edge of the letter against the background. A serif is the finishing stroke that emerges from the main strokes. A **sans serif** typeface is one with no finishing strokes.

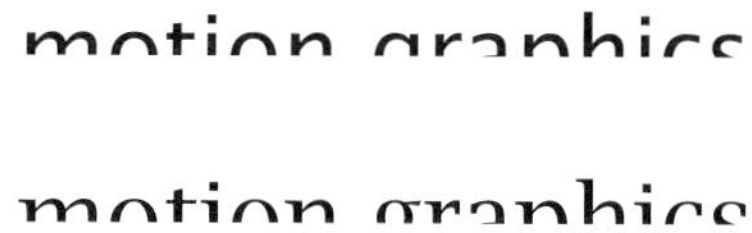

figure |4-8|

The serifs on a letter help a person see the shape of the letter and word.

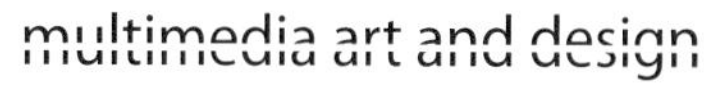

figure |4-9|

It is easier to distinguish the top half of letters than the bottom half.

Contrast

The process of letter recognition makes the level of contrast between foreground (the type) and background very important. At a low level of contrast it is very difficult to decipher the edges of the letters. If the contrast is too high, with a light foreground against a dark background, there may be a halo, or glow around the edges of the letters, which will likewise make it difficult to decipher the edges of the letters.

Mixed Cases

Since we use a visual process of word recognition, it seems apparent that it is easier to read words and sentences with mixed cases, upper- and lowercase letters, and not only all capitals. Sentences with mixed cases help us recognize the word shapes because of the varying height of the letters. The **ascenders** and **descenders** of letters offer visual aid to seeing the shape and determining the word. Ascenders are the strokes that rise above the **meanline**, the invisible line that sits atop the lowercase letters. Descenders are the strokes that fall below the **baseline**, the invisible line that the text sits on.

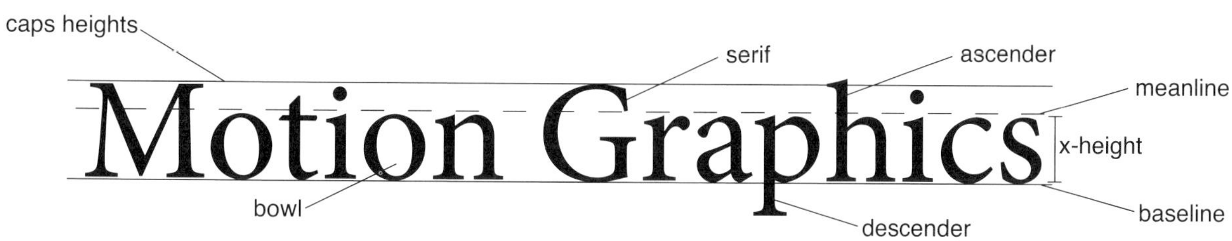

figure |4-10|

The basic components of type anatomy.

how do we read

HOW DO WE READ

figure |4-11|

It is easier to read sentences that use mixed cases—capitals and lowercase letters—because the ascenders and descenders help us scan the shape of the words.

Choosing a Typeface Based on Audience Needs and Expectations

If a typeface is hard to read, it makes it harder to classify and interpret the information. This is not to say never experiment with hard-to-read typefaces, but know your audiences and have a thorough understanding of their abilities, limitations, and expectations. For example, in creating a motion graphic design for children who have recently learned to read, remember that they will not all be quick to recognize the shape of each letter nor have an extensive vocabulary catalogued and visualized. Therefore, you will want to use a typeface that is easily recognizable, without extra flourishes that would look unfamiliar and be harder to decipher. Also, capitalizing on a strong contrast between the edges of the letters (foreground) and the background will aid in readability. When designing for individuals with sight impairment, you will need to take into account their specific needs. Someone with impaired vision may have a problem seeing the contrast between the foreground and background, therefore using high contrast will not work. Making the characters bigger with enough space between each to easily distinguish the letter edges will most likely enhance readability for this audience.

| NOTE |

Remember, viewers do not have the luxury of reading type at their own pace in a motion graphic. They are forced to read it in the time it appears on the screen, as designated by the designer. Using type that can be easily read and deciphered is extremely important.

DEVELOPMENT OF TYPEFACES

There are two aspects to reading. The first is word recognition based on letter shapes and the second is the letter style. Not only do we see the word made up of individual letter shapes, we also associate meaning to specific typefaces, based on the context of the type used in history. If we see a typeface that has a particular association with a historical period, we may have preconceived ideas about the message behind the type style. Throughout history different typefaces have been popular, each with their own distinct style. The following typefaces represent a different period in history.

When developing moveable type for the printing press in 1455, Gutenberg based his choice for the typeface on the style popular at the time, black letter. Scribes used black letter in handwritten books; it was the typeface of choice and was easily recognized by all. Black letter, a heavyweight typeface with extreme flourishes, is difficult to read by today's standards, but people in that time could easily identify the letter and word shapes.

times new roman	transitional
myriad	humanist sans
arial	neo-grotesque
eurostile	geometric
LITHOS PRO	glyphic
brush script	script

figure |4-12|

Examples from different type families.

In 1475 Nicholas Jensen designed a typeface based on the humanistic style of lettering that developed during the Renaissance, taking inspiration from classic Greek and Roman styles. These characters moved away from the very heavy width of black letter and look very similar to the standard serif typefaces we use today.

Sans serif typefaces first came on the scene in 1957. Helvetica, a popular sans serif typeface today, was developed by Max Miedinger and Edouard Hoffman. It is widely considered that serif fonts are easier to read in print, whereas sans serif typefaces are easier to read on screen, but this idea is changing. Most likely this became a general rule of thumb simply because we were used to reading printed text with serif typefaces and screen text with sans serif typefaces. Now that more studies have been done, it appears that this rule of thumb does not always hold true.

TYPEFACES DEVELOPED FOR DIGITAL TECHNOLOGY

Initially, typefaces for digital technology, such as the old LED typeface often used on signs in airports or train stations, were serving technology more than catering to audience considerations. Design was constrained by limited technology. As technology caught up to design, special consideration was given to typefaces developed for digital applications, such as personal digital assistants (PDAs), cell phones, and television. Designers had more options in choosing a typeface that suited the design.

Every time a typeface is designed for a digital technology, both the intended application and users' expectations must be considered. Readability and legibility affect how typography for motion graphics is read on the screen. Consider whether viewers have control over the device settings. Can they adjust the screen contrast to enhance the foreground/background relationship? Can they change the screen resolution to make type larger or smaller? Can they pause or rewind if there is interference? These are essential questions to ask before embarking on designing a typeface for the digital medium. Consider the answers to these questions as well:

- How long will it take the average viewer to read the message?
- What distance will the viewer be from the medium?
- Will the viewer also be in motion while reading?
- Will the surrounding environment affect the viewer's ability to read the message?
- Will the viewer be in control of the device controls and settings?

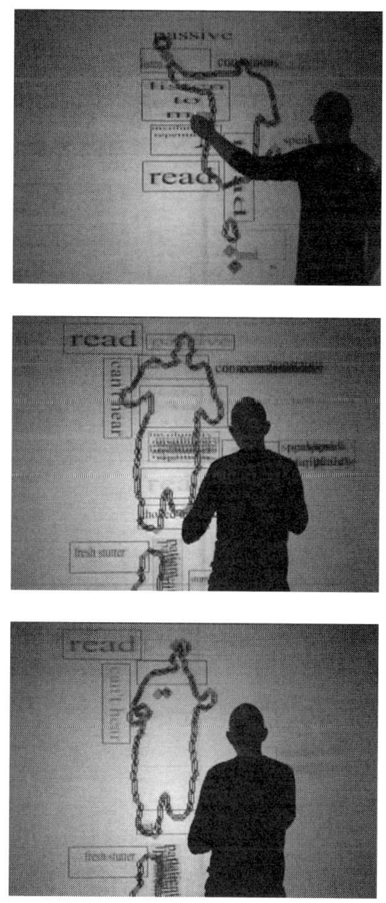

figure |4-13|

Typography designed for screen display, used in interactive art piece.

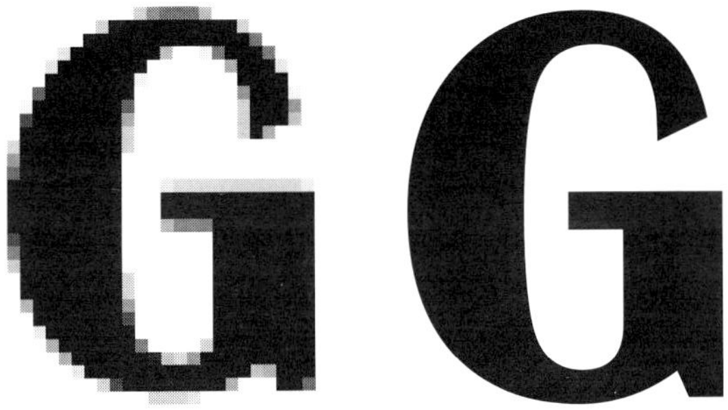

figure |4-14|

Raster graphics (left) are made up of pixel information, and vector graphics (right) are made up of computer code.

Raster Graphics

Screen graphics, referred to as **raster** or **bitmap**, are made up of pixels. Photoshop and ImageReady are two examples of software applications that use pixels. A **pixel**, short for picture element, is the smallest unit of information. It is an individual dot of the larger graphic image, such as type, picture, or color shape. All screens are composed of millions of pixels that are arranged in rows and columns, and the pixels are squeezed together in this grid format. Each pixel can be a different color, and when they are placed close together, they appear to be connected and form a clear image, with distinct but smooth color fields and shapes. There is a finite amount of pixel information in each image, so if a raster graphic is scaled up (made larger than the original) it will look distorted because extra pixels cannot be added where they did not originally exist. The end result is an image that is pixilated and of poor quality. Avoid using pixilated images in your designs.

Vector Graphics

Flash and Illustrator use **vector graphics**. Vector graphics are made up of computer code consisting of 0s and 1s instead of pixels. These codes instruct the computer how to "draw" the graphic on screen. The vector is defined by its start point and end point, not by the individual points, and unlike raster graphics can be enlarged or reduced without distortion. Vector graphics are very important to motion graphics in web design because they greatly reduce file size, therefore making for faster download times and a better web viewing experience.

CONTROLLING HOW WE READ

Knowing that words are read visually, by shape and not by sounding them out letter by letter, is important to motion graphics because it allows designers to take more liberties with moving type. The movement of graphics can attract and direct the eye to read the information in the order that the message requires. By controlling how and when the words appear on the screen, the designer dictates the manner in which the message is read. When reading a static poster that has three lines of information, viewers can scan the poster in any order they choose. If the same three lines of information are presented in a motion graphic, and each line flows onto the screen in a specific order, the viewer will be forced to read the information in that order.

ADDING MOTION

When adding motion to type, consider not only the principles of type discussed so far in this chapter but also the environment in which the viewer will read the message. The viewer will have a limited amount of time to decipher the letters and read the words, so they need to be clear and easily recognizable, from the appropriate distance. If added motion is going to hinder the proper communication, you may need to leave the words on the screen for an extended period of time to compensate.

With the advent of automobiles came street signs. And with street signs came the necessity to apply type to designs that would be read while people were in motion. For advertisers street signs were a new medium to entice people to buy their wares. For designers they were a new medium to experiment with. Designers had to consider how much could be put on a sign to convey all of the information and still be readable by people in motion. They had to consider how to lay out information in such a way that it could be read by the average individual in a limited time and without too much distraction from extraneous information.

Until the late nineteenth century, many advertisements were very text heavy with few or no visuals. Advertisements explained what the product or service was, and why it was a good investment. Ads were not the visual candy they have become today, meant to entice viewers with abstract ideas of how life could be improved by purchasing the product or service. The fact that drivers have a limited amount of time to read street signs led designers to figure out a way to pare down information in a creative, visually enticing way. Designers today are faced with the same dilemmas when designing motion graphics.

As technologies developed, motion graphics developed. Movies and television shows used scrolling text to list all of the cast and crew, an early use of type in motion. Television commercials used type in motion to supply additional information about the product or service for sale. It was a method used to get all of the necessary information into a very short span of time. Designers needed to consider how to adapt and creatively use each new technology while still maintaining high levels of readability and legibility. Remember the goal is a properly communicated message.

Because typography is the main focus of the motion graphic that holds viewers' attention, the details of each letter must be considered. Ask not only how does each letter read individually and as part of the word, but does the typeface convey the meaning of the word, or the emotion of the word? When moving words, breaking apart words and letters, or otherwise distorting them, determine where the point is that the words or letters are no longer readable or legible. Consider whether the viewer has had enough time to decipher the message and receive the communication. Adjust the movement of the words or letters as needed to ensure that there is no interference.

Today we see type in motion all around us. Websites apply moving type in ads or splash pages, movies and television run sophisticated title sequences using advanced techniques of moving type, and digital billboards abound in public spaces such as airports and train stations. Highway signs use moving type to communicate travel messages.

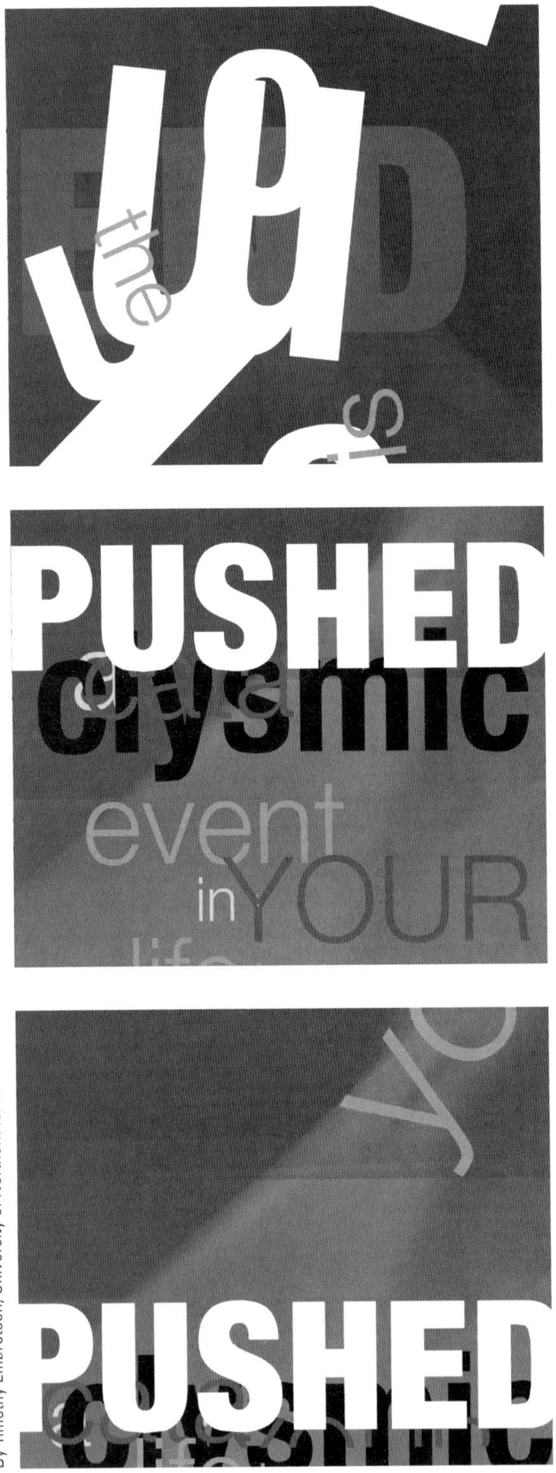

By Timothy Embretson, University of Northern Iowa

figure |4-15|

Using a word in a manner that mimics the action in the physical world.

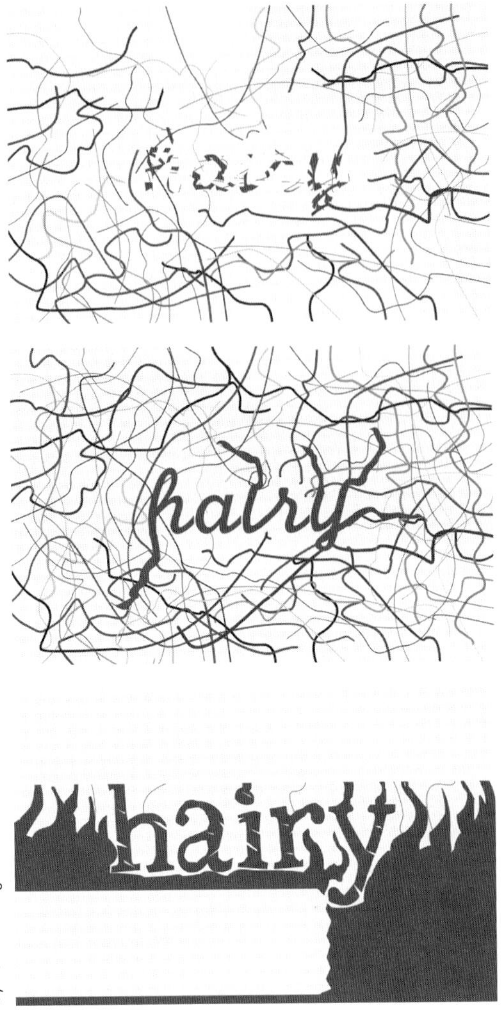

By BJ Alumbaugh

figure |4-16|

The letters in this example take on characteristics of what the word stands for.

| NOTE |

Splash pages serve as introductions to a website. They are often used to set the tone of the website and create a high level of interest with the viewer. When designing a splash page it is a good idea to offer the viewer the option of skipping the introduction and allowing them to enter the website when they please.

▷ Case Study ◁

Type in Motion

The SciFi Channel promo by Dorian Compo uses After Effects and Illustrator videography to achieve the effect of white type being revealed by a black cloud. The word *believe* is slowly exposed as the black cloud flows into the frame. The illusion of type being revealed is created by an interesting use of the foreground/background relationship of white type floating on a white background. Only as the black substance slowly spills into the frame are the letters shown to us. The pace in which the word slowly materializes out of nothingness is smooth, mimicking the supposed movement of a viscous cloud of black ink in water.

Compo designed this motion graphic for television broadcast, dictating the use of the horizontal frame. He uses the frame in such a way that one could imagine she is looking into a glass case filled with a clear viscous liquid while a black fluid is injected from the side. This offers the illusion of watching some type of scientific experiment, out of which the word *believe* appears.

Notice that although the black cloud enters the frame from the right, opposite of how we read, the letters, and therefore word, are revealed from left to right. By following the principles of how we read, Compo has created a design that is not only visually engaging, but easy for the viewer to decipher. There is no great challenge to the viewer to decipher words, and once the entire word appears, it remains on screen for a moment to ensure that all are able to read it. Only then is the smooth tranquility on the screen interrupted by a barrage of static that distorts the text. This text distortion emphasizes the unknown, reinforcing the identity of The SciFi Channel. The choice of the sans serif typeface further reinforces this identity and evokes a future time.

Compo says of his work,

> *My overall intentions for creating the SciFi promotion were to create a compelling and engaging design that portrays the identity of The SciFi Channel.*
>
> *I have always been intrigued and inspired by the design of the SciFi Channel's promotion. Their design aesthetics followed the same rules and guidelines that I depict through my own designs. I wanted to convey an alien-like feel, as if the organic substance was invading your television and creating a malfunction within its circuitry. The SciFi Channel often uses alien motifs with the conviction that life exists on other planets. That is the feeling I wanted to communicate with my design, and that is why I conclude the sequence with the work "Believe."*

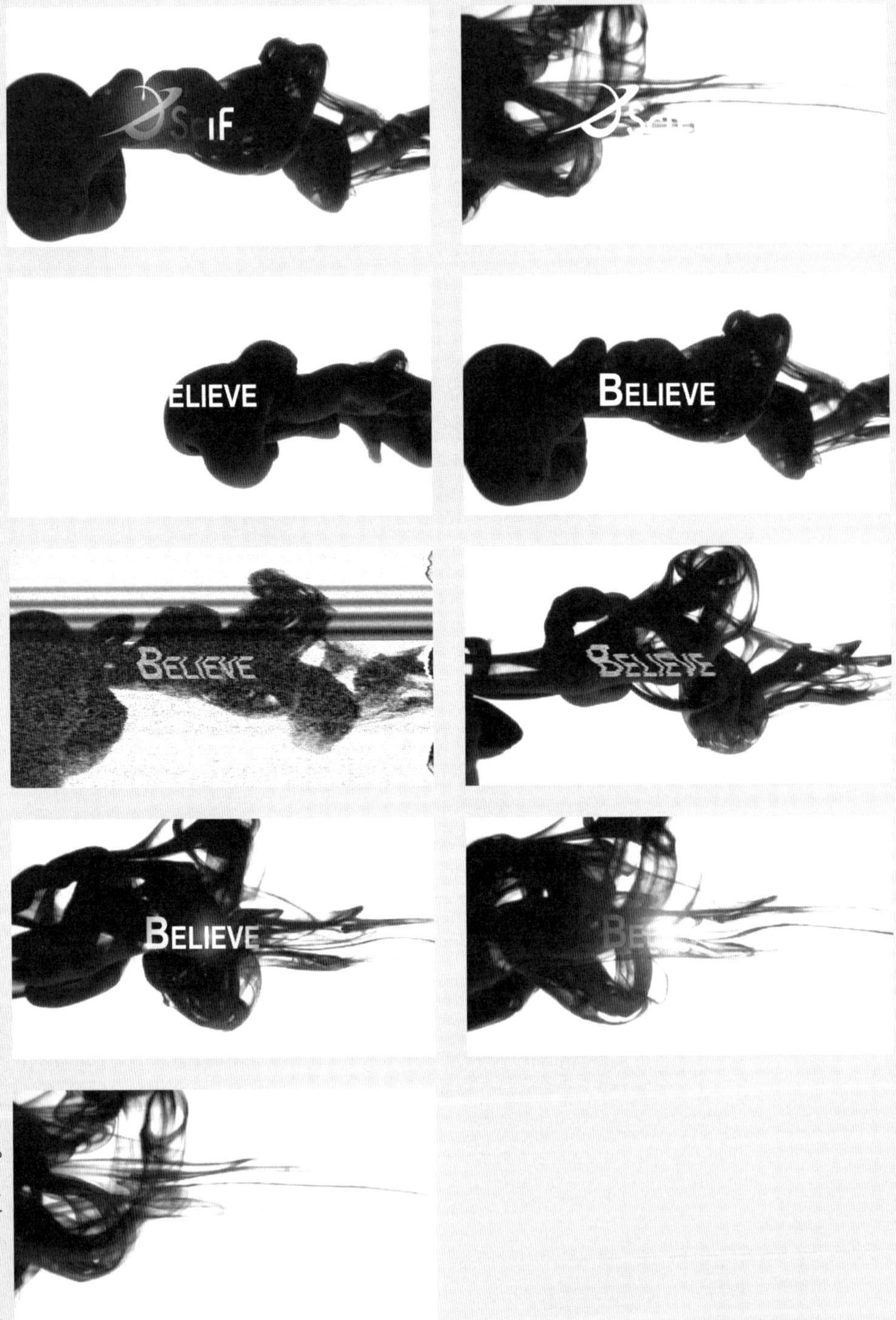

By Dorian J. Compo/Designer/www.rekonstrukt.com

figure |4-17|

Promo created for The SciFi Channel.

SUMMARY

We start learning letters early in childhood and thus become very familiar with the shapes of letters. If you stray too far from the original, recognizable shape of a letter, your audience will have to work that much harder to decipher your message. It will take viewers more time to discern the letters, then the words, then the message.

We are much less dependent on handwriting today with all of the digital communication devices at our disposal. Even so, lettering has a long history, and if you study the importance lettering once took on, you can apply those ideas to your motion graphics. You may also use the familiarity of handwritten words as an element of your design, as there are numerous typefaces available that mimic handwriting.

Initially, viewers were in motion while signs were static. Eventually that changed. Today we often stand still while what is around us is in motion. The principles of type remain unchanged, though you are challenged to communicate a message that occurs in a limited or structured amount of time. Using electronic media with motion graphics means visual communications and typographic design does not have to conform to linear constraints originally developed for traditional typography and moveable type.

Today designers add motion to many digital graphics. Billboard ads dance, highway signs flash, and PDAs are programmed with animated greetings. How we add motion, fast or slow, repetitive or chaotic, reflects the emotional undertones of the message. We respond to these universal ideas of what certain ways of moving mean.

in review

1. What is the major difference between a pictograph and an ideograph?
2. Which society initially developed the alphabet?
3. What are the main characteristics of typography?
4. How do we recognize letters and words?
5. What needs to be considered when developing a typeface to use on a digital device?
6. How do we read type on a screen?

exercises

Exercise 1

Type in Motion

This exercise will reinforce basic typography skills, while enhancing awareness of the emotional impact of different typefaces.

Task

Animate the letters of a word in a manner that reflects the meaning of that word.

Goal

Complete a simple animation in which the typeface, type size, and movement all reflect the emotion of the word.

Software

Flash

Design It, Step-by-Step

Choose one of the following words and find a typeface that is supportive of the emotional connotation.

- Livid
- Ecstatic
- Crabby
- Sad
- Silly

1. Select the type tool and click anywhere on the stage.

> **TIP**
>
> The workspace is referred to as the stage in Flash.

2. Select the typeface and type size in the Properties window. Leave the type black so that color does not influence the emotion of the design.

3. To animate the individual characters in a block of text, you need to place each character in a separate text block. Select the selection tool and click a text block. Select Modify > Break Apart. Each character in the word is placed in a separate text block, and the text stays in the same position on the stage.

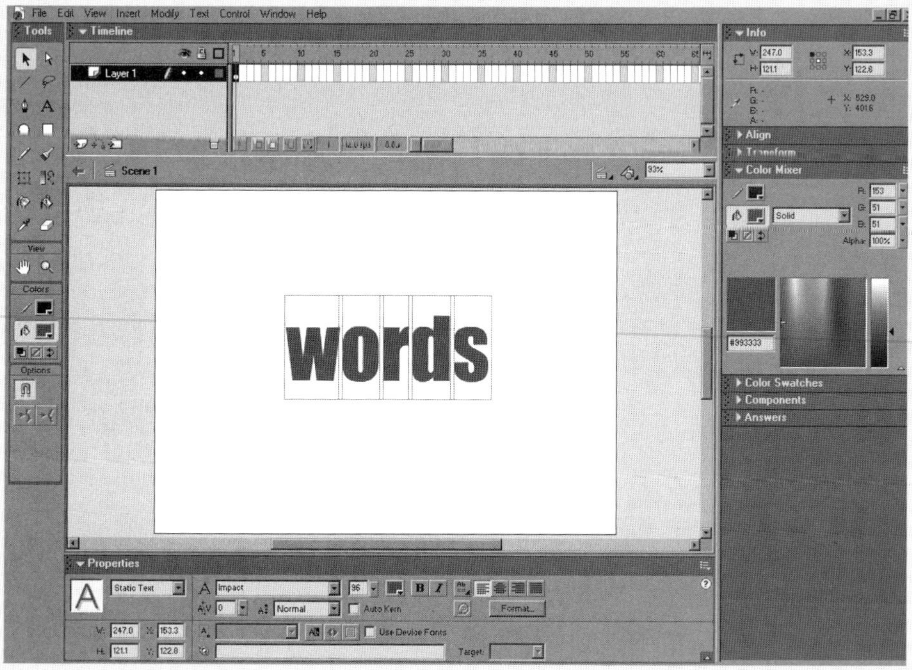

figure E4-1

4. To add different animation characteristics, such as scale and position, you will need to put each character on its own layer. To do this select Timeline > Distribute to Layers.

5. In each layer you will need to create the starting and ending keyframes for each animation (for each character). To do this target the desired frame for that layer in the timeline and select Insert > Timeline > Keyframe, or F6 on the keyboard.

| TIP |

Keyframes indicate the beginning and end of an animated sequence.

6. Target the first keyframe of the layer in the timeline. Move the letter to the desired start position, where you want it to appear at the beginning of the animation.

7. Target the end keyframe and move the character to the desired end position, where you want it to be at the end of the animation. Target any frame in between the two keyframes, and in the property inspector click the Tween drop-down menu and select "motion." Repeat this process for each character of the word.

8. Save the file.

Exercise 2

Animation Used for Education

Use the range selector tool to animate letters in a manner that one letter pops up from the rest. This can help children remember the visual shape of the letter while speaking it out loud. This technique of combining visuals and audio to aid in the learning process is often used in educational television and video.

Task

Animate the letters *a–z* for use as a visual aid when teaching English as a second language to college students.

Goal

Create an animation that could be used for educational purposes.

Software

After Effects

Design It, Step-by-Step

1. Open After Effects and make a new composition: Composition > New Composition. Name the composition *Alphabet*, and select the preset NTSC DV, 720 × 480.

2. Create a text layer. Select the text tool from the Tools palette and click in the Composition window. Type the letters of the alphabet.

3. Choose the typeface size, face, and color that work for this project. Choose a typeface that will be easy to read on screen. Consider the principles of typography discussed in this chapter and audience considerations from Chapter 3.

4. Expand layer 1 in the Timeline to position the animator. Choose Position from the Animate pop-up menu in the text layer's Switches/Mode column. Position will now appear in the Timeline.

5. Set the Range Selector. In the Composition window, drag the triangle on the right vertical selector line. Move it to the left until only the letter *a* is highlighted. Next to Position there are two coordinate points, now at 0.0, 0.0. Enter a y Position value of –75, so it looks like 0.0, –75. You will see that the letter *a* is now positioned above the rest of the text.

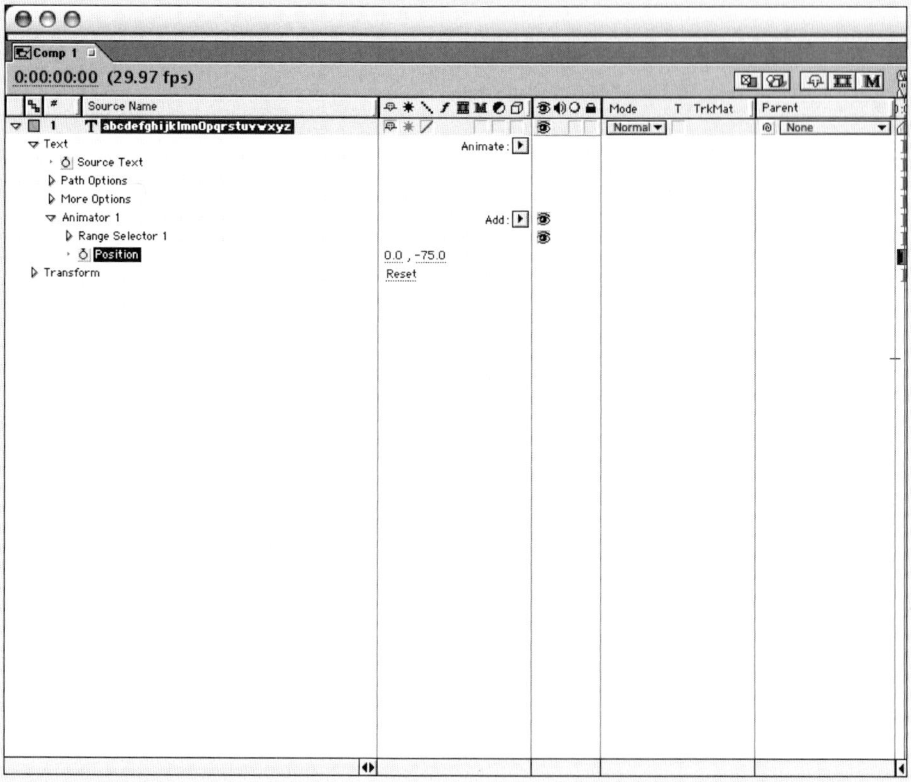

figure E4-2

6. Expand Range Selector 1. Move the playhead or time indicator to 1 second and click the stopwatch icon next to Offset. In the Composition window drag the right selector line, while holding down the Shift key, to the left. Both selector lines are now on the left side of the letter *a*. Move the playhead or time indicator to 15 seconds. While holding Shift, drag the left selector line all the way to the end of the alphabet until it sits to the right of the letter *z*.

TIP

Notice that a keyframe is automatically inserted because we have the stopwatch checked.

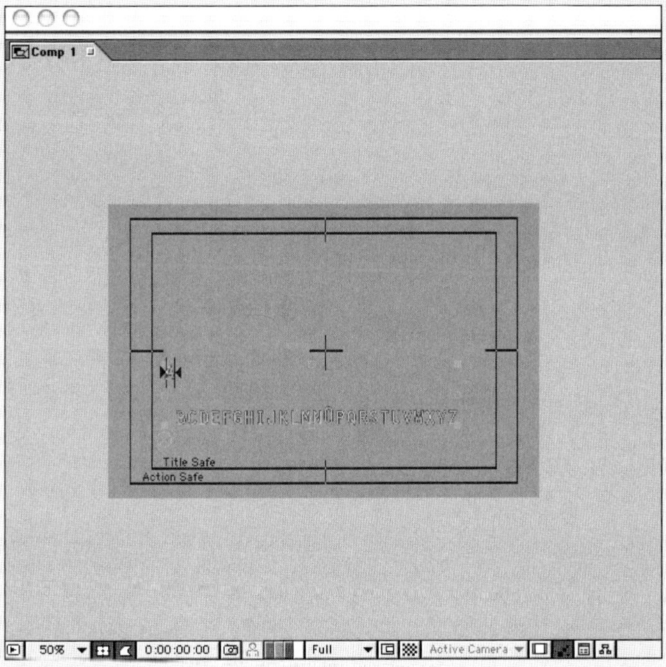

figure E4-3

7. Add color, opacity, and scale effects to the animation. Move the playhead or time indicator back to the beginning. In the Add pop-up menu in the timeline choose Property then Scale, Opacity or Fill Color (when choosing Fill Color opt for RGB). Once you have added these features, they will appear as a new layer under Range Selector 1. You can add values there. Make adjustments that add to the design of the project.

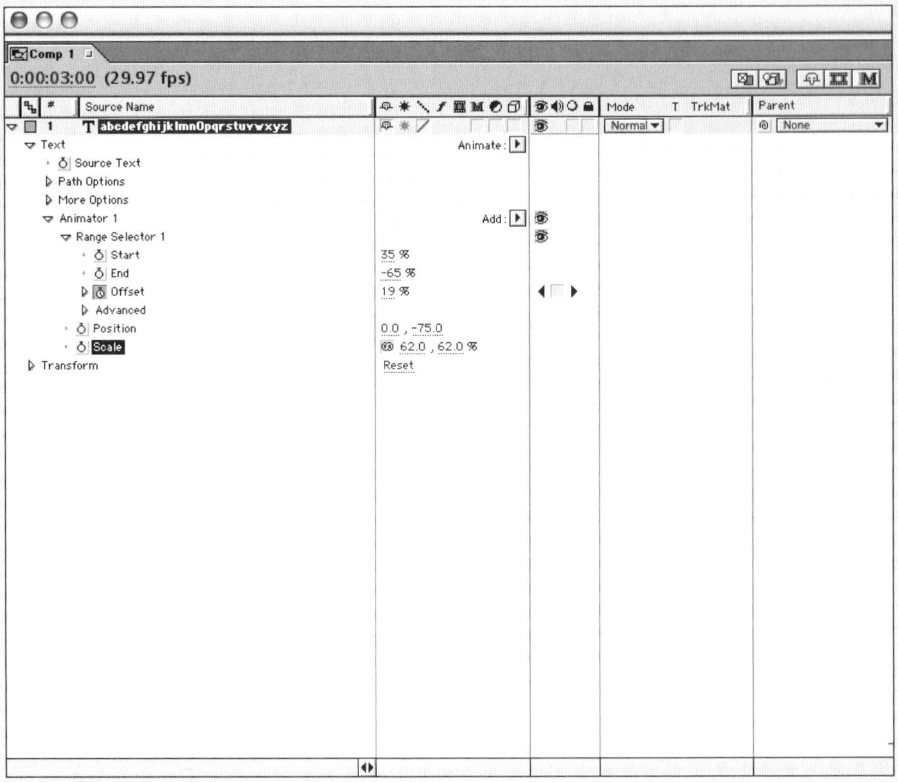

figure E4-4

8. Move the playhead or time indicator back to the beginning. Expand the Advanced submenu. You can adjust the Smoothness and set the letters to move less smoothly, making them appear to bounce a bit.

9. You can preview the animation by placing the playhead at the beginning of the timeline then play it by going under Composition > Preview > RAM Preview. This will play your graphic in the Composition window. Be sure to save this project by clicking File > Save As and choosing a name.

Design It, Advanced Techniques

1. To export from After Effects complete the following steps:
   a. If you do not already have the alphabet project open, open it now.
   b. Choose File > Export > QuickTime Movie.
   c. Click the settings button. In the Video pull-down menu, set it for DV/DVCPRO—NTSC. Set Settings to Best Quality. Deselect sound since we have not used sound, and deselect Prepare for Internet streaming. Name your file and save it as a .mov file.

2. To import to Final Cut Pro, complete the following steps:
   a. Open Final Cut Pro. Import your .mov file.
   b. Drag it onto the Timeline on the top video track.
   c. Select the button in the Canvas window and select Image & Wireframe. Now you can move your motion graphic into place in the lower-right quadrant of the frame.
   d. In order to see the motion graphic in Final Cut Pro, you will need to render it first. Choose Sequence > Render Selection > Video. Before you render it, though, you will need to save the project.
   e. Now you can view your motion graphic in Final Cut Pro.

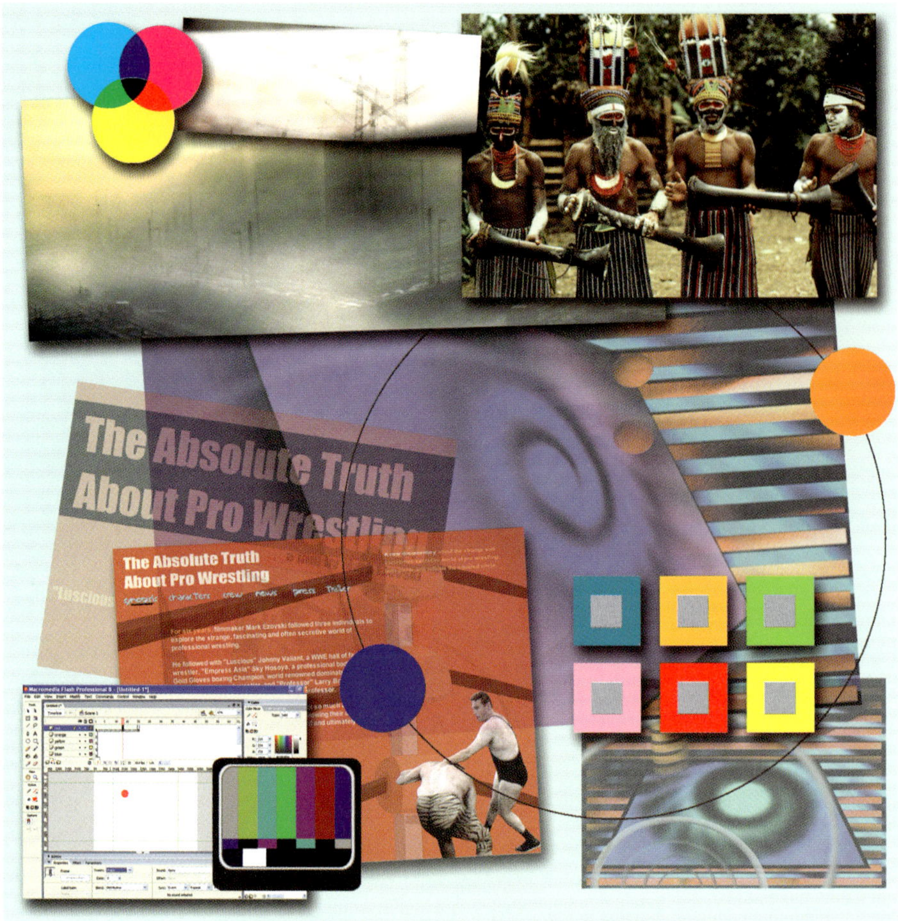

CHAPTER 5

Chapter Objectives

Discover how we perceive color

Learn basic color vocabulary and the different color systems

Explore the impact different color schemes may have on your motion graphic design

Recognize how we respond emotionally to color

Learn how to use color for emphasis and balance

Introduction

Our ability to perceive and analyze (or interpret) is what sets us apart as a species and makes it so much fun to be a designer. As a motion graphics artist, you are orchestrating a message with graphics, color, sound, and motion. Color adds emotional impact to any motion graphic; it is a stimulus that triggers a reaction in the viewer. Depending on the choices you implement as a designer, you can use color to manipulate a specific response from your audience.

USE OF COLOR IN HISTORY

The earliest forms of multimedia communication integrated color with motion to narrate a story and send a message. Colors carried very specific meanings and were pulled from a shared cultural experience. Different groups would identify themselves with specific color combinations. Clans, royal families, and the military all grouped themselves by wearing like colors. Men in Ireland wore kilts with color schemes specific to their clan, thereby clearly defining their loyalties. Royal families displayed coats of arms, designed to tell the story of their heritage, in which color played an important visual role. At the time of the American Revolution, the British Army wore red uniforms and was thus referred to as the Red Coats. In addition to

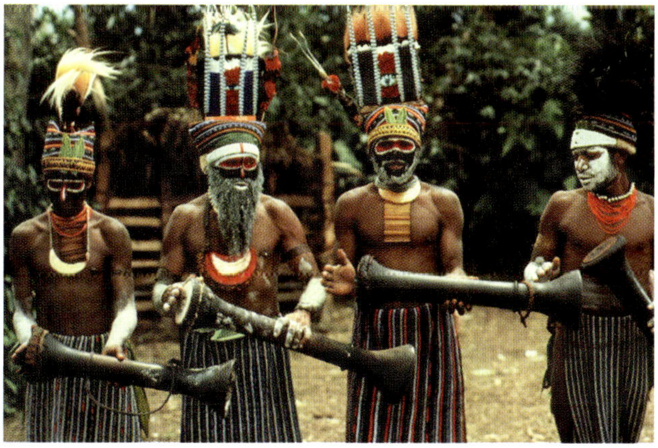

figure | 5-1 |

Individuals use color paints to decorate their bodies for ceremony.

COLOR

using color in clothing or objects to signify their connection to others, many groups throughout history painted their faces and bodies with different colors that held special significance within their culture.

HOW WE SEE COLOR

Sir Issac Newton, a seventeenth-century physicist, was the first to document the range of colors we see and determine that they are the property of light. While looking at light refracted through a glass prism, he was able to record the colors we see on the **spectral band**: red, orange, yellow, green, blue, and purple.

figure |5-2|

The color spectrum shows all light visible to the human eye.

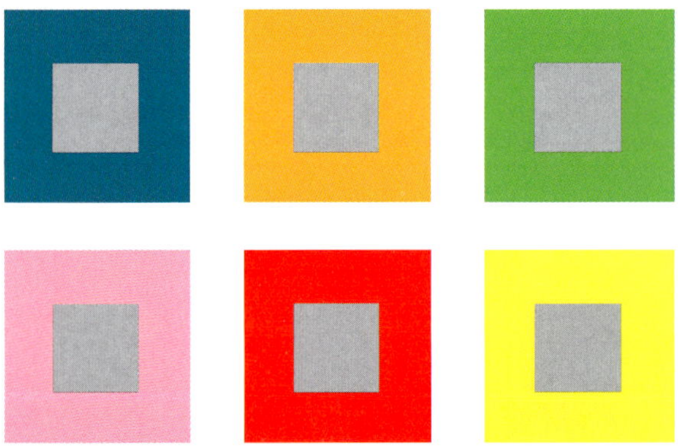

figure |5-3|

Our perception of color may change depending on the colors in the surrounding environment. The gray squares are all the same color but appear slightly different in relationship to the surrounding colors.

Red, green, and blue make up the majority of the spectral band; they are therefore the **primary colors** of light. The color that we read in objects is determined by the amount of light reflected or absorbed by that object. White objects reflect all light back to the viewer, making the object appear white. Black objects absorb all light, reflecting none back to the viewer, making the object appear black. Therefore, white is all of the visible light, or 100 percent of the light reflected back to the viewer, and black is the absence of any light, or 0 percent of the light reflected back to the viewer. All other visible colors are variables of reflected and absorbed light. Objects viewed under different light sources may appear to be different colors when in fact they are the same. Other colors that surround the object being viewed also affect our perception of color.

COLOR SYSTEMS

We will look at three color systems: **pigment** (or **traditional**), **additive**, and **subtractive**. Each color system is used for different media and clearly shows how primary colors, when combined, form secondary colors. Red, yellow, and blue are the three primary colors in the pigment system. The other colors of the basic color wheel are called **secondary** and **tertiary colors**.

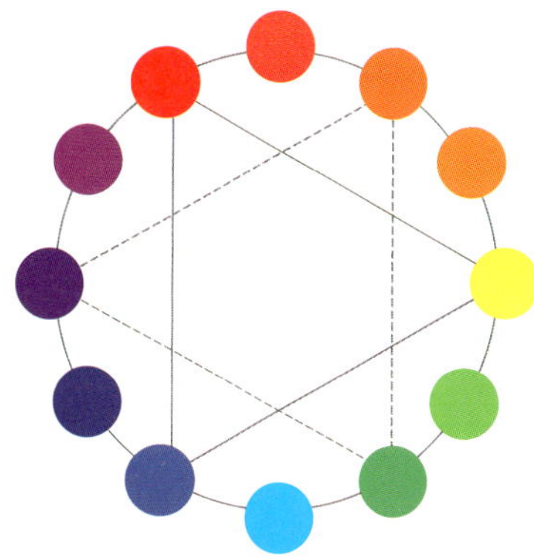

figure 5-4

Traditional color wheel.

The **color wheel** system dates back to the eighteenth century and is used to show color relationships. The three secondary colors are green, purple, and orange, and tertiary colors are all colors that fall between primary and secondary colors. The pigment system is traditionally used in two-dimensional media such as painting and drawing.

In the subtractive system, used in the four-color print process, cyan, yellow, and magenta are the primary colors. Standard ink jet and laser printers use four ink cartridges—cyan, magenta, yellow, and black. Printers refer to these as CMYK.

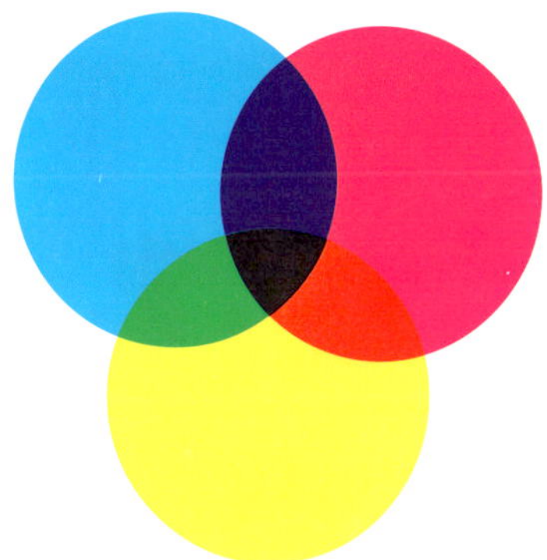

figure 5-5

Cyan, magenta, yellow, and black use the subtractive color system.

Cyan and magenta ink combine to produce blue, yellow and cyan combine to produce green, and magenta and yellow combine to produce red. Red, green, and blue are the secondary colors of the subtractive color system. If you combine cyan, magenta, and yellow each at 100 percent, they form black, and when you use each of the pigments at 0 percent, no ink is applied to the paper. Since no ink is applied, you simply see the paper. Other printing processes use more than four colors, such as the six-color process, which also uses orange and green ink cartridges. These advanced printing processes are often used when printing high-quality photographs; the orange and the green make the magenta and yellow more vibrant.

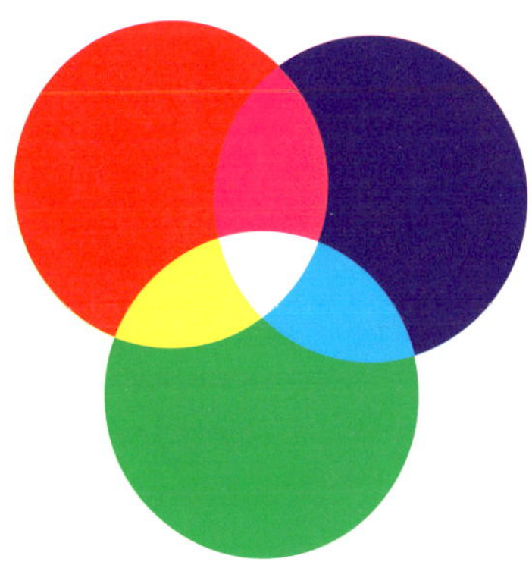

figure 5-6

Red, green, and blue use the additive color system.

The additive color system follows the properties of light in which red, green, and blue are the primary colors. Using various combinations of red, green, and blue creates the millions of colors we see on screen. When red and green light are combined, we see yellow. When red and blue are combined, we see magenta, and when blue and green are combined we get cyan. Cyan, magenta, and yellow are the secondary colors of the additive color system. When red, green, and blue are used at 100 percent, white appears. When there is a total absence of all colors, we see black. As a motion graphics artist, you never leave the confines of the screen; therefore, all color choices you make will be based on the additive color system of red, green, and blue light.

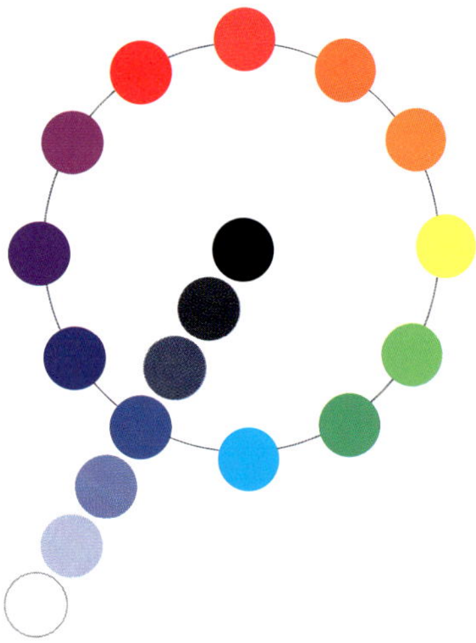

figure 5-7

Levels of brightness showing shades and tints.

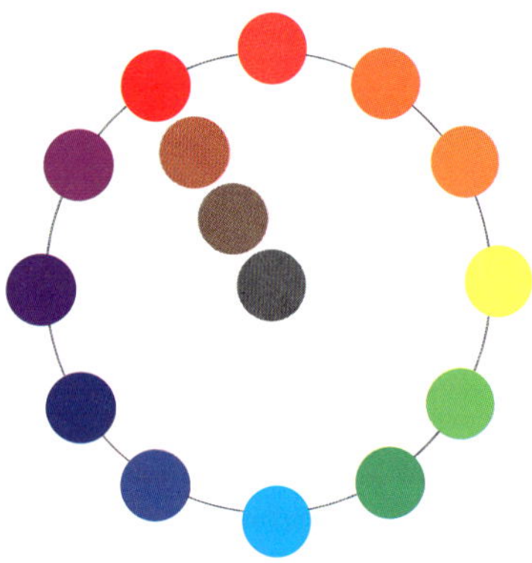

figure 5-8

Saturation values, from middle gray.

Properties of Color

The three properties of color are **hue**, **value**, also referred to as brightness, and **saturation**. Sometimes the terms *hue* and *color* are used interchangeably, but hue refers to the visible colors on the color spectrum, while **color** refers to the hues, including all variations of saturation, **tints**, and **shades**. Value refers to the overall darkness or brightness of the hue and produces the many tints and shades of each color.

Saturation refers to the intensity, or amount of pure color of the hue. The amount of gray added to a color determines the saturation level. A hue can be completely **desaturated** when gray has been added until there is no color left. Adding white or black to the hue creates shades and tints. Shades are created as black is added to the hue, and tints are created as white is added. Since value is the lightness or darkness of the color, a very saturated color can still be very dark if the value is lowered. Using hues, tints, and shades in your design is a very effective way to elicit a sense of depth. Brighter and bolder colors appear to come forward, or to be in the front, while darker, less saturated colors appear to move away, or to be in the back of the design.

Screen Considerations

Remember that pixels are the units that make up all images, graphics, and text on the screen. Each pixel unit contains the three primary colors of light: red, green, and blue. The color of each pixel is determined by the properties of light, which can be clearly seen by accessing the Channels palette in Photoshop.

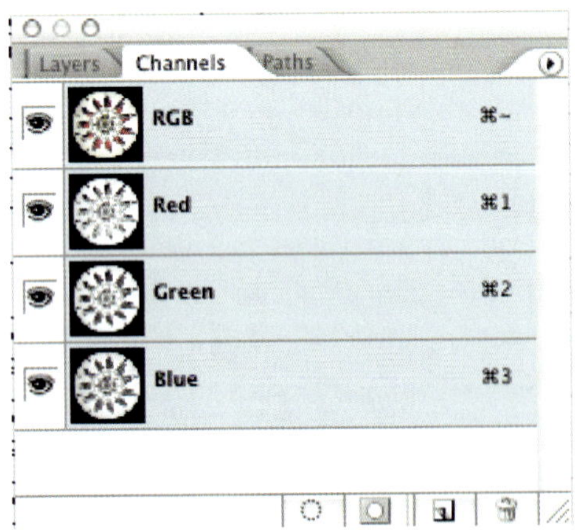

figure 5-9

The Channels palette in Photoshop shows the composite RGB channel in addition to the individual red, green, and blue channels.

Each image has a composite channel, RGB, and three individual channels, red, green, and blue. In some instances there may also be an alpha channel that is used for selections and transparency. The alpha channel contains no color information. Selecting each channel individually reveals how much red, blue, and green are in the image.

Digital designers are at the mercy of other people's computer monitors or device settings. Every screen is calibrated slightly differently, so if you have found that perfect green, do not count on your viewer seeing the same beautiful subtleties. There are also differences between the way a Macintosh computer and a PC display color on the monitor. Generally speaking, the color on a Macintosh computer always appears lighter than on a PC. This is an important distinction to know, because although the design and film world is filled with Macintosh computers, many of your viewers will likely be looking at your website animation on a PC. You will need to make adjustments to the color levels of brightness and contrast where necessary.

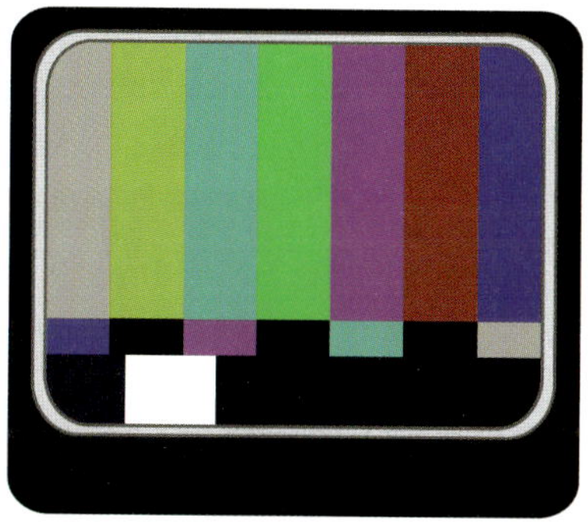

figure 5-10

Color bars are used to ensure broadcast quality.

On a video screen, colors with high saturation levels look like they are bleeding together, even though they may have looked fine on your computer monitor. The range of colors that are not prone to bleeding are called broadcast colors and are used to match colors from different sources, such as cameras, monitors, and other video. **Color bars**, used to ensure broadcast quality colors over television and between video viewing devices, appear at the beginning of all recorded material. Red is the worst culprit of color bleeding. The saturation and brightness can be adjusted to make the color broadcast quality.

COLOR THEORY

The colors used in any design need to support the emotional tone of the message. We recognize color before we read the text or see the images in a design. We see the red of the stop sign before we read the word *stop* and because we read the color red as a warning, we stop the car. Use color as a tool to impart the emotion of the design onto the viewer, guide them in understanding the content, and use it to create impact and help them remember the message. To control the emotional undertone of the graphic, choose a color with the same emotional weight of the message.

Color Schemes

An infinite number of color combinations can be used to induce a psychological reaction from the viewer. Color schemes are organized to show different color relationships, and all colors can be used in their respective shades, tints, or saturation levels. A light color scheme is one that uses tinted colors; conversely, a dark color scheme is one that uses shades of each color. A vivid color scheme is made up of highly saturated colors, and a dull color scheme is made up of desaturated colors.

As you look at the different color schemes that follow, think about your initial emotional reaction. Are the colors warm or cool? Do the colors make you feel calm or excited? Does a specific brand, object, or location come to mind when viewing the color? All of these color schemes are based on colors from the pigment system color wheel.

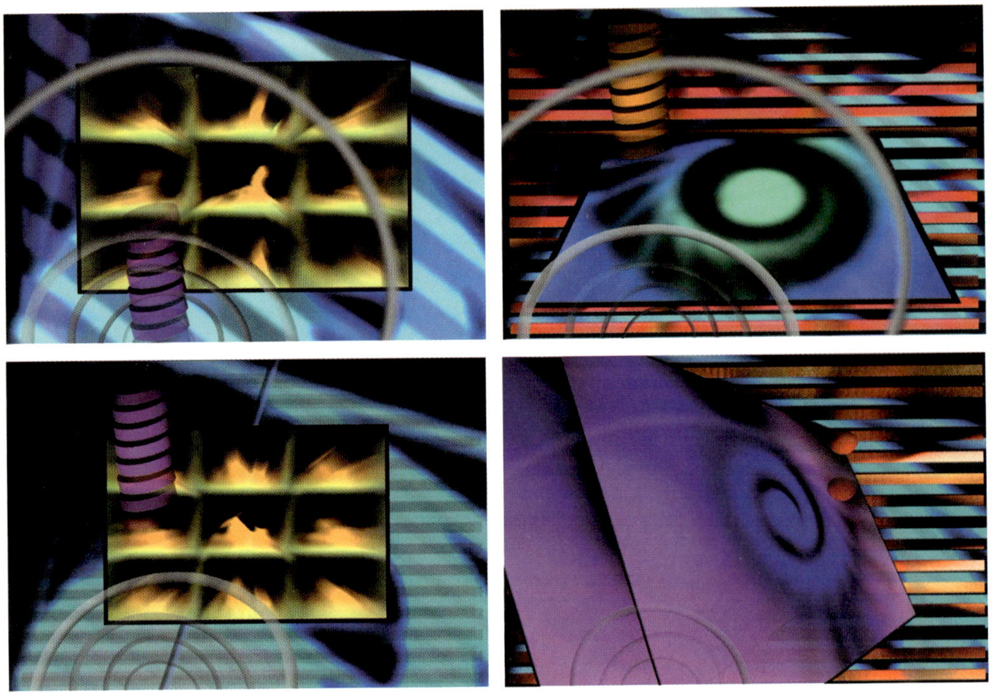

figure | 5-11 |

This motion graphic uses vivid colors to create dynamic play between the elements.

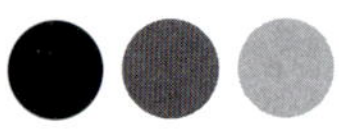

figure | 5-12 |

Achromatic colors.

Achromatic: In this scheme there is a complete absence of color and only black, white, and shades of gray are used. An achromatic look may elicit a feeling of looking at something historic, sophisticated, or outdated, so it should be used with care and purpose.

Monochromatic: This scheme uses only one hue, or shades and tints of the hue. The monochromatic look can have an interesting effect, often one that is tranquil because there is no demand for attention, but it should be used sparingly as it may not leave a lasting impression on viewers. There is no dynamic play between the colors, which can make for a flat design if not balanced by other elements such as scale, depth, or texture.

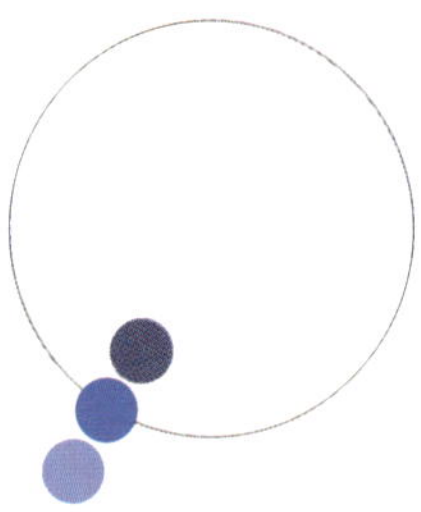

figure | 5-13 |

Monochromatic colors.

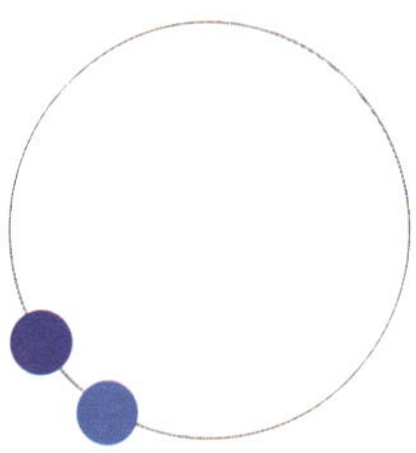

figure | 5-14 |

Analogous colors.

Analogous: This scheme is seen when colors directly next to each other on the color wheel are used in combination. This can be very effective when used thoughtfully, and using the tints and shades of the hue as well can create a sense of depth. The analogous look can lack impact though, because there is only a subtle shift of color. A subtle shift may not be able to grab and hold the viewers' attention. There is not an immediate push-pull among the colors, again opening the possibility for a flat design.

Complementary: This scheme uses colors that are opposite each other on the color wheel. Complementary colors placed next to each other in a design appear more brilliant than if used alone. Using complementary colors creates dynamism and a lasting impression on the viewer.

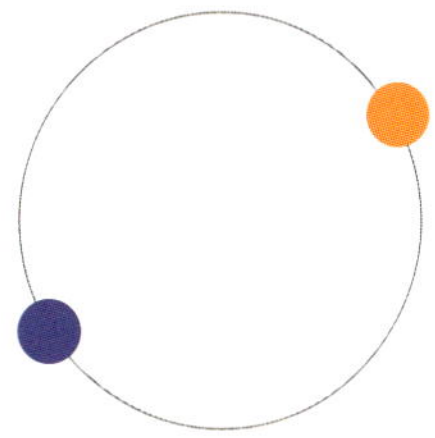

figure 5-15

Complementary colors.

Split complementary: This scheme uses three colors and is a variation on the complementary scheme. Choose one color plus colors from either side of its complement on the opposite side of the color wheel. The effect is similar to using complementary colors, but the brilliance is not increased as dramatically.

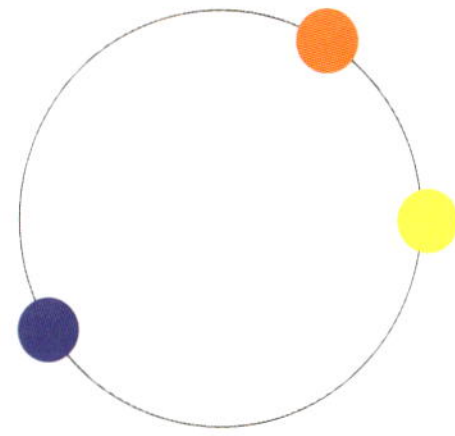

figure 5-16

Split complementary colors.

Clash: This term implies that the two colors of this scheme will not be visually appealing, but by using one color plus the color directly to the right or left of its complement is an often-used scheme that has a dramatic effect. The clash scheme should be used as needed to support a design created to grab viewers' attention with two strong colors fighting to be the focal point.

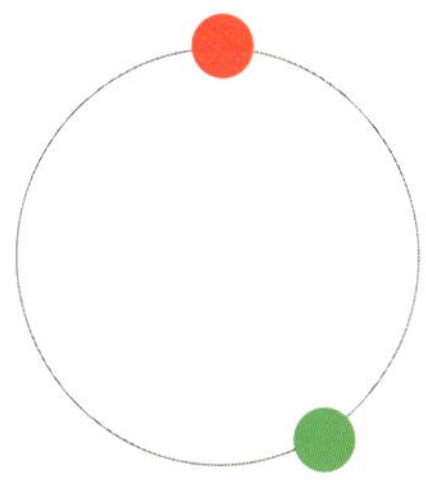

figure 5-17

Clashing colors.

Primary: Many manufacturers of children's toys and craft supplies (paints and crayons) use the pure primary colors red, yellow, and blue.

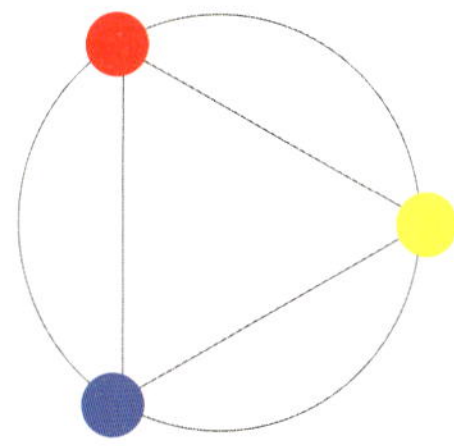

figure 5-18

Primary colors.

Secondary: The pure secondary colors, orange, green, and purple, are warm and earthy.

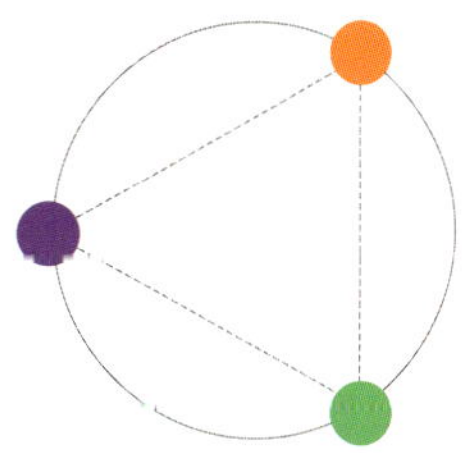

figure 5-19

Secondary colors.

Tertiary: This scheme uses three colors that are not one of the primary or secondary colors, all equidistant from each other on the color wheel. There are many combinations of tertiary colors.

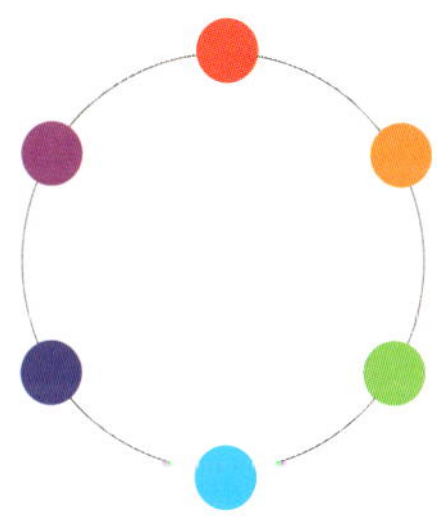

figure 5-20

Tertiary colors.

Attracting the Viewer by Way of Color

Breaking out and using unexpected color schemes can grab viewers' attention and engage them in the motion graphic. When choosing to go with the unexpected, remember the general color principles and select your colors wisely. You want to engage viewers, not turn them off from your design by using too many colors that fight for their attention and detract from the message.

Considering the ultimate placement of your motion graphic design is especially important when you will be competing for the attention of viewers against all of the other media that constantly vies for their notice. If you have created a piece for a digital billboard anchored in a busy area, you are immediately competing with all the other billboards, storefronts, and signs. You will have the advantage if you effectively use color in a way that grabs viewers' attention.

EMOTIONAL COLOR

Our first reaction to a color is physical. The physical reaction to, say, yellow, may be that you recall the last time you were at the beach under a warm sun, and "feel" that warmth again. An emotional response is an overall feeling that the color elicits, not a specific memory or

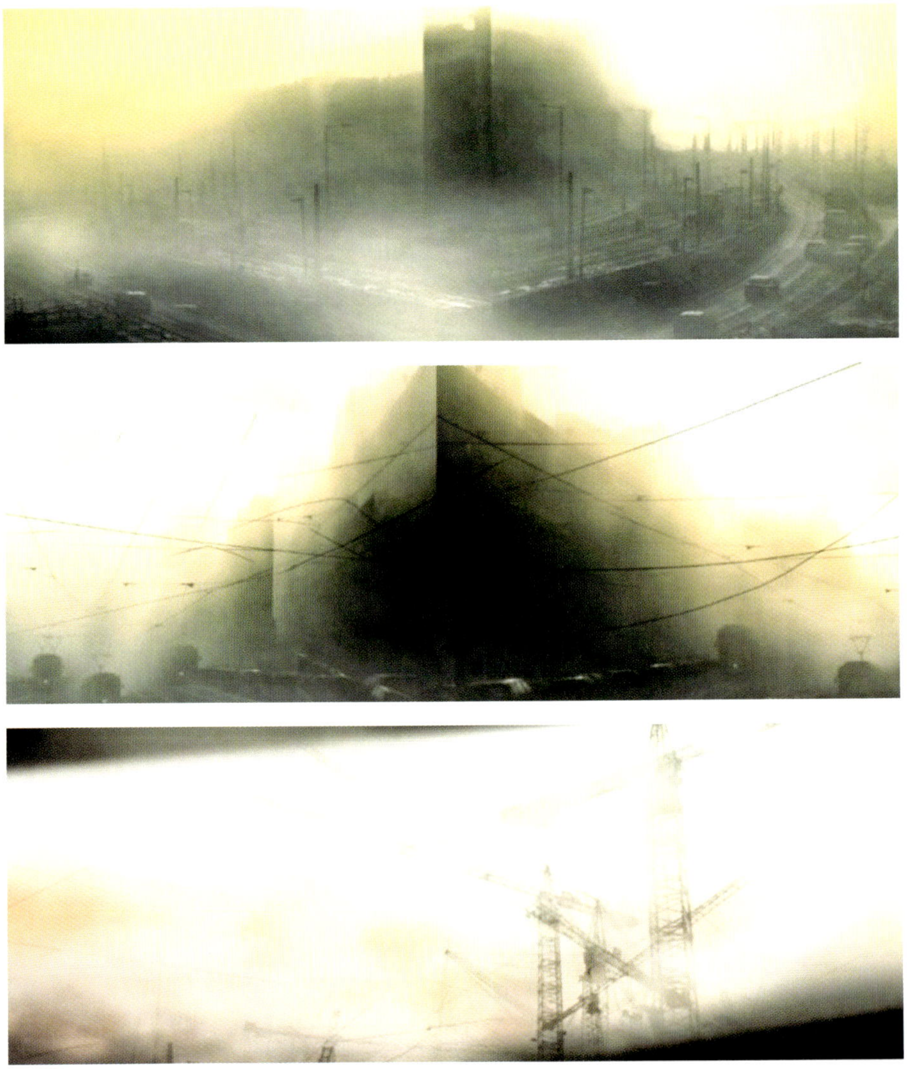

By Patrick Doan

figure | 5-21 |

The muted, murky colors used in this motion graphic signify daybreak and speak to a feeling of a "new dawn." There is an emotional response associated with these colors.

association with a physical thing or place. In a psychic reaction we express our emotional response to that particular color. The psychic reaction to yellow could be happiness, outwardly expressed by a smile. Some colors hold very clear emotional responses.

Whether physical or psychic, people have an immediate emotional reaction to color. Since it is this emotional reaction that will set the tone and will affect the viewer's response to the design, you need to make sure that the colors support the message of the communication, and remember that the shifts in the intensity of the color when saturation and brightness is adjusted will change the emotional impact. For example, our response to pure red is to feel excited and energetic, but what if you have a red with less saturation? A desaturated red will not carry the same level of energy because the color is more subdued. A less saturated red will be less dramatic and bold.

Universal Responses

Although specific colors will not elicit the same response in every viewer, it is fair to say that many emotional responses are based in universal connections and associations. Some universal responses to color are based on the physical sensation that is mentally tied to the color. No matter where in the world, a fire is composed of reds, yellows, and oranges, and it is hot. Water is some shade of blue, and it is cool. Here the basic colors, based on the color pigment system, are listed with some of the emotions most likely to be tied to them.

Red

Pure hue: Angry, Passionate, Dynamic

Tints: Romantic, Sweet, Girly

Shades: Regal, Refined, Velvety

Orange

Pure hue: Vital, Energetic, Tangy

Tints: Friendly, Funny, Inviting

Shades: Solid, Vital, Autumnal

Yellow

Pure hue: Warm, Lively, Sunny

Tints: Illuminating, Happy, Soft

Shades: Tart, Dusky, Comforting

Blue

Pure hue: Contemplative, Cool, Wet

Tints: Serene, Refreshing, Tender

Shades: Dignified, Authoritative, Cold

Green

Pure hue: Healing, Fresh, Natural

Tints: Verdant, Caring, Soothing

Shades: Eloquent, Quiet, Peaceful

Purple

Pure hue: Royal, Spiritual, Sensual

Tints: Delicate, Aromatic, Nostalgic

Shades: Elegant, Luxurious, Exotic

White

Pure, Innocent, Virginal

Black

Powerful, Mysterious, Oppressive

Cultural Responses

Some response to color is based in cultural attitudes. Because emotional responses are powerful, a designer must be mindful of the use of color in eliciting such responses. In the United States and other Western countries, black is the color of mourning, but this is not true for all countries. In India white is the color of mourning, and in China it is red. In the United States white is the color of purity and hope, used for rituals of love such as weddings, and red is the color of passion and energy, used in other rituals of love, such as roses on Valentine's Day. Use color responsibly and deliberately, knowing that the viewer will have an automatic emotional and sensory response. This is to be used to your advantage to manipulate the viewer's response to the intended emotion of the message.

Branding with Color

Some cultural responses can be seen in the power of color in marketing and advertising. With major brands expanding in world markets, they too are becoming universal, but many are still steeped in cultural awareness. There is a clear method of conveying meaning and message through instant recognition of emotional ties to color. When you think of Coca-Cola, what color do you think of? Coca-Cola conjures up thoughts of the color red. The red used by Coca-Cola is an energetic, vibrant color that successfully advertises the sweet, bubbly product. The National Milk Mustache "got milk?"® Campaign, jointly launched by America's milk processors and dairy farmers—The Milk Processor Education Program (MilkPEP) in Washington, D.C., and Dairy Management Inc., in Chicago—uses milk's white color to symbolize purity and innocence. In the ad campaign all models (celebrities and actors) were photographed with a thick white milk mustache. The white mustache became a symbol and branded milk as a product not only for kids or something you poured into your morning coffee, but as a beverage that should be enjoyed all by itself. Both of these examples illustrate a different manner of using color to brand consumer goods, and both are equally effective.

Case Study

Intentional Color

The Absolute Truth about Pro Wrestling by Mark Ezovski is a documentary made for multiple audiences and is promoted through a website intended to offer practical information about screenings and press as well as entertainment with the visuals. The filmmaker's goal is to tell a story about wrestlers and the wrestling industry while appealing to an audience larger than just wrestling fans. In addition to focusing on a storyline that speaks to anyone following a dream—not just one of becoming a pro wrestling star—the filmmaker employs experimental and artistic techniques in the editing process. When designing the website, Ezovski applied this aesthetic as well, creating a fully developed identity system and brand for this documentary. All of the work was created in-house and was developed to consciously and unabashedly follow the raw essence of old-school professional wrestling.

The website uses an abundance of red with grainy, desaturated photographs. The red elicits feelings of pain, fury, and raw energy while conjuring images of blood. This bright, saturated red of the website is contrasted and balanced by the treatments applied to the photographs. The photographs, originally in full color, are brought into Photoshop, and the saturation is lowered using the Hue/Saturation dialog box. The remaining color is also slightly adjusted to create a uniform cyan cast. Using these complementary colors creates contrast on the page and initiates a visual play, making the photograph pop off the page.

The photographs and the motion graphics of the website are used in the same manner as in the film, creating visual continuity between the two media. When the webpage initially loads, the primary color is bright red, then the photograph moves in from outside the frame and has a soothing effect.

These color treatments speak to the childhood connections Ezovksi had from watching pro wrestling on television and reading about it in the specialty magazines. It was all very low-tech, often with poor-quality photographic reproductions in magazines or poor-quality television broadcasts. It also was not uncommon to see a wrestler in a match, or picture of a wrestler in a magazine, with blood streaming down his forehead and cheeks. These visuals greatly influenced the choice of color palette for the website.

| TIP |

To create photographs with a similar look in Photoshop, follow these steps: make a Hue/Saturation adjustment layer (Layer > New Adjustment Layer > Hue/Saturation). Click the slider for saturation, and move it to the left to take out most, but not all, of the color. Then click the slider for hue, and move it to the right to slightly colorize the photograph. Click OK when satisfied. The next step is to create the pattern (Layer > Layer Style > Pattern Overlay). Lower the opacity of the overlay so you can see the image below, and choose a pattern. Click OK when satisfied.

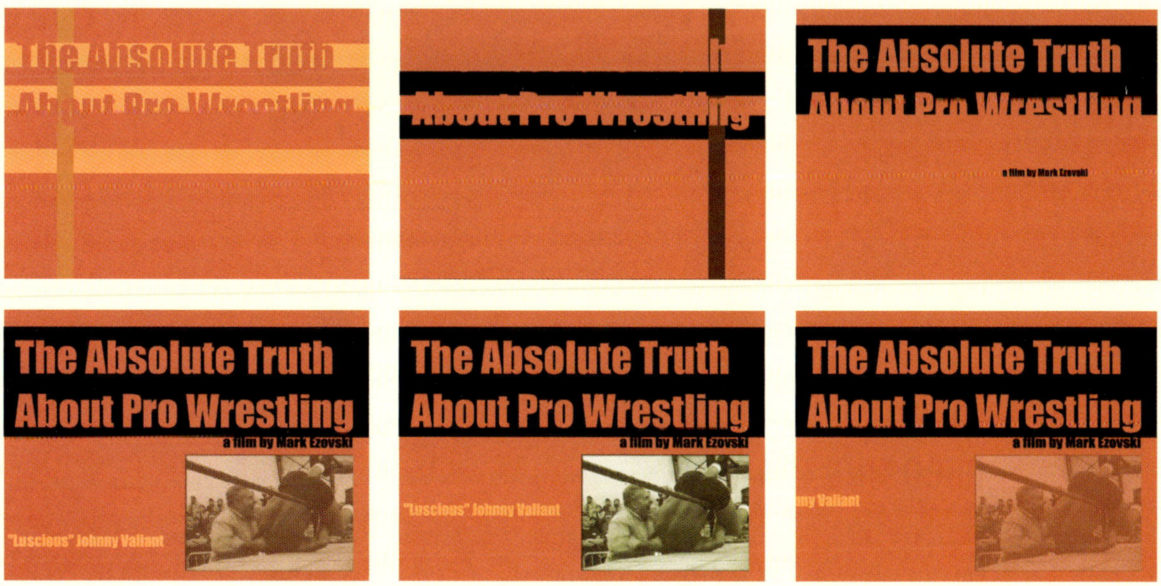

By Mark Ezovski Productions/Diabolical Brain

figure |5-22|

Screen shots from the animated splash page of the website for *The Absolute Truth about Pro Wrestling.*

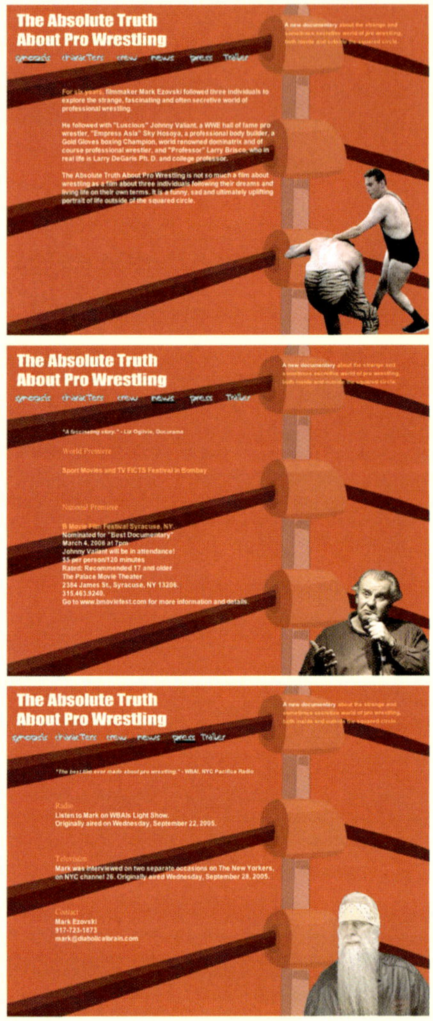

By Mark Ezovski Productions/Diabolical Brain

figure | 5-23 |

The color treatment is also used with photographs on the static webpages.

CHOOSING COLORS

One task when beginning a new design is to determine a color palette. First, decide what the emotional colors of the product are and what colors the audience will respond to. Choosing color can sometimes be overwhelming with all of the limitless possibilities, but by breaking it down into the following categories and basic guidelines, color selection becomes much easier.

- Determine whether colors should come from the warm or cool side of the color wheel.

- Select a color theme to follow: analogous, complementary, monochromatic, and so on.
- Select a primary, or main, color and one or two accent colors. The primary color will be used for the majority of the design, and the accent colors will be used for supporting elements that are not the main focus.

For example, colors in an ad designed to attract tourists to Florida for a family vacation should speak to fun and excitement. Choosing what are referred to as **warm colors**, the reds, yellows, and oranges on the color wheel, will impart these feelings and potentially conjure memories of past enjoyable experiences. On the other hand, **cool colors** would elicit a different emotional response and would not support the message of the ad. There are a number of ways to include the warm colors in the overall design, and each, in their own way, will support the message. Guide the viewer through the ad by highlighting specific words in the design with the warm color, emphasizing the message that Florida is exciting and fun. Use a warm color to create a visual impact, perhaps by drawing a giant sun that fills the frame. Using a warm color in this manner will have a lasting impact on viewers because it is a familiar symbol with a pleasing color and is easy to remember. Each time they see the ad with the large warm sun, they will recall the message of the ad without having to read it again, and they may dream of traveling to Florida.

In this example a warm tone is used to signify fun and excitement. These tones may also be used to signify a great number of other emotions, such as passion or elatedness. Cool tones, on the other hand, are more subdued and often associated with calm, sad, or quiet, and would not be a strong color choice for the Florida vacation ad. If color is misused and does not support the message, you will send a confused message to the viewer. Make sure the color choices support the overall message.

Many designers use color books and chips, such as Pantone® guides or *Color Harmony* for assistance. Although you could use color books with swatches specific to screen colors, we recommend that you use the color spectrums in any design software. This will give a more accurate assessment of how the color will appear on screen.

Using Color to Create Emphasis and Balance

Color is used in motion graphics to bring focus, group elements, emphasize information, and add visual interest. How color is implemented will also aid in developing a visual hierarchy, creating a map for how the viewer should read the design. Color used as emphasis shows what the most important element of the design is, thereby helping to communicate to the viewer what the most important part of the message is. Recall the example of the ad for a Florida family vacation. In this example a warm color was used to emphasize individual words and to highlight the important information while imparting emotional associations. By using color to create a visual hierarchy in your design, you ensure that the viewer reads the message as intended.

You can use color for emphasis in a number of different ways. Bold, bright colors generally stand out from other content on the screen. A strong color immediately grabs the viewer's

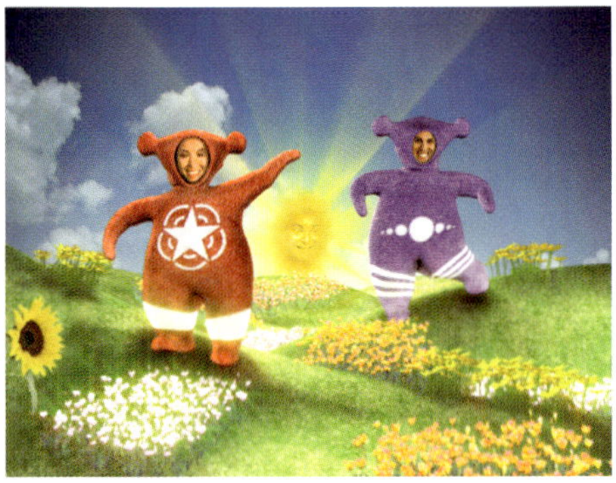

By Joel Lava, Green Towel/Transistor

figure 5-24

A music video sequence uses color to put emphasis on the dancing bears. The designer chose bright, warm colors to use throughout the scene, but still manages to emphasize the bears by using clash colors for their fur.

attention and takes all of the initial focus; remember we see color before anything else in the design. You can emphasize a part of the screen by choosing a bold or dynamic color, one that is bright and stands out from the background and other type and pictorial elements. You can use a photograph with strong, bold colors that will also stand apart from the rest. You could also emphasize certain words by stroking or filling the letters with bold, bright colors. When using color to create emphasis, the options do not have to be limited to bold, bright colors. Emphasis can also be created by using color for one element in the design among a sea of elements of another color. Think of looking down from the third floor of a building on a rainy day. If everyone on the street wields a black umbrella, then no one stands out among the crowd, but one person carrying a white umbrella will certainly be noticed. White is not a bold or bright color, but when used with an individual element in this manner that element is emphasized.

Using Color to Create Visual Play

Whatever colors you choose, the goal is to create a visual play among all of the design components. Creating a visual play is using color in specific elements to develop a sense of contrast, conflict, or tension against the other elements. Although this color play makes a visually interesting design, be careful not to choose too many colors that, in the end, fight with each other for the viewer's attention so that the message becomes secondary, or gets lost altogether. The best way to ensure that this does not happen is to choose one main color and then two or three supporting, or accent, colors.

Color may also be used to balance a design. The balance of a design is determined by looking at the two sides of the vertical axis. A piece of paper folded in half will show the two sides of the vertical axis. When looking at color and balance, first determine the overall color categories: light, dark, vivid, or dull. See if the colors are used uniformly throughout the piece or if one side is lighter, darker, more vivid, or duller than the other. If all of the colors in the design are of the same category with little variation, they will all have the same visual weight, or impact on the viewer. No color, therefore no element, will stand out, or pop, from the rest. A solution may be to add an additional color to the scheme, and add it sparingly as an accent color to important elements and information. In another scenario, there may be an overuse of one color on one side of the vertical axis dragging viewers' attention to only that side of the design. To combat this problem, use a small amount of a contrasting complementary color on the other side of the axis. Even this small amount of color will create a balance in the design. Use color to create a focal point on the important element for the viewer.

SUMMARY

All visible colors are derived from light, primarily red, green, and blue, which make up the majority of the color spectrum. Color may appear to look altered in different environments, when in fact it is simply that we perceive color based not only on the light reflected off of it but also of the light reflected off of the colors surrounding it. This will potentially cause the viewer to have a different reaction than that intended by the design. Some colors and color combinations have specific cultural associations, while others are considered more universal. From a very young age we are conditioned to respond emotionally to the colors we see. When we see color it is not just the light that we react to; there is also a distinct impression left by the emotional association. It is this emotional association that will create a lasting impact on the viewer about the motion graphic design. Since we are conditioned to respond to color stimuli, it should be used to manipulate your audience so it responds appropriately to the emotional ties within your message.

in review

1. What are the three main color systems?
2. Which color system do motion graphics designers use?
3. What are the properties of color?
4. What are some of the color schemes, and what is the impact of each in the larger design?
5. Why do we respond emotionally to color?
6. How can you use color to create emphasis or balance?

exercises

Exercise 1

Color Schemes

This exercise allows you to look at your surroundings and categorize the color schemes based on examples from the chapter.

Task

Find examples of specific color schemes used on professional websites.

Goal

Bring screen shots from three different websites and discuss the use of color in class.

Research It

Find examples of websites that use the following color schemes:

- Analogous
- Complementary
- Monochromatic

Answer the following questions about the website:

- Does the color scheme match the emotional content of the website?
- How does the chosen color scheme support the message?
- What if any accent colors were added to the website?

Exercise 2

Color Wheel

This hands-on exercise will further develop your animation skills using keyframes and tweens and will reinforce properties of color, specifically hue and saturation.

Task

Make a traditional color wheel that is animated. At the end you may decide to add additional elements, such as animated tints and shades, and label the color wheel with vocabulary from the chapter.

Goal

Create an animated, traditional color wheel that illustrates levels of saturation for each hue.

Software

Flash

Design It, Step-by-Step

1. Open a new document and set the document size to 550 × 400 pixels.

2. Make twelve new layers in the Timeline window and label them to correspond with the twelve colors of the traditional color wheel.

   - Red
   - Red Orange
   - Orange
   - Yellow Orange
   - Yellow
   - Yellow Green
   - Green
   - Blue Green
   - Blue
   - Blue Purple
   - Purple
   - Red Purple

> **TIP**
>
> To add a new layer, go to Insert > Layer. A new layer will appear in the Layers palette. To rename the layer double-click the words *Layer 2* and type the new name.

3. Set guides on the stage to mark the center. Set the horizontal guide at 200 pixels and the vertical guide at 275 pixels. You need to pull the guides down from the rulers, so if your rulers are not showing, go to View > Rulers.

   Set guides to mark the outer rim of the wheel. Set one horizontal guide at 50 pixels and the other at 350 pixels. Set one vertical guide at 100 pixels and the other at 450 pixels.

4. In the Color Picker palette, set the fill color to middle gray, R = 216, B = 216, G = 216. Be sure the stroke color is set to none; you only want to use a fill color.

5. Draw a 25 × 25 pixel circle directly in the center at the axis point of the guides positioned at 200x and 275y. To draw a perfect circle, hold down the Shift key while dragging the cursor.

TIP

You can draw the circle first and then adjust the width and height in the property inspector. The shape must be selected in order to do this.

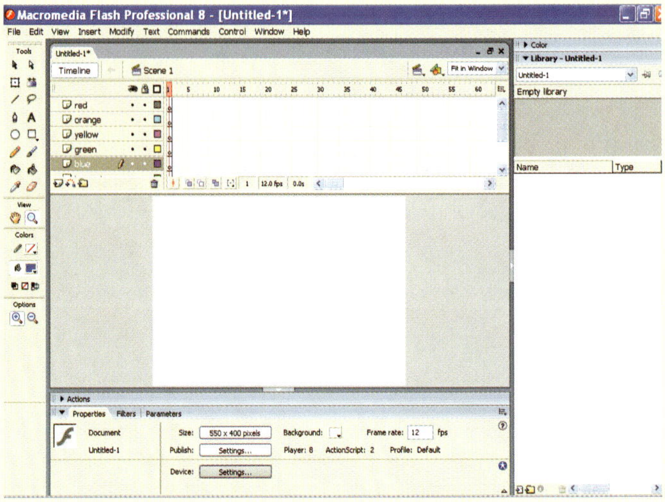

figure E5-1

6. Convert the shape to a symbol: Modify > Convert to Symbol. In the dialog box be sure *graphic* is selected and name it "small gray circle."

7. Target the Red layer and drag the symbol from the Library onto the stage.

8. Be sure the Red layer is still targeted. Add a keyframe to frame 20 by targeting frame 20 on the Red layer. Insert > Timeline > Keyframe, or hit F6 on the keyboard.

9. While still targeting frame 20, and making sure the small gray circle is selected, move it away from the center, straight up to the horizontal guide set at 50 pixels.

10. While still selecting the small gray circle at frame 20, scale it up to 50 × 50 pixels.

11. Be sure the large gray circle is still selected, and in the Properties window, select Tint from the Colors pull-down menu. Change the fill color to a red hue.

NOTE

All symbols are stored in the Library, which can be accessed through Window > Library, Ctrl+L (Windows) or Cmd+L (Mac). Using symbols keeps the file size down and allows you to use the same elements in multiple layers without re-creating them from scratch each time.

TIP

To see the scale option in the property inspector, or change the color, you must have the shape selected.

12. Position the playhead anywhere between frame 1 and frame 20, and in the Properties window select Motion from the Tween pull-down menu.

TIP

When a tween is successful, a solid arrow will run between the two keyframes. A dashed arrow indicates that the tween does not work.

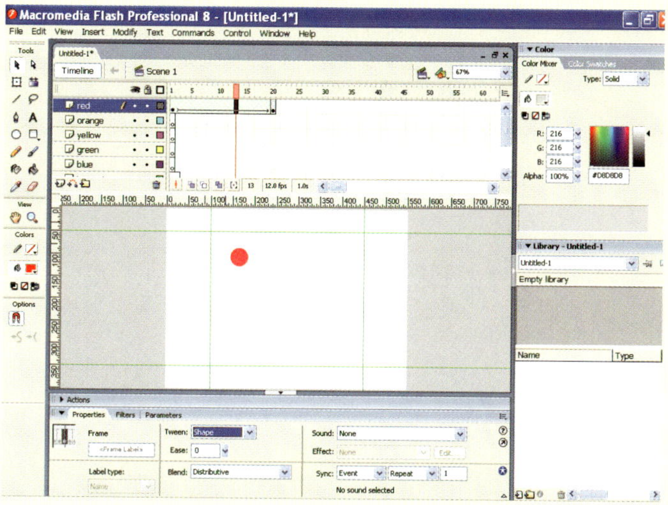

figure E5-2

13. Target the Orange Yellow layer. Add a keyframe to frame 1.

14. Drag the symbol and center on stage.

15. Add a keyframe to frame 20.

16. While still targeting frame 20, and making sure the small gray circle is selected, move it away straight from the center right to the vertical guide set at 450 pixels.

NOTE

Tween is short for in between. In other words when you tween between frames, the computer recognizes the different location, shape, or color, and adds the transition information to all frames in between the two keyframes.

17. Scale it up to 50 × 50 pixels.

18. Change the hue to orange yellow.

19. Position the playhead anywhere between frame 1 and frame 20, and in the Properties window select Shape from the Tween pull-down menu.

20. Target the Green layer. Add a keyframe to frame 1.

21. Drag the symbol to center of stage.

22. Add a keyframe to frame 20.

23. While still targeting frame 20, and making sure the small gray circle is selected, move it away from the center straight down to the guide set at 350 pixels.

24. Scale it up to 50 × 50 pixels.

25. Change the hue to green.

26. Position the playhead anywhere between frame 1 and frame 20, and in the Properties window select Shape from the Tween pull-down menu.

27. Target the Blue Purple layer. Add a keyframe to frame 1.

28. Drag the symbol to center of stage.

29. Add a keyframe to frame 20.

30. While still targeting frame 20, and making sure the small gray circle is selected, move it away straight from the center, left to the vertical guide set at 100 pixels.

31. Scale it up to 50 × 50 pixels.

32. Change the hue to blue purple.

33. Position the playhead anywhere between frame 1 and frame 20, and in the Properties window select Shape from the Tween pull-down menu.

34. Now you have a grid to follow. Complete the preceding steps for the remaining eight colors. Place them so they form a circle.

35. Add the remaining colors:
    - Red Orange
    - Orange
    - Yellow
    - Yellow Green
    - Blue Green
    - Blue
    - Purple
    - Red Purple

36. Save your animation: File > Save As.

37. To view the animation move the playhead back to frame 1, and press Enter (Windows) or Return (Mac) on the keyboard. It will play on the stage. To preview it in the player, go to File > Publish Preview > HTML, or Ctrl+Enter (Windows) or Cmd+Return (Mac).

TIP

It is helpful at this point to add another layer, below the rest, and draw a circle. This will help with the placement of the other color circles on the wheel.

Exercise 3

Emotional Color

This exercise will strengthen your intuitive use of color. Focus on how the motion of color elements is used to support the emotion and innate rhythm of that color in conjunction with the overall theme and design of the piece as a whole.

Task

Put together a composite of photographs, color graphics, and type.

Goal

Create a digital collage that could be exported and used in a motion graphic.

Software

Photoshop or other photo compositing software

Design It

Choose one of the color schemes listed in this chapter—monochromatic, split complementary, analogous, and so on. Choose a base color and accent color. Begin by creating the color collage in Photoshop, putting each element in a separate layer that can be brought into After Effects for animation. Make a new document, 320 × 240, in Photoshop. Use typographic elements, photographs, drawings, and scanned elements, but always only using the colors from the palette you chose. Each element that you want to animate should be in a separate layer. Once you are happy with the digital collage, save your work as a .psd file.

Ask yourself the following questions while animating the color shapes, pictures, and type:

- How do the colors of this palette move?
- What is the emotional association to these colors?
- What do these colors represent?

Design It, Advanced Techniques

Import the Photoshop file into After Effects: File > Import > File. Browse for your file. In the dialog box, select Composition in the Import As pull-down menu. Open the composition by double-clicking on it in the Project window. Use the Timeline to create a simple animation in which the movements support the emotion of the chosen colors.

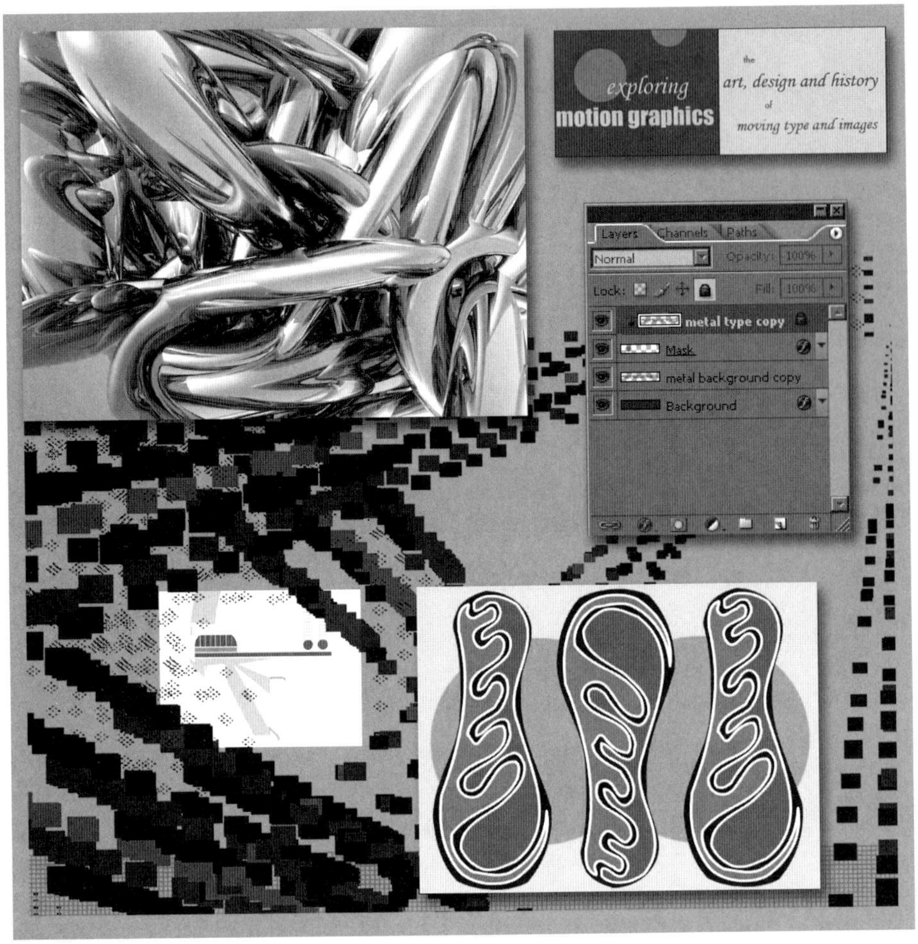
exploring
motion graphics
the
art, design and history
of
moving type and images
Layers
Channels
Paths
Normal
Opacity:
100%
Lock:
Fill:
100%
metal type copy
Mask
metal background copy
Background

CHAPTER 6

Chapter Objectives

Study visual vocabulary and principles of graphic design

Explore how to create strong composition

Learn frame transition techniques

Recognize where to look for inspiration

Understand how to apply texture to add emotional impact

Understand how to integrate sound to add emotional impact

Introduction

Style is defined as a distinctive manner of expression or custom of behavior. It is also a particular technique in how something is done or created. Here we are discussing style as a manner of expression and technique. Every designer develops her own style as she works toward a unique design vision. Stellar designers combine personal vision with cultural trends and traditional design theory to make trendsetting visual communications. You most likely have a particular style that you ascribe to as well. Sometimes you will use your personal style in your design while other times you may have to put that aside in favor of your client's and audience's style. Style, after all, is an elusive concept and is subjected to the likes and dislikes of individual viewers.

When designing for certain clients, you may have less freedom to impart your personal style. The client may dictate the ultimate design, and therefore style, and you will need to adapt your style to fit with the existing brand, look, and feel of the product. Then there are the projects that allow you to develop and create everything from the concept through finished product. In this case you can develop the sensibility of the brand and impart your own style. These are the most fun projects where you are responsible for developing the style. Through them you get to show your unique vision and implement your own stylistic thinking.

Style permeates all aspects of our lives. Looking back to the Baroque period of the seventeenth century, we can see the same use of elaborate and ornate design in clothes, interior design, furniture, gardens, jewelry, typography, and much more. While popular, this style was applied to all aspects of European life, but once it went out of fashion, it seemed out of place and misused.

While some design styles are fleeting and are simply attributed to trends in pop culture, other elements, more classical styles of design, are tried and true and can be used for many applications. It is your responsibility as a designer to stay up to date with visual trends and understand how best to apply them in tandem with your unique style. If you use a popular, trendy design style for a project that will be used for a prolonged time, you risk that the chosen design will go out of style and your work will lose its impact. For any design intended for long-term use, such as a company logo, incorporate traditional design laced with contemporary style. The design should look fresh, but include mainstream visual elements that allow it to outlive any fleeting trends. On the other hand, when designing for a specific, one-time event, capitalize on the current design trends if it will enhance the final design and message.

DIGITAL ART

Before computer graphics were largely used by the general public, artists and scientists experimented with digital motion using color and sound. They analyzed how our bodies interacted with the new machines and how data transmitted from them was perceived. In other words, user-interfaces were explored as well as the viewer's emotional reaction to the message.

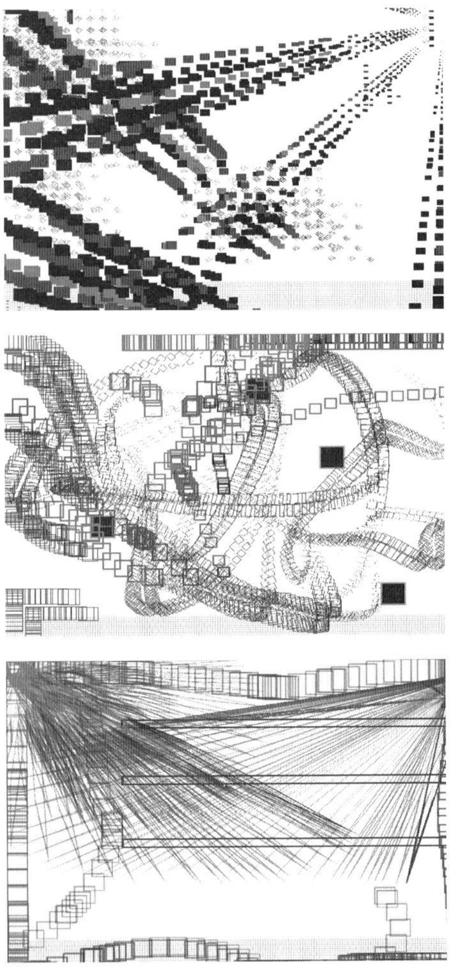

By Vera Bighetti— São Paulo—Brazil/www.artzero.net

figure 6-1

This interactive work combines sound and music to allow viewers to act as both graffiti artist and DJ.

Artists were experimenting with digital art as early as the 1960s, long before computers entered many people's homes and offices. Michael A. Noll was among the early digital artists who began to incorporate technology into his work. Noll, of Bell Laboratories, was primarily a researcher who experimented with computer-generated images. His image, *Gaussian Quadratic*, created in 1963, was included in the 1965 exhibition, *Computer-Generated Pictures*, at the Howard Wise Gallery in New York. He and other artists of the time anticipated the interest people would have in creating art in the digital realm.

As the number of artists interested in this new medium grew, collaborations between artists and programmers grew as well. A need for a centralized place for the two groups to come together brought about the formation of Experiments in Art and Technology (EAT) in 1966. EAT was founded by Billy Klüver, who worked with such artists as Andy Warhol, Robert Rauschenberg, and Jasper Johns. These partnerships between technician and artist were showcased at the World Expo 1970 in Osaka, Japan. The collaborations that Klüver initiated are imitated in today's world of design and motion graphics. Designers, developers, and writers team up, often with many others as well, to create and produce contemporary works of motion graphics that fully bridge the gap between art and design.

Contemporary digital artists continue to experiment with computer art and human interaction. Emerging artist Vera Bighetti created *Gr@fite*, an interactive piece that allows the viewer to act as graffiti artist or DJ by altering the colors and graphic shapes on screen, which in turn affects the output of music. The programming behind the graphics acts like a graffiti artist with a can of spray paint or a DJ with a turntable. According to Bighetti, "Gr@fite is a reactive, generative and interactive use of the software, where the applications figure as an amusement, a game where the user enters, and the rules are given so the user can make its choices of action." Bighetti creatively uses programming, interactivity, color, and sound to entertain and allow the user to experience the actions of a graffiti artist and DJ.

VISUAL VOCABULARY

To develop a cohesive, well thought out sense of style, there are certain principles a designer should know in order to understand the implications of how viewers see and read the message of the design. Design has its own language that defines the manner in which a design is composed, framed, and edited. This vocabulary refers to the rhythm and flow, or the emotions elicited by the design. Some of the vocabulary describes the subtle visual nuances and how and why a viewer interacts with a design. Other vocabulary describes what happens in the frame and between the frames. Then there is vocabulary that describes why the audience reacts in specific ways to the design.

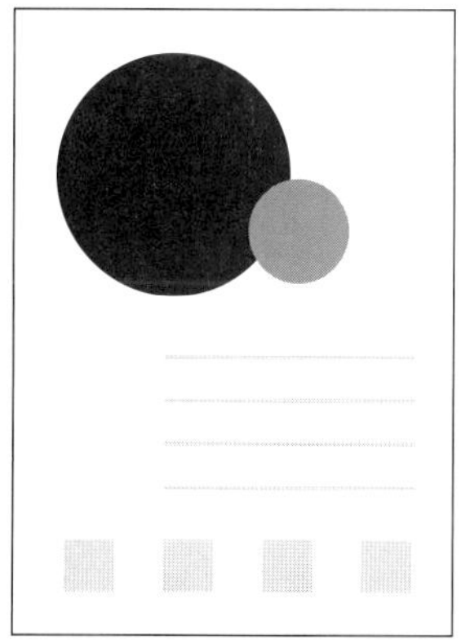

figure |6-2|

The large, dark circle in the upper left of the example is the most important element in the visual hierarchy.

Principles of Graphic Design

Every design has a **visual hierarchy** that is implemented to guide viewers through the message and help them to understand what information is most important. A clear distinction between the primary, or most important, information and the secondary and tertiary information is what defines a strong visual hierarchy. This dictates which elements of the design will be emphasized and how it will all be laid out.

For example, when designing an advertisement for a specific event, begin by breaking the information into groups. What is the event? What day is the event? What time does the event begin? Where is the event held? The "what" information about the event is the most important piece for the viewer. This is what will initially interest viewers and should take visual priority. Information about the day and time are secondary information and should carry less visual weight. Information about the location is also important, although slightly less so, and should carry even less visual weight. Although the secondary information is necessary to successfully communicate the message, it is not what will initially interest and excite the viewer the way the name of the event will.

One way to achieve visual hierarchy is by applying a larger type size to some copy, such as the name of the event, and a smaller type size to other copy, such as date and time, and an even smaller type size for the location. By applying a different visual weight to each information group, a clear and visually pleasing guide that offers the viewer an initial focus and a natural path to follow is created.

The principle of **closure** belongs to the larger category of **Gestalt principles of perception**. Gestalt refers to how we perceive what we see. Can we see depth in a two-dimensional plane or see movement in a static frame? We do not really see it because it is not tangible, but we can perceive it. Closure refers to a tendency to perceive a set of individual elements as one recognizable pattern. Individual elements are visually grouped together and become a new element.

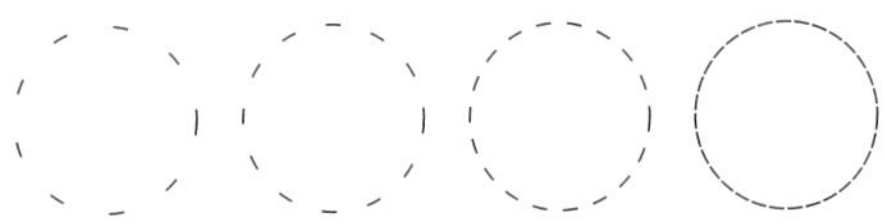

figure 6-3

The principle of closure is demonstrated here by our tendency to view all four elements as circular shapes.

The closure principle is especially important in understanding how viewers perceive the flow and movement of motion graphics design. We tend to fill in the missing pieces in visual design in an attempt to make the motion seamless. For example, imagine seeing a series of illustrations of a person walking up a flight of stairs. In each successive illustration the person appears further up the stairs. The illustrations do not show each movement of the figure, but since the movement of lifting the leg off one step and placing it on the next step up is such a familiar motion, we create a mental picture of the missing movements, which illustrates the principle of closure.

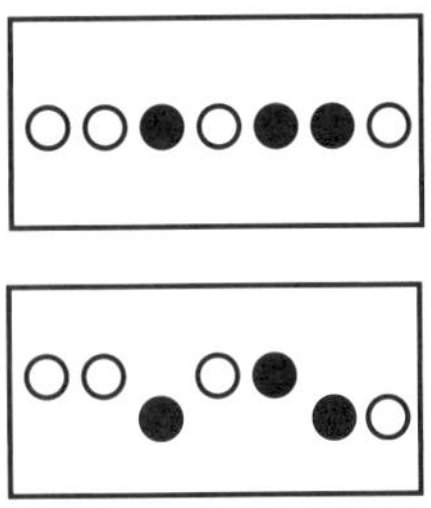

figure 6-4

The principle of common fate is demonstrated in the second grouping of circles in that it is seen as two separate rows.

Common fate is another principle belonging to Gestalt that says objects moving in the same direction are perceived to relate to each other more than objects moving in different directions. In designing motion graphics the objects in motion must flow in a set rhythm and space and be arranged in a calculated manner. If objects flow across the screen or move about in the frame with no distinct purpose or method, the design will be perceived as chaotic and disordered with all of the elements disconnected. Capitalize on the notion of common fate by moving related information through the frame in the same direction.

The **golden ratio** refers to the ratio of elements within a form, such as the width of the Parthenon to its height. Instances of golden ratio have long been documented in history and are seen in art, architecture, and nature. It is thought that we are subconsciously drawn to objects with this ratio, because we inherently prefer the aesthetic quality. Apple's iPod is one modern device that follows the golden ratio rule, seen

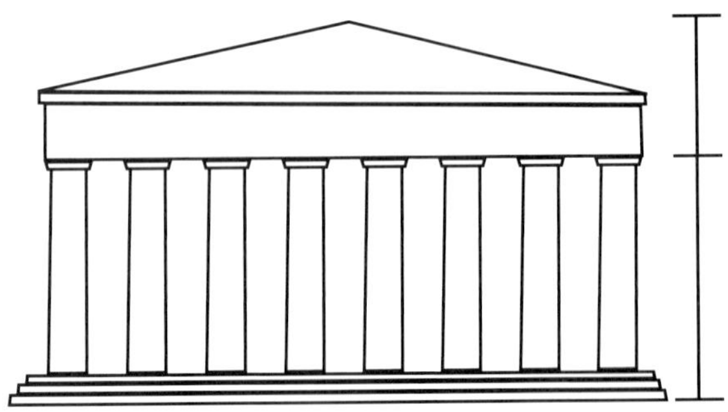

figure 6-5

The drawing of the Parthenon illustrates the principle of the golden ratio.

in the ratio of the LCD screen to the rest of the body. The golden ratio may also be applied to design elements in a two-dimensional plane seen in the ratio of picture to text. The aesthetic effect will be the same: more visually pleasing, therefore easier for the viewer to engage with.

Although not rules that must be followed, these principles are fueled by years of research and analysis of human behavior. By thoroughly understanding and applying these techniques in conjunction with your own sense of style, you will develop a method of creating strong, communicative compositions that will both entice and inform the viewer.

Composition

After determining a hierarchy of information, a composition needs to be designed. In designing a composition, your decisions on how the elements, typography, images, and graphics will be grouped together will determine the layout.

When all elements are grouped together in one quadrant of the frame, it is called **gathering**. Movement may be implied, depending on how and in what form the elements are gathered. The elements may appear to be flying out of the frame or diving into the frame. Different configurations can be used to create these visual illusions.

Dispersion is seen when elements are scattered about within the frame. Elements composed in this manner may convey a sense of chaos and disconnectedness. To bring the viewer into the design and create a focal point in what may appear to be a random sea of graphics or images, use color to make the main element stand out.

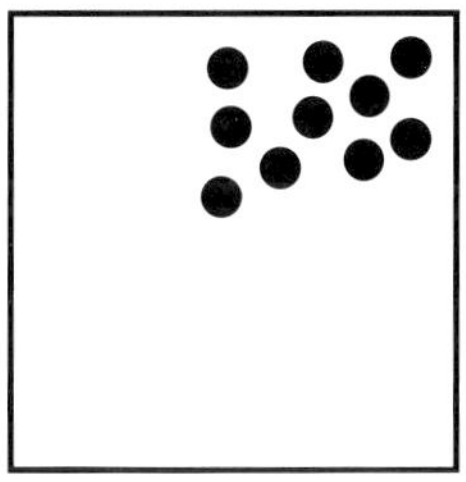

figure 6-6

All elements are gathered in the upper right quadrant.

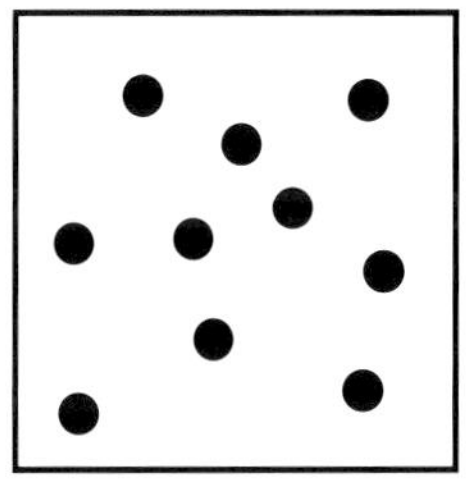

figure 6-7

All elements are dispersed in the frame.

Exclusion is when all elements are clearly grouped together, except for one. That one element is excluded from the rest, therefore making it a focal point of the design. Although the grouped elements fill a larger portion of the frame and create a visual pattern, it is the lone element that will draw attention simply because it does not fit within that pattern.

Chunking is the term for grouping like elements together. Chunking is thought to help viewers retain the information. This composition is regularly used with information graphics where there is much for the viewer to see, read, and remember. Any like elements may be grouped together; group by color, shape, size, or type style.

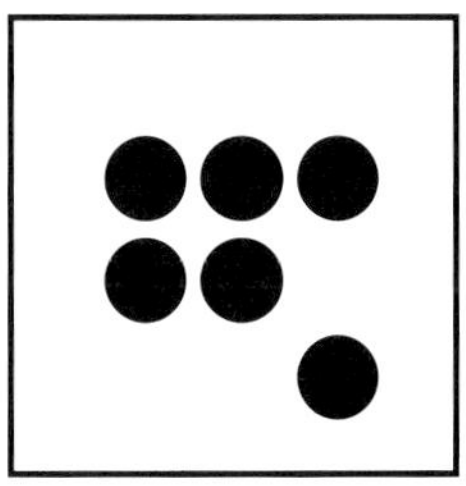

figure 6-8

All elements are evenly grouped, save one that is excluded from the rest.

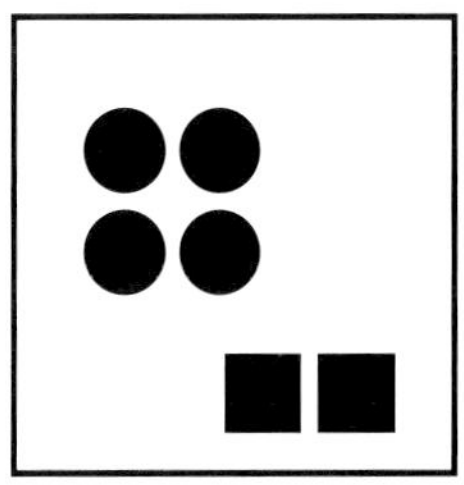

figure 6-9

Elements are chunked, creating two distinct groups.

The term **optical center** refers to the natural center we see when looking at a design. When the center point is

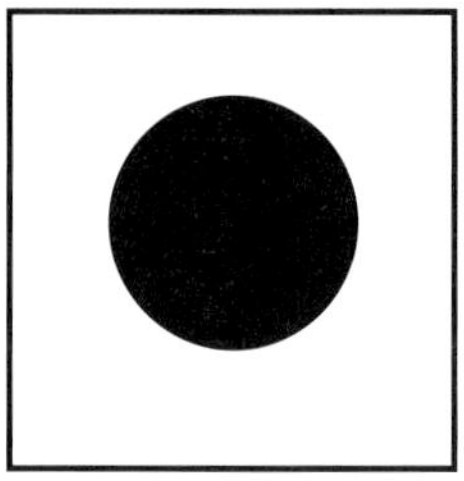

figure |6-10|

The circle is optically centered in the frame.

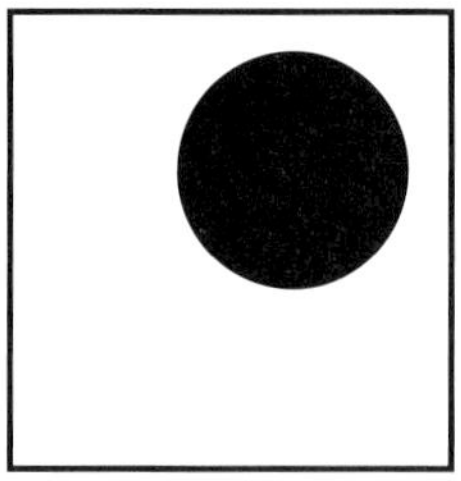

figure |6-11|

The circle is placed off-center in the frame.

measured and an object is placed at that point, it will often look too low and off-center. This is because it is more pleasing to the eye to shift the element up a bit higher, to the optical center. When creating a composition where the focal point is at the center of the design, be aware of the optical center and shift the focal elements to that point.

A focal element placed to one side, or in one corner of the frame is **off-center**. Creating a composition with the focal element off-center sends a message of playfulness and fun. It is not seen as stagnant, but energetic. This composition style works in many applications, but there must be a sense of balance with the other elements in the frame, otherwise it will be too heavy on the side with the main focal point. Off-center works best when the element is set to either side of the frame, as opposed to top or bottom.

What makes a strong composition? Although our likes and dislikes are subjective, following the principles of graphic design in creating a composition will allow for a truly successful and visually appealing motion graphic. Every element put on the screen will not only be seen for its individual qualities but also for how it works and plays with, or off of, the other elements on the screen.

Frame

Composition is what is done inside the frame. How objects move inside the frame needs to be determined. Motion graphics are composed in individual frames, each representing a set amount of time on the two-dimensional plane of a screen. Composition within the frame is constrained by four visible sides: left, right, top, and bottom. In addition, a designer may choose to work with depth in the frame, either through the use of optical illusion or through the use of scale coupled with animation to create the illusion that type, graphics, or pictures are moving away from the viewer into the depths of the frame.

figure |6-12|

An optical illusion of squares fading off into the background.

figure |6-13|

An optical illusion of squares pushing into the front.

A designer can create the impression of depth in how elements are layered. Take the example of the layered squares. The set of squares with the top layer at the bottom left and the bottom layer at the upper right leave the impression that the squares appear to be fading away in the distance. In reality the squares are all the same size and composed on a two-dimensional plane. The other set of squares with the top layer in the lower right and the bottom layer in the upper left appear to be coming forward. This optical illusion occurs because of the eye movement that takes place when reading the design; remember that we read from left to right.

In the first scenario, we begin to read the design from the left edge of the frame, and the first square we see is positioned in the lower left. As our eyes move over the design and we continue to read the squares, they move up to the right-hand corner, thus leaving the impression that the squares are fading to the background. Likewise, when reading the second scenario, our eyes travel from the top, or optical back, to the bottom, or optical front. How elements are layered together determines how we read the design.

Motion graphics are constrained within existing technologies, that is to say, the frame is always predetermined by the technological device of the user. When designing for the web, television, and video, the frame is horizontal, dictated by monitors that are wider than they are tall, but when designing for a PDA or cell phone, the frame is most likely vertical, again dictated by the physical makeup of the device. With this preexisting physical frame in mind, you need to decide how to frame your composition. Consider whether the font will be large enough to read on the screen at typical resolution settings. Will the chosen colors offer enough contrast between foreground and background elements? And will all of the information be immediately visible or will the viewer have to work to get to it?

How the composition is framed also speaks to the underlying tone of the message. How the elements are placed in relation to the frame edges should help support the appropriate tone. Elements crowded into the frame, and pushed to the edges, may create the illusion that they are bursting out and the frame is unable to contain them. Or, this example may create a feeling of claustrophobia as the frame tightly contains the elements.

Elements that are neatly inside the frame, with some space between the edges, read as calm, controlled, and ordered.

If the elements are very small and placed very far away from the edges of the frame with a lot of space, they will appear to be disconnected, overshadowed, and overwhelmed.

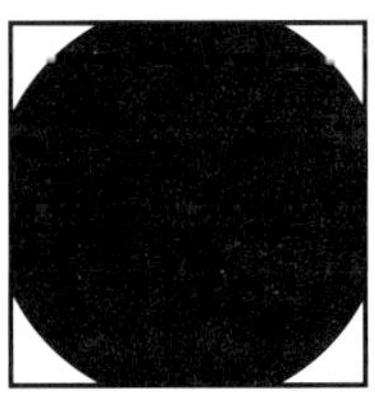

figure |6-14|

Design elements crowded in the frame.

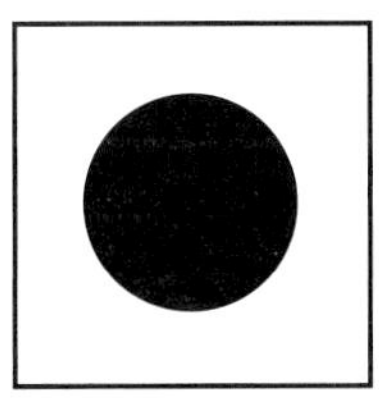

figure |6-15|

A design element peacefully positioned in the frame.

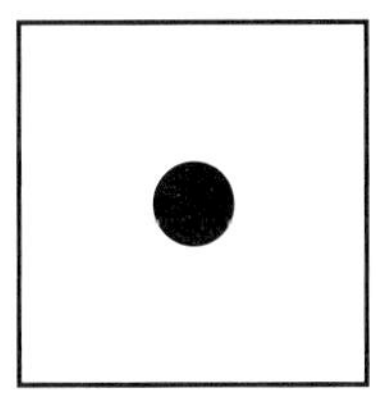

figure |6-16|

Object that appears to be disappearing into the abyss of the frame.

Flow

Designers talk about flow in a number of different ways. Your eye flows over the screen as you take in the information, elements flow within a section, and frames flow as they are edited together. Flow, in general, refers to how easily we internalize the information. Think about rafting on a river. Some rivers are slow and smooth, others are fast and smooth, and others are fast and rough. Each river has its own flow, and as you ride along you feel it. This idea is applied to the reading of motion graphics and how we feel when experiencing the design. Did the elements and frames speed along, flowing quickly? Did the motion graphic move through information slowly? Was the flow bogged down by too much information? Did you encounter something unexpected that slowed your internalization and understanding of the message? If so, that would affect the flow in that you had to stop reading the design and take extra time to decipher the unexpected bit of information; the flow was interrupted. How you compose the whole work and lay the frames together, and transition between them, affects the flow of the entire piece while also supporting the emotional delivery of your message. You can piece together your composition and transition between frames with the following transition styles. In the following examples source refers to a group of frames with the same design elements.

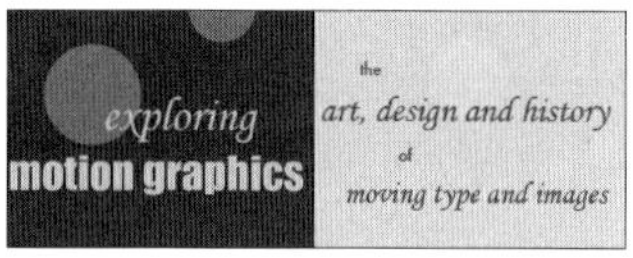

figure |6-17|

Transition using a cut.

Transitions

An instantaneous transition from one source to the next is called a **cut**. This is a standard, often used transition and should appear to be seamless. When done correctly the viewer does not even notice the change in source elements. When applying a cut, the second source should contain new information.

A **dissolve** is made when two overlapping sources have the levels of opacity altered. As source one gradually becomes fainter, or opaque, source two gradually becomes less opaque, eventually filling the screen as the only source visible. In other words, one picture dissolves into the next picture. This transition is apparent to the viewer and should be used when the visuals of the two sources complement each other, so that where the visuals overlap they will not create a visual contradiction, but work together. There should be a strong visual relationship between the elements of the two sources.

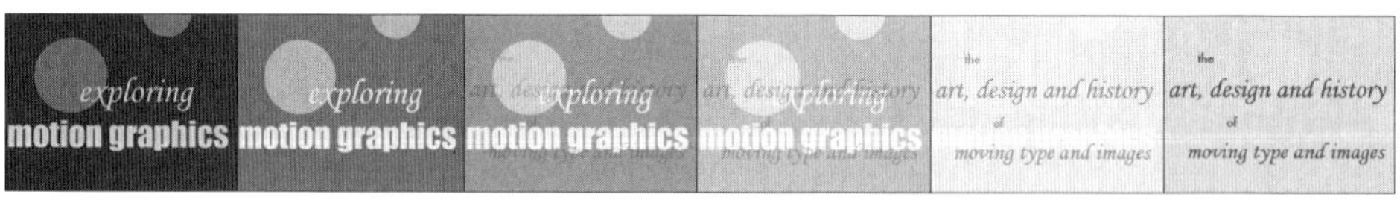

figure |6-18|

Transition using a dissolve.

A **push** transition is when one source is pushed out of the frame by the second source. This push can come from any side of the frame: top, bottom, right, or left. Depending on the direction of the push, the transition will elicit a different feeling in the viewer. A push that comes in from the top will feel oppressive, pushing down on the other source. Pushing from the bottom has a more lighthearted feel, bumping the source out of the way for a turn on the screen. Pushing in from the left feels natural, as that is how we read. A source that comes in from the right is dynamic, moving against our direction of reading.

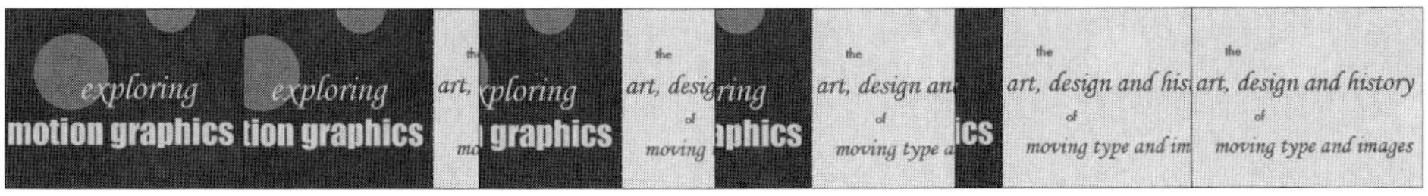

figure | 6-19 |

Transition using a push.

At first glance a **slide** transition may look like the push transition. The difference with the slide is that source one remains static while source two slides into the frame. Source two may slide in from any of the frame edges. When one source is sliding in from the left or the right, it may appear to be sneaking up on the other source. When it slides down from the top, it may appear to be covering up the other source, like pulling down a window shade. When it slides in from the bottom, it also looks as if it is covering up the other source, but in a more caring manner, like covering someone with a blanket after she has fallen asleep.

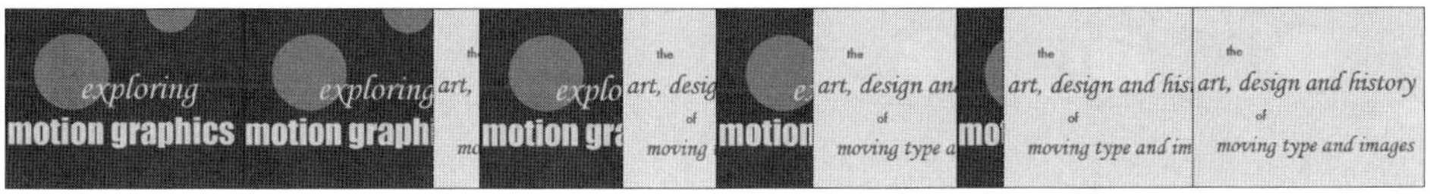

figure | 6-20 |

Transition using a slide.

A **wipe** is used to either reveal or obscure one source from another. A typical wipe will be in the shape of a rectangle, circle, or other simple geometrical shape. Source one may be obscured as a circular shape in the middle of the screen grows to reveal source two. Wipe transitions are common practice and are built into most motion graphics software. A wipe key, also referred to as a moving matte, is used to create the illusion that an object in one source reveals the second source as it moves across the screen. For example, as the tip of a marker slides across the screen, it reveals the second source, as if painting it into the screen.

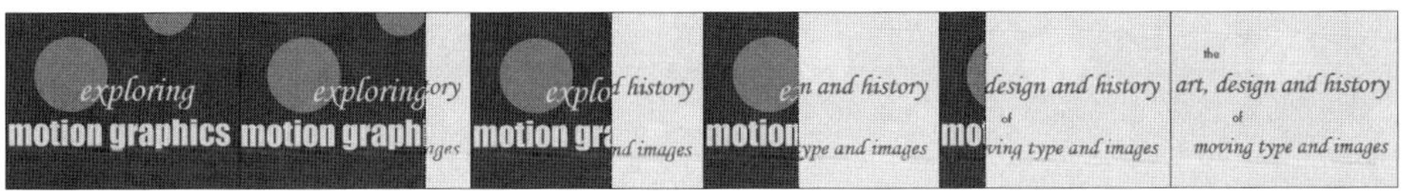

figure | 6-21 |

Transition using a wipe.

In addition to these basic transition styles, you may want to experiment with more complex ones using compositing and layering. Compositing refers to using elements from multiple sources, including pictures, type, graphics, and sound. Layering is the order in which the elements appear to be from back to front. Many software programs used for motion graphics have custom transition effects that you can apply to your graphics, or you can create your own.

Some of the transitions, such as flare or glow, require the two sources plus a special effect applied at the cut point. Other transitions, such as overlay, require the two sources with a third source added at the transition point of the two initial sources. The page turn is another popular transition used in video and on the web. It creates the illusion that the transition is made from one source to another when the page of a book is turned. Often, when applied on the web, the viewer is given control of turning the page with the use of the computer mouse. How you apply any of these transitions to your motion graphic, at what speed or opacity and with what source footage, will add to the emotional tone.

Texture

The word *texture* is often used to describe a tactile object, such as a velvet sofa that is smooth and supple, a piece of sandpaper that is rough and scratchy, or a kitten's fur that is silky and soft. Digital designers also use the word *texture* when describing work. Visual texture is created when you use color value and patterns to produce the impression or illusion of texture. Texture can be used as a design element or to elicit a sense of depth and dimension and add to the visual aesthetic of the work.

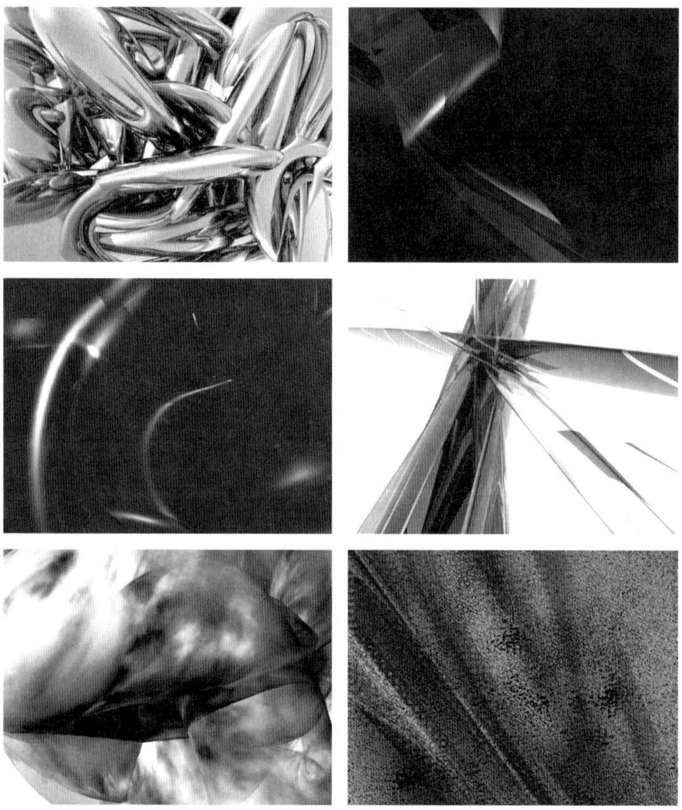

By Danny Glix/dannyglix.com

figure |6-22|

Digital textures may be used as a background element or part of the typography or other graphic element.

Textures should be applied with the same considerations given to color application. Different textures elicit different emotional responses. The goal of a texture is to give the viewer the feeling that she could reach out and touch the surface. A smooth, shiny texture made to look like highly polished metal will give off the feeling of a chill because tangible smooth metal surfaces are often cold to the touch. A texture designed with sharp, pointy angles will push the viewer away, creating a feeling of distance, because if we encountered that texture in the physical world we would shy away from touching it for fear of being hurt. Textures designed using variable transparency levels evoke smoke or clouds. Depending on the colors, this texture can allude to different associations within the physical world. A darker color may make you feel like the design is closing in on you, like smoke, while a lighter color may make you feel like you are in an open space, looking up at clouds on a beautiful summer day. We visually read textures even though they are not tactile.

| TIP |

Use the Pattern Overlay in Photoshop to easily add texture to images or type: Layer > Layer Style > Pattern Overlay.

Many software programs come with a texture library or with filters that can be applied to photographs, graphics, or type. Texture filters are extremely versatile and can be used in any number of applications. Some standard texture filters are metal, smoke, and burlap. Designers who work often with textures build up their own library to have on hand for any project.

SOUND

Sound waves bounce off the eardrum and cause vibrations that we then interpret as words or notes. Matching sounds, music, spoken word, or incidental sounds to visuals is beyond just laying the track. When Michael Silvers and Randy Thom won an Oscar at the 77th Academy Awards for Sound Editing for *The Incredibles*, Thom said, "Certain Academy Awards like Sound and Visual Effects and Editing are sometimes referred to as technical awards. They're not technical awards. They're given for artistic decisions." We are fundamentally affected by music and sound, and the designer and editor are fully in control of the emotional impact it will have on the viewer. In all applications, film titles, DVD menus, video games, or websites, sounds and music set the tone.

We respond emotionally to what we hear and impart that emotion onto what we see. The sound a designer chooses to use in the motion graphic must support the emotion of the message. Even the sheer thought of sounds can have an impact on us. When I write the words *fingernails on a chalkboard*, what do you "hear"? How do you feel? Do you shudder when you think about it? Sound is a very powerful tool to use with motion graphics, and equally important with typography and color.

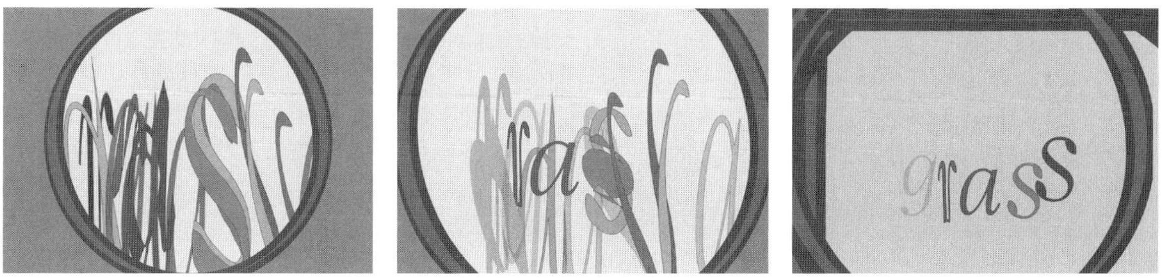

By Sally A. Kueker

figure |6-23|

As the grass sways the sound of it rustling in the wind plays in the background and is used to create an experience of sitting outside.

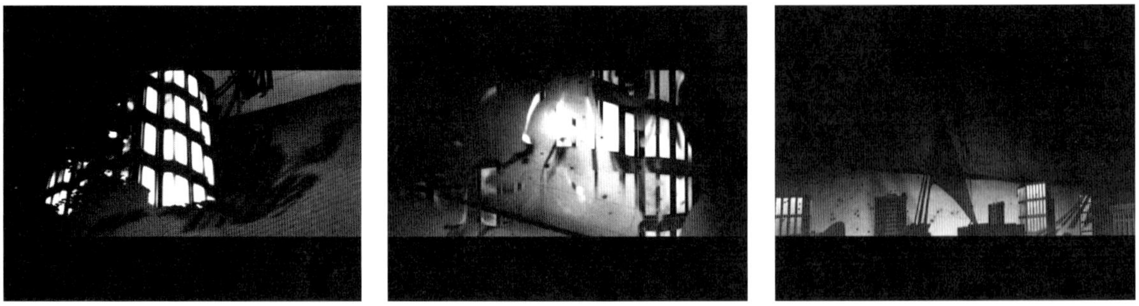

By Jan Mathias Steinforth (mateuniverse)

figure |6-24|

The graphics in this video took inspiration from the psychedelic art of the 1960s in direct response to the sound of the music track *Dirt Empire*.

EMOTION

Emotion is an extremely powerful tool for a designer and comes forth in direct response to the style of your design. You want audiences to feel something from your motion graphic; you want them to remember it and have the message stick with them. A sticky message is one in which the viewer remembers the visuals, tone of the message, and product or service for sale. The best way to accomplish this stickiness is by making an emotional connection. Stickiness of any message, a commercial, song, or website, for example, can be measured by having viewers answer poll questions. Many of us remember bits and pieces of everything we see and hear, but with such an excess of information viewed every day, there is much that we filter out; therefore, we often do not retain the full message. Viewers might remember a visual, jingle, actor, or tagline from a product, but none of that matters if they cannot remember the meat of the message—the product or service for sale.

As a visual communications designer using the medium of motion graphics, it is your job to convey a convincing message in a short amount of time. We are all conditioned to respond to emotion and imbue our communications with emotion as well.

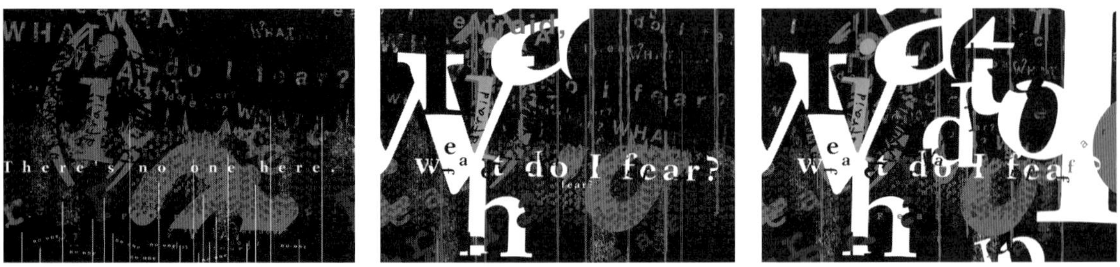

By Soo C. Hostetler, Assistant Professor, University of Northern Iowa

figure |6-25|

The use of sound similar to that used in horror films, the style of jagged typography, and the movement of the words as they push into each other communicates an emotion of fear and stress.

To convince the viewer to buy into the message there needs to be an appropriate emotion. If you design a station ID for an intellectual, sophisticated station but use elements that convey a playful emotion, such as bright, sunny colors and a fat, rounded typeface, you will not successfully communicate the feeling, therefore message, of the station. Instead, elements that speak to the serious nature of the station should be employed in the design, such as dark colors and a mid-weight serif typeface. Every motion graphics piece you create will have its own emotion.

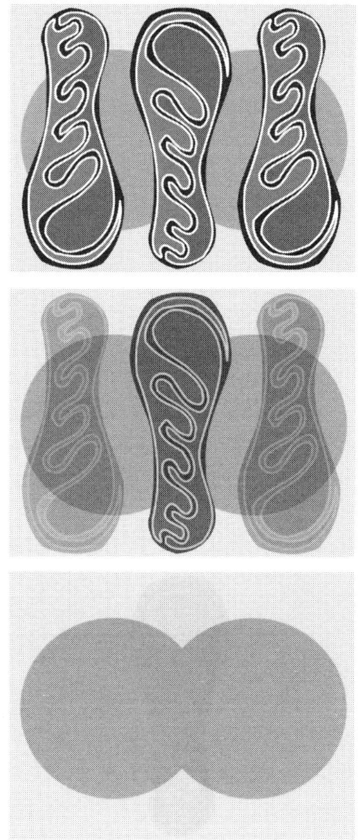

By Phillip Julian, Artist

figure 6-26

The design of this piece is influenced by the art of expressionist painter Henri Matisse. Specifically, Matisse's use of color and line inspired Phillip Julian's motion graphic and his desire to use positive and negative space to unify his art.

INSPIRATION

Every designer is inspired in different ways, and you should look to everything around you to get ideas for your next project. Inspiration may be found in other designs, art, music, stories, furniture design, nature, and just about anything else you may think of. Many designers have a full library of design books that they will often reference for inspiration. Just looking at things will inspire new ideas. One suggestion is to keep a shoebox and collect images, writings, or objects of interest to refer to when looking for the next new idea.

The first thing to tell new clients to do is collect objects that inspire them. Suggest that they collect pictures, words (have them write the words on a piece of paper), paint chips, wallpaper samples, found objects, natural forms such as leaves or flowers, and anything else that intrigues them. This helps to break the creative ice, so to speak, and get the ideas flowing and to help the designer begin to visualize the design of the project.

▷ Case Study ◁

Personal Style

Danny Glix initially created this untitled motion graphic for the website Altsense. It is a visual experiment that explores the idea of motion and object as shape. Glix has spent much of his past ten years as a designer developing lasting brand strategies, identity systems, and digital graphics for many companies. This project allowed him an opportunity to use his personal style in both design and application.

Glix used Flash for this project. By using keyframes he was able to show different images that seem to be moving but are in reality static graphics. Every object is broken into multiple graphic components, many reminiscent of either mechanical devices or digital devices. Some visuals look like wheels and gears, while another takes the shape of a gun and another a CD. One graphic appears to flow into the next with a

By Danny Glix/dannyglix.com

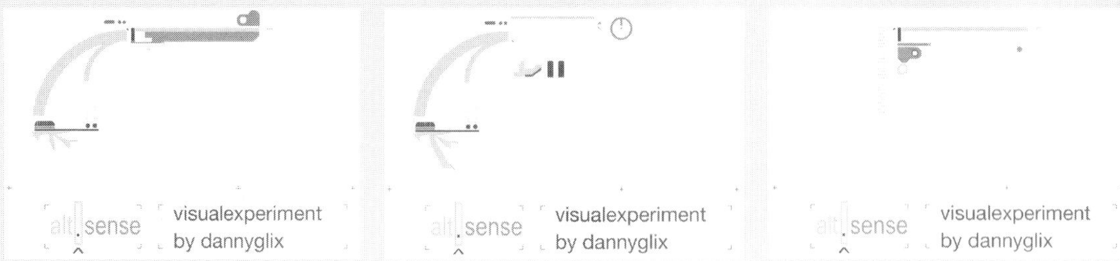

figure |6-27|

Visual experiment created for altsense.org, using vector art in Flash.

rapid metamorphosis between them. The graphics never break the frame, but live within it. They all appear from within, not emerging from outside the frame. The motion is smooth, never jarring, and although fast-paced with some flashes of lines and shapes, the color palette is one that elicits a feeling of peacefulness. The palette of neutrals and pastels balances out the sense of urgency that builds up from the quick movements. The texture is smooth, which complements the feeling of calm put forth by the color choice.

This motion graphic is also successful because of our desire to see a complete cycle even where none exists. In applying the principle of closure, we are able to see the graphics in motion, see them spin, and see familiar objects in and among the lines and shapes. The principle of closure and persistence of vision (discussed in Chapter 2) explain this phenomenon of seeing the illusion of motion where there is in fact none. Glix has creatively and stylistically put these principles to use in this example.

SUMMARY

Style is how you design and what your design looks like. The visual vocabulary describes how a design looks, functions, and communicates. Strong compositions with clear visual hierarchy are successful in communicating the intended message by visually guiding the viewer in understanding what elements are important and where they should initially focus on the design. This focus is determined by the emphasis afforded to each element, using color, texture, movement, and sound. As you continue to develop as a motion graphics designer, you will develop a unique style that you will carry through all of your projects.

in review

1. What are the principles of graphic design?
2. What are the different styles of composition?
3. What role does the frame play in motion graphics?
4. What are the different transitions you can use to move from frame to frame?
5. How can you impart emotion into your designs?

exercises

Exercise 1

Banner Ad

For this exercise you will incorporate texture and transitions techniques to create a stylized banner ad.

Task

Use a moving matte transition technique to illuminate stylized metal type.

Goal

Create an animated .gif file and save it for the web.

Software

ImageReady (This may also be done in Photoshop, using layers and the Animation palette.)

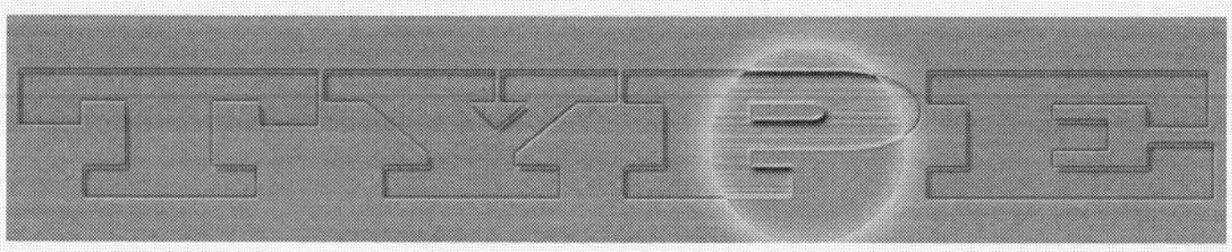

figure | E6-1 |

Design It, Step-by-Step

1. Create a new document. Choose web banner, 486 × 60 pixels.

2. Fill the background with the hexadecimal color #003366: Edit > Fill and select color from the pull-down menu. The Color Picker dialog will open. Be sure "only web colors" is checked. Type the color code into the box next to the pound sign. Click OK. Then click OK in the Fill dialog box.

> **| TIP |**
>
> Using "only web colors," or hexadecimal colors, ensures that all monitors will read the color values the same, with little or no variation.

3. Unlock the background layer. Press Option (Mac) or Alt (Windows) and double-click on the padlock icon in the layer. Rename the layer Background.

> **| TIP |**
>
> Always name your layers clearly. It is a good habit that will make editing the work easier.

4. Target Background and choose Pattern Overlay from the Layer Styles pop-up menu at the bottom of the Layers palette and set the following: Blend Mode—Normal, Opacity—59%, Pattern—Brushed Metal, Scale—883%.

   You can also access the Layer Styles palette through Layer > Layer Styles > Pattern Overlay.

5. Copy Background and rename it Fill 1: Layer > Duplicate Layer. You now have two layers.

6. Use the type tool to add a type layer. Type in a word or phrase, choosing a typeface and character size.

> **| TIP |**
>
> Use a typeface with wide letters, such as Impact, for best results.

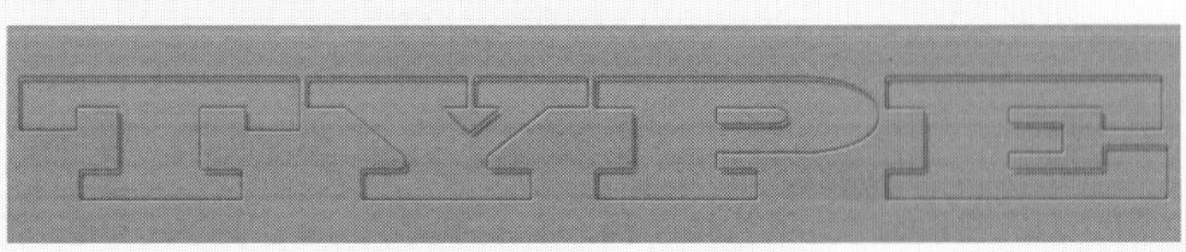

figure | E6-2 |

7. Add an Inner Shadow Layer Style to the type layer: Layer > Layer Style > Inner Shadow. Enter the following settings for Inner Shadow: Blend Mode—Color Burn, black, Opacity—60%.

8. Before closing the dialog box, choose Bevel and Emboss from the menu on the left. Choose Pillow Emboss from the Style drop-down menu.

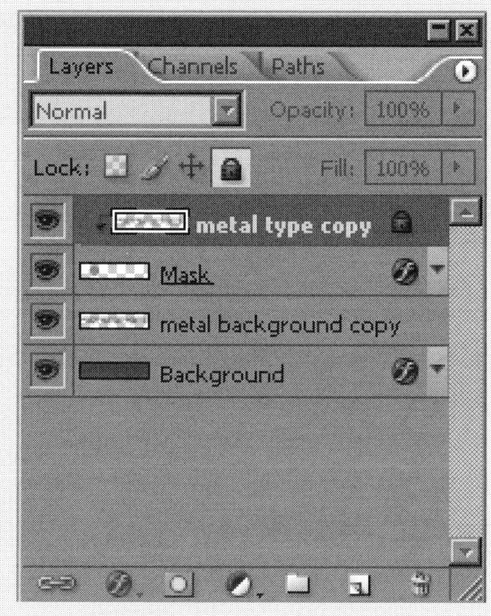

figure E6-3

TIP

Make sure your layers are in the correct order:

Fill 1

Type

Background

To reorder the layers simply click and drag on the layer you would like to move. Release the mouse when a thick black line appears between the two layers.

9. Clip Fill 1 to the type layer. This will fill the type with the patterned background and mask out the rest. To clip the layers hold down the Option key (Mac) or the ALT key (Windows) and click on the line between the two layers. The cursor will change when it is directly over the two lines.

10. Duplicate the clipped layers and rename them Fill 2 and type 2. Be sure to move the two new layers to the top of the layers palette if necessary.

11. Fill Fill 2 with the color #6699CC.

TIP

Both layers can be duplicated simultaneously by selecting one layer, holding the Shift key, and selecting the other layer.

12. Merge Fill 1 and type 1. Merge Fill 2 and type 2. Merge the layers by selecting the two you want to merge, then go to Layer > Merge Layers.

13. Add a new layer and name it Mask: Layer > New > Layer. Position it between the two merged layers: Fill/type 1, Mask, Fill/type 2.

14. Make sure the Mask layer is targeted. Use the circle marquee tool and draw a circle. Hold down the Shift key to make a perfect circle. Fill the circle with color #003366.

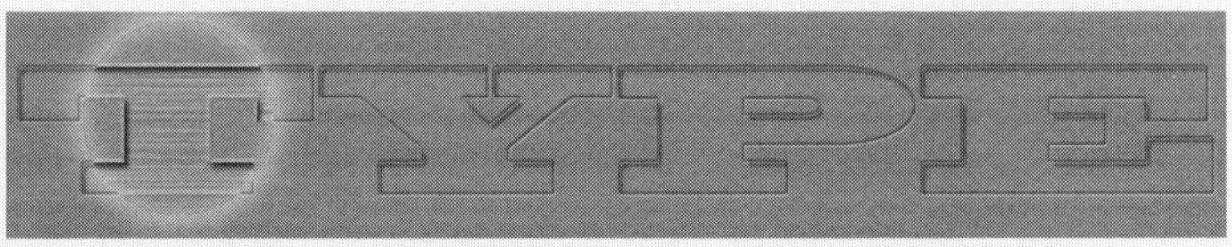

figure |E6-4|

15. Clip Fill 2 to the Mask layer you just created.

16. Save the file as a .psd file: File > Save As.

17. If the Animation palette is not open, go to Window > Animation. By default the first frame of the animation is activated.

18. Target the first frame in the Animation palette and target the Mask layer in the Layers palette. Using the move tool, position the circle where you would like it to be at the beginning of the animation. Be sure to only move the circle and nothing else.

| TIP |

The file is saved as a .psd so the layers are retained. In order to make an animated .gif file, we must keep all of the layers.

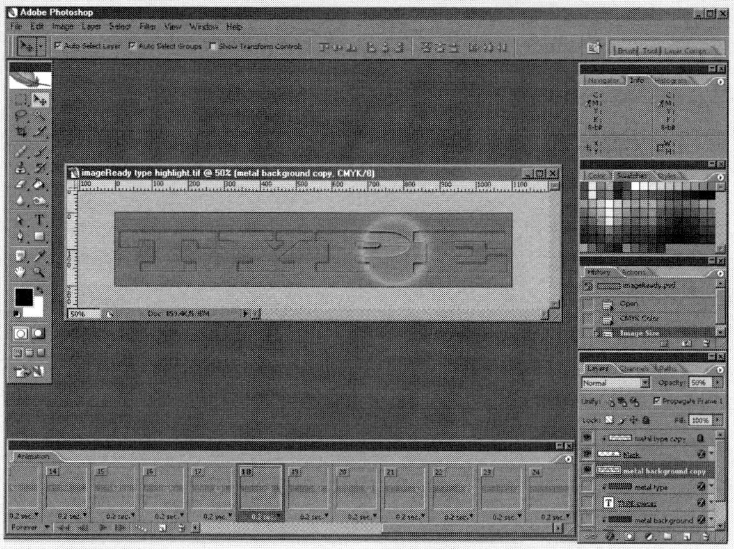

figure E6-5

19. Add a new frame after the first. Choose New Frame from the submenu in the Animation palette.

20. Target the second frame and target the Mask layer. Using the move tool, position the circle a bit away from where you positioned it in the first frame.

21. Select both frames and apply a tween. Select Tween from the submenu in the Animation palette. Set the tween for 3 frames, All Layers, and set the Parameters to Position only.

22. Add new frames. Repeat steps to make tweens until the highlight circle has flowed across all of the type. You want to make multiple tween sequences to allow for more movement of the circle.

23. Save for the web: File > Save Optimized As (or File > Save for Web in Photoshop). Optimized As reduces file size and prepares it for web viewing. Save it as a .gif file with 256 colors.

Exercise 2

Visualizing Music

How do you visualize your favorite song? This exercise will reinforce the methodology of combining multiple media and help you develop a sense of style. This project may be done on the computer or on paper, in the form of a storyboard.

Task

Using only color, shape, and texture, make a motion graphic to accompany a song of your choice.

Goal

Design visuals to accompany music that support its message and emotion.

Design It

Ask the following questions before beginning the design and animation:

- What do I feel, physically, when listening to the song?
- What pictorial associations do I make when listening to the song?
- Are there certain words in the song that stand out and speak to the emotional message?

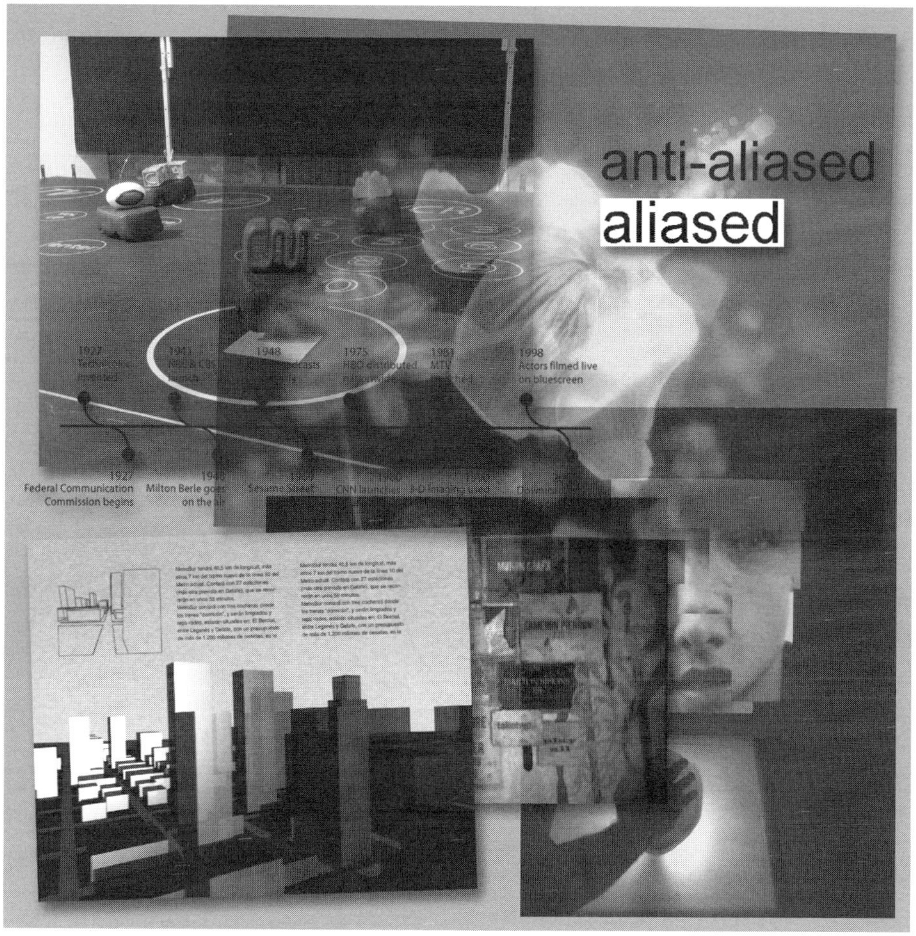
anti-aliased
aliased
1998
Actors filmed live
on bluescreen
1927
Federal Communication
Commission begins
Milton Berle goes
on the air
Sesame Street
CNN launches
3-D imaging used

SECTION

2

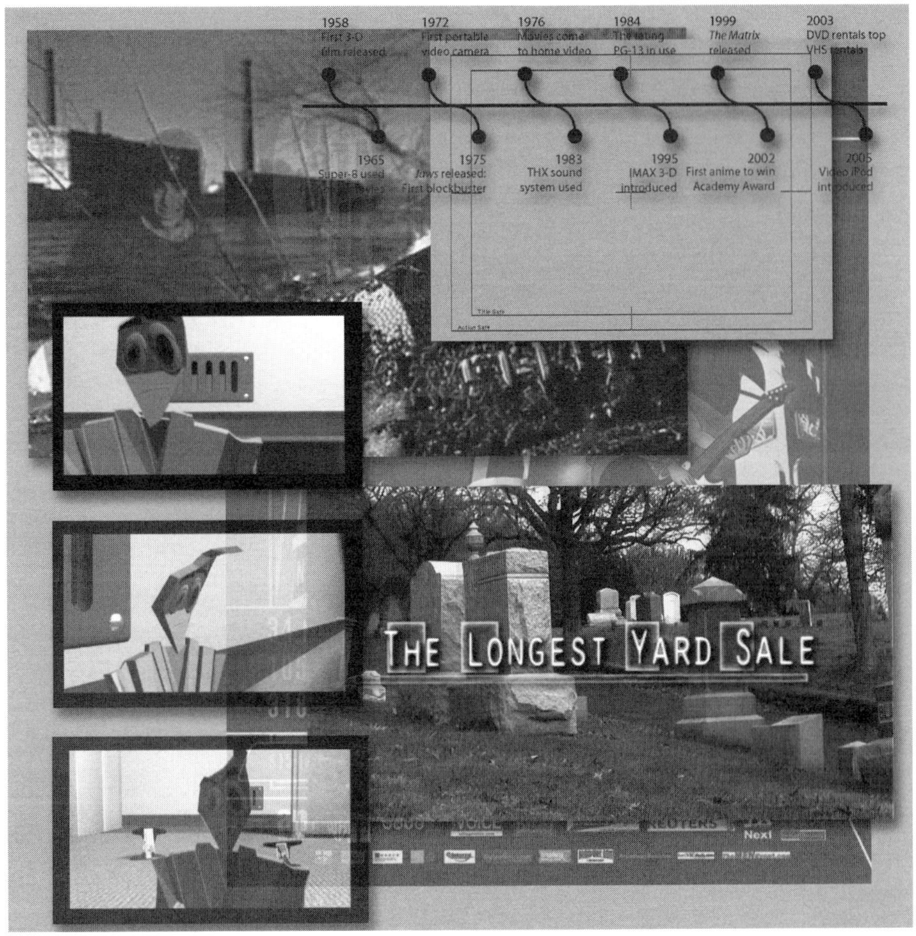
1958
First 3-D
film released
1972
First portable
video camera
1976
Movies come
to home video
1984
The rating
PG-13 in use
1999
The Matrix
released
2003
DVD rentals top
VHS rentals
1965
Super-8 used
1975
Jaws released:
First blockbuster
1983
THX sound
system used
1995
IMAX 3-D
introduced
2002
First anime to win
Academy Award
2005
Video iPod
introduced
THE LONGEST YARD SALE

CHAPTER

7

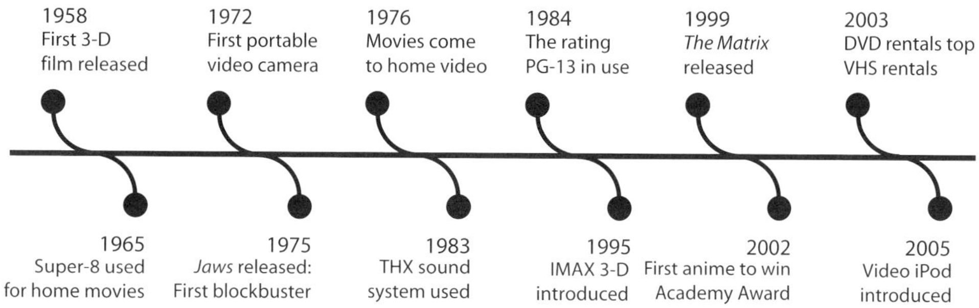

Chapter Objectives

Learn the cultural impact of film and video

Understand the role of a title sequence

Understand the technical and audience considerations for a title design

Discover where to look for inspiration when designing for film and video

Introduction

Movies are an American pastime. Since the founding of Hollywood, we have been enthralled by movies and movie stars and have flocked to see the newest releases. People are intrigued by film because it captures motion, sound, and plays back with special effects what could never have been produced on stage. Although theater attendance has been declining since its all-time high of the 1950s, we still cannot get enough of our movies. We simply have more options for where to view them and frequently choose to enjoy them in the comfort of our homes on television and through home rentals.

Moviemaking was originally a vocation that belonged only to Hollywood. It was not until 8mm film, invented by Kodak in the 1950s, became popular with the average individual that the act of filming and making a film belonged to the masses. The 1950s marked the beginning of experimental, or avant-garde, filmmaking.

Stan Brakhage, a pioneer of the medium, was known for his methods of editing, often quick and sometimes jarring, and for his style of compositing, using layers of light and shadows caught on film in conjunction with other techniques such as hand painting on the frames. One of his best-known works, *Dog Star Man* (1961–1964) has an opening sequence, titled Prelude, which uses the colors of light against shadowy backgrounds, quick jerky edits, and no sound. The effect is jarring and unexpected; done, it appears, with the intention of visually upsetting the viewer.

In 1965 Kodak introduced Super 8 film, which instead of being wound on a reel was housed in an easy-to-load plastic container. This ease of use made it a favorite for recording home movies. During the 1980s home video cameras became very popular, and people routinely recorded every special event or milestone in their lives. Today, we take it for granted that we can pick up a video camera and record our surroundings. A digital video camera is considered an essential technology to have by some. The ability to record moving images is standard on most digital still cameras and many newer cell phones. Because we have grown up watching movies, we have internalized the vocabulary of film shots. We know that a close-up means intimacy and a wide shot gives a better view of the world inside the film. As a result, this is a generation that is quite adept at using film language to tell its stories.

DESIGNING FOR FILM AND VIDEO

All of what we know about the design of motion comes initially from film and the visual experiments that brought this medium to the forefront of the entertainment industry. Much of the vocabulary and techniques employed in motion graphics were developed for film. In film and video there are three primary uses for motion graphics. They are used in title sequences at the opening of the film, in credits at the end of the film, and sometimes within the film. Motion graphics are used in narrative films to identify a location or time essential to the plot, as pictorial elements, or in documentaries to visually present integral information or quantitative data to help the viewer better understand the message.

The title sequence at the beginning of a film leads viewers into the movie and sets the emotional frame of mind in which they will watch it. The style and use of motion graphics at the start of a film should support both the film's genre and theme and set the overall tone and emotion of the movie. This is done by creatively combining music, typography, and visuals from the film.

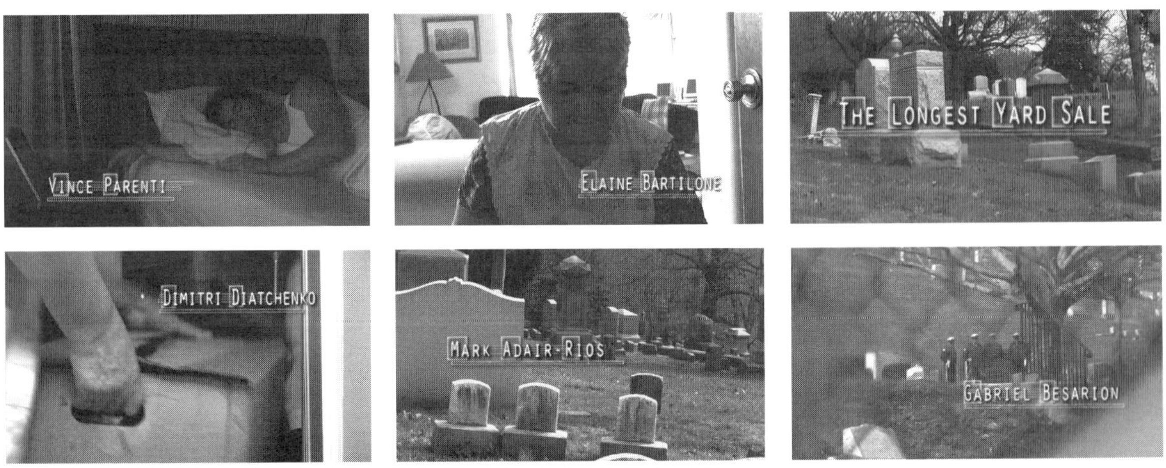

Courtesy Reverie Pictures, Vince Parenti

figure |7-1|

The title sequence for *The Longest Yard Sale* introduces the characters and offers the viewers a background story.

Title sequences have not always been so elaborate or tone-setting. In the early days, film title sequences consisted of no more than large pieces of cardboard with hand painted titles that were photographed and later cut into the film. Recall from Chapter 2 that title sequence design as we know it today did not begin to flourish as an artistic medium until the 1950s when Saul Bass began to design the opening sequences for Hollywood films. Think for a moment about the different films that you like and recall their opening sequences.

- What tone or mood did the opening sequence set for the film?
- What techniques were used to set the mood and emotionally prepare you for the visual story to follow?
- How was type used?
- How did graphics flow across the screen?

In addition to their use in title sequences, motion graphics frequently appear in film as a pictorial element used to enhance the viewing experience. This is not something we expect to see in a feature film, and when married to the other film elements, it creates a rewarding experience. In *The Hitchhikers Guide to the Galaxy*, for example, motion graphics are integrated as part of the text of an intergalactic travel guide used by the film's characters. These graphics not only grab viewers' attention but also are integral to supporting the plot of the characters' wild travels through the galaxy. Whenever the book is opened, the motion graphic sequence begins and fills the frame, leaving the impression that we are looking over the character's shoulder and following along.

Motion graphics are often used in documentaries to illustrate a point or visualize quantitative information to the viewer. *Supersize Me* employs motion graphics to show statistical information in an interesting way. The opening sequence of the film uses motion graphics during a narrative exploring the evils of fast food, specifically McDonald's. With no visuals to stimulate the imagination, this information, though interesting, would be dry. The filmmaker combated potential boredom with creatively applied motion graphics. When telling the audience how many McDonald's restaurants there are in the world, a map appears and quickly becomes overpopulated by individual golden arches on a stick, which then spiral down to reveal many golden dollar signs. This use of motion graphics creates a powerful visual that gives the message more impact and draws the audience into the story.

The Hitchhiker's Guide to the Galaxy and *Supersize Me* are just two examples of how motion graphics can extend beyond title sequences to engage an audience and to enhance its understanding of a film's overall message. They also show how motion graphics sequences act as organic parts of the whole film. Because motion graphics serve as a piece of a larger work, it is important that the motion graphics designer work closely with the film's director and editor to ensure that the graphics fit into the film's overall theme, while also doing the work that they are created to do. They must catch the viewer's attention, be legible, and disseminate information to the audience.

DESIGNING TITLE SEQUENCES FOR VIDEO

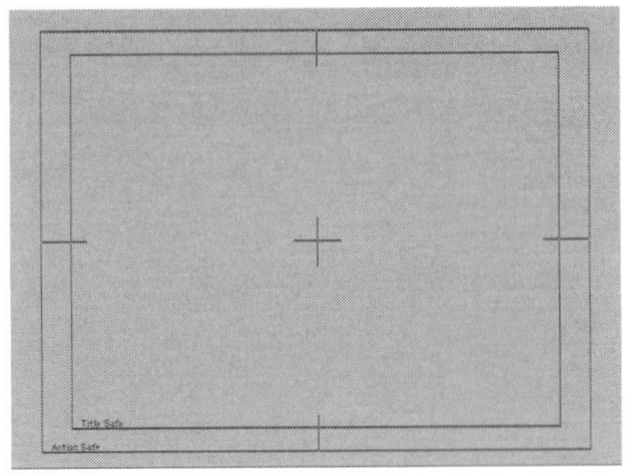

figure 7-2

When designing title sequences for video you cannot place type or other graphic elements right at the edge of the screen. A computer screen allows you see the entire video window, including the border that does not appear when viewed on a television or other video screen. These screens overscan all images and the edges get cut off. Lines that run around the border of the window in any video editing software designate the safe areas to work in. The outer lines designate the **action safe** area, the outer most point any image will reach before getting over-scanned. The inner lines designate the **title safe** area, the outer most point to which type will be displayed without risk of distortion. Be sure to work in the title safe area.

A motion graphics designer may be hired for film or video to add a title sequence, copy to support a scene in the film, or add information graphics. In any scenario the designer will need to look to the artistic style of the movie and use a typeface and graphic style that is representative of the existing material. The designer's goal is to relay information to the viewer in a clear, yet visually interesting and exciting manner.

▷ Professional Profile ◁

Henry Ferrini

Background

Years in industry: 27

Education: I came from a music background. I was studying music through college and realized that I didn't want to end up teaching so I made a lateral move into film and video. There are lots of musicians who did that because it's sort of a time-based art. Music and film have many similarities; among them is the fact that they both move rhythmically. Rhythm and pacing and those things that music has in common with film have become a big part of how I approach my work. You know the rhythm is an important aspect of that, and the graphics end up becoming a rhythmic element. Charles Olson, who is my current subject, says in a poem, "An actual world of value to construct one, from rhythm to image, and image is knowing and knowing, Confucius says, brings one to the goal: Nothing is possible without doing it."

Draw of the Industry

Right from my childhood, I've always been a film fanatic, a cinephile. Film and music worked in tandem, so I figured if I'm not going to perform music, I want to make film. I just insinuated myself into the scene and tried to do as much as possible, because I didn't like the teaching part of the scene.

First Project

I experimented in college with Super 8 and some 16mm equipment but never completed a project. I'd helped out friends. Then 1978 was my first gig. I talked myself into the job. During the Carter administration there was a program called CETA (Comprehensive Employment and Training Act) that provided jobs to the unemployed, and in many cities it employed artists. I convinced the person in charge that the city needed a program for the high school about environmental responsibility in Gloucester, MA. I rented a 1/2-inch black and white portapack video—it was the small format tool that created the video revolution, because it made stuff portable and allowed people to go out on location rather cheaply—and I produced a meditation on environmental responsibility. A lot of the docs that I've done have sort of sprouted from that first seed, because many of my films are about place. It was received very well and played on a smattering of public TV channels and was supported by the Boston board of library commissioners. It was sent to Massachusetts libraries.

Design Process

Motion Graphics Design

I really deal with the graphics after I've put together the sequences or constructed the majority of the piece. For instance, now I can talk about it in terms of the piece I've been working on, *Polis Is This: Charles Olson and the Persistence of Place*. The graphical stuff is certainly motivated from the photography. But this guy was a poet and very concerned about how the text looks on the page. It's also layered in after I've constructed the sequence. The title is about how the poet viewed the place he lived—how he viewed reality through the lens of the place where he lived—he lived in Gloucester, MA, but it could be New York or North Dakota or Shanghai. Everybody views reality through the places that they live. It is important that the graphics reflect that. I've been dealing with how to make that happen—text coming out of landscape, what it's going to be filled with. This process comes at the end. I don't think about that at the beginning, unless I get hit with something during the filming process that I find kind of interesting. It's really in the finishing room that I come up with this.

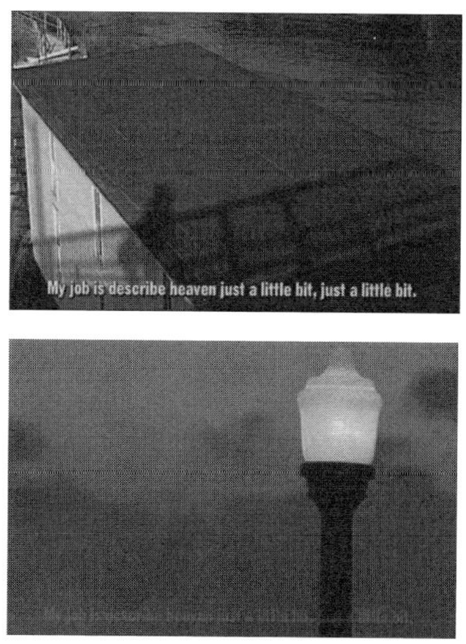

By Henry Ferrini

figure | 7-3 |

Type emerges from landscape, from *Lowell Blues*.

You deal with your title. I know the name of the film at the get-go. Sometimes it doesn't come until the end, but that name gets translated graphically from the start even when writing a proposal. Saved with the image, the logotype, you're dealing with that and maybe it's on a subconscious level; it's always there. This film title, *Polis Is This: Charles Olson and the Persistence of Place*, is the title I started with, but then I changed the title, and now I'm going back to that because it's stronger. The issue was that some people don't know what the word *polis* means. That's a problem when you're trying to make a film for people, but also you want to raise the bar. I've got something blocked out now that I'm playing with. I usually need to work with the thing, and see it, and try it until I know.

I usually bring on a graphics person at the latter end of the process. The reason for that is simply an economic one. If I could afford to bring a graphics artist on earlier, that would be wonderful, but I have to watch my pennies, so they come on at the end. When I have ideas formulated, I talk about how to best accomplish those ideas, and then try to bounce around ideas that my graphics person may have as well. In this piece we talked about trying to use the same typeface that Olson used in his books. Then we researched that and found that he didn't have a favorite typeface as we thought.

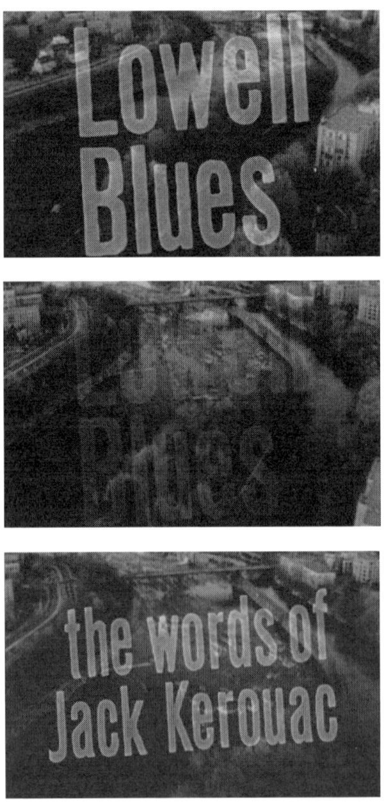

By Henry Ferrini

figure 7-4

Main title sequence from *Lowell Blues*.

The huge problem of type on screen is you want to make sure you have a style, but you also want it to be readable. Always a concern at the forefront of it is that people aren't going to have a problem reading things.

Audience Considerations

If you think about your film out there—specifically, most of my stuff is on public television—if you think about what it takes for someone to tune in, you have a certain amount of time to hook your viewer—about one or two minutes. If in that period of time there is a graphical aspect to your show, then that can help hook them. Usually the title.

There's always been this idea that you don't start anything with graphics—if you can't show the person and you have to tell them through graphics, then you're not a visual artist. I don't agree with that. I think graphics are a part of your visual vocabulary and they can be as persuasive as image.

In the first ten seconds of my film, there's a graphical image. That graphic is "man must rediscover the earth or leave it." That was stated by my subject, and it really sort of says what the rest of the sixty minutes of the film is about. That's sort of a condensation of everything in that statement. And I suppose if I had my subject saying that—and it's very important to me that it be up-front—that little statement is going to act like a cosmic transmission and fly out from the earth and out to the viewer's eyes, and I hope that it will be effective and engage the viewer visually and maybe intellectually as well. I think motion graphics can do that and that they are very strong.

Olson wrote a book called *Projective Verse*, and it was really a theoretical manifesto about poetry. He used the page like action painters use the canvas, opened it up and did things very differently from what was happening. For this particular film, using graphics and type was very important to my subject and reflects back on the whole film, so it's really important for me to spend as much as I can afford working on this stuff.

I usually spend weeks messing around on the graphics, depending on the budget and how long I can defer payment and how busy the graphics person is. It's a dance with all of those things. I will also work with it and pick up some slack too.

Good Film Title Design

If you had Saul Bass to work with, then you wouldn't have to worry, like *North by Northwest*, having those titles come out of the architecture. It's got to have something to do with the film. It can't just be plastered on without anything to do with the film; that's why *North by Northwest* is one of my favorites.

With my film on Kerouac, Kerouac was out there bouncing off the boundaries, pushing the boundaries. Those were some of the thoughts behind the making of it and the titles that appear to bounce. He also bounced around Lowell, his hometown where the piece is set. What makes it good is if people are enhanced by it and in the moment. If your audience is in the moment, then you've done your job.

Another one of my favorite openings is from a Russ Meyer film, *Good Morning and Good Bye*, where he basically put all the graphics on mailboxes and the camera pans, chasing this fast car and at the end of the title sequence, the car arrives at the first scene of the film. I thought it was one of the most brilliant, cheapest ways of having a very effective graphic title sequence.

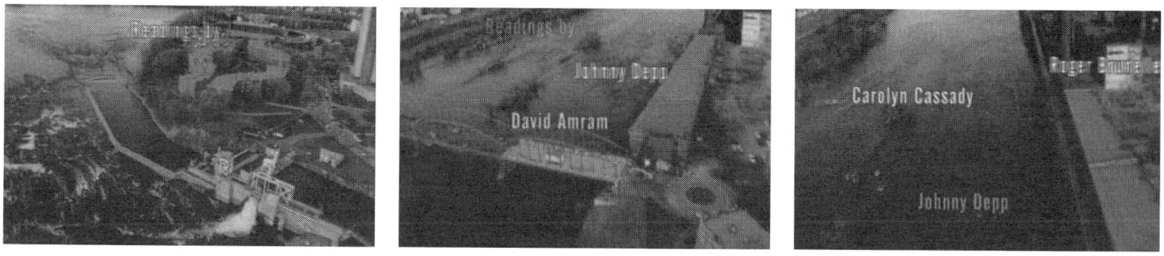

By Henry Ferrini

figure | 7-5 |

From the main title sequence; the names appear to bounce along with the rhythm of the river.

Challenges of Movie Title Design

The signature component is the cinematography and the photography. I labor over and shoot a lot of material in my films. I want the graphic component to have as much care as I put into the photography and to blend with it—although it can work against it. It can play. It has to be a dance between the two elements. When creating that dance between the photography and the graphics, if it swings, then it's working. If it's clunky, then I try to do something else. But it's important that it comes from the photography. The photography comes first because that's my first interface with the subject matter—except for that subconscious thing with the title, then the title becomes almost a glyph.

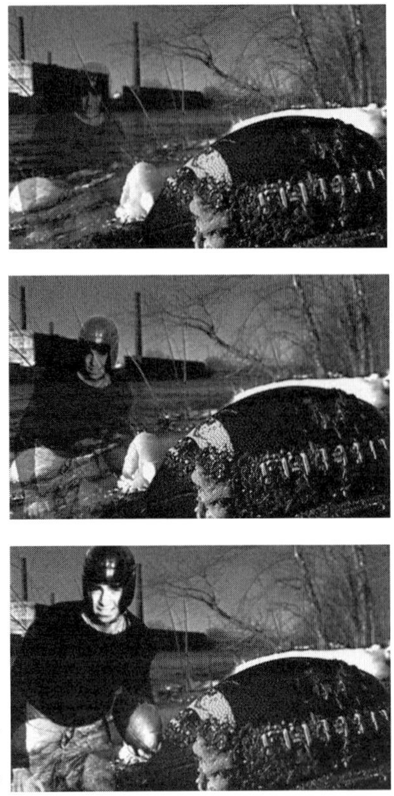

By Henry Ferrini

figure |7-6|

Graphics are used to further illustrate a message in the scene and blend in with the photography of the film.

Changing Technology

In the past I would do everything myself. I think my first piece that I did, I went and got a Letraset—press type stuff from the seventies—and pressed that out by hand and made my titles and then shot them. And if I wanted movement, I would do that with the camera. The first motion graphic in my first film, I wanted the wave that came up to wipe the title on. I shot at a low angle and wanted the photography and graphics to mingle. I had the camera on the ground shooting a wave about to crash, and just as the wave broke, it revealed the title. And then I did some sort of luminance key so that it appeared and came into focus. I pressed it out with Letraset. Back then you bought sheets of it in whatever font, and you would lay them out on graph paper. Then I'd shoot them.

Now we have these incredibly powerful home computers that can do everything. My brain is a little stiff to deal with all of these programs. I can deal with editing and Photoshop. I know about After Effects but am not an After Effects geek. Those programs are really, really deep; you really need someone who works with them all the time and knows the nuances. I work with other people. You gain production value when you deal with people who know what they're doing. Early on it was more DYI—do it yourself—filmmaking. Young kids doing it today, they have such facility with these programs, but they have little history.

How Old Technology Has Influenced Current Ways of Working

It gives one a better understanding and a better way to communicate with graphics people about how you see the finished product. It gives you a vocabulary.

| PROMOTIONAL VIDEOS |

Promotional videos are a long-form commercial created for specific groups of people, often a potential client. *Client*, in this scenario, is a broad term that refers to anyone who will use or interact with the product or service touted on the video. These videos often employ the use of motion graphics to engage the client, communicate their message, and sell the product or service. Pseudo documentary with a stylized, polished finish is often used for the presentation style of the video. Although often not as glamorous as films, they offer a good way to get some experience and develop your own style.

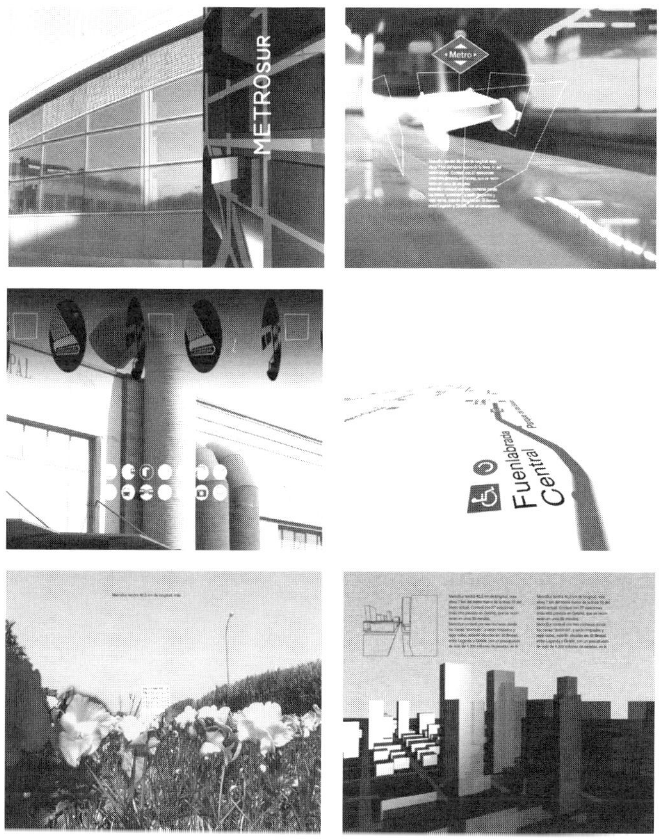

By Jan Mathias Steinforth (mateuniverse)

figure |7-7|

Industry video created for Metro Madrid for the Expo Ocio Fair 2003, designed to encourage people to use the subway in Madrid.

I really am kind of a nut about the graphic thing because it is SO, SO visual. When shooting, I totally have this reflection fetish. Type, in particular, is exciting to view when undulating on the surface of water. Of course, when you shoot it, it's reversed, but with a computer you can flip stuff and then you get this readable graphic with a reflection. But this movement that the computer could never emulate, natural movement, I use it in snippets; especially with this writer stuff, I work words in. I like looking for graphics in the landscape—looking for the way they're hidden. How their meaning changes when they drop a letter. I find that fun in a way. That's informed by my having done all of this stuff in the past, having worked setting up titles. It's part of my vocabulary. ◄

▷ Professional Profile ◁

| *Jeffrey Sproul* |

Background

Years as a designer: 2

Education: BA in theatre and philosophy from Colorado State University, and an Associate of Applied Science degree in Digital Media Communications from Katharine Gibbs School—New York.

The Draw of Design

I had always liked drawing, but for many years I never really considered going into the design field. I had come out to New York to be an actor, and although I was able to stay pretty active, I made very little money. I eventually decided to go back to school to learn a skill I could not only make money with, but would allow me to be creative. Working in coffee bars just wasn't cutting it for me anymore. I went into the Katharine Gibbs Digital Media program figuring that it would give me some nice groundwork in different areas of the digital arts, and I could eventually pursue what areas interested me most.

First Design Before Becoming a Professional

I've done a lot of sketch comedy in New York. Back in 2000, I wrote a multimedia comedy (video and live segments) called "Minutes Later. . . ." There were some serious budget limitations, so I ended up doing a lot of design work for it myself. I also did our poster art, which allowed me to use my drawing skills. We also had a lot of props, or fake products, such as flyers in the actual show, so I ended up doing most of that design work as well. Considering I hadn't studied design at that point, I'm actually pretty proud of how it all turned out.

First Professional Design Job

I became the graphic and web designer for the 2004 New York Musical Theatre Festival. It was their first year and they didn't have a lot of money, so they were looking for

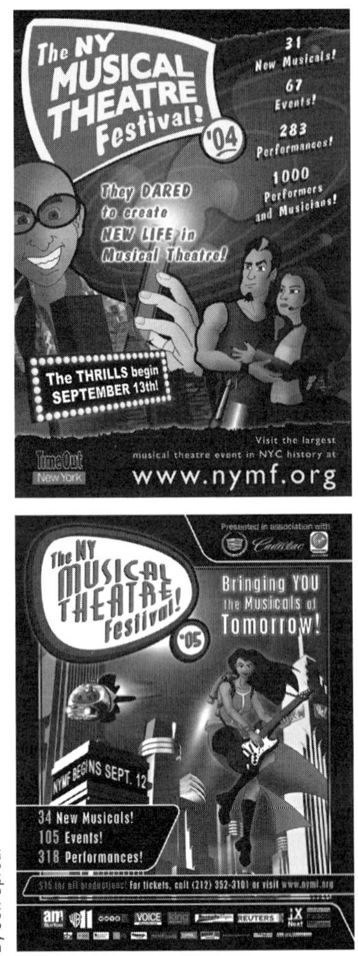

By Jeff Sproul

figure |7-8|

Posters created for 2004 and 2005 New York Musical Theatre Festival.

a designer who was more interested in the portfolio pieces and résumé credit than a fat wad of cash. I was just out of school, so that person was me. I knew I was the new guy, so it was all about paying my dues. It was a lot of work, but I'm proud of how it came out. I learned a lot from the experience.

Design Process

Conceptualizing a Design for a Title Sequence

You must of course have a thorough understanding of the film itself. You look at everything—the genre, tone, cinematography, themes, music, lighting, on and on. All of it can have an influence on the titles. It then becomes your job to effectively compress the essence and spirit of the film into the title sequence. It's as much a part of the overall film as anything else, and should therefore feel as if it truly belongs there.

What Makes a Strong Designer

What makes someone a strong individual is what I believe makes them a strong designer. The best work comes as a result of the designer doing the work as only he or she could. This means trusting your instincts as well as your skills. Perhaps it's a nebulous way to describe it, but I think it's about really putting yourself into the work. My best work is always what feels the most like me. It's not just about knowing the craft (which is of course essential), but also knowing what makes you unique as an artist and using it.

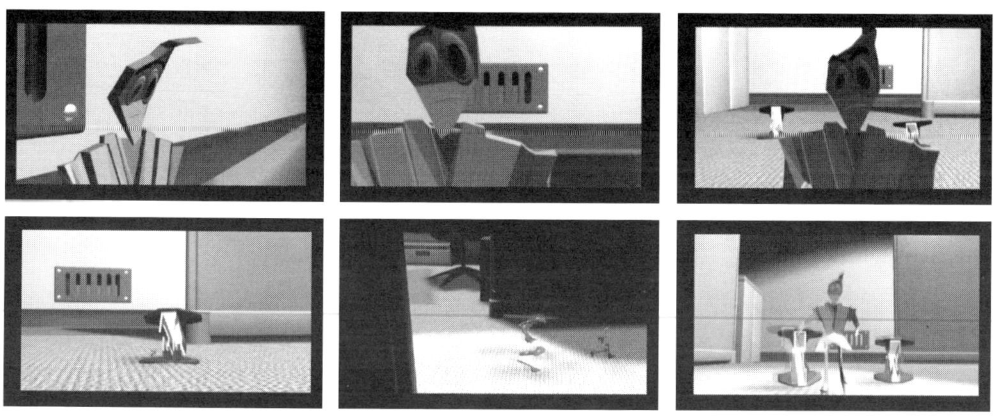

By Jeff Sproul

figure |7-9|

Scenes from a short film, *Johnny Origami*. Done in 3-D, it is the story of Johnny Origami, a piece of paper, that has to escape from the evil office supplies—scissors, staple remover, paper clips—if he wants to survive the night. This short reflects the designer's unique style.

Collaborating with Clients

The goal is ultimately to give the clients not only what they wanted, but make it even better than what they originally had in mind. You're not always going to agree, but there are plenty of times when the collaboration can lead you into some new and exciting areas, because you're forced to come at it from an unexpected direction. It's those times when you can really grow.

Challenges of Title Design

It's ultimately about how to best represent the film in its entirety. You ask yourself what will feel the most natural to the viewer and at the same time serve the intent of the filmmaker.

Viewers' Expectations from a Title Design

I think they typically see it as a natural part of the overall film. They expect it to be a seamless part of the whole. Sometimes it's like a book cover of sorts, meant to help generate a sense of excitement about what's to follow. Other times it almost seems parenthetical and woven into the story, which is already moving forward. It depends on the individual film. You pick the style that will most serve it.

Design Signature

It's my personal sense of playfulness. It's the part of me that still loves toys and cartoons. I've worked on many different types of projects, but if there's a through-line to them, I'd say it's a sort of deadpan sense of humor coupled with a love of small, fun little details. I like to give the impression that there's all sorts of fun stuff going on just behind the scenes.

Role of Title Sequence

It announces the beginning of a particular journey that you're about to sit through.

The Future of Feature Films

I'd like to think that eventually more filmmakers will begin to relax and see all this technology as a means to merely serving the story. So often these days the technology is clearly the only reason the project was made. ◅

SUMMARY

Many of the motion graphics techniques used today were originally used for celluloid film. A title sequence has just as much importance today as it did then, and it plays the role of engaging the audience with the storyline, introducing characters, and creating a sense of anticipation. In addition to the opening and title sequences in films, motion graphics can appear during the film to enhance the narrative by clarifying a plot point or providing additional information.

in review

1. What contributed to the public's ability to make its own movies?
2. What is the purpose of the title sequence?
3. What other purposes can motion graphics serve within a film?
4. What makes for effective motion graphics in a film?

exercises

Exercise

Design a title sequence for a documentary about your favorite band. It should reflect the emotional content of the film and be visually consistent.

Design Process

For ideas and inspiration look into the band:

- What do they represent?
- What does the audience expect from them?
- What is their style?

In addition to the band's style, also look to the style of the film for guidance.

- How is it shot?
- How is it cut?
- Is it glossy? Gritty? Slick?
- Does it look professional, like something you would see on an entertainment channel, or is it more guerilla style, reminding you of a home video?

After initially viewing the film, brainstorm for a while. Remember when brainstorming, there are no bad or wrong ideas. Think practically, but also push the envelope and don't be afraid to write down ideas that at first may seem utterly ridiculous. In the end you may find these to be some of your best ideas.

Inspiration

Now is the time to begin making decisions about the design of your title sequence.

- Do you want titles over black or titles over footage? If you choose to use footage, what kind of footage? Would you use photographs? Rehearsal footage? Concert footage? Or by contrast, footage of the band when they are not in "band mode"?

- What kind of audio do you want for your title sequence? Should it be the band's music? Should it be music that contrasts the band's style? Perhaps you might consider using audio from an interview with the band, or audio from the fans.
- What is the band's logo? Do you want to incorporate the type style from the band's logo into your titles?

Decide which footage and which music you will use for your opening sequence, because this will help to frame the rest of your decisions for your title design. The footage will impact the type, color, and movement of your titles, and the music will help to define the rhythm of your sequence.

Decide what information needs to be conveyed in the title sequence:

- The name of the band
- The director of the film
- The cinematographer
- The editor
- The crew
- Any additional performers or special appearances

The band's logo is also an important element to consider. Decide whether you want to work with the colors and type of the logo. You could decide to work against them depending on the message you want to send in the opening of your film. Whatever your decision, your choices must reflect the content of the film.

Look at the footage that you have selected and listen to the music again. Think about the most effective way to integrate the information of the title sequence with the footage and the music. Now you can:

- Choose your colors
- Choose your type
- Begin to sketch out your design

Method

1. Do a rough pencil sketch of your titles, making sure to block out the type and the movement, if any, of your words. Include any additional graphics in the sketches. You want to pay close attention to the framing of your elements. In fact, this is a good opportunity to play with your framing in order to settle upon the best composition. Also, keep in mind the rhythm of the accompanying music.

2. When you are satisfied with your pencil sketch, do more complete digital storyboards in color. Use either Photoshop or Illustrator, depending on whether you want your graphics to be raster or vector-based. Be sure to storyboard the entire opening sequence.

3. While in Photoshop or Illustrator do a screen-size or larger version of your type to make sure that it reads.

4. When you are satisfied with your storyboards, edit your opening sequence in Final Cut Pro, and execute your titles in After Effects. As you edit, allow the music and the video footage to guide your cuts and determine the pacing of your graphics.

5. Import your titles from After Effects into Final Cut Pro.

6. Color correct your titles, setting them to the color bars of a video monitor, rather than the computer monitor, since the colors on the computer screen may not be true to the NTSC colors.

7. Print your title sequence to tape.

8. Watch the final tape on a television monitor. Compare your titles on a video monitor and a computer monitor. You will see that the colors will never match exactly, but the emotional impact of the colors should be the same in either format.

Now that you have completed your title design, show it to an audience. What is your audience's impression? Do you think the band would like it? Is it a fitting introduction for the rest of the film? Are there any elements that you would change? What did you learn from completing this process?

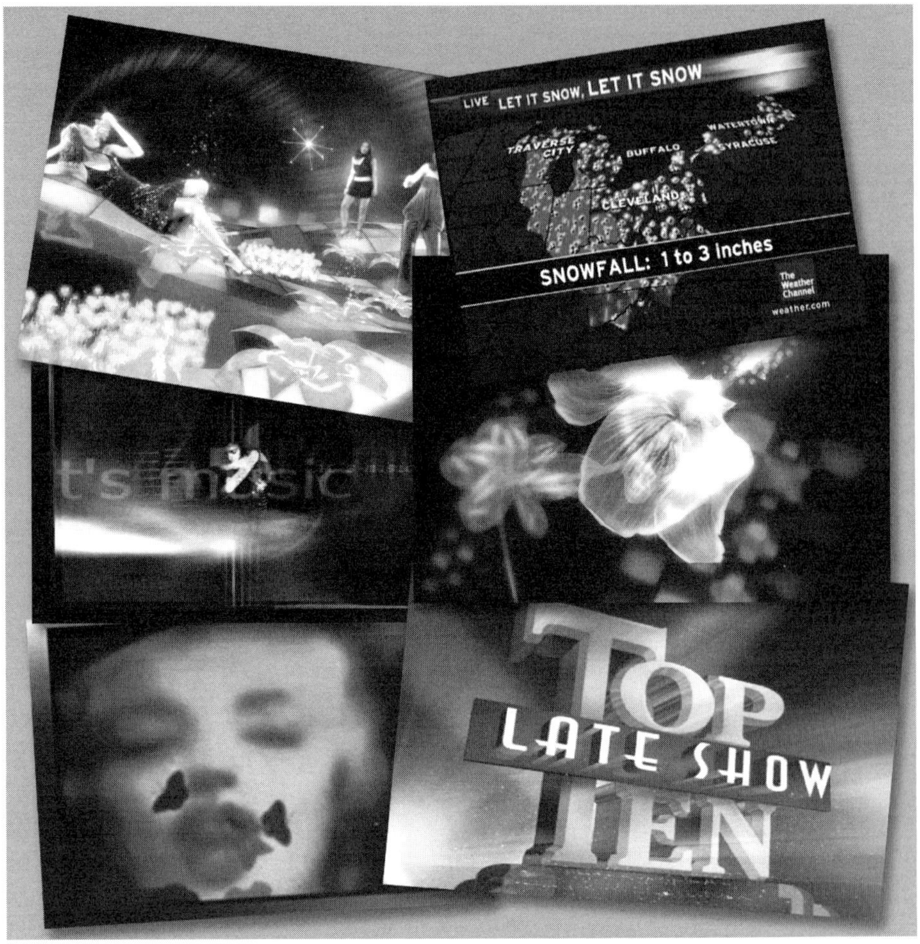
LIVE LET IT SNOW, LET IT SNOW
TRAVERSE CITY
BUFFALO
WATERTOWN
SYRACUSE
CLEVELAND
SNOWFALL: 1 to 3 inches
The Weather Channel
weather.com
t's music
TOP
LATE SHOW
TEN

CHAPTER

8

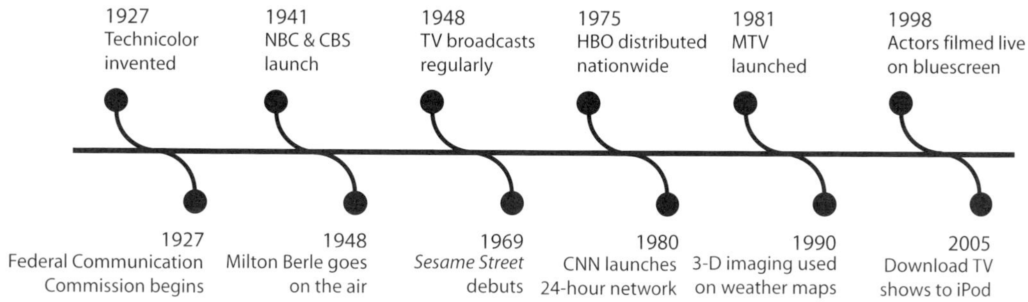

TELEVISION

Chapter Objectives

Understand the impact of television in society

Learn to apply the principles of graphic design to motion graphics design for television

Understand the technical and audience considerations that go into television graphics design

Look at different roles of the television graphics designer

Learn how to create successful broadcast designs

Introduction

Although in use in the 1940s, television did not captivate American audiences until the 1950s. Commercial stations came on the air in 1941, but when World War II resources were limited, broadcasts ceased. Television stations began broadcasting again after the war, and many families bought televisions for their living rooms. This period in the 1950s is often referred to as the Golden Age of Television. People were enthralled by the technology and content, and television replaced other forms of entertainment such as movies and radio. Where people once may have stayed out for dinner and dancing, they now rushed home so they would not miss the newest episode of their favorite show, such as *Dragnet*, *The Jack Benny Show*, and *I Love Lucy*. Television dictated the flow of modern society as more and more people looked no farther than their living rooms for entertainment. Initially, television shows followed the same format as theater and vaudeville with many popular variety shows.

Over time, television shows took on many formats—drama, comedy, talk show, reality show, mini-series, soap opera—all of which brought a unique audience following. This opened a new avenue for advertisers who now had a captive audience to sell their wares and services to. They could determine the most successful way to manipulate viewers, and design the most persuasive ads, by gauging viewers' likes and dislikes based on the type of show they watched. Television forever altered and dictated the social aspects of society and opened new doors for the design of motion graphics.

Courtesy of The Weather Channel

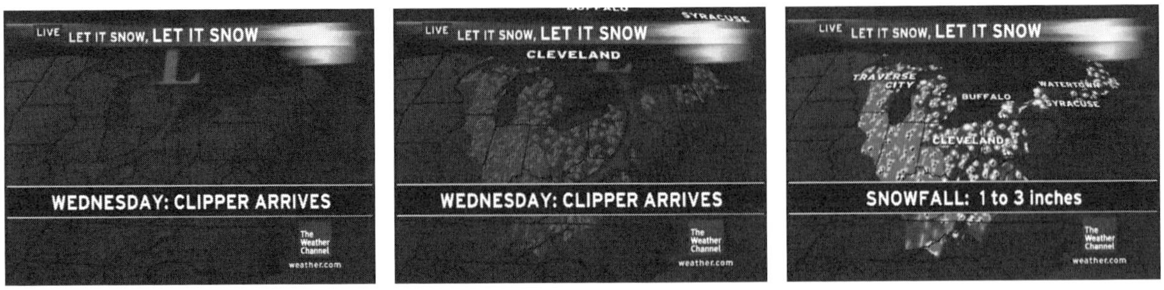

figure 8-1

Motion graphics used in a weather graphic from a broadcast on The Weather Channel.

DESIGNING FOR TELEVISION

Motion graphics are used in many capacities on television, such as news broadcasts, commercials, sports broadcasts, and other programming. In a television show motion graphics communicate with the audience as a prelude, and in news programming they can enhance a news segment or highlight a sports maneuver. The job of a motion graphic on television is to serve as both information and entertainment no matter where it is applied.

As with films, the opening titles used to introduce a television show to its audience consist of graphics, text, theme music, and video, which set the tone and draw the viewer in. The information in the title sequence tells the audience the name of the show and the key people involved, such as the stars, writers, producers, and directors. Beyond being informational, it also sets the stage and mood. In the brief amount of time given to a title sequence for a television show, the designer must use elements of design to hook the viewer and keep her tuned in. Also, by using the same opener every week, for each show, the title sequence design is repetitive and offers a sense of familiarity.

Many television shows such as *Numb3rs* and *CSI* also use motion graphics within the show. These crime dramas use a good deal of technical terms, and the motion graphics help viewers, who might not otherwise understand what the characters are talking about, visualize the story. In *Numb3rs*, the FBI uses mathematical equations to solve crimes. Mathematical jargon is often used, so to keep viewers engaged and enhance

By Violetta S. Kraja, CADA/NYU Gallery

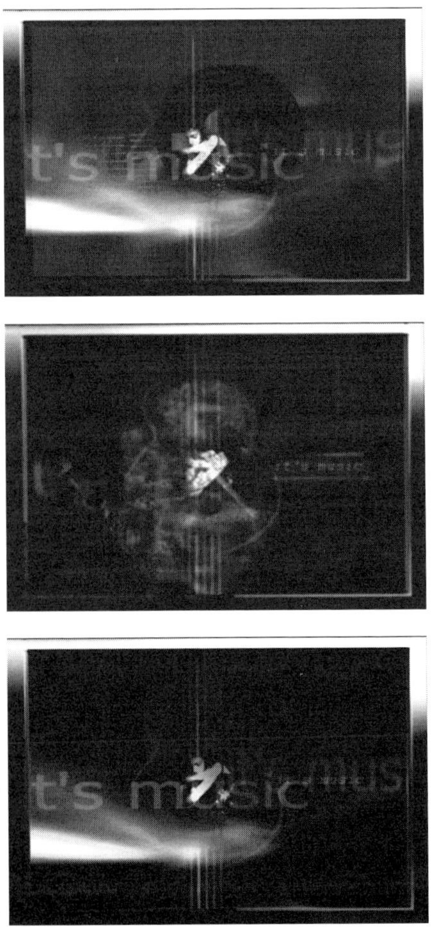

figure 8-2

Show opener for *It's Music*.

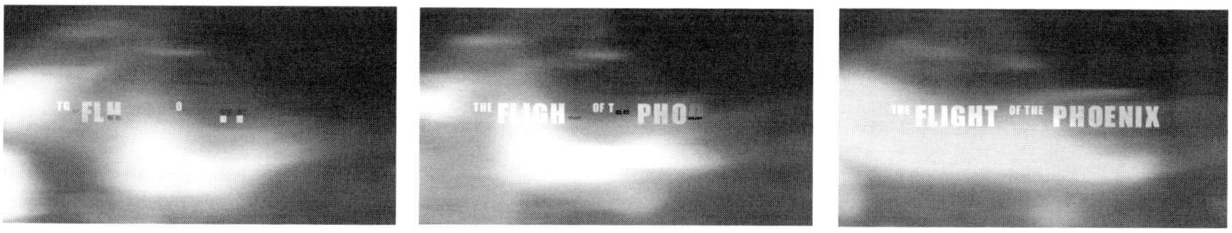

By Dorian J. Compo/Designer/ www.rekonstrukt.com

figure 8-3

This sequence for CineMAX focuses on typography to highlighting movies the station airs.

their understanding of the events, the show uses composited visuals of handwritten equations, diagrams, and textures. *CSI*, a forensics drama, uses motion graphics to create visuals to accompany the medical and other technical language used by the morticians and crime scene investigators. Without these motion graphics, viewers' attention would wane, but with them the shows' writers have more freedom to include genre-specific dialogue, making for a more realistic story.

Motion graphics are also often used in advertising on television. Whether advertising a product, a show, or the television station, the motion graphics in commercials draw viewers' attention to the brand. This may be done by animating the name of the product or brand logo or by animating graphics and text that inform the viewer about specifics of the product. It is important that the choice of graphics, typeface, type treatment, rhythm, flow, and transitions reflect the theme and existing emotion of the station or product. These elements should support the existing brand and reinforce the viewer's feelings about it.

Motion graphics designers who design for television are often faced with the challenge of creating a very short sequence that must relay information to the consumer in an environment where the consumer is not required to stay tuned to that particular station during the commercial breaks. The designer must use attention-grabbing graphics that will immediately interest consumers so they will pay attention to the message.

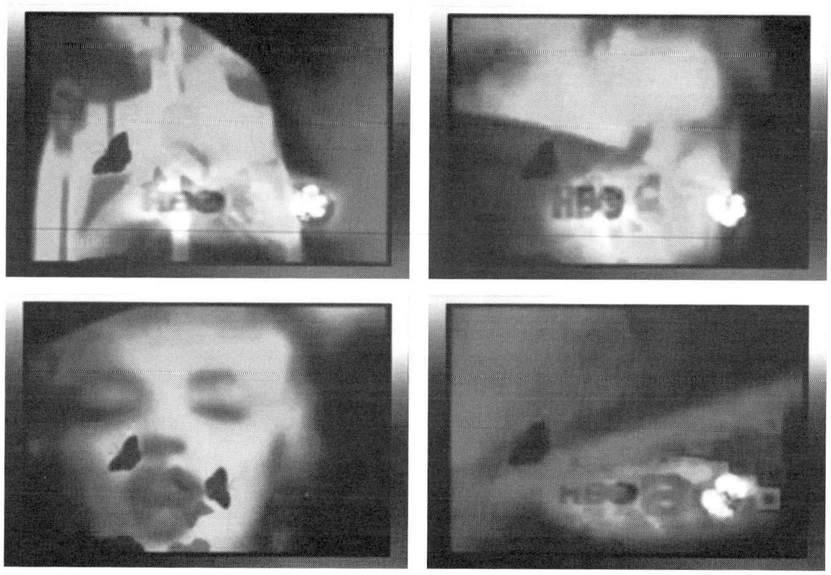

By Violettta S. Kraja, CADA/NYU Gallery

figure 8-4

This sequence for HBO uses a lot of texture that reinforces the station's exciting, raw energy.

DESIGNING COMMERCIALS FOR TELEVISION

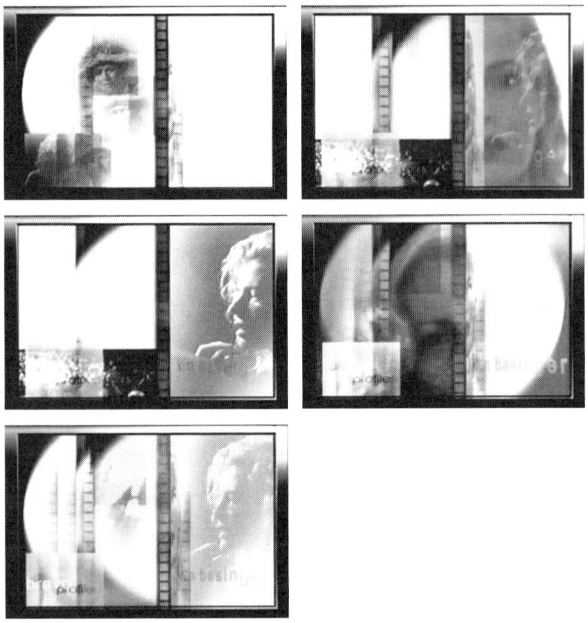

By Violetta S. Kraja, CADA/NYU Gallery

figure 8-5

Eventually, with technological advancements in routing advertisements to specific viewers, this promo for Bravo could be sent only to viewers interested in the series or in Kim Basinger.

Television commercials, or spots, run for a minute or less, which does not leave much time to convey crucial information. It is the designers' responsibility to combine design elements in such a way that will hold viewers' attention. There are so many channels to choose from, and if we get bored with what is on one channel, we can easily flip to another, and thus avoid listening to the intended message.

Advertisers are looking for new and better ways to communicate with potential consumers, and one technological development has great promise. Generally, commercials are aired to a vast number of viewers, with no control to air them in only certain neighborhoods, to specific groups of people. With a new technology that allows information sent over cable lines to be routed to specific neighborhoods, advertisers are able to create commercials tailored to very specific demographics. Now designers have the freedom to create motion graphics with colors, typography, and images that will appeal to specific groups.

Commercials, with the aid of motion graphics, are created for the sole purpose of selling a product. They need to be packaged in such a way that the viewer is entertained, visually stimulated, and convinced, after watching it, that she simply must have the product or service. The new routing technology will make the designer's job easier.

▷ Professional Profile ◁

Roger White

Background

Years as a designer: 20

Education: BFA from Parsons in illustration, graduate studies at School of Visual Arts, Pratt and The New School in computer graphics

The Draw of Design

I wanted to be a zookeeper until I worked at a zoo in high school and cleaned up lion and monkey crap for a few months. Then the second semester of senior year I went to a custom car painting place and painted designs on motorcycles and cars and that got the art side going. I was doing Jags and Corvettes—higher-end cars from dealerships. I would mix five gradients of golds and browns on the hoods or have very tasteful ivory blending into silver down the side of a Cadillac, as opposed to the tattoo art you see on motorcycles—although I did do tattoo art on airboat helmets. So that got me interested in applying to art schools.

First Design Before Becoming a Professional

There was a contest for a show poster for *Funny Girl* in high school. My poster was chosen, and then it was stolen. And so then I figured it must be really good if they were asking me to do it again.

First Professional Design Job

I was a staff artist for *Late Night* and *Saturday Night Live*, but that was after a year of getting out of school and struggling and hoping and wishing and taking part-time jobs selling theater tickets. Honestly, it was a hard year, a year of feeling like you're a total failure and everybody else had a job of some sort, and I was trying to make ends meet selling tickets part time.

The job had come up on the school placement board. The art director at *Late Night* was also a Parsons alum. So I got it through the school.

Design Process

Working with Clients

When I begin a design project, I always start out with a pencil sketch. I'll listen to the clients' description of the project, ask many questions, and get an idea of whether they are open to other suggestions. Some clients have a clear vision of what they want; others will type out a three-page description but have no clear vision. I'll begin with rough pencil sketches or storyboards to quickly establish that we are on the same page. This usually opens a concept dialogue—what I call banging heads. This is a great place for me to interject some of my own ideas while incorporating theirs. This quick process gives the client confidence in my work before they spend the big bucks. I'll tell them in the first meeting there is no obligation to continue if they don't like the sketches.

With *Late Show*, I work with the director of the show, and I get my work approved by him and he gets his approval from Dave. So all of my work is a collaboration with the director because he doesn't mind my adding ideas to a project, and we collaborate very well. I usually start out in sketch form, pencil sketches to concept. Then from there, I go to the color realm and then to video realm with the storyboards. Once those things are resolved, Dave will look at the storyboards and will then decide whether to pay $100,000 for sets, camera, lighting, costumes, and so on. Storyboards approved, I will then become art director and take it to a post house

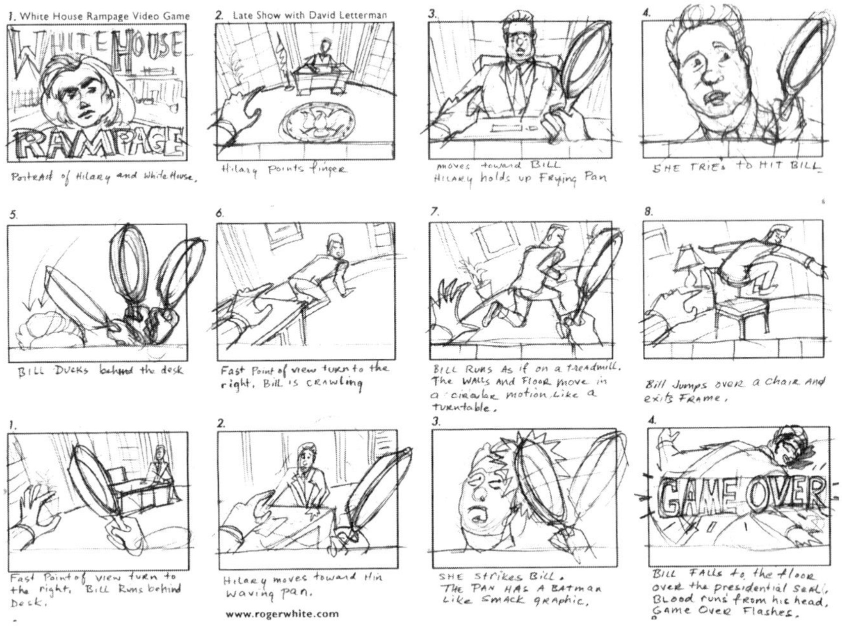

figure |8-6|

Roger White's pencil sketches for "White House Rampage."

and art direct my design for the show. I will deliver daily tapes to update the director, and we will discuss what needs to be changed—and all of that needs to be approved by Dave. If it's an animation that airs on the show within the show like "White House Rampage," then I will do it myself on my Mac.

Audience Influence on Design

How does your audience influence your design? Knowing your audience is the most important factor to overcome. I have worked in entertainment for so long that I tend to throw in too much pizzazz when I'm hired to design a news piece. Art directors at *Time* and *Colbert Report* will tell me to pull back on the comedy quota.

The Colbert Report or *Time* is a straight depiction of the subject. You're not adding anything. You're just putting lip gloss on it. With Letterman, or more the entertainment side, you tend to interject—not comedy, because comedy is in the writing as I'm always reminded—but it is serious with a wink. It's dressing it up, but you wouldn't necessarily laugh at it unless it had the joke to go along with it.

Inspiration

Good art in a museum or on a CD cover inspires my design. Album covers are always a favorite. Roger Dean and Pink Floyd. Today it's the type design of a lot of the rap CDs like Nelly or 50 Cent. They're more about the type design and photography and less about the illustration because CDs are smaller.

Nature's colors like beach sunsets inspire my color choices. I keep a folder of good magazine advertising and logo design. When a project comes up, I'll look through my collection for inspiration. I rip them off! Using color combinations from one and the type design from another. You don't need to reinvent the wheel with every project. By the time you incorporate your own ideas and style, the design is no longer a copy but your own unique work.

Most Important Design Element of Television Graphics

Transportation. The way an artist makes us feel and moves us through the design. A true artist can lead us visually through a piece by moving design elements in such a way that the eye is always following something. As one element is leaving a scene a new element is emerging. The biggest problem I see with young motion designers is a static screen, causing our eye to wander about looking for a ride. When I do the storyboard going from the pencil sketch to the color storyboard, I literally move my hands around as if they are pieces of the composition. As one leaves, another moves into position. I try to give my own work the look and feel of riding in a luxury car rather than a bumper car.

Technology and Design

My first job after college was creating graphics and illustrations at NBC. For eight years I drew and painted traditional artwork that was placed on a camera stand for *Late Night* and *Saturday Night Live*. The older artists still wore suits and ties to work. When we got a Xerox machine I could scale and duplicate, but a color reproduction still took two days at the photo lab. When Letterman moved to CBS, they asked me to design a logo for *Late Show*. The art supply store no longer carried the press on type I requested. NBC had just gotten a Mac, and the *Late Show* logo and marquee became the first projects I ever designed on a computer.

Even though all of my graphics and animations are created on a computer, every project begins with a cup of coffee and pencil sketches. A sharp brain and sharp pencil are the most important tools I continue to use.

What Makes Roger White Designs Unique?

On the surface it's usually a 3-D environment with metallic shiny textures. But what a client asks for is not necessarily what I would call my look. TV graphics have been stuck in a 3-D rut for years. Every news program now looks like *Entertainment Tonight*, which looks like a video game graphic. No matter what project I am working on, I am concerned with its color and composition first. If it looks good on a storyboard, it will look great as an animation.

My traditional background really helps because you think more about color and design. If the design doesn't look good as a still, then it's not

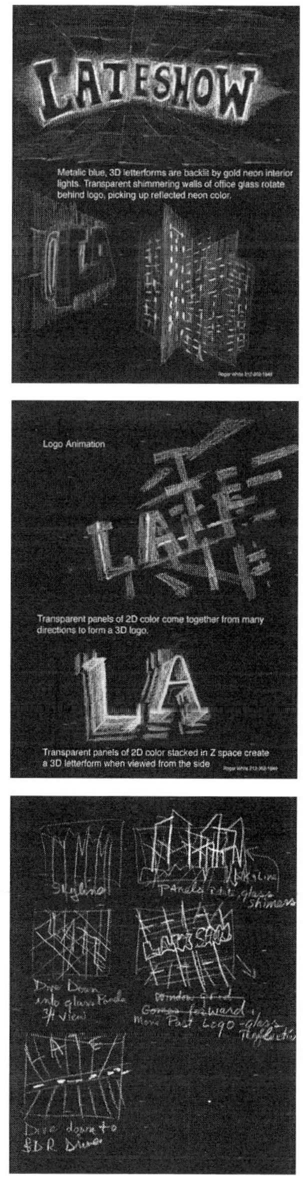

Artwork by Roger White. Logo copyright courtesy of Worldwide Pants, Inc. The artwork shown is for demo purposes only; no endorsement or sponsorship by the owners or subjects is implied.

figure | 8-7 |

Color sketches of the logo for *The Late Show with David Letterman.*

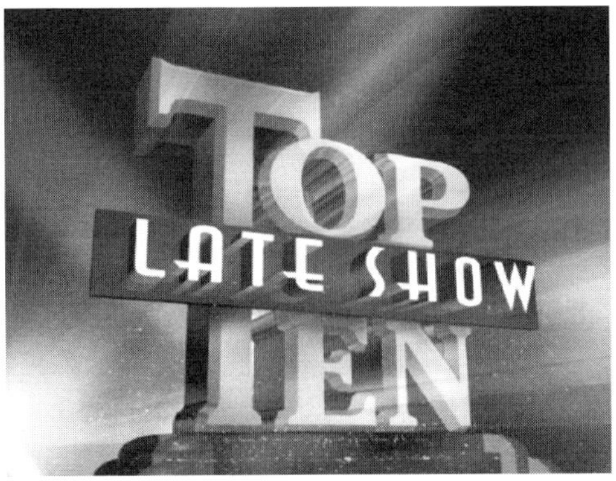

figure |8-8|

The Late Show Top Ten.

going to look good as an animation. If your design skills aren't there, you can't fake it by making it move. It has to look good before it ever moves.

Switch to Digital Television in 2009

My wallet will be thinner because I'll need a better computer and monitor. The new aspect ratio just gives me more room for design. I think text fits better in a rectangle than in a box shape. And I'm happier that the graphics will be sharp and clean, unlike the fuzzy analog image. ◁

▷ Professional Profile ◁

| *Bill Byrne* |

Background

Years as a designer: 5

Education: BA from Richard Stockton College of New Jersey in visual arts photography; MFA from School of Visual Arts in photography

The Draw of Design

I started using After Effects as part of artwork in graduate school. I had been animating Photoshop montages when developing my After Effects skills. People saw my work and said I should move into motion graphics work because I'd get paid for it, and so I tried it and that's how I got that ball rolling.

First Design Job

I didn't do design until college. While I was in grad school I got hired—actually, I was interning—to animate the introduction to a Japanese web television show. It was a five-minute-long weekly documentary. And then I ended up getting hired. This was in 1999—I was using After Effects version 4.0. So I got hired by that company and worked there from 1999 to 2002. It was streaming media to the Internet for Japanese businessmen to watch reports on Palm Pilots. It was a lot of technology and news websites. I was shooting, editing, and doing motion graphics for these little documentaries.

First Broadcast Design Job

I had just been hired at PS260. On my interview I had spoken about my work on After Effects, so they asked me to animate a logo based on a drawing. It was a flower growing inside of a house, and the commercial was for a company that helps people get loans to buy a house, Neighborhoods in Bloom.

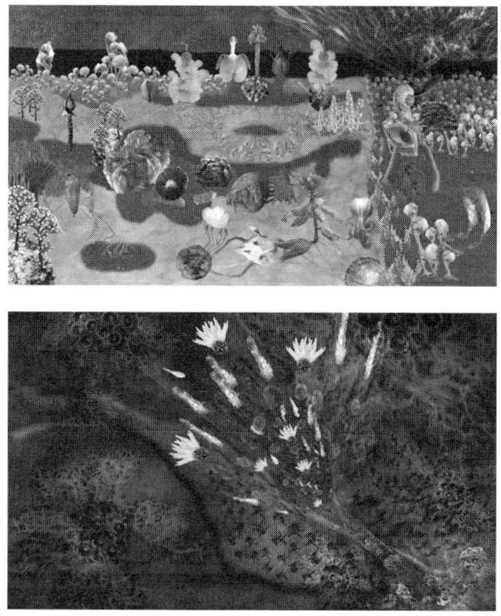

By Bill Byrne

figure |8-9|

Digital artworks.

Design Process

Designing for a Client

The way that I've worked those jobs, most of the time you either get a script or storyboard that describes what they are looking for. I always do their version first. I pretty much build what's on the paper, and then that's usually just a springboard for me to introduce my own ideas. I've had a very good success rate, but you have to feel your clients out, and you have to see how much of a collaborator they want. Some people want you to be very engaged. They want you to feel like an audience member. And others want an After Effects monkey, and that's fine, too.

I much prefer to be inspired by the material I'm working on and to feel comfortable collaborating. I much prefer that situation to being sort of a robot, but at the same time, I do feel those jobs where I'm being a robot I'm still informing the process, and I'm still learning. Every editor and designer has felt that, and they have varying amounts of freedom on a project. The bottom line is you are getting paid for a service, so if they want you to execute a script, then that's what I'll do if that's needed.

Long-Distance Collaboration

I worked on a Skittles commercial in the early stages. I sat with the client and my friend Bryan Wetzel, who was editing it. The client was describing to me how the fish were flying around. He had cartoon fish that he drew that he wanted me to animate in After Effects. When we were done, we sent the commercial to a third-party company in L.A. They took the After Effects fish that the client had done with me, and they then animated the real fish. So I've done stuff like that. But I'm usually working on the final product.

Designing for an Audience

There's a couple things that come up. One thing is will they understand the meaning behind what we're doing? That's the big issue. When you're just throwing type around, it doesn't have the same meaning as if it's not moving. You're trying to build a little world with motion graphics, and it's a whole little world where things are happening. So you have to ask, will the audience understand the definition of what we're doing? And that's

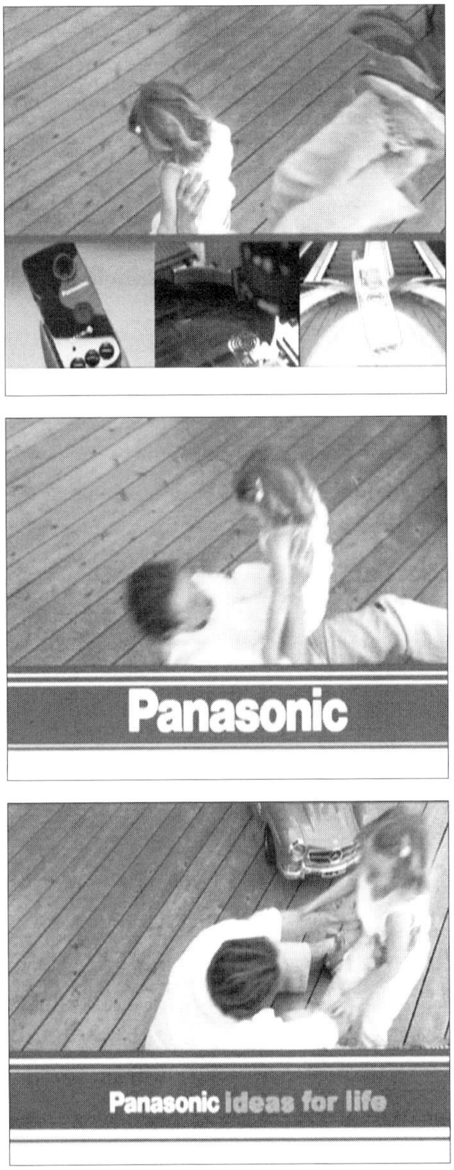

Courtesy Ocean Group, graphics by Bill Byrne

figure |8-10|

Panasonic commercial.

the distinction between plopping down effects that look cool and making something that's actually meaningful.

The graphics you make can be memorable—more than just another lens flare. One thing that definitely helps make it meaningful is also part of the editor's process, which is sitting back and watching it as an audience. Stepping back. Even if I just make a DVD or tape of something and watch it on a different screen, I catch different things. Walter Murch talks about this in his book *In the Blink of an Eye*. He has to turn around to see the monitor to watch his edit play back, so he is reminded to watch the work as an audience. I took his advice, and I apply it to motion graphics. I think in some cases, it's more important to watch it in the role of an audience member, because when you're creating something in motion graphics, it's more abstract.

Convincing a Client Something Doesn't Work

The first thing I would do is just make the argument of why it doesn't work. I pretend to be playing devil's advocate. If I can convince them the design's not working, then it's great. But if I can't, it really depends on who the client is and whether I can present the argument. You don't want them to walk and work with someone else. But you want to trust your instincts, and if you feel something is not right, you have to see how much you can get away with, with that client. There's been a few things I've worked on that have elements that I don't feel are the right decisions. But that's one of the reasons there's a hierarchy, and there's a director. You pick your battles, and if you don't win this one, that's part of being a collaborator. And frankly, I've been wrong a few times.

Challenges of Broadcast Design

Time is always a factor because you can never get anything done fast enough. Another issue—especially with commercials when you are designing a motion graphic with a commercial—is that there is a list of things that the motion graphic has to say. And then you've got a time frame in which to fit it. What's happened to me is that the edit and the motion graphic are happening simultaneously, so the window is shrinking and growing. The commercial has to be exactly thirty seconds to the frame, so while I'm working, I'm thinking about time and space. It's like a donut and the hole to fit the graphics in is shrinking and expanding. This is the case when I am doing the motion graphics and someone else is editing.

I've been an editor and a motion graphics designer. It's easier when I do both because I'll have simultaneous set-up in both programs. It's easier to integrate with the technology, and I can work on the graphics and edit a little more simultaneously.

His Fine Arts Background and Signature Style

I think that's where you get the style that is "Bill Byrne." It's very organic. I always think of ways in which I can fight the computer to get things to look more organic. I don't like motion graphics that look too cold or robotic or stiff. I always try to make my graphics life-like. I think that that's a more interesting direction to go because the materials lend themselves to being more robotic. With the installations that I've done when I was working on artwork that was machine parts, I always looked for ways to make it look like it was growing or floating. I am always trying to make something look life-like that by its nature isn't. I know the computer can get me what I want. I just have to figure out how to get it done. I love machines and gadgets; it's just a matter of what I think is interesting.

For clients, one thing that I do when I start a job is I look at what the rule system is for what's happening in the graphic. Are there solid walls? Ground? Are things floating or flying? Is the background always this particular color? And then I make my own rules of physics for each scene depending on how much it's needed. What is this thing's function?

Future of Motion Graphics

I feel like the jobs of the motion graphics designer and editor are becoming the same job. Everything is so graphics heavy that you're basically editing and designing graphics at the same time. Movies like *Ice Age* and *Lord of the Rings* you can't edit without the graphics. It's the same thing with music videos, between designing the graphics and moving them around and then building scenes. The growing trend is that the editor and motion graphics designer are becoming the same job.

Most commercials have moving typography and graphics at the same time as footage. On commercial music videos or something like that, the graphics are so heavily integrated into the editing that it's very hard to distinguish that they're two separate jobs. This change has a lot to do with the fact that the software is easier, more affordable, and it's faster.

Even if you go out looking for jobs as an editor, they almost assume that you know how to edit and ask, "What else can you do? How good are you at After Effects and burning DVDs?" It's almost a shame because being a good editor is getting lost in a lot of ways.

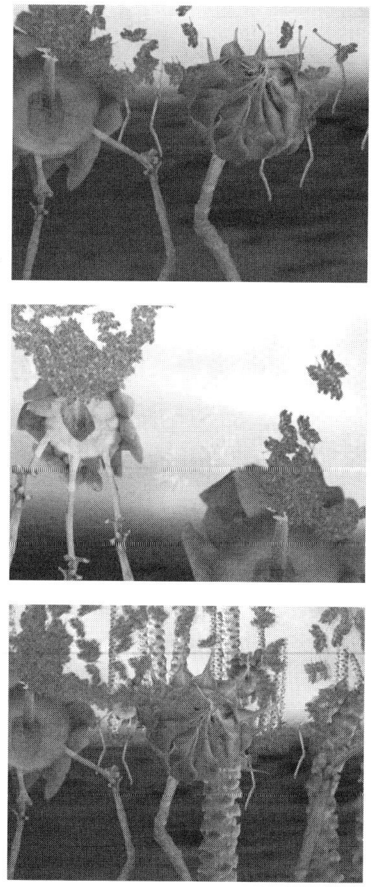

All About House Plants written by Amy Fasseman/Michael Hearst/Joshua Camp; Published by One Ring Zero Publishing (BMI); Performed by One Ring Zero, ©2004 Urban Geek Records; Used by Permission

figure |8-11|

Music video for *All About House Plants* reflects Byrne's fine arts background and appreciation for organic elements in his designs.

An example of this is I just edited, did the graphics, and composed the soundtrack for a commercial. On the commercial end of the business, commercial budgets are smaller and they have old footage they want to re-purpose. I was given footage from an old infomercial with a graphics treatment idea. I edited the old footage and combined it with graphics that I made. I basically took elements from another job to make it a completely new commercial, and I did it all myself. Not too long ago, this would have been the job of four people or more.

MOTION GRAPHICS DESIGN FOR MUSIC VIDEOS

The style of design and editing of music videos offers a great deal of creativity in the application of motion graphics. In music videos the visuals are used to enhance the connection between the song and the audience. The song is developed, written, and performed first, with the graphics developed specifically to help the viewer visualize the lyrics as intended by the musicians. The visuals support the song's theme and tell a story. The rhythm and flow of the graphics should follow not only with the lyrics of the song, but with the beat as well. When there is a transition from one graphic to the next, the transition should generally correspond with an accent in the music. In other words, the rhythm of the graphics should seamlessly mesh with the beat. If the graphics do not flow smoothly with the song, the viewer will be thrown off, unable to get into a rhythm with the song, and therefore not enjoy the experience. Spend time listening and imagining visuals that could accompany what you hear.

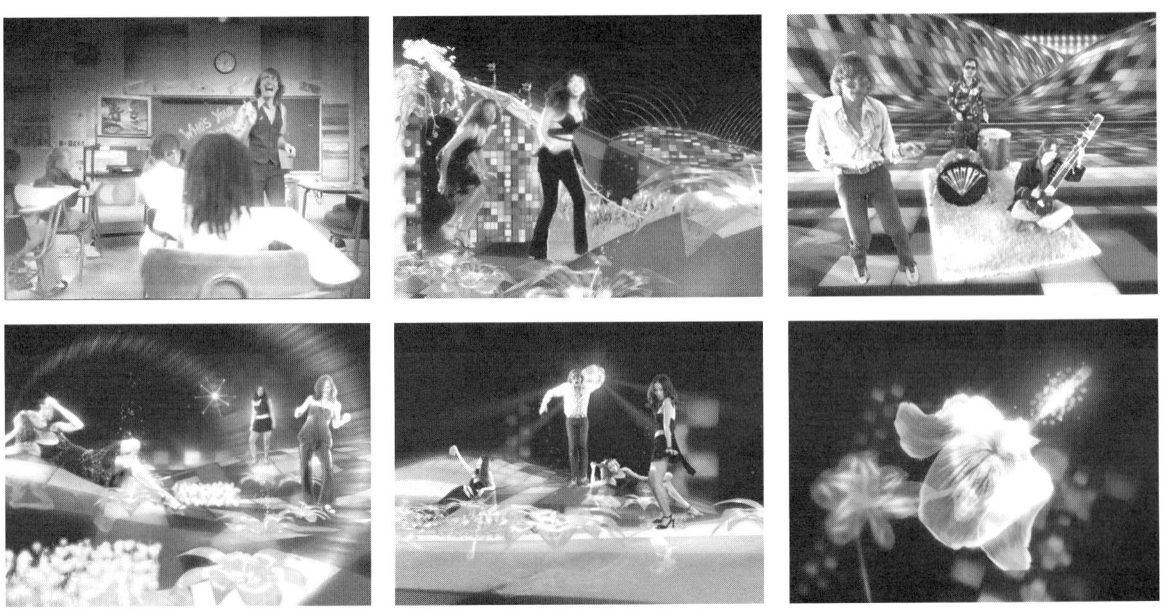

By Joel Lava, Green Towel/Transistor

figure | 8-12 |

Motion graphics used in a music video for *Your Mama* by Kennedy. The motion graphics are used to illustrate a fantasy world and enhance the lyrics of the song.

Another thing in the future is digital paper—paper that can capture video—a flat surface that can capture video. When you can have a flat surface that people can read like a magazine, that's going to change motion graphics to a huge degree.

What Makes a Good Motion Graphics Designer

Obviously being creative, obviously being technical, being patient, and being a collaborator. A little bit of confidence doesn't hurt—apple *s*, apple *z*—being willing to try something and experiment. I've always learned a lot from going into a project I didn't know how to do and figuring it out. One technique that I use—people should do this more often—is doing a Google search for tutorials.

Good Broadcast Design

What makes a good design is the design being appropriate to the material and aesthetically pleasing. If it doesn't look good, it doesn't matter how appropriate. If it looks good but isn't appropriate, then it calls into question content because it's not communicating. You're communicating to your audience just by choosing a font. You're communicating before you worry about the words, and that goes back to "will the audience get what I'm saying?" The look and feel of the design is already communicating before the audience has read any of the words. ◅

SUMMARY

Television first replaced many other forms of entertainment and mass communication during the 1950s; a period often referred to as the Golden Age of Television. Since then television has served audiences by delivering news, talk shows, serial shows, movies, reality shows, how-to shows, and music videos. The role of the motion graphics designer for television is often a challenge in that they must design a sequence that will immediately grab the viewers' attention and keep them tuned to the same television station. To accomplish this, the designer must create a sequence that is entertaining to satisfy the viewer and informational to successfully relay the message.

in review

1. What was the impact of television on society?
2. What makes a strong motion graphics designer for the medium of television?
3. What are the technical considerations for motion graphics design when applied to television?
4. How do motion graphics aid in the selling of a product?

exercises

Exercise

Design a bug and station ID for your favorite television network. The design should be consistent between the two, but your bug will be stationary, while the station ID will be in motion.

Process and Research

Before you begin your design, first determine two important points:

- Who is your client?
- Who is your audience?

Since this is a class assignment, you can model your client after a television network that you watch often. In thinking about the network's image, you should consider the following questions:

- What is the general attitude of the network and how is that reflected in its programming?
- What kind of programming appears on this network?
- Who are the network personalities?
- What does the current station ID look like and how has it evolved from past IDs?
- What were some of the station IDs from the past?
- Does the network have a slugline that you want to work into your ID or bug?

The answers to these questions will not only tell you about your client, but it will also give you a very good sense of the network's audience as well. Whether the network has a wide range of programming, thus targeting a wide audience, or it specializes in one particular type of programming geared to a very specific audience will impact how you proceed with your design.

In addition to the list of questions outlined in Chapter 3 to determine your audience's demographics and lifestyle, here are some additional questions to ask about your audience:

- Is your audience hip? Modern? Conservative? Traditional?
- What is the audience's level of sophistication?
- What attracts your audience to this network?

Conduct some research, both by watching television and by searching Internet websites to view current competitors' logos, as well as past logos for your network. There are sites that give a very comprehensive history with video and pictures of station logos, bugs, and on-air promotions for most long-running network and cable channels.

The Internet or trade magazines such as *Daily Variety* and *The Hollywood Reporter*, as well as your local paper, can give you information regarding the network's ratings. These are also good sources for learning the demographics of your network. One final thing to consider before you begin to design is that some networks use different logos for different times of the day to reflect their diverse audience. This may be something you would like to try. Whatever you decide, you must be specific about the audience you will target with your ID and bug. If you choose to target a specific niche, then your design should reflect the characteristics that appeal to that niche. If you decide to appeal to a wider audience, then your design should have universal appeal that will offend few and attract many. Use your knowledge of the audience to guide you in your design choices, while staying within the network's current branding campaign.

Inspiration

The current station's logo should serve as a guide to your design, whether you decide to update and modernize it or to try something entirely new. It is, after all, how the network has chosen to represent itself. Naturally, the elements of the current design will factor into your choices of color and type, particularly if you decide to work with the current logo.

Another visual element to consider with the station ID is the kind of background you want. Do you want it to be solid, or do you think it would stand out more against an image? And if you decide to use an image, would it be a still or moving one?

Finally, when thinking about making the elements of your ID move, you will want to think carefully about audio and how it will accompany the movement. Would you use your network's theme song, if it has one, or would you introduce new music to the mix? These are all things to think about as you continue to sketch out your ideas.

The choices you make for your station ID will help with the design of the station bug, since there should be consistency with the branding. Because the station bug is placed at the bottom of the screen during a show in progress, your design will have to take into account the fact that the background will always be moving and changing. So how will you optimize the image to stand out?

Once you have answered all of the relevant design questions, you can continue to make rough sketches of your ideas.

Method

1. Do a rough pencil sketch of your station ID and bug, making sure to block out the type and the movement. Each time you introduce a new graphic, add a new frame to your storyboards. And each time your logo or an element of your logo changes places, you must draw a new frame of your board. Remember to think about composition and rhythm as well.

2. When you are satisfied with your pencil sketch, do more complete digital storyboards in color. Use either Photoshop or Illustrator, depending on whether you want to use raster- or vector-based graphics. Be sure to storyboard the entire station ID sequence.

3. Create a mock-up for your bug, which is stationary. You will want to make sure that the colors allow it to stand out from the constantly changing background but also allow for play in grayscale.

4. When you are satisfied with your storyboards, you can execute your station ID and bug in After Effects. As you put your ID together, allow your audio to guide the pacing.

5. Color correct your work, setting it to the color bars of a video monitor, rather than the computer monitor, since the colors on the computer screen may not be true to the NTSC colors.

6. Print your work to tape.

7. Watch the final tape on a television monitor. Do you think it is ready to air?

Show your work to an audience. What is your audience's impression? Can they see these logos actually playing on your favorite network? Compare and contrast your logo to the network's current logo. How is yours as good? Where does yours need improvement? What have you learned from completing this process?

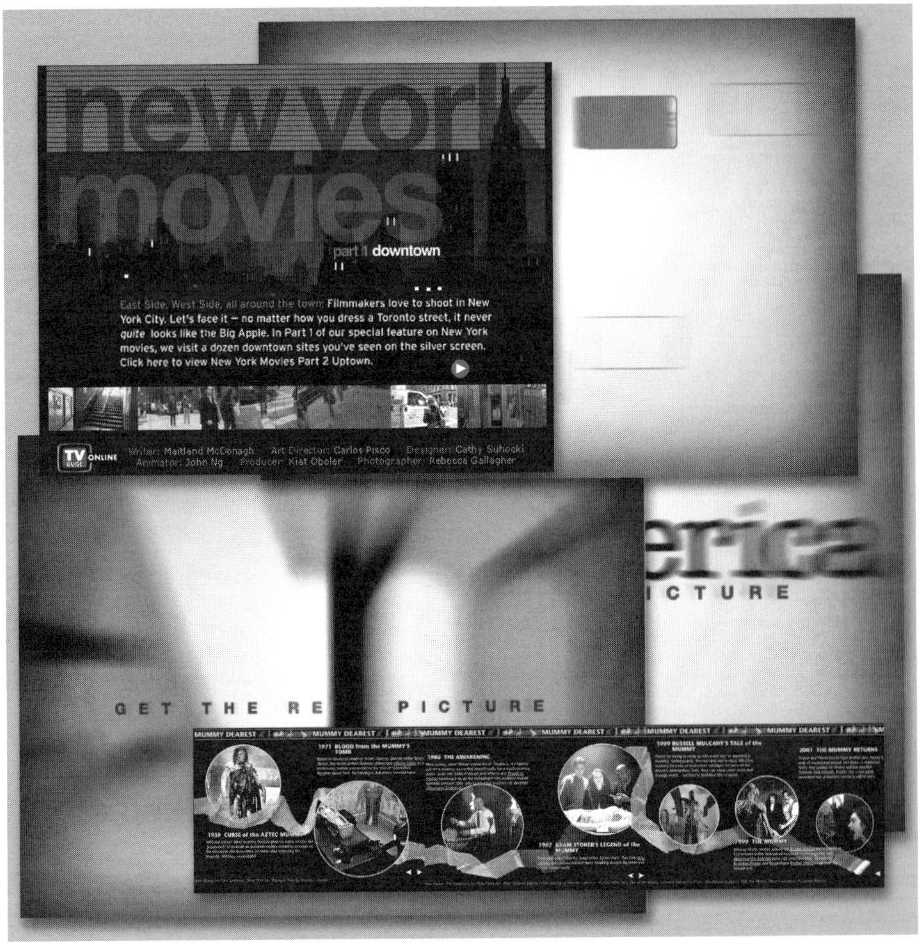
new york
movies
part 1 downtown
East Side, West Side, all around the town: Filmmakers love to shoot in New York City. Let's face it — no matter how you dress a Toronto street, it never *quite* looks like the Big Apple. In Part 1 of our special feature on New York movies, we visit a dozen downtown sites you've seen on the silver screen. Click here to view New York Movies Part 2 Uptown.
TV GUIDE ONLINE
Writer: Maitland McDonagh Art Director: Carlos Pisco Designer: Cathy Suhocki
Animator: John Ng Producer: Kiat Oboler Photographer: Rebecca Gallagher
GET THE RE PICTURE
ICTURE
MUMMY DEAREST

CHAPTER

9

1957 Funding for ARPA approved

1969 ARPANET established

1972 First e-mail sent via ARPANET

1973 Term *Internet* is coined

1989 Development of the web starts

1993 First browser, Mosaic, released

1993 52 registered web servers

1994 829 registered web servers

1994 World Wide Web Consortium

1995 First TV program debuts via web

1996 Set-top boxes debut

1999 Napster debuts MP3 file sharing

Chapter Objectives

Learn the history of the World Wide Web

Recognize the impact of the World Wide Web on society

Learn how motion graphics are used on the World Wide Web

Understand the technical and audience considerations that are applied to design for the World Wide Web

Introduction

The Internet has forever changed the way we interact within society. We have instant access to information from around the globe, we can regularly communicate with anyone around the world in real time, and we can readily download music, movies, or other types of entertainment in our homes. The Internet has changed how we interact with colleagues, friends, and family. We also do not have to engage with people in the same way; we can remain anonymous or housebound. We can do just about everything on the Internet from home, such as working, grocery shopping, and chatting with friends.

We are eager to use the Internet to the full extent of its capabilities, including e-mail, research, and entertainment. This opens up a wonderful opportunity for designers to experiment with the medium and push the boundaries, adding new means of user interaction in both function and form.

BEGINNINGS OF THE WORLD WIDE WEB

The Internet was conceived by a group of scientists. They wanted a way to quickly and easily share their scientific findings with each other. Funding for the Advanced Research Projects Agency (ARPA) was approved by President Eisenhower in 1957. In 1969 the ARPANET was developed and established by the United States Department of

Defense. It was a closed system and unavailable to the general public. At this time, the home computer had not yet entered people's lives.

For two decades not much advancement was made to the network. Then in 1989 Tim Brenners-Lee proposed the development of an open network—a place for the general public to converse, share ideas, and communicate. He presented his vision of the World Wide Web at a conference, and he foresaw the vast power and potential of such a network. That same year the World Wide Web was opened to commercial traffic. With the dawning of this new network, the world began to change—slowly at first. The web was not as user-friendly as it is today. To use it you had to understand computers, which had only become common in American households a few years earlier, and you had to understand some of the background processes of how the Internet worked. In order to navigate through the network, you had to understand how to find the page and type in the proper pathway.

ADDING GRAPHICS AND MOTION

The World Wide Web contained very limited features and minimal design when it was first introduced. Creating a website was very taxing and often visually unrewarding. In the beginning there were no graphics, no pictures, and certainly no animation. There was a time when the only way to view a picture through a website was to download it to your hard drive, then open it. In 1993 Marc Andreessen, at the National Center for Supercomputing Applications, released the first browser, called Mosaic. Over time other technologies developed, and the ability to add more graphics to webpages along with basic animation became a reality.

Animation came to the Internet in the form of an animated .gif file, which allowed the designer to create a graphic with a transparent background and add motion with a frame-by-frame animation technique. Image mapping, the process of invisibly breaking down a picture or graphic into clickable hotspots, was added to the web arsenal around the same time. The ability to add image maps and fully integrate graphics and photographs into the overall design of the site took the web to new levels and excited users around the world. Now not only is there full design control, but you can access the web from almost anywhere from any number of devices.

We use the web for information, communication, and entertainment. Motion graphics have become an expected and welcome element of the medium. We access the web from computers, cell phones, and PDAs. In each instance the design and content layout needs to fit the specific needs of the device and meet the expectations of the user.

USES OF MOTION GRAPHICS ON THE WEB

With the development of scripting languages such as JavaScript, designers started to explore new methods of adding motion to the page. One of the simplest examples of early motion graphics on the web is rollovers. A rollover, by definition, works when the user moves the cursor over a button or graphic, which causes a computer reaction. The original image may be swapped for another, or the illusion of a very basic animation is created—the button text or button shape may change. The button or graphic becomes an interactive element, not just static information.

As web software and browser capabilities and connection speeds improved, it was possible to develop more complex animations for use with buttons, banner ads, splash pages, or simply integrated into the page as part of the overall design. Once designers had been reluctant to populate the webpage with too many images because of slow download times; now they were adding more complex composited and moving images.

With the introduction of Macromedia Flash the art of motion graphics for the web came into its own. Flash allowed designers to create advanced animations with small file sizes that carried a short download time. Designers were excited about the greatly expanded possibilities for animation and the control they now had. Flash gave web designers the freedom to choose from a longer list of typefaces and much more control over how the design was laid out on the webpage. They could add sound and motion by using keyframes and more advanced, interactive navigation menus. This new application of motion graphics to a relatively young medium opened up the doors for a vast amount of experimentation and allowed designers to take new liberties in what had once been a very static medium.

The web has become an extension of just about every industry and as a result has grown in its sophistication. Businesses use websites to provide information to their clients, while also providing an alternative form of communication. Retailers use websites to sell their products outside of their brick-and-mortar stores, and publications use websites as supplements to highlight features in their print versions and attempt to drive up subscription sales. Websites also make for wonderful educational tools and are used as a supplement to material taught in the classroom, or are used to teach online courses, again outside of the brick-and-mortar education system.

Websites are also used toward less tangible goals in the world of entertainment. They act as interactive advertisements for films, musicians, and television networks. A website designed for publicity purposes serves an array of functions, some of which will provide revenue, such as the sales of CDs, DVDs, or downloads of songs or television shows, or to act as a draw to attend a performance, screening, or tune in for the next television airing. When websites are used in this capacity, they provide additional information about the movie, show, or project by including trivia games, interactive games, live chats with the stars, biographies, fun facts, and much more, all of which is designed to build the audience's interest.

In recent years, even the layperson has found a voice on the Internet. With the proliferation of personal websites, chat boards, and blogs, there is no shortage of content on the Internet, whether it is a site dedicated to finding the perfect mate, planning a wedding, or selecting rare wines. The abundance of information available on the web, therefore, makes it that much more imperative for website designers to create motion graphics that stand out and help a site to compete.

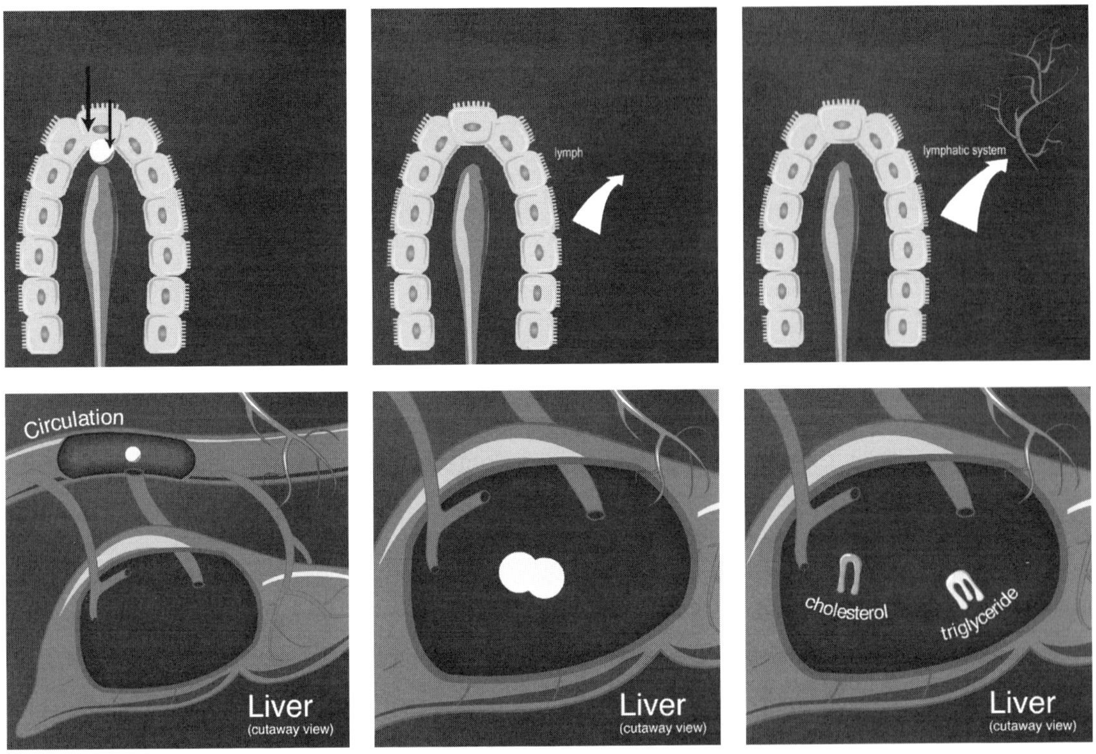

By Sharon Gorman, Production Director; Kevin Mackett, Project Lead and Lead Programmer; Clint Forrester, Lead Designer and Animator; Jason Robinson, Programmer; Ben Kirby, Assistant Art Designer; Thomas Lon Owen, Ph.D., Content Expert/Instructional Designer/Narrator, Professor of Biological Sciences, Northern Arizona University

figure |9-1|

Motion graphics are a wonderful tool for educational instruction as seen in this example: Bio 320 Lipoprotein Transport interactive learning module.

One challenge a designer faces is how to provide a large amount of information in a way that is both captivating and easily digestible to a particular audience. This means breaking the information into logical chunks while also making sure to choose fonts that both complement the overall style of the website and are easy for the audience to read.

Usability is another key issue of design. The website must be easy for the viewer to use, and the navigation from one page to the next must make sense, be easy to understand, and be consistent. If it is difficult for a viewer to find information or to move from one page to the next, then the design is not successful. An e-commerce website, for example, must have clear links from products to their descriptions and prices. If this information is not easily accessible, the shopper may search for a new e-commerce website that sells the same product but is easier to use. Usability is also tied in to the overall design of the website. Not only should it function easily, but there should be an overarching aesthetic that ties all of the pages and navigational buttons together. The navigation system needs to be consistent. The buttons should be labeled the same on each page, act the same on each page, be located in the same place on each page, and always link to where they are supposed to. The overall plan, after all, is for each page to work well as part of a greater functioning whole.

The role of the designer is to create a website that is both functional and engaging. Even professionals face obstacles created by technology and client demands. Expectations differ according to clients and their audiences. The ability to meet these expectations stems from experience and the ability to work well with a design team.

Successful designers overcome challenges presented by technology and client needs by relying on their sound understanding of design along with their freedom to try new things.

| THE ELDERLY AND THE INTERNET |

A 2003 study showed that higher percentages of the elderly use the Internet than teenagers, due to their tendency to use it for e-mailing and receiving photographs from family members. A series of interviews with a random sampling of elderly members showed that many used the Internet for getting news and health information from Yahoo!, as well as from some newspaper and news channel websites. Some enjoy shopping, and some go beyond getting news to getting more information about their special interests. At the end of the study, the researchers concluded that the elderly were not prone to web surfing, but were more interested in sites with which they were already familiar. Moreover, because many of them watched TV or subscribed to newspapers already, the best way for media sites to draw them in as users was through easier navigation.

SOURCE: Michael L. Hilt and Jeremy Lipschultz, "Elderly Americans and the Internet: E- mail, TV News, Information, and Entertainment Websites," *Educational Gerontology* (2004).

▷ Professional Profile ◁

| *Carlos Pisco* |

Background

Years as a designer: 12

Education: Degree in civil engineering with classes in fine arts and computer science

The Draw of Design

Graphic design was a natural combination of my studies in engineering, fine arts, and computer science. Civil engineering focuses on the physical layout of structures, or on designing something, and combining that with computer science and fine arts naturally led to graphic design. For the web, people have to have a lot of sense of architecture—information architecture. A solid experience in information architecture is more important for online than print design.

What drew me into design is I really have a great passion for photography and typography. I am constantly paying attention to type on subways and in magazine ads, because the type plays a strong role in the way the message is communicated. Every designer I talk to is a little obsessed with type.

First Design Before Becoming a Professional

I designed bottle labels as an art project. When I moved to New York I was very aware of the obsession with the body, especially in the gay culture. So I did a series of "power juicy labels" for an art project. I had a gallery show during the Gay Games in 1994. It was a series of almost 150 bottles with different labels. The titles were things like "E-Z Growth," "No Pain, No Gain," and things like that.

First Design Job

I did business reports for Exxon. They were so boring. There was no image. They were typed on that old computer paper with green and white stripes. I did that for four years in Brazil along with online systems. I was designing for online but it was only text driven. It was before people were using laptops. This was at least ten years before people started using the web.

Design Process

Collaboration with *TV Guide*

In terms of edit and art, there are about twelve people—a small team. I have a designer and three photo editors; one of them also helps with the design. We produce a couple of special features a month, and we update content and photographs daily. The layouts, however, do not change daily. We update about 300 photos weekly, so we do a lot of photo research.

Basically, I usually present the editors and senior staff with a couple of design options, and we discuss the possibilities. Being part of the team for eight years gives me a good sense of what works and what doesn't for us.

| PHOTO ACQUISITION FOR WEBSITES |

Photo research and photo editing is an important job in design. It is imperative to choose pictures that enhance the other elements in the design and support the message. There are many ways to obtain pictures; you could take them yourself if you are confident in your abilities, you could hire a photographer, or you could buy them from a stock photo agency. Stock photo agencies offer two general categories of photographs to purchase: royalty free and licensed. Royalty-free photographs are generally less expensive because the photographer will not receive any compensation for their usage. They are also generally less interesting and very generic. Licensed photographs, on the other hand, can be very pricey because you are not only paying the stock photo agency but also paying a royalty fee to the photographer. Tvguide.com uses a great deal of licensed photographs of celebrities and classic movie stills.

I also have a very strong sense of content, so when someone gives me a headline or copy to work with, if the type doesn't work for me I have a very hard time. I'd rather cut my hand off than use three exclamation points at the end of a sentence. When I get a bad headline, I go back and talk to the editor. I suggest, "Maybe you can say this in a different way just to add more punch or be more direct." Visually, you have to get the real message across. The challenge designers face is to have a strong grasp of the content and how to convey that visually.

Collaborating with Clients on Freelance Work

New clients need to see more versions of the design, and they need to see more options. The challenge is that I have to be more creative. I need to spend time to understand their needs and to see what the competition is doing. I ask them questions—what do they like and what do they dislike about the competition. If they tell me up front, "We don't like the look," then I'm not even going to go that route.

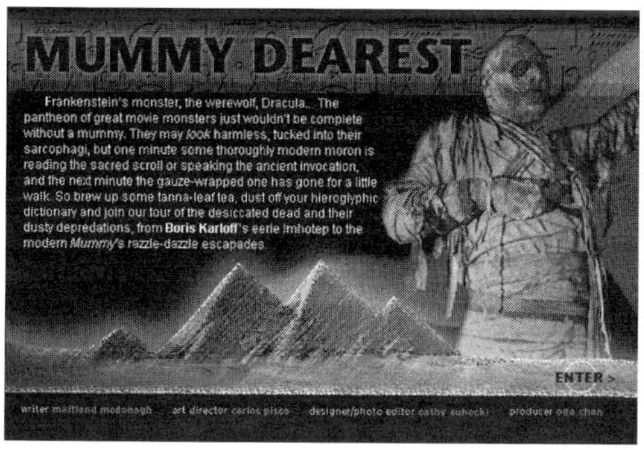

Audience Considerations for Design

These days we try to put a strong emphasis on photos because we know people love to click on photos. So I try to keep the design very low-key so that the design doesn't overwhelm the photos. Another approach we have here, especially on the home page, is

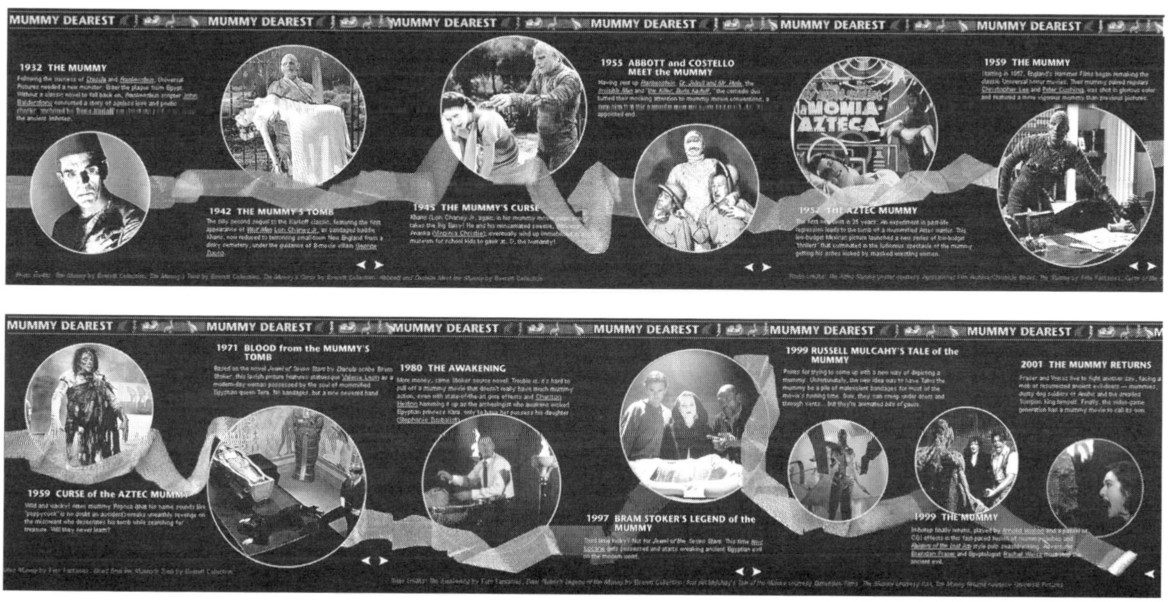

Courtesy tvguide.com

figure |9-2|

Mummy Dearest.

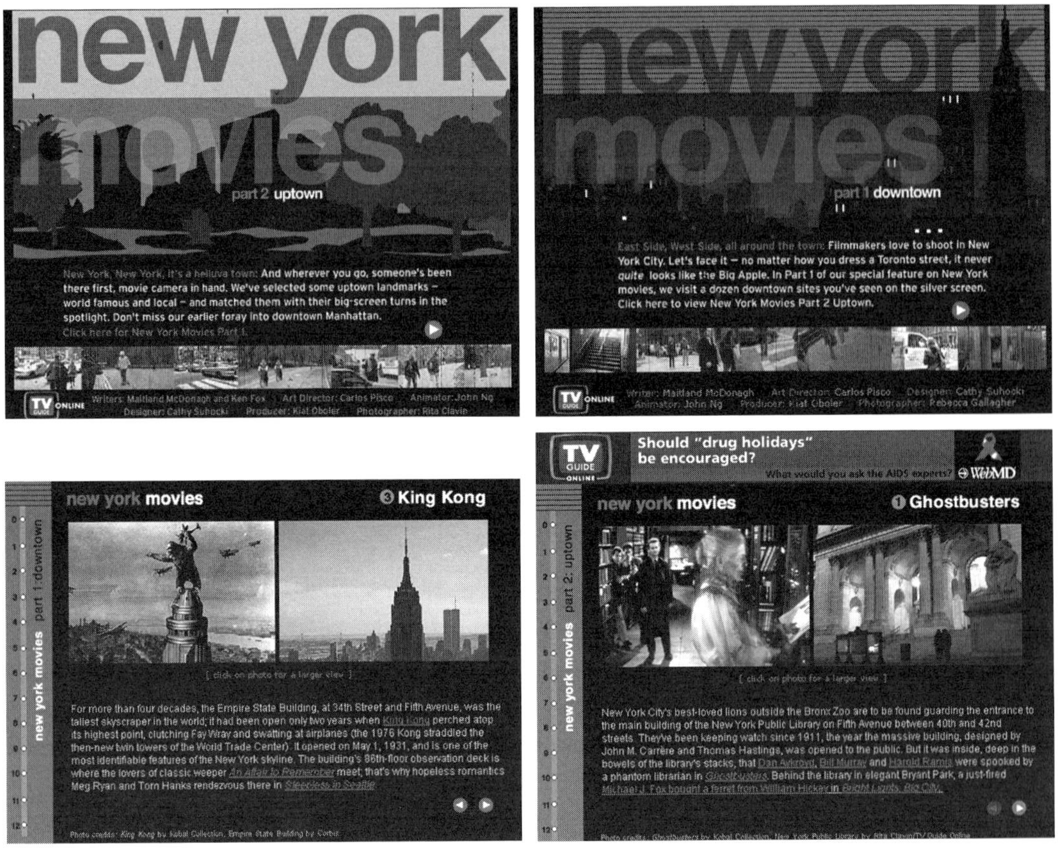

Courtesy tvguide.com

figure |9-3|

"New York Movies" lines the bottom of the screen with photographs on the splash pages and enlarges the photos on the interior pages.

not to put too much content, because if you put too much content on a page, then the viewer doesn't know where to begin. It's basically to keep the pages uncluttered with an emphasis on photos.

Also, having a lot of photos on the website makes people stick to the website. Stickiness, which represents the time people spend on the website, is a very good way to measure the success of a website. We are trying to find a way to make the site be found by search engines like Yahoo! and Google, so we keep those things in mind when designing the website. For example, we have to make headlines more prominent in terms of placement. Each page has one catch point to trigger search engines to find our page and bring new users to the site.

What Makes a Strong Web Design

At one point during the early days on the web, designers would spend lots of time on animations and flashy intros, but they found that most people are not interested in spending time on the fluff before going to the site. We are cutting down on flashy intros. We want information to get to the viewer as soon as possible, so we don't lose him. People have a very short attention span when it comes to the web. If they don't get what they're looking for, they will go somewhere else.

One of the goals in our designs is to avoid information overload. The first way to accomplish this is to think of how many pages do I have to break the content into to make it more enjoyable? If I have a list of fifty movies, instead of putting fifty on one page, maybe it's better to break it into two or three pages—grouping and dividing the information in a way that makes sense.

We also have to think about, in terms of user experience, readability of the page. Sometimes people use Flash. The fact that type in Flash is not as sharp as type in HTML might have a negative impact on the user experience. If it's a lot of text, nobody wants to read a lot of blurry text. We also have to decide that if there is a possibility that the user might want to print the page, then we need to create a printer-friendly version of the page.

It's also important to make sure that within a certain website, the navigation remains consistent from one page to the next and that the labeling is consistent. If a viewer clicks on a button that says "Movie Reviews," then he must be taken to a page that is very clearly marked "Movie Review."

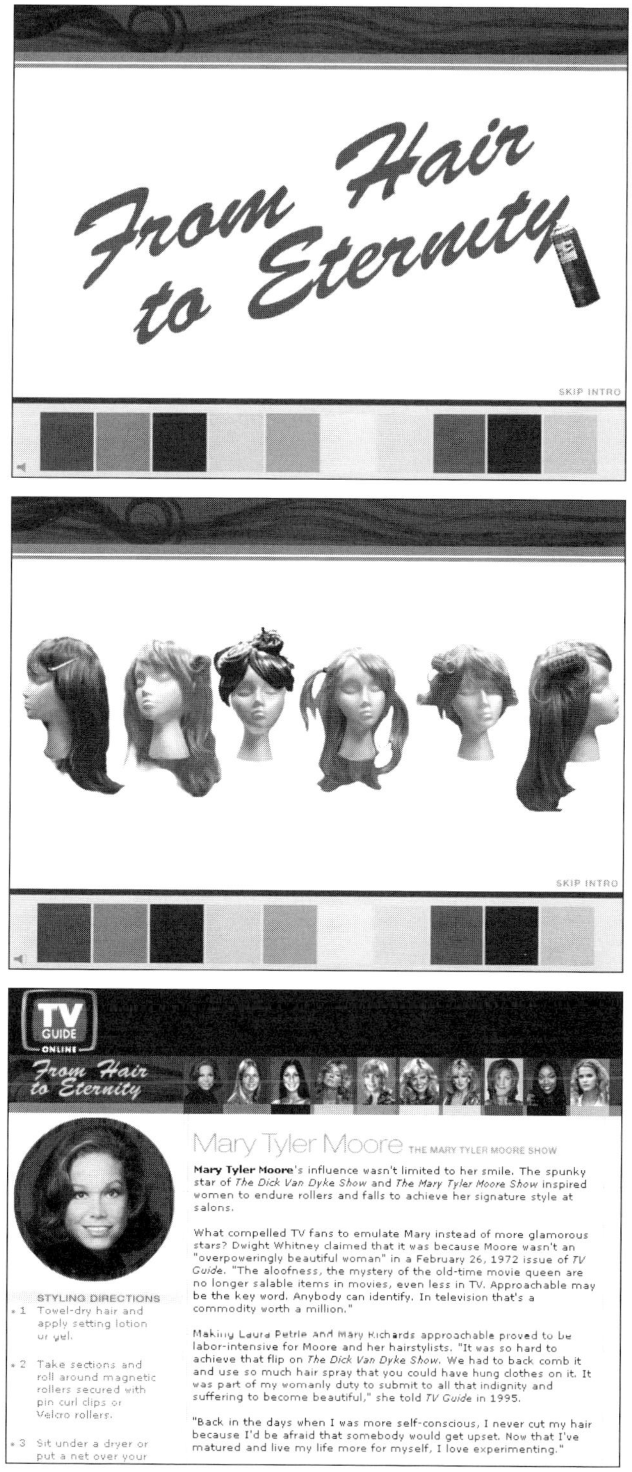

Courtesy tvguide.com

figure 9-4

From "Hair to Eternity" successfully incorporates large chunks of type into the design.

THE UNITY OF MULTI-PAGE WEBSITE

Although each page in this example from tvguide.com looks different and does not appear to follow the rule of consistent usability and design, certain visual elements are used throughout that tie the pages together, and each page serves a different purpose. The first page in "What Were They Thinking" is part of the animated introduction and effectively serves as the title sequence for the web feature. The second page acts as the introduction and explains the premise of the feature to the viewer. The third page is the meat and potatoes of the feature and offers photographs and text to complement background information on each television show highlighted in the feature.

Even though each page serves a very different purpose, the visual elements tie them all together and underlie clear site usability. The logo for "What Were They Thinking?" uses consistent type style and color, so although it is placed in a different place on each page, the visuals remain consistent, therefore allowing viewers to remain confident that they are still looking at the same special feature on the website. Colors and graphic shapes are also used repeatedly. A warm, analogous color scheme is employed in the design. The rectangular color shapes, which mimic the shape of a television screen, are used as the main graphic element on the opening page, and as a supportive graphic element, but in the same arrangement, on the second page. On the third page, each rectangle is used separately, as a button element for the navigation on the left side of the page. This is a creative application of design elements, successfully used, that provides good usability.

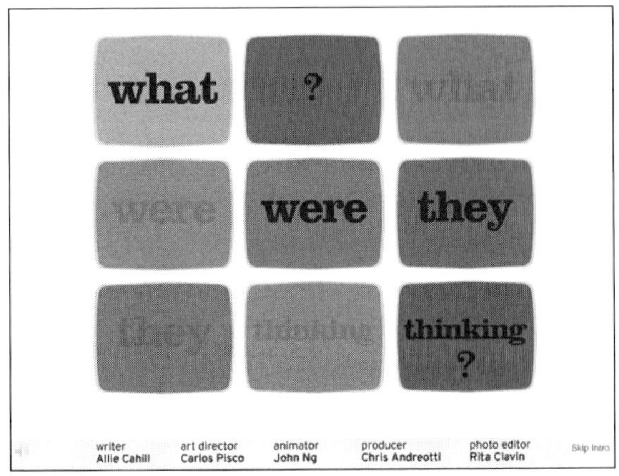

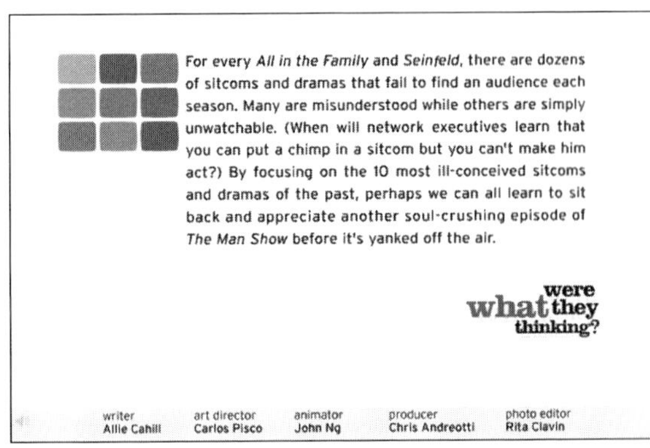

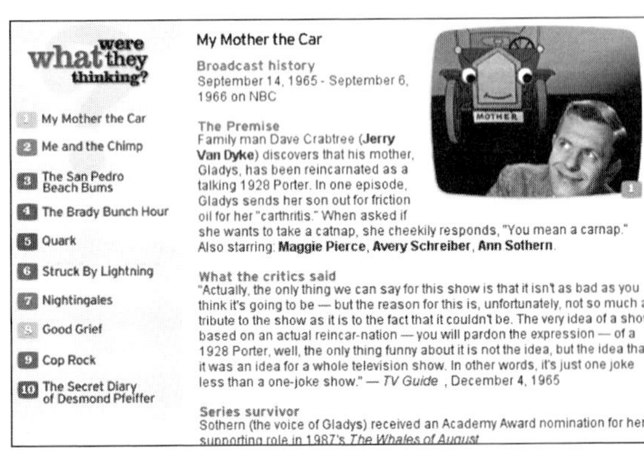

Courtesy tvguide.com

figure |9-5|

"What Were They Thinking?"

Challenge of Web Design

One of the biggest problems that I face everyday is that my content is constantly competing with ads. The bulk of content is only 60 percent of the real estate, and the rest of it is ads. In order to strike a visual balance between the ads and the content, I tend to keep the content layouts simple. I cannot make my content try to compete with the ads because it would turn the site into a circus and scare people away. Less is sometimes better to make the reader stay focused on the content.

| NOTE |

Content real estate refers to how much space you have for pictures, text, navigation, logos, and so on.

Signature Design

When people talk about my work, they say it's a very clean, elegant design. I avoid the use of 3-D graphics, buttons that look like 3-D video game spheres. I avoid that because the web medium is in a flat surface, so I don't think it's necessary to use those tricks—drop shadows and 3-D graphics—to grab people's attention. Just keep it simple.

The Future of Web Design

A lot of content will be built in a programmatic way. When people design for a magazine, they know their word count. Web is more flexible. Design that can expand and grow with less text or more text, or with fewer images, will be the future. ◀

▷ Professional Profile ◁

| Carlos Lema |

Background

Years as a Designer

About 15 years at it. I started professionally at *Entertainment Weekly* magazine. For six and a half years I got the chance to work on all sorts of design projects, from photo retouching to marketing collateral—that is when my love affair with advertising began. I started working for Young and Rubicam, one of the most recognized ad agencies worldwide. I worked with the best in the industry, so inevitably my strategic and creative skill sets sharpened. With my itching desire to learn, I turned my eyes to the web, which at the time was totally dismissed by the big players. I recognized the potential that an online medium offered to the marketing mix, so I started freelancing for several agencies, including Elipze, Atmosphere BBDO, and Agency.com.

| TIP |

Many motion graphics designers will create an animated logo that is representative of their design style.

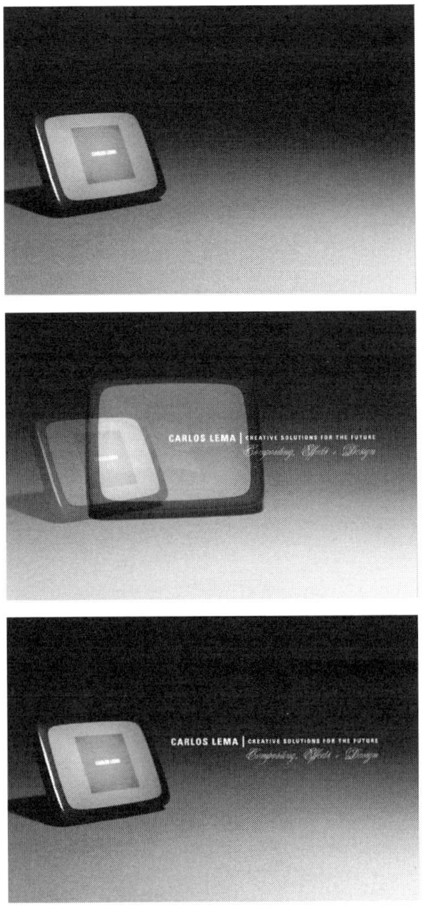

By Carlos Lema

figure |9-6|

Motion graphic used to illustrate personal design style.

Education

Electrical Engineering, Harmony and Music Composition—a strange combination that still makes perfect sense to me. When I was designing my own amps to play in a band, I was fooling around with fonts, colors, and textures—I figured that I can change people's perception about a product. Music in itself was the catalyst to graphic design. While I was working with synthesizers, samplers, and sequencers, it forced me to look at computers more closely. At the time, the coolest and most affordable computer was the Atari ST 1040. After a while I said to myself, well what else can this computer do for me? 512 colors was the most impressive painting palette, and Type 1 fonts were nonexistent, nonetheless it was a huge canvas to play with, literally. 3-D applications were extremely limited and rudimentary. Apple just came out with their flagship computer, the SE and their WYSIWYG promise, which later revolutionized the whole design industry. Photoshop 1.0 fit on a single floppy disk, Illustrator 88's vector design was a new concept, and Motion Works certainly was a foreign tool kit.

Design Process

Importance of Language in Design

I believe there are two schools of thought when it comes to design—design for art's sake and design with purpose. Fortunately or unfortunately, I never went to design school; nevertheless, I learned about designs that sell a product or a

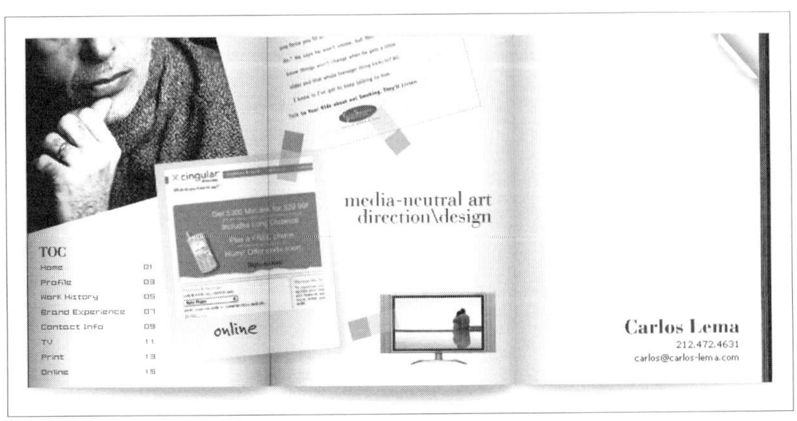

By Carlos Lema

figure |9-7|

Portfolio website designed for both art and with the purpose of attracting new clients.

service. In terms of a language, it all depends on the strategy and the message, which are translated into designs that work across the board.

Audience Considerations for Design

Age group, gender, psychographics, demographics, and marketing touch points. From a media placement perspective, one has to be aware of how to leverage the media surroundings so that the message is well received. If you're talking about TV, what type of programming, channel, how many times per day the spot will be played? On the web, you must take into account whether it is niche-specific or general audience-driven. How many times is the same banner presented to the same person, using in place or over the page technologies? All of this has an impact on how the message is perceived. Sometimes I might have a company's ad that goes to one particular segment and another ad that goes to another segment. I have to be thinking about what is going to resonate with people in order for them to have a positive response.

Getting Inside the Audience's Head

I do a lot of research and it all depends upon the product or service the brand has to offer. Consumers are shrewd and well informed. They recognize their buying power and their power to bring a global company to its knees.

Inspiration for Attacking Design

The first thing I look for is an appropriate image or a sequence or texture that conveys the emotion that I want to project. For example, I wouldn't use a sports director to do a make-up commercial, unless I am trying to launch a new line of sports make-up. I look everywhere for inspiration—magazines, TV spots, even radio. I have a library of elements that inspires me. When the time comes, I look over the library and sometimes I am surprised that a tiny little icon somewhere sparks my creative juices. That is why when I do storyboards or mock-ups, sometimes I use cutouts from magazines to present the idea to other people.

Roughs and Storyboards

Sometimes I do my own rough sketches, but when it comes to client approvals, I usually have a professional hand-drawing illustrator do the storyboards. But it all depends on budget and the turnaround.

| BRANDING AND CONSUMER EXPECTATIONS |

Carlos says, "Consumers' life-long relationship with a brand is composed of good and bad transactions—ultimately if the company's brand promise is in line with their needs, they will be loyal. Look at many successful brands with a huge following: Harley Davidson, Nike, BMW, Coca-Cola, to name a few—they have one thing in common—these companies deliver their brand promise by providing, without hesitation, a product or service that fulfills their consumer's needs. For example, Discovery Networks in the United States is the premiere provider of real-world media and entertainment, offering a distinctive mix of compelling stories, high-end production values, and vivid cinematography that consistently represents quality and excellence for the American consumer."

To successfully design a motion graphic for a company such as Discovery Networks, your design must also deliver on the brand promise and meet audience expectations in terms of quality of production and use of design elements that fit within the existing look and feel of the product. To maintain customer loyalty it is important to understand and meet the audience's expectations.

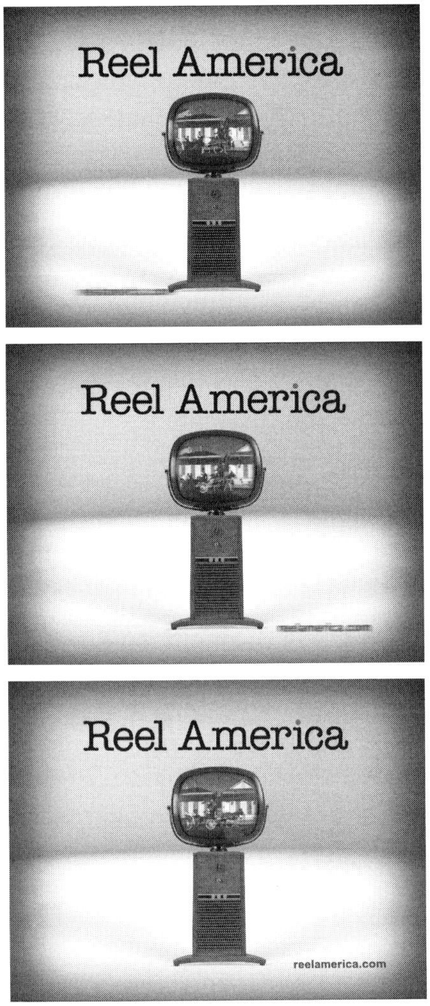

By Carlos Lema

figure |9-8|

Designed to meet the expectations of Reel America's audience.

The goal of the storyboard is tri-fold—it keeps everyone on the same page; without much fuss everyone sees if the idea works; and it is the blueprint for the final execution. When I don't work with storyboards, I wander around aimlessly—it's kind of like dropping me in the middle of a country without a map. I have no idea where to go, so many roads and places to investigate. All of a sudden, a week or months go by and I have nothing to show—that is a problem, especially when you're dealing with a client's budget. I am also dealing with timelines and a team of twenty or so people who are counting on my designs. The storyboards are my roadmap to making sure that everything happens the way I want it—as a designer, as an art director, as a creative director, whatever.

Roughs for the Web

When I am working for the web, the first thing that I do is nail down the project scope. Let's say, a simple website redesign. Getting the site map approved is my top priority, which also identifies my high-level pages. Then I concentrate on the overall look and feel, and a handful of designs. I do my initial exploratory in Adobe Illustrator. Since it is resolution independent, I can move, resize, and reshape without loosing any quality. At that point, everyone including the client can understand what I am trying to accomplish and provide comments that reshape the final outcome. Once the client approves these final designs, I can start the production phase.

Teamwork

I depend on experts: illustrators, programmers, directors, editors, gaffers, and colorists. Sure, I can program in PHP, but I would not have the resource and knowledge of a programmer that breathes and dreams about code—everyone has an innate talent. I know my strengths and limitations. I am an art director coming up with ideas that help sell a product or service. Once the client buys into this idea, then I pass it on to whomever else is going to produce it, regardless of medium. An idea might be a simple line of copy or an elaborate 3-D animation. The goal is to convert something intangible that lives in my mind into a tangible element that everyone else is able to see to approve or disapprove. Then, I simply let the real artist take that idea to the next level.

How Updated Technology Has Affected Work

Sometimes programs are either not doing what I need them to do or they are so mind-boggling that I am overwhelmed by things that the programs can do. Some programs are designed for the general consumer and fall short when it comes to professional needs. Nevertheless, there are very specialized high-end systems that not many people can afford. For example, Adobe After Effects is a fantastic program, but it lacks so many features that high-end programs like Discreet's Flint or Digital Domain's Nuke or Quantel have at their disposal. The end result might be somewhat similar, but the workflow is more intuitive, fully integrated with external devices and real-time, even while working at HD or Film resolutions.

How Technology Has Affected Creativity

Well, it gives me more options, but it also hinders my creativity with so many options. At one point I worked with a handful of fonts, now there are over 65,000 of them on my library! There is an array of tools that help me in my design process—the more tools I have at my disposal the easier it is to solve a problem. Many times I've been in After Effects wanting to try something in 3-D, but somehow it is not possible or it is more convoluted than it should be, so I switch to Lightwave or SoftImage. Somehow it evolves to places I would not have imagined—happy mistakes I call those. It is like smearing two primary colors and coming up with this cool color.

Most Important Component of Graphics

The Message. Look at the Superbowl back in 2000; you had tons of beautiful commercials that didn't say a thing. People remember some of the commercials but do not remember what brand was behind it. Even today, we have beautifully done commercials, but you have no idea what they're advertising. That's the difference between having a good ad agency and a bad agency. Visuals are the hook that captures people's attention. The message is what they walk away with in their mind. There are many people out there who are incredible at what they do—designers, filmmakers, and motion graphic artists—they are driven by art, or wanting to tell a good story or creating something beautiful without purpose—that is very different from advertising.

Design Challenges of the Web

Most of the limitations are technology related—bandwidth used to be a huge issue, but it is disappearing thanks to broadband. We still have the browsers' disaccord. You have to customize the code for designs to look good in everyone's computer.

Challenge of Designing for Agencies

It all comes down to chemistry and communication within the team. Everyone on the team is extremely important for the success of a project.

Collaboration of the Design Team

The core creative team is made up of the associate creative director, art director, designer, and copywriter. The team brainstorms approaches and concepts in line with a creative brief that the account or creative executives have devised beforehand. Once the general direction is established, the team disperses. The copywriter comes up with the copy for the message and the art director and designers work together to find appropriate visuals, type styles, and treatments to present the concepts. Once everyone within the team says "this works, this is exactly what we want" then it gets presented internally to senior executives, who in turn provide feedback. Once their feedback is implemented, it is then presented to the client. The copywriter and art director are always a team. Very, very rarely does something happen in a vacuum. For online advertising, the cycle is about six to eight weeks. For TV and print it is about three to six months. Project managers are key to keeping the whole process within the project's time constraint.

Signature Design

Clean and simple—message is king in my book. I think about how I can present an idea in the least intrusive way. I don't believe in having lots of cuts or lots of clutter all over the place—in the end it just blurs and buries the message. I remember a while ago interviewing at an agency; my work was labeled as "functional." I thought, what is the point of having a highly conceptual ad if it doesn't sell?

I spend a lot of time looking for the right visuals; whether working with a photographer, director, illustrators, or animators, I'm always making sure that we have the same vision. I try to keep up with what is going on in the world, being sensitive to what is happening around, and being sensible about how I am communicating a message.

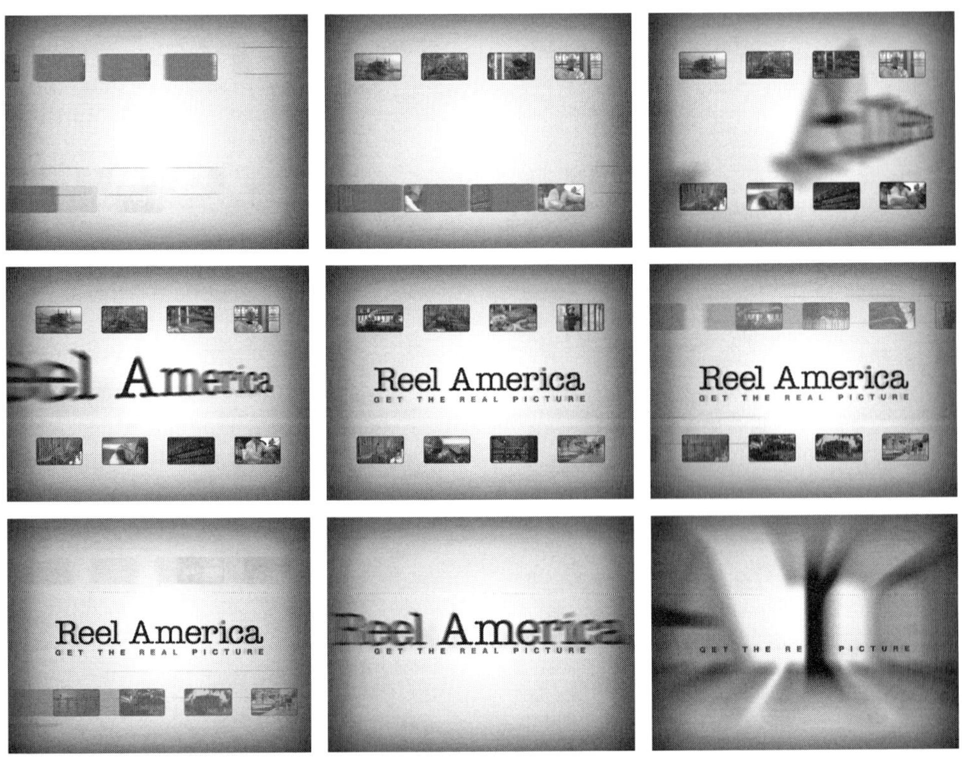

By Carlos Lema

figure |9-9|

Motion graphic sequence designed and produced for Reel America.

The Future

I believe that within the next ten to fifteen years television is going to become what AM radio is today, thanks to the rapid broadband adoption. Television or print or radio is not going to go away. The web is going to claim its rightful place as the dominant player in the media mix. The web allows you to have bi-directional communication with the consumer. We are able to acquire knowledge that other mediums do not provide.

I believe that designers should think more about messaging while keeping a medium agnostic philosophy. They have to think about the big idea and then figure out how that's going to work across all the different mediums.

I am not married to any medium—I have fun doing pretty much anything that has a message that makes sense behind it. Whether it's TV, print, or online, it's just fun. I truly enjoy doing what I do. The funny thing is I would never call myself an artist—maybe a creative person helping a client sell its product or service. ◀

SUMMARY

With the Internet we have instant access to information, can download entertainment, and can communicate with people over long distances without leaving our homes. The first websites were difficult to build and lacked pictures and graphics. An early form of the internet, ARPANET, was funded by the military in 1969 and was unavailable to the public. Twenty years later the World Wide Web was open to commercial traffic, though it was more difficult to use than it is today. First JavaScript and later Macromedia Flash gave designers the freedom to create more sophisticated motion graphics on the web. The role of the web designer is to create websites that are easy to use, functional and engaging to the user.

in review

1. How are motion graphics applied to the World Wide Web platform?
2. What are the technical considerations for motion graphics design when applied to the World Wide Web?
3. What has been the impact of the World Wide Web on society?

exercises

Exercise

Design a banner ad for a small, neighborhood hardware store.

Process and Research

Before you begin, you must know the following:

- What type of product or service are you selling?
- Who is your audience?
- On what websites would this banner appear?

In order to develop a way to sell your product, you must know your product or service well. This will, of course, require research into your product and into the competition.

- What does your product have to offer?
- What are the advantages and disadvantages to your product?
- Who is the competition?
- What can the competition offer?

Research into your audience is also necessary for the success of your product. In addition to the questions outlined in Chapter 3 for learning about your audience's demographics and lifestyles, here are additional questions to answer:

- Does your audience need this product?
- Does your audience regularly use this product?
- Does your audience use the competitor's product? If so, why?
- What impresses this audience?

If your audience does not regularly use this product, or if it uses the competitor, your job will be to devise a sales plan to convince it to use your product or service. The kinds of websites your audience frequents may offer you a clue for how to win it over.

- What kind of content runs on the websites your audience frequents? News? Music? Technical information? Shopping?
- How is the content presented? Is it easy to navigate and easy on the eye, or is it complicated and packed with information that is difficult to find?
- What is the style of the website? Is it fun and upbeat with rollovers and buttons that reveal information? Is it formal and straightforward with easy-to-find links? Is it disorganized and complicated?
- Are there a lot of colorful photographs?
- Is it mostly text?
- Are there options to play video and audio on the site?
- What language is the site in? Does it give options to run in other languages? Which languages?

Once you have gathered all of this information, you can brainstorm and begin to synthesize it into a concept to sell your product.

Inspiration

Your design should be for 800 × 600 pixel screen resolution. Having a good sense of your product's strengths and weaknesses, its competition, and the preferences of its audience, you can begin to sketch out ideas for your sales concept. Because your ad is going to be either on the side or at the top of a working website, your design choices must be ones that are interesting enough to draw your audience away from the website it is browsing. Knowing what attracts your audience will certainly help you in making strong design choices. For example, if your audience likes rollovers, or likes to click on photographs, then you should probably consider incorporating them into your design. In addition, you will be working with less space than if you were designing a full-scale web page, so this also an issue in your design.

Additional design considerations:

- Should you include animation on your banner ad, and if so, what kind?
- Should you include sound or music? What kind?

In order to convey as much information in as short a time and as little space as possible, focus your attention on information hierarchy. This goes beyond simply composition. Seriously plan out how you will structure the information you are presenting to your audience, so that it can view it and process it as efficiently as possible.

Information hierarchy impacts your color and type choices, in particular because the colors and type style can make your message more digestible. What is the most important part of your message, or what is the part of the message that is most likely to *sell* your product?

- Is it the name of the product?
- The price?
- The deadline for purchasing your product?
- What your product can do?
- A photo of your product?
- Your product's slogan?

Whatever the most important selling point is, you will want to make that the focus of your banner. Your design must attract viewers' eyes to these points so that they can eventually act on the ad. Make sure to include contact information so that the audience can actually purchase the product.

Method

1. Complete pencil sketches of your design. Pay special attention to information hierarchy and presentation of your product, as well as navigation through buttons or rollovers.

2. If you are animating any part of your ad, complete frame-by-frame sketches of the animation in storyboard format.

3. When you are satisfied with your sketches, do your color mock-ups in Photoshop or Illustrator.

4. Decide whether you want to execute your ad in Flash or Dreamweaver. Remember to consider the advantages and disadvantages of both and that the key is readability and usability of this ad.

5. Check your design on both PCs and Macs and in different browsers—Explorer, Mozilla, and Safari—to verify that the motion graphics load properly and the colors look acceptable on both platforms.

6. Show your banner ad to an audience.

What is your audience's impression of your banner ad? Are the viewers attracted to it? Do they want to buy your product? What have you learned from this process?

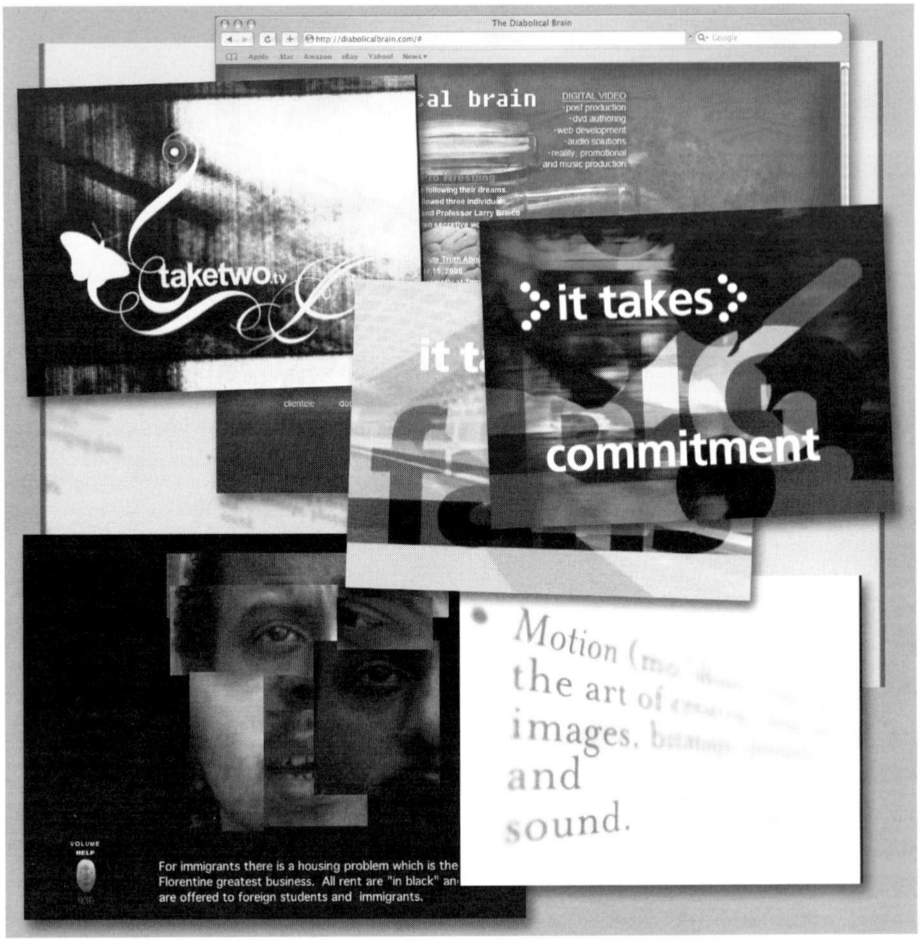
The Diabolical Brain
http://diabolicalbrain.com/#
DIGITAL VIDEO
·post production
·dvd authoring
·web development
·audio solutions
·reality, promotional and music production
taketwo.tv
it takes
commitment
Motion
the art of
images,
and
sound.
For immigrants there is a housing problem which is the
Florentine greatest business. All rent are "in black" an
are offered to foreign students and immigrants.

CHAPTER 10

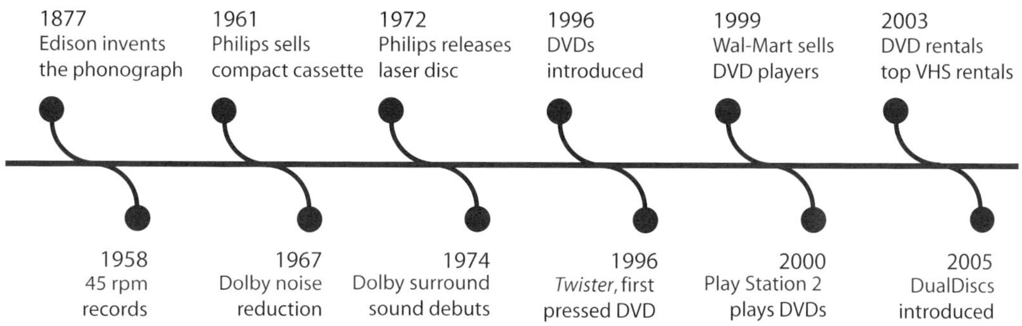

Chapter Objectives

Learn to apply principles of graphic design to motion graphics for DVDs

Understand the role of DVD title design

Explore the techniques used to create successful DVD interface design

Introduction

Until recently, DVDs were the fastest selling new technology. They are much less unwieldy than their predecessor, the laser disc, which was the size of a vinyl record. Philips introduced laser discs in the late 1970s, but they never became a household item. VCRs were still a relatively new product at that time and few households had one. Laser discs were large and bulky, but relatively little information could be compressed onto the disc. Both sides held media, so it had to be flipped halfway through the movie. In the 1990s DVDs were introduced, and by 2003 DVD movie rentals outnumbered VHS rentals. The picture quality on a DVD is far superior to that of VHS, which helped push sales to the top.

DVDS AND A NEW DESIGN APPLICATION

With the advent of DVDs a new application for design was born. Material on a VHS tape is presented in a linear fashion; the only options for the viewer are play, fast-forward, rewind, and stop. With a VHS the movie experience starts when the movie starts and not before. With a DVD the movie experience starts the moment you put it into the player, at the DVD menu. The role of the menu is to both inform and visually entice viewers.

Courtesy Katharine Gibbs School, NYC

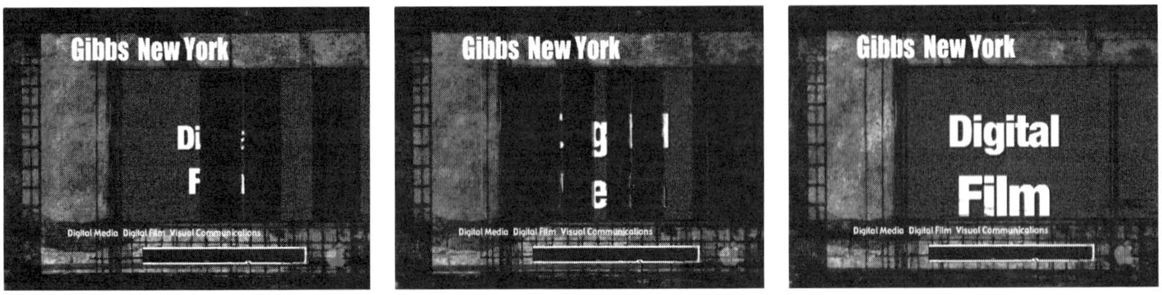

figure |10-1|

The DVD menu highlights the film and animation sequences, giving viewers a sneak peak at what they will see.

The elements incorporated into the menu need to be carried from the film's design, emotion, and flow. This means more than just using visuals from the film. The rhythm of the elements in motion on the menu should reflect the rhythm of the film. The color scheme for the typography and other graphic elements needs to support the film's aesthetics and visuals. Think about the emotional associations of colors and tie those emotions to the theme of the film. The graphic elements should be considered in the same way. Typography is very important in a DVD menu. It is essential in communicating the interface and showing viewers how to navigate through the selections; for example, view the film, see the extras, or listen to commentary.

By Roberto Bocci

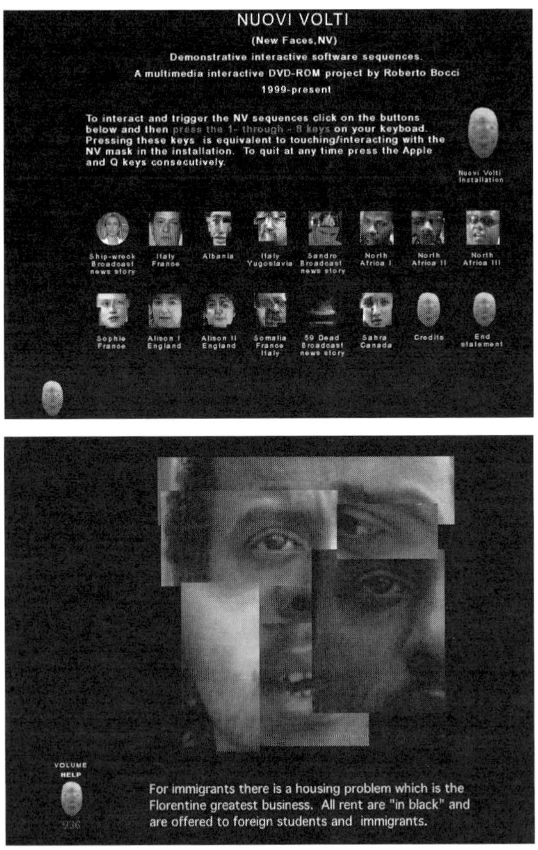

figure |10-2|

The DVD menu for *Nuovi Volti* presents a large amount of visual information in a well-organized, easy-to-understand design.

The DVD menu is the first part of the film a viewer experiences, even before the title sequence. You should consider it as a welcoming mat. The viewers' experience with the menu will dictate their emotion going in to the movie. If they are frustrated by the lack of ease of navigating through the menu or cannot figure out which button to push to view the movie, they will be less likely to be fully engaged in the film experience. As technology improves further and DVDs are able to contain even larger quantities of data, the interface will get more complicated. Narrow down what the most important access points or entry points should be, such as Play Movie, and make those buttons the most visible. Other access points should have buttons in the subsections so as not to present too much visual information and create confusion in the interface.

A designer for a DVD menu has the responsibility to look to the movie for visual inspiration and create an interactive experience for the viewer; one that mimics the experience of the movie. Many DVD menus not only use icons from the movie, but use clips from the movie as well. The clips act as mini trailers for the movie the viewer is about to watch, building excitement and interest.

▷ Professional Profile ◁

| Mark Ezovski |

Background

Years in the industry: 10

Education: BA in Art and BA in English, with a minor in Sociology from The University of Rhode Island. MFA from University of South Florida in Tampa. They have a real sports program there now, so people actually have heard of USF. Ten years ago it was like, "Is that the one in Gainesville?"

The Draw of Design

I guess I thought I was going to be a lawyer or something, so I majored in English with a Sociology bent as well. I always enjoyed books and reading and ideas about stories and telling stories; a lot of people tell me that I should be an actor because I tend to play the different roles when I tell a story.

I started taking a couple of art classes just to fulfill general elective requirements, and I think I just enjoyed the freedom of the art classes. My sculpture class was early in the morning, 8:00 a.m. if I recall correctly, and for me that's really bad. It was Monday morning as well, which normally would have been a death sentence for a class. As it turned out, I didn't mind getting out of bed for it—that was kind of new and different for me. I'd roll out of bed and get a big coffee and go and slop around in the wet clay while this weird a cappella jazz show was playing on the university radio station. There wasn't a lot of structure, so as long as you were getting your work done it was all good. It felt really different from anything I had done before, and I really started getting into it. It gave you time to think without being told you had to think; just personal space to think and figure and feel strange inspiration from strange music and the energy of other people working around you, and that was really attractive to me.

I think it tied in all the different kinds of thought processes for me, from the very mental to the very physical and visceral, maybe even some kind of spiritual and natural connection in there too, who knows? Thinking about these kinds of abstract thoughts—the nature of lines and what they make a piece of sculpture say kind of turned my brain in a new direction. This was never the kind of thing I had thought about. I was always analytical; I always wanted to know how things worked. Now it was "What is the nature of space? Why do things feel the way they feel mentally and psychically?" Weird stuff. I started spending all of my time around the art building. I got a work-study job in the printing lab and just started thinking and talking about this stuff all of the time. I took a film class the next semester and my fate was sealed.

First Design Before Becoming a Professional

I always did things for myself. My parents never helped with school projects; you know, dioramas and that sort of thing. My dad never showed me how to use tools; I just picked them up and figured it out for myself. I was always making things. I used to make all kinds of little additional items and accessories for my Star Trek or Batman action figures; whatever I would see on the shows or in the comics that they didn't have for sale in the stores. When the first *Star Trek* movie came out in 1979 I was like, "Wow, those new uniforms they have in the movie are awesome. The ones they wear on the show are really boring." So, I made new uniforms for Captain Kirk and Mr. Spock that looked just like the ones in the movie. I think I cut up an old sweatshirt or something.

My sister and I used to always make different paper dolls also, sometimes characters from different TV shows. Once again, stuff that you couldn't go out and buy. We each had Dr. Who and his companions and some of the villains, complete with a Kleenex box for "Tardis" (that's his time capsule for those of you unfamiliar with the show).

In high school, my friend Pete and I built a lighting setup for our rock band. We had seen another local teen band play somewhere and they actually had some lights as well as a P.A. system—it seemed pretty professional to us, more professional than our band, and we didn't want to get left behind. We had no idea how to do electrical work, but we scraped together maybe $20 or $30 and hit the hardware store, buying all this wire and colored light bulbs and plugs and sockets and switches. We rigged the whole thing up on a Saturday afternoon, and I have to say that even to this day I have no idea how we got it working so well or even to work for that matter. We used the lights live a couple of times and they were impressive—all different colors coming from five or six different boxes that we set up all around the stage. We are lucky, however, that we didn't start a major fire. We had all of the lights running through a single regular household dimmer switch—we're talking two dozen lights. When the lights were all on that dimmer got unbelievably hot. You could actually hear the lights over our guitar amplifiers. When the lights were dimmed, the noise got softer, when they were turned back up, the noise got louder. Yikes, kind of scary! Basically, I was never satisfied to not have something. If I wanted or needed it and couldn't get it, I made it.

First Professional Design Job

Right after I got out of grad school I worked for a one-person design firm for the summer. I had landed a job in New York as an assistant to a documentary film editor but I wasn't due to start until September. Since I had nothing else to do for the summer I decided to stay in Tampa. A woman who I had been in school with was also moving away, so she hooked me up with her old position. The boss was a single mother and I worked alongside her out of her home office. I remember she had this giant mean parrot that would get mad and try snapping at you when you went by its cage. Well, you had to go by the cage to get to the bathroom so it got mad all day long. I must admit that sometimes I would go up to the cage and egg the parrot on so it would bite at the cage hoping to get to through so it could bite me. Anyway, she did interior decorating and design. It was an okay job, pretty low-key until her six-year-old son got home from soccer camp and then he would run around yelling and causing trouble and she'd be yelling at him across the house to quiet down and behave. That really got on my nerves a lot.

Her main client was the Salvation Army. This is 1996, around the time when it was getting to be cool to buy "vintage" clothes so I think the Salvation Army was trying to gussy up its stores a little and make them hipper. I was really new to computers but was learning pretty quickly. I did some Photoshop design and lots of office work. The computer would crash very often when I used "Background Printing," which meant you were setting aside additional RAM so that you could actually print while you were performing another task on the computer. Wow! How forward-thinking of the folks at Apple! If more than two applications were open at the same time, the computer would crash or run unbearably slowly. Photoshop would constantly run out of memory, and I would have to reboot just about every hour to get it back up. Those coming into the business nowadays don't know how good they have it—computers ten years ago were a real pain. I remember in particular, designing some neon signs for the different departments of the Salvation Army store—Men's, Women's, Housewares—and I also remember updating her contact database in Filemaker Pro for an entire week while she was on vacation. Just sitting there doing data entry for eight hours a day made me know that I needed to do creative work. The administrative work was definitely not for me.

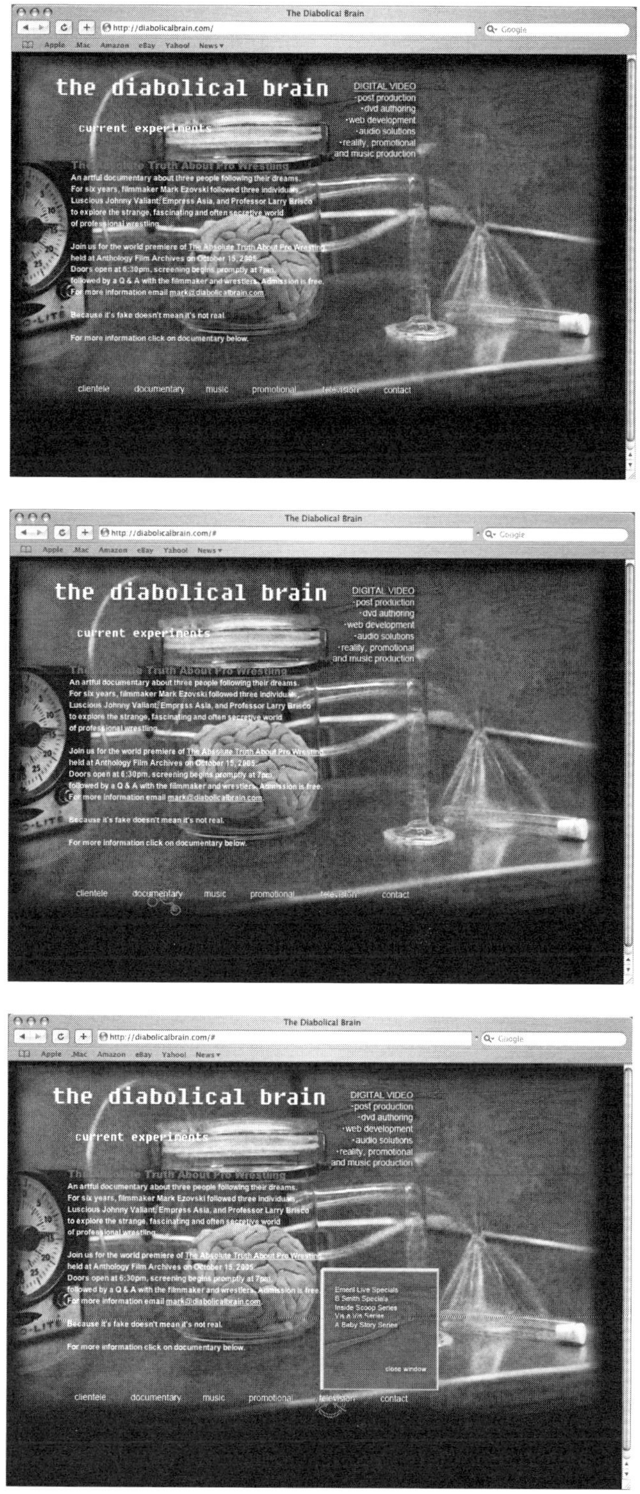

By Mark Ezovski Productions/Diabolical Brain

figure |10-3|

The technique of layering and compositing pictures with textures is carried over into the web design.

Design Process

Inspiration for DVD Design Menu

I don't think I ever sit down and ask myself what something should look like. I rarely change a concept. I'll revise a concept, maybe even overhaul it, but rarely do I find myself in a position where the concept must be completely changed. It's almost like the film or show on the DVD in some way has defined how it should be represented. Every show has a feel to it—visually, emotionally, rhythmically. These things get into my head and create the package on their own.

My mother used to tell me how her family was fairly poor when she was a kid. They didn't have money for any extras. It was a special treat in the winter when the milkman would leave the milk. If it was cold enough, and this is the 1930s so it's well before 2% milk and all of that, the cream would rise out of the milk and sit at the top of the bottle and freeze. She and her siblings would scrape the frozen cream off the top of the milk in the bottle and enjoy it like it was ice cream. It's like that. The good stuff—the interesting and compelling stuff—climbs to the top and sits there. You cannot get past it to get to the rest of the stuff, just like in the milk bottle; my mom couldn't get to the milk without scraping the cream off the top. The good stuff from the show becomes the DVD menu. It's a package, a whole, an entity, so it's got to fit and be representative. It should be a treat visually and interactively. It should be cool and fun.

I like movement; there's always movement in my menus. If a DVD menu doesn't have movement I will go so far as to say it's "wrong." Not that there needs to be all kinds of crazy things flying around, but there needs to be something that happens to make the viewer/user rethink the menu at given intervals. It's not just information, it's entertainment as well. It's not a slideshow, that's why movies were invented—it should be compelling with variations on visual themes. I tend to make all of the menus on any given DVD very similar but add certain twists and changes along the way—modifying the visuals without modifying the emotional quality. I like layered photographic images mixed with graphic elements and sound. There has to be sound also. Why would you want silence? Since the dawn of film, people tried all kinds of ways to add sound to film whether by live orchestra, announcer, or some guy standing in the wings of the theater doing sound effects. Finally, sound is technologically incorporated

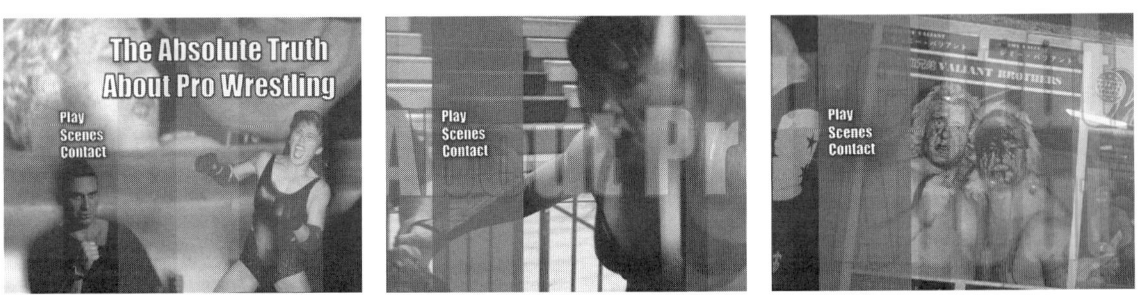

By Mark Ezovski Productions/Diabolical Brain

figure | 10-4 |

DVD menu for *The Absolute Truth About Pro Wrestling.*

seamlessly into the cinematic experience and seventy years later we have folks removing it as an element in DVD menus? I don't get it. It doesn't make sense. The DVD menu is part of the whole experience. Treat it like one; don't treat it like it's the disposable shrink-wrap covering the DVD box.

What Makes a Strong Designer?

A mind for details. Being crazy-obsessive about meaningless details, elements that no one else would notice but that are important if not vital to the subconscious mind upon viewing? It's hard for me to say because I call myself a filmmaker even though I do all of this other work. I suppose it all comes from the same place—can you tell a story? Any kind of media you create is a kind of story even if it's not a literal story. A sense of the theatrical wouldn't hurt. If there is a real aesthetic at work behind the creation of the story, I think you're on the right track. A distinctive vision, even if it's a bit sloppy, unrefined, over the top, et cetera, can make something better than it would have been if it were treated with too much care. I suppose that really believing in your vision is part of this also. If you can work without too much concern, there is a degree of fluidity that can come forth. If you believe that your story is interesting and will not bore the audience, I think you can then tell it in a way that will interest others even if the story itself isn't really that interesting. Like The Who said, "It's the singer, not the song, that makes the music move along." As the designer, you are the performer; you are imbuing energy into whatever it is you are creating.

| COLLABORATING WITH A CLIENT |

Does your process change depending on whether you are working on something for yourself or for a client? How do you adapt your process for collaboration?

When asked about his experience of collaborating and working with clients, Ezovski said "I hate collaborating. Let me rephrase that—I enjoy collaborating but not much collaboration is true collaboration. To me collaboration is designing together, not reworking separate ideas so that they can be presented as a single idea. That's a drag. 'Okay, I have this idea that I really like and I have to combine it with an idea that YOU really like.' There's a *Simpsons* episode, one of the Halloween specials, where someone, I think an evil Bart, created a pigeon/rat. They were sewn together back to back. The rat ran across the floor, the creature flipped over and the pigeon flew away with the rat thrashing about upside down in the air. That's most people's idea of collaboration—a really bad Frankenstein monster fighting with itself over how it should operate. When I work for clients, they call the shots. That's the way I want it. I may rein them back in if they are getting too far away from a sane or executable concept, but the concept is up to the client. I will add little things here and there—touches, flourishes, details—but I see my job as bringing the clients' ideas to life. If I am specifically asked for input, I offer it along the lines of what they are thinking. I will not try to talk anyone out of an idea they feel strongly about. Just because an idea does not fit my aesthetic does not mean the idea holds no value. I try to find the value in any idea and tweak it, if need be, to make it work."

Challenges of DVD Design

One of the challenges that bothers me most is adjusting image size and scale. Websites often have tiny font size; it's a common design practice and "look." Tiny fonts allow you to use larger fonts as a contrast enabling you to quite easily create a visual hierarchy in you text. There are two issues that make this visual hierarchy difficult to achieve on a DVD. The first issue is that the DVD will very often be viewed from a distance. On a computer screen, 8 point font will read next to 48 point font. Put that 8 point font on a screen five to eight feet away and you are in trouble. The 48 point font will read fine, but the small font will be lost. The second issue is compression. When graphics are compressed to mpeg2 files for DVD, type tends to get very noisy and often falls apart into a blob of pixels if it's too small. Using 20 point as your smallest font doesn't give you a lot of latitude in your type design. If you start using really large type, the entire screen is filled before you know it, leaving no room for image content, which to me is the more important aspect of DVD menu design. Color, font choice, and effects become a much larger issue when size cannot be readily used in your design arsenal.

Another problem that can deflate a great design is the difference between how video is viewed on a regular television versus a plasma TV or computer. On a regular TV, there is a portion of the image that is not displayed due to technical limitations of a television picture tube. This portion of the image is a border around the outer edges of the picture diminishing the presented image by about 10 percent of its actual size. On a plasma TV or computer, the entire image is displayed. What does this mean? It means that there is a "frame" around the image that cannot have any important information in it, as oftentimes it will not be seen. The image can look very different depending upon how it's viewed, sometimes appearing to have a giant border depending upon the design. It can be tricky to navigate this spatial concern and diminish the frame on a plasma TV or computer without making the design look too "stuffed in" on a television.

Viewer Expectations

I don't know that viewers/users have expectations yet. There are so many DVDs that have uninteresting menu designs that I don't feel like people know what is possible yet. It's kind of weird because if you look at web design as an example, there are so many sites that have all kinds of interesting animations, rollover design, et cetera. I saw this dog food website not long ago that blew me away. It was awesome and it was a simple e-commerce website through which to buy dog food. I don't understand why things coming out of Hollywood are not as interesting as dog food websites. Someone is missing something. Raise the expectations by bringing principles of cinema into the DVD menus, make them something that viewers/users want to spend time with and enjoy and not get through so they can watch the movie and the deleted scenes.

Is There a Signature Mark Ezovski Design Component?

I don't really think so. It's kind of all the same bag of tricks, you know. Different proportions maybe. I do have a certain style. I use the same kinds of fonts and colors and graphic layouts

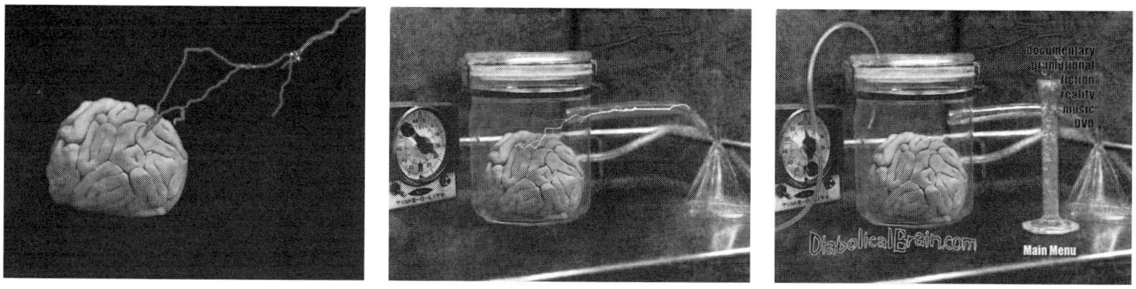

By Mark Ezovski Productions/Diabolical Brain

figure 10-5

DVD menu for promotional reel that uses Ezovski's signature design. A reel highlights your accomplishments and is sent out to perspective clients to generate new business.

and presentation from project to project, but I don't think it's something that really sets my work apart from the work of others. Maybe I use layered images with opacity changes more than others. I like combining pictures in this way, I like ghostly tendrils overlapping and informing other images, but I don't think it's something new. It's just the way my brain works and what looks pretty and enticing to me. When you're doing something like a DVD menu you are often using the work of others as the starting point. You are trying to get at what the movie is already. It's just trying to add a bit of your voice or psychological lean to the images to give them a different sort of life than the creator might have originally anticipated.

The Role of the DVD Menu

A DVD menu is not the same as a website, although they are similar in many ways. Certainly, you want coherent navigation in both media. You've got to be able to lead the viewer/user where you want and need her to go. They both should be visually interesting but I see websites based more on information transfer. A DVD is based more on visual stimulation and entertainment. The DVD menu should support the movie or programming that is presented. The movie is the main feature; everything else is support so the menu should not usurp that position. It's a fine line to tread.

The Future of the DVD

It's interesting because it could go either way. DVDs as media could become more or less important depending upon how things go—maybe in the immediate future far less important and then as technology develops far more important than ever before. It's all

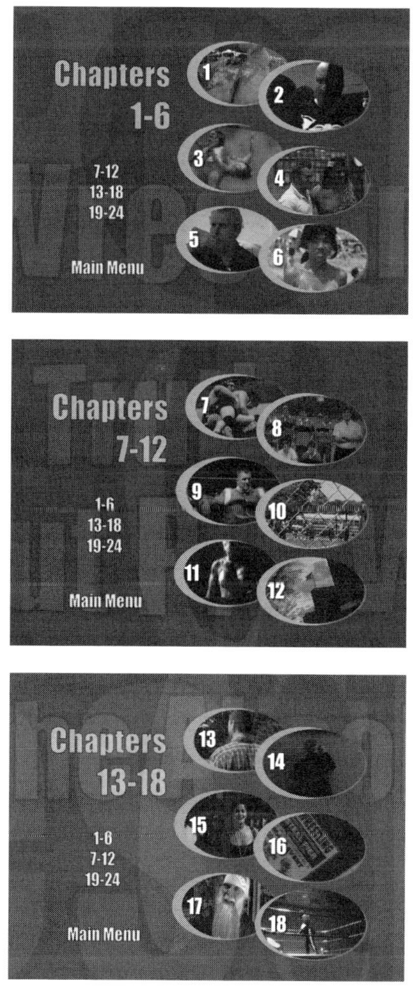

By Mark Ezovski Productions/Diabolical Brain

figure 10-6

Chapter selection menu on DVD for *The Absolute Truth About Pro Wrestling.*

about choices in media intake. If you think about a movie on VHS tape, it's all in order. The FBI warning comes on, the logo for the film company comes on, the previews come on, the movie starts. Very linear—just like one would see in a movie theater. Unless you fast-forward, it will be the same every time. With a DVD menu there are a lot more choices in terms of media selection and order. Most DVD releases have some kind of extra material, something that was not viable for a VHS cassette, especially in terms of voice-over commentary. As physical space on DVD media gets larger and larger, the role will expand. Not long from now, the "season" box sets that are popular will be available on a single disk or an easy download.

On the other side of the coin is what we are seeing with the new iPod and PSP. High tech is, in a way, going low tech—small screens and bad resolution. On the video iPod, video artifacts are readily viewable. This isn't even the case on VHS—you'll never see blocky artifacts, glowing colors, and bad contrast. If disturbances in the actual picture were part of the VHS technology, Beta certainly would have won that war. Now, all these years later, we are back to the basics in a way, stripping down to a bare-bones minimum so the technology can work. File size versus quality, the oldest struggle in media. In a few years, the portable video devices will display video as pristine as anything on a top-notch plasma TV of today. The process of getting to that point will be interesting to follow. I am old enough that all of this stuff was a Star Trek sci-fi fantasy. It's still so very amazing to me and I'm curious to see how it all turns out. ◁

▷ Professional Profile ◁

| *Darton Simons of TakeTwo* |

Background

Years as a Designer: 13

Education: Bachelor of Arts in Commercial Design from Graceland College in Lamoni, IA.

The Draw of Design

It was more practical than a career in fine art (which is where I was headed). I took a couple of computer design courses and was hooked.

First Design Before Becoming a Professional

I worked in the campus Publications Production Center (PPC) as a student designer. We produced playbills, pamphlets, catalogs, sports schedules, and other various collegiate collaterals.

First Professional Design Job

Money Mailer of Mid America hired me as their senior designer. I produced cooperative direct mail (junk mail coupons) for four to five years. I used my free time to develop my portfolio. That portfolio eventually led to my current position as a graphics designer/graphics animator for TakeTwo.

Design Process

Collaborating with a Client

Every project begins with communication either with the client or project producer. It's critical that you establish a rapport with every client. You need to make sure that not only do you understand the clients' needs and expectations, but that they trust you to do your job. Our editors oftentimes work under direct supervision. I have always worked best unsupervised. It just suits my personality—all the more reason to have excellent communication skills, especially when you're billing $300/hr.

Being versatile in your design style is essential. You can't apply the same treatment to a retirement center that you used for a snowboard manufacturer. There are valuable lessons to be learned from every project. Viewing each job as an opportunity is a valuable quality.

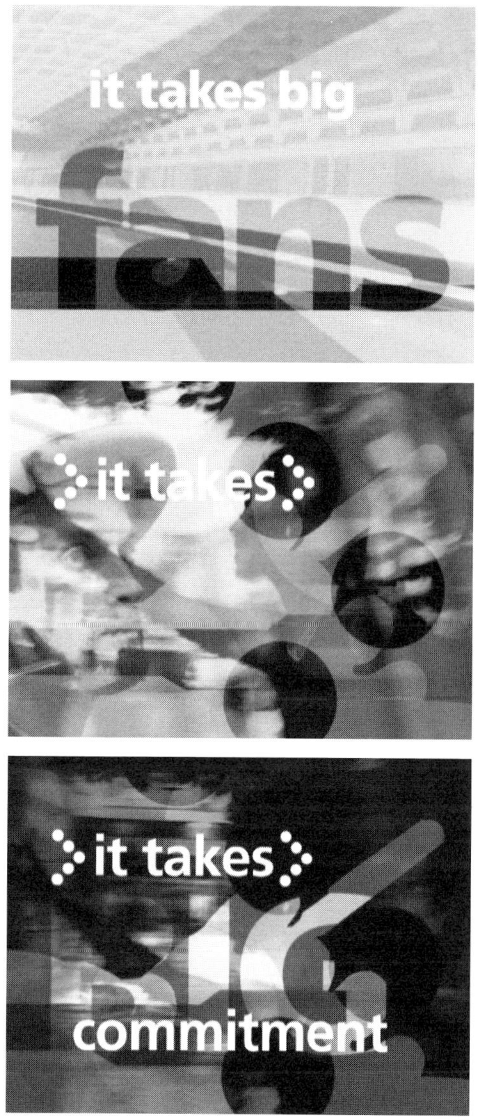

By TakeTwo—Kansas City

figure |10-7|

This motion graphic sequence sums up the commitment and versatility TakeTwo has toward design.

Inspiration

Inspiration is everywhere but especially in the visual mediums of cinema and television. I'm always on the lookout for new type treatments and visual special effects that I'd like to emulate. My co-workers and I constantly push each other to go beyond our comfort zone. They are an invaluable resource when it comes to getting respected feedback on your work. Only slightly less important are sources of 2-D design. The work in *Communication Arts* magazine has driven me to excel for years. The projects between the covers of

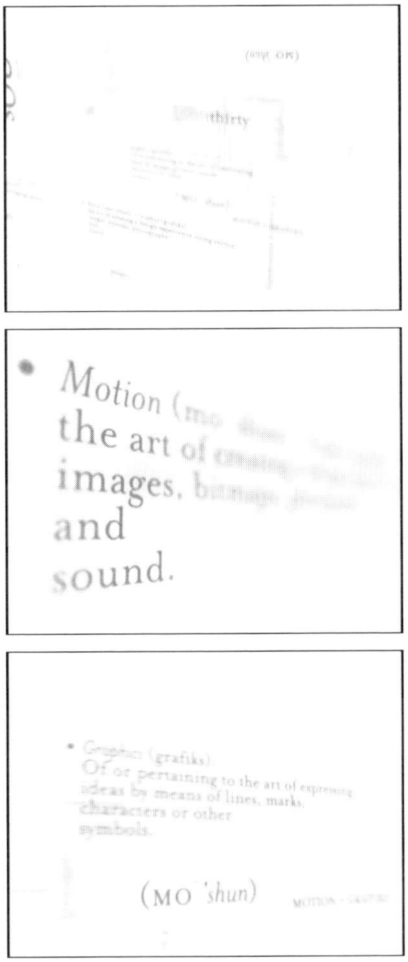

By TakeTwo—Kansas City

figure |10-8|

In this motion graphic, which uses only type and no graphics, it is apparent that TakeTwo is as equally skilled and creative with the use of typography as it is with graphics and graphic treatments.

their design annuals are there for a reason. It's some of the best work being done. *Archive* magazine is excellent as well.

The Influence of Changing Technology

When I started designing, we saved our files to floppy disks. In the PPC we still used the traditional paste-up techniques requiring X-Acto knives, tape, and "film spotter" to paint over pin holes in the film. We shot the films for the layouts on an ancient stat camera and developed it by hand. My senior year I got to use a scanner one time just to see what it was like. I learned Photoshop, Freehand, and Quark Xpress after graduating from college. Now I use Photoshop, Illustrator, and After Effects.

The advancements in technology are amazing and frustrating. The more powerful a program, the more demands we place on the machines. The most limiting factor in my life is the sometimes agonizingly slow processing speed of my machine. It often dictates what I will and will not do on a project.

Regardless of your access to technology, you should be able to do award-winning design with the most rudimentary tools in desktop publishing software: type tool, circle/square tool, and the ability to manipulate color. Everything else is gravy. I am the successful designer that I am today because I built my career on a foundation of fine art: drawing, painting, photography, 2- and 3-D design, and ceramics. That is where I developed my sense of balance, harmony, unity, eye movement, and color theory. I depend on this foundation every single day. On a more pragmatic subject, if you can't type well on a keyboard, you are going to suffer. Typing is one of my most useful skills.

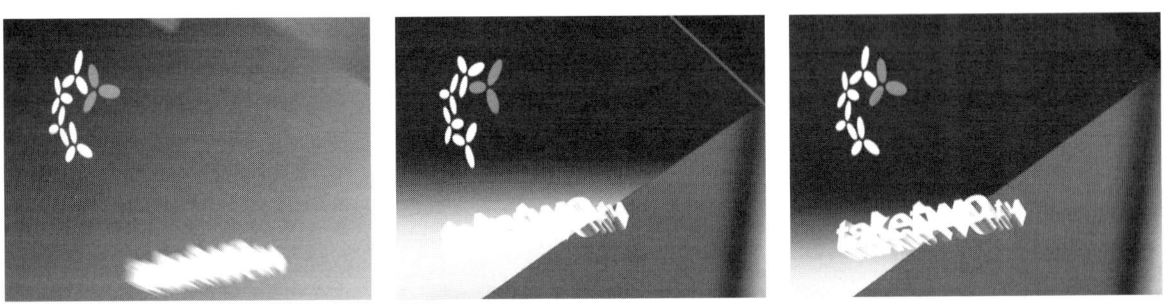

By TakeTwo—Kansas City

figure |10-9|

Working with extruded elements, such as "taketwo.tv" in this figure, may slow down processing, but often the resulting effect is worth it.

By TakeTwo—Kansas City

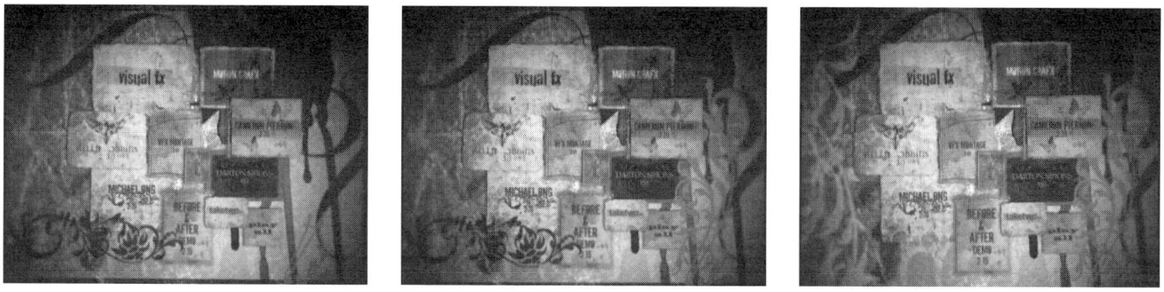

figure 10-12

The DVD interface for TakeTwo's promotional reel.

Changing Technology and Its Impact on Design

The depth of the programs and the speed of the machines running them is at least double. Much less of the final execution takes place by hand; this speeds up the completion of the process and increases its productivity. However, I've still held onto my initial approaches to a project's workflow. I try to do as much research and preliminary sketching as I can by hand. This frees me to try several different ideas without feeling the constraints of technology.

Challenges of DVD Interface Design

DVD interface design is challenging due to the restraints of the medium. These challenges demand the programmer and designer work together to create a seamless interface that is both technically accessible and aesthetically pleasing. Adequate planning and testing are essential to creating a successful DVD.

Signature Design

Our work embodies several different styles, techniques, and personalities. Most importantly, however, they all come together to form client-specific solutions. It is this collaboration that distinguishes TakeTwo and is prevalent in our work.

By TakeTwo—Kansas City

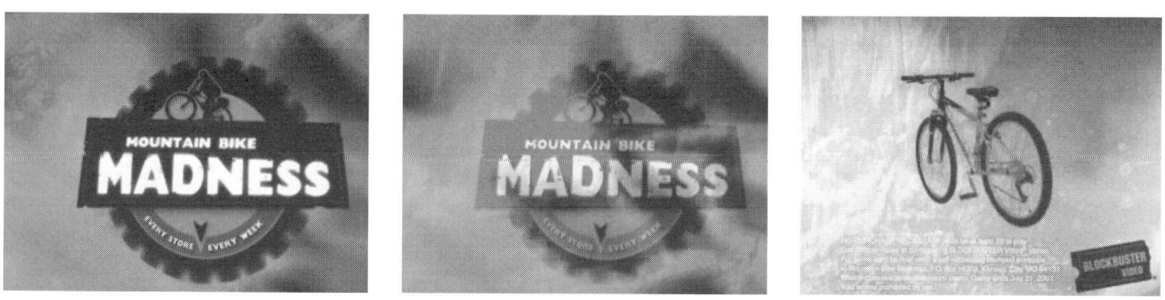

figure 10-13

This motion graphic designed for a promotion for Blockbuster shows how many styles can come together to form one unique, cohesive, well thought out design.

The Future of DVDs and Interface Design

The future of DVDs will be even more affordable, versatile, and media rich. The discs continue to grow exponentially in terms of data size and consumer accessibility. DVD authoring continues to become more user-friendly as newer and more mainstream applications become available.

SUMMARY

With the invention of DVDs a new venue for design was born. Since the advantage DVDs hold over videotape is the ability to move nonlinearly throughout the material, the role of the DVD interface is to provide navigation for the viewer. Because it is the first thing the viewer sees, even before the opening titles, it must also act as a welcome mat, guiding the viewer easily to the control buttons.

in review

1. What makes a strong motion graphics designer?
2. What is the role of motion graphics in DVD design?
3. What is the role of a DVD menu?

exercises

Exercise

Design a DVD menu for your favorite film. Be sure to include all of the special features you would want to enjoy.

Process and Research

Watch the film again, thinking about the theme and style and how you can incorporate them into a menu design.

- What graphics and fonts have already been used in the film and in the film's title design?
- Is there a gimmick or a theme from the film that you can translate into a frame for your menu? (i.e., if your film takes place in the theater, you could use a stage and the curtains as a frame.)
- Are there any historical or technical motifs from the film that could be incorporated?
- Is there a signature scene or a character that should be included in the menu's background design?

Inspiration

The main function of the DVD menu is to help your audience navigate the DVD. Since usability is a key issue, first lay out the features that will ease viewers' use of the menu:

- PLAY MOVIE
- SCENE SELECTIONS
- SPECIAL FEATURES

- LANGUAGE SELECTION
- SUBTITLES
- GO TO NEXT SCREEN
- GO BACK TO PREVIOUS SCREEN

Accessing some features may lead you from the main menu to an additional menu. For example, the Special Features button on some DVDs can take you to a special features menu with a director's commentary, storyboards, "the making of" documentary, or cast and crew information. Decide which additional features you want to include in your DVD interface and where they will be located in the menu. Group your menus in a logical way so that your audience can follow easily.

In addition to seeing that features are clearly stated for easy access and are organized in a coherent way, you will want to devise an engaging presentation that ties into the style and content of the film.

- What background images do you want to use from the film? Do you want them to be still or moving video?
- Do you want a video introduction before the menu becomes active?
- Which scene shots from the film do you want to use for your scene selection menu?
- When navigating between pages, what kind of transition would you like to use? Wipe? Dissolves? Cuts?
- Do you want to include audio from the film?

Your choice of colors and font will most likely be dictated by the colors in the film and the type used in the title design, DVD cover, or film's promotional materials, but they should not interfere with the viewers' ability to read and understand the menu.

As you plot out your design, pretend you are designing for someone who does not use DVD players often, in order to ensure simple navigation.

Method

1. Complete pencil sketches first for your main menu design. When you are happy with it, continue to sketch out the designs for the additional menus. The design should be consistent among them.

2. Do mock-ups of your menu in Photoshop. Import video stills if you are including them in your menu.

3. Execute your design using a program like DVD Studio Pro, or other similar software. Import any video or stills into the program. Pay attention to audio levels of your footage. You can adjust them in DVD Studio Pro.

4. Burn your menu onto a DVD.

5. Put your DVD into a player and test it to make sure that the buttons link to the correct menu or footage.

6. Show your DVD menu to an audience and have audience members navigate.

What was your audience's impression of your menu? Did members find it easy to navigate? Did they find it visually interesting? What did you learn from the design process?

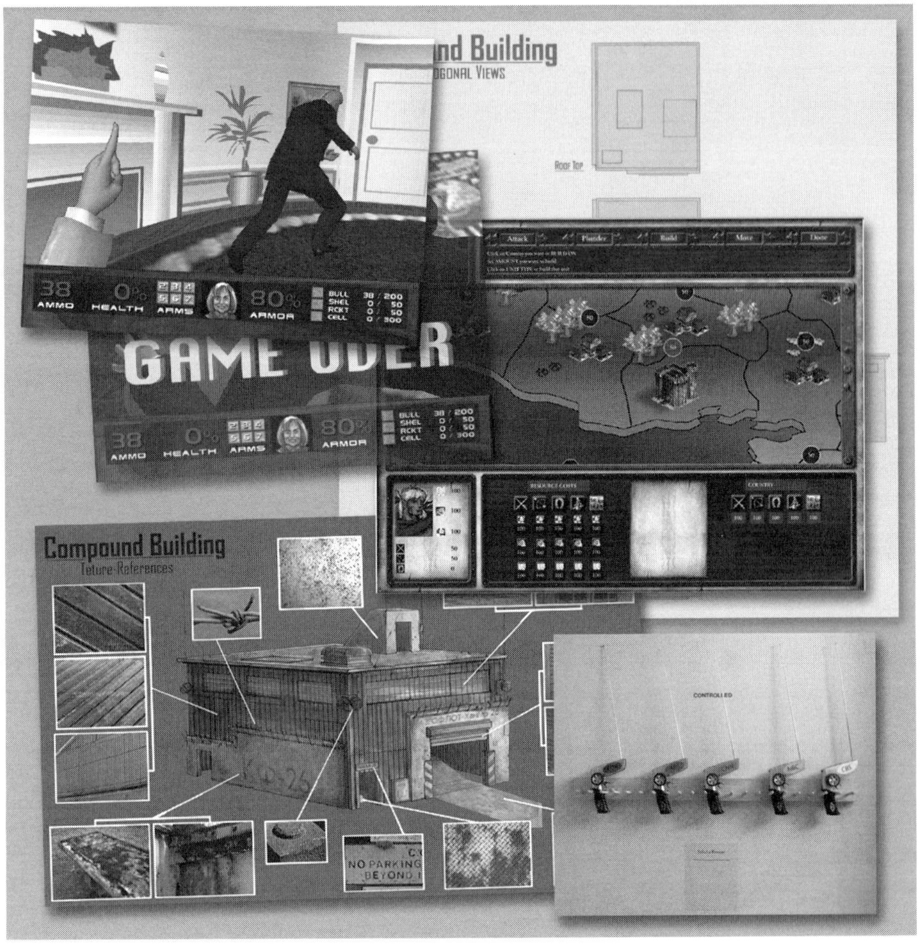

CHAPTER 11

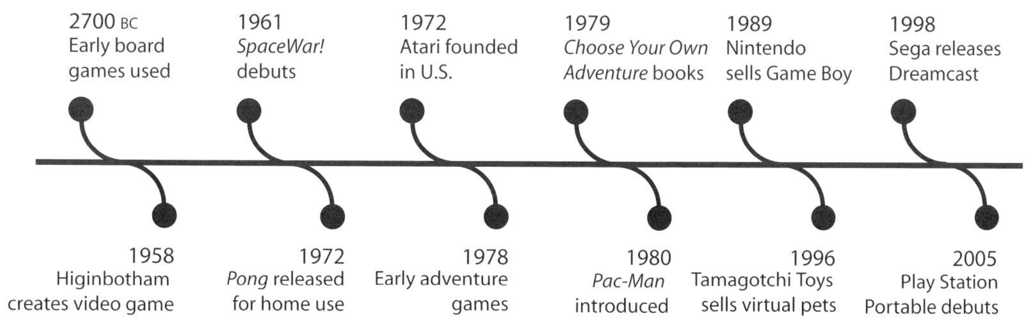

Chapter Objectives

Discover how user expectations affect the design of a video game

Understand how to apply the principles of design to creating motion graphics for video games

Learn how to develop a concept for a game

Introduction

Games have long been a source of fun and entertainment. We play games in groups or teams, one opponent against another, or an individual against a machine. We play intellectual games, requiring wits and strategy, or combative games, requiring physical strength and cunning. No matter what we play, conflict is inherent in the game and the desired outcome is to win. There are rules to follow, dictating what you can and cannot do, and what feats of cunning or strength are needed to win the game. The quality of interaction with the game, which is dependent upon the motion graphics, is one factor in determining the popularity of the game.

HISTORICAL OVERVIEW OF GAME DEVELOPMENT

The first video game, designed by William Higinbotham in 1958, was an early version of table tennis and contained no real design qualities. He developed the game to entertain visitors to his lab, and the game was never released to the public. In 1961 *SpaceWar!* was developed and released. Used primarily on college campuses, it was distributed for free among interested parties. Computer technology was still in its infancy, and the graphics and overall design of video games were very simple, with no color or depth.

In 1970 *Pong* swept the nation, despite its simplistic graphics, and the video game craze was born. Although previous games had been available to the general public via computers and shareware, *Pong* was the first game sold for home entertainment.

Early video games relied heavily on the viewer's imagination, in a world where, quite often, the main character of the game was not more than a few square pixels, such as in the Atari 2600 game, *Adventure*. Shortly after the game's release, Atari became a household name.

At the same time video game consoles for home entertainment were becoming popular, video arcades began to pop up in cities and towns across America. Playing video games became a national pastime. Portable, personal gaming devices became the rage with the release of Nintendo's Game Boy in the 1980s, which changed the way we interact with video games. People's love for video games has not lessened one bit since 1970. For the 2005 release of Xbox 360™ avid gamers waited outside stores for days to get one before they sold out.

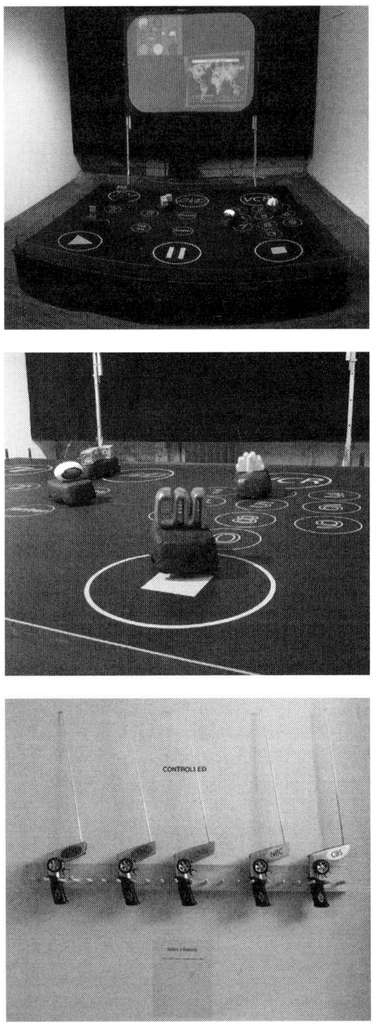

By Scott Michael Conard

figure |11-1|

Controlled creatively combines digital technology with the look of a traditional board game to send a message that viewers have little control over the media. Using interactive technologies, the user initiates action and receives a response. The user is required to select a remote from the wall in order to activate the console.

DESIGN CONSIDERATIONS

As interest in gaming continued to grow and technology became more sophisticated, so did the graphics of video games. When video games first appeared on the scene, computers were slow and had limited storage capacity, which meant that even if game designers were capable of designing more visually enhanced games, the average player would not have the hardware, a computer or console, capable of handling the advanced software. Today's video games look as well styled and sophisticated as any other media with smooth, film-like motion of more complex figures and are able to enthrall players for hours at a time. Not only do users want a strong plot with developed characters, they are also visually mature and design savvy.

Video game designers use 3-D software, such as Maya and 3ds Max, more than any other motion graphics designer. Three-dimensional software aids in creating high-quality, realistic looking graphics for the characters and environment. Environment refers to all scenes in the games, and many games provide a library of environments to choose from. Gaming characters are highly developed and appear only slightly less realistic than TV or film characters.

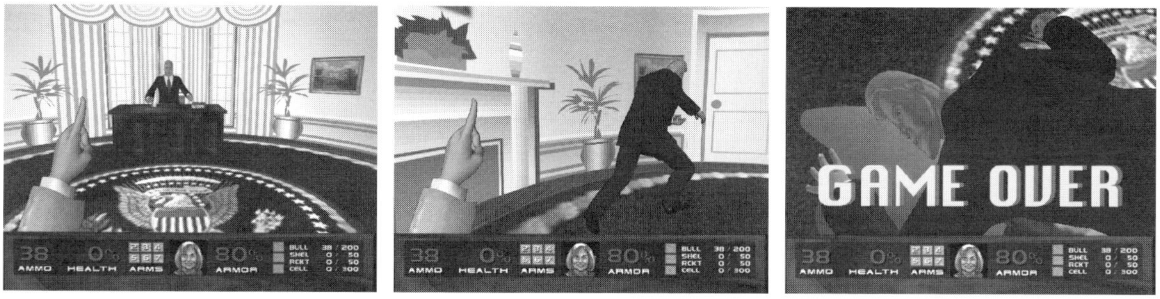

By Roger White

figure |11-2|

"White House Rampage" is a game that uses 3-D graphics to show the President running from his angry wife.

Graphics created in this software use wireframes that act as the three-dimensional framework of the character or object, which help to develop more realistic shapes and movements.

When designing for games, you need to create graphics that visually enhance the game, create an easy-to-follow narrative, and are clear with concise direction. Players enjoy the game when they understand how to interact with it and are enthralled by the graphics. They expect exceptional motion graphics and animation no matter whether the game is delivered via console, computer, or cell phone.

Video games rely on motion graphics to tell a story, support the action, and communicate rules and game status to the user. The motion graphics are presented to a user engrossed in the interaction with the medium of the digital game, so the message has a very high probability of being communicated successfully.

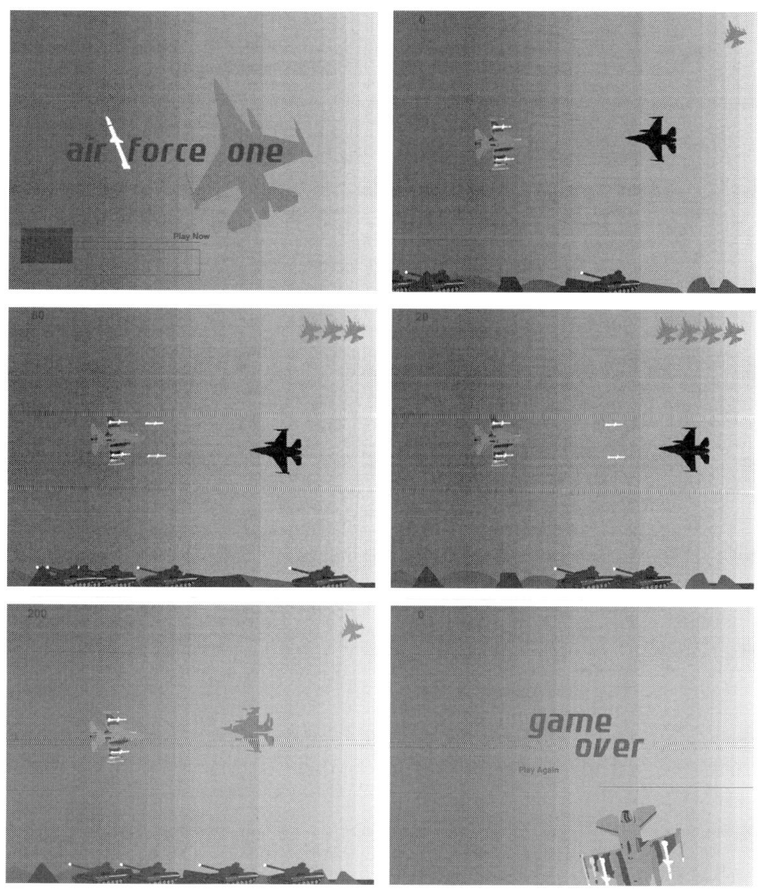

By Leonardo Silverio

figure |11-3|

Air Force One uses simple graphics that clearly communicate the actions of the game to the player.

THE DESIGN TEAM

Because video games are interactive in a way that film, television, and even websites are not, video game design requires a larger team of professionals to create logic and realism in a virtual world that is controlled by an unknown player. While it is the designers who develop the concepts of the game—the object, the characters, the environment, the obstacles—they must also have a working understanding of the underlying technical components that go into creating the game. Whether working closely with the game artists, animators, and programmers, or actually programming the game themselves, designers must be aware of the technical limitations to their game's world in order to focus on the most crucial aspects of what will lure players and engage them enough to keep on playing. In other words, they have to know which concepts to keep and which to lose in the event that the technology cannot support every idea.

Video game artists and animators elaborate on the designers' sketches and storyboard ideas, first by putting pencil to paper, and then by using the computer. Artists and animators create characters by using modeling software. The simplest component of a video game character's structure is a **polygon**. Artists manipulate these polygons by combining them, pulling and shaping them into wire mesh frames of their characters. Once the frame is covered with "skin," the character is ready for animation, either by the artist or a separate animator.

A character animator can create motion by using key beginning and ending poses and then allowing the computer to fill in the movements in between. Often they build models out of fiberglass or clay and then scan those objects into the computer. Another method animators use to create realistic motion is motion capture, where a real person is put in a body suit and hooked up to the computer by connecting sensors to pivotal parts of the body. The motions the person makes while engaged in an activity such as skateboarding or playing tennis is captured digitally. These motion sequences are then used in the game, thus creating smooth, realistic motion. This method is used often in the sports genre of video games to create the most realistic football tackles, basketball slam-dunks, or hockey goal blocks.

When animating **cut scenes**, intermission sequences that play at set points during the game, the animation can be more detailed because the player is not determining the movement. The animator is more restricted by the movements that the anonymous player creates because they are controlled by a joystick or a menu and are chosen by the player.

The artists in charge of the texturing of the characters and the environment have to be as detailed and specific as the animators in creating believable elements of the world. They also use 3-D software to "build the set" or to scan in textures to give surfaces a believable look. However, due to the capabilities of the device on which the game will be played, there is only a certain amount of memory to hold each detailed element. It will be up to the programmer, in conjunction with the designer, to figure out how to get all of this information into the game. And in many cases, it may mean making choices about which components are most necessary and which should be given up so that the game can still function fast enough to keep up with the player.

Video game programmers often use C and C++ software to translate the designers' and artists' concepts into a game that functions and follows a player's commands. One of the key roles of the programmer is creating the **artificial intelligence** of the characters playing against the player. Artificial intelligence determines the characters' responses to the player, and as with other aspects of the game, needs to be both realistic but also engaging enough to keep the player in the game.

Not only do programmers determine how quickly a game runs by the code they write, but they determine everything else from how quickly graphics appear to how animated characters and objects run in different environments. The more details and features, the more demand on the memory of the gaming console. However, the more efficient the game's code, the more information and features are able to appear in the game. The more details that appear in the game, the more realistic a world is created, and the more likely the player is to come back for more.

Professional game designers not only have a strong design sense, but they have a feel for fun and are excellent collaborators. Audience expectations, as well as technical limitations, are ever present as they complete their tasks. Luis Cataldi and Prithvi Virasinghe, two design professionals, discuss how they work and how they address challenges that arise on the job,

| MAKING THE GAME MORE FUN |

Video game publishers, the companies that fund and distribute video games, naturally want to convince their audiences to purchase upgraded versions of already popular games. The element that they often capitalize upon is realism. Each upgrade seems to find a way to convince the player that in this new version, more than ever, the player is actually there *in* the game, which makes the game more *fun*.

Madden NFL '06, released in the fall of 2005, is a perfect example. The designers incorporated camera angles that give the player new perspectives of the football field, while not interfering with the player's point of view. In addition to camera movements that dolly around the player as he kicks the ball, there are "trench cameras," which present a "worm's eye view" of the field and camera features that mimic what a viewer might see on a television broadcast of a game.[1]

Additional changes were also made to the environment to make it more realistic and include shots of the coach looking down on the game, as well as shots of players without their helmets watching from the sidelines. Because Electronic Artists, the company that publishes Madden, has a license from the NFL, they were able to use head scans of 150 NFL players for their game's characters. And because such details as facial expressions, scars, and bruises contribute to the realistic effect, they even programmed the game to have these features recess as the characters got further away from the camera (McEachern).

Like other sports-inspired video games, such as NBA Live 06 and NHL 2K6, Madden animators take advantage of motion-capture sessions with professional athletes in order to make the plays look more realistic. With all of the lifelike elements, including the details of professional players' faces and movements, game designers face the challenge

1 Martin McEachern, "The Art of the Deal," *Computer Graphics World* 28, no. 10 (Oct. 2005).

of how to keep the game processing at a high speed. Programmers minimize the less important details (i.e., features of background players) in order to capitalize on the more important details, such as the faces of the opponents directly involved with the player or any other element that enhances the player's experience at that moment.

▷ Professional Profile ◁

| Luis Cataldi |

Background

Years as a Designer: 12

Education: BFA in Department of Broadcasting & Cinema, University of North Carolina at Greensborough

The Draw to Design

It was the desire to study filmmaking—theory, auteur directors and scriptwriting, and a little production. At my college it was very difficult to get your hands on expensive production equipment like one might get at a university like NYU. Rather than trying to enroll in programs I couldn't afford, I decided to try to learn about camera and lighting by experimenting on a computer in 3-D space. I decided to explore being a filmmaker in a virtual world. That's what inspired me to seek out 3-D computer animation and design.

You can approach 3-D from a number of ways: one way is traditional animation background, and another is from a broadcast and filmmaking background. Back then, if I wanted to shoot film in an alley, I'd have to worry about how to light that alley and shoot it well with no money, whereas I could build that alley virtually in 3-D space and light it and frame it any way that my current skills could achieve. You can play with the shutter speed to get motion blur as you whip pan, and a big difference is that you're sitting in your living room.

First Design Before Becoming a Professional

I tried my hand at dance choreography. What I discovered is that I sucked as a choreographer.

First Professional Design

I started getting paid to do computer graphic work in 1993–1994. I was still in my last years of college. At the time, I was doing an internship as a computer network assistant. As it turned out, I did some work for a company that needed a multimedia guy; after demonstrating some skill, I applied for the job and got it. At first, I was making fancy images and setting up PowerPoint presentations. At one point, I was asked to show how an airbag deploys from its housing. I tried to do it with still images but they wanted a more dynamic visualization. I considered trying to shoot it live action in slow motion but I did not have the equipment or the know-how to pull that off. Plus, I was really interested in 3-D animation so I pitched the idea to my boss that we visualize it with 3-D animation. He asked me to do some research about it so I investigated high-end 3-D hardware and software, which at the time could cost in the neighborhood of $50,000. I looked at Alias, Wavefront, and Softimage, all of which cost a small fortune for hardware and software. I presented this to my boss and after he stopped laughing, he said "here's $5,000, get it done." The reality was that for what we needed, I didn't require all that power. I needed to make a good animation but there where other choices. While doing my research I had also discovered a less expensive piece of software called 3D Studio, which ran on an inexpensive DOS computer. Though it was not as fancy as I might have liked, I did the animation and they liked it.

Because I had developed some skills in 3-D working for those guys, I started getting some freelance work. One of my first freelance jobs was for a company that repaired medical equipment like endoscopes for endoscopic surgery. They were very intricate, expensive devices that need frequent servicing. This particular company hired me to create an endoscope in 3-D and to animate a camera in and around it to show how it was to be cleaned and maintained. Now the reality was that none of that was what I wanted to do, but it afforded me time to learn on the job and to learn how to use the tool set.

Design Process

How Video Game Design Differs from Designing for Other Media

One of the biggest differences between game design and film or broadcast is that with film and broadcast, you only have to shoot the stuff that's relevant. You only make the front of something because the camera doesn't see the back or sides. You don't do work that you don't need to do. A game is very different because you've giving the camera to the audience, and they can look at things however they want. You have to maintain their suspension of disbelief while the camera's in their hands. You don't get the "behind the curtain" that you do with film or broadcast; video game audiences demand to have the freedom to move around. You don't want to pull them out of the experience by showing them something that doesn't work anymore.

Initial Approach to Game Design

The game industry is very fascinating. There is often a designer or lead designer who sets the parameters. The

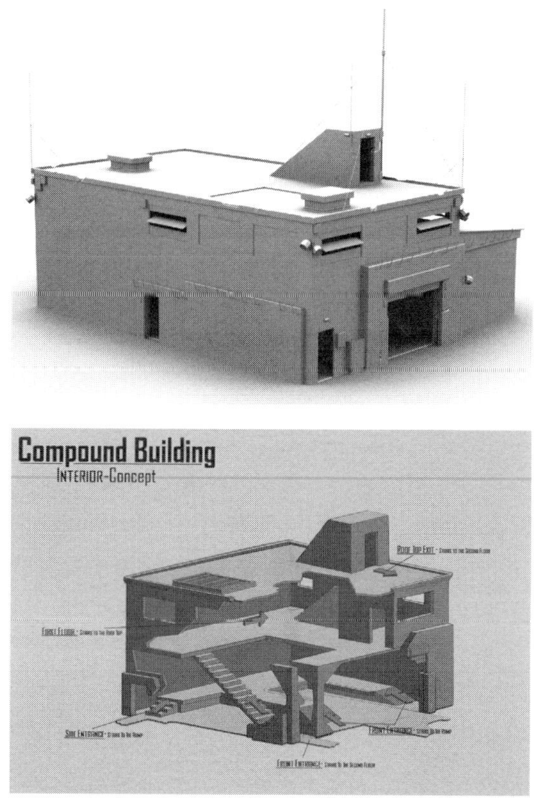

By Luis Cataldi

figure |11-4|

Diagrams showing both the exterior and interior of a building.

designer and/or the story designer will both do a bunch of research before they set the stage. Generally, they will create a design document that will tell us where we are, who will do what, how they will do it, and how they will accomplish it. At our company, after the initial ideas between the designers on a specific portion of the game, we come up with a template form that has all of the appropriate questions we need to answer. We have found that you have to ask the important questions, or at least if you structure the way you ask the questions, then you have a way to find the answers. This document is literally three to four pages. What this tends to do is allow us to get to the big picture sooner.

Video Game Design Process

The map or level template has all of the relevant information for the rest of the team like the time of year, which is going to help us define the color of the sky, the color and type of dirt, are the trees full of leaves or bare, how much haze is in the distant sky, whether there's snow on the ground. . . . From this information, we can come up with a color palette in which to unify the world. It also sets the stage for what's happening in this environment. What are the times we're in? Desperate? Happy? Magical? Are the cars clean or are they broken? Once the template is filled out and we all sit around and talk about the answers, we refine the answers and sometimes the questions, and then we can start defining the design vision.

A level designer, who lays out the maps, might take the document and from that draw a two-dimensional topographical map in Photoshop of the environment and structures. Then he might go into the game engine and build the environment with very primitive shapes. This is called a brick-out. With this, the team can quickly begin to see if it is attuned to the design of the game. The level designer might capture a couple of still images of his brick-out and take it over to the concept artist. They will do loose concept drawings suggesting what the sky, terrain, and the buildings look like and start to play with a couple of different color palettes. The concept artist might experiment with the color palette to see if he could come up with different moods for the level.

We'll take these concepts and elaborate on them before anyone in 3-D starts to work on it. After we iterate on this process, the level designer will start to make it a little more realistic, put the hills, structures where they need to be and put in structures to give a sense of reality. Then from there it's time for the art team to replace the stand-in objects with things that actually represent what was drawn in the concept drawings. We iterate and iterate until we come up with a world that is cohesive in terms of color and design. We ask ourselves if this is the environment we want to play the game in.

Within the template we also ask how the story is delivered. Who delivers the story? Is it a voice-over? Who is giving the exposition? Is it told by a narrator? Is it someone you walk up to and ask a question? Are there signs on a wall? All of those things are answered in the mission template. If this part of the story revolves around a particular character, we start asking relevant questions like who this character is and what is important to notice about him. What does he look like? How old? What social standing?

We often take the answers to these questions to a concept artist who will flesh out on paper what is described in the mission template by doing a series of quick thumbnail sketches that depict a scene or character. We then meet about which thumbnails capture the feel for what we need. We suggest a little more of this, less of that, and we flesh things out a little further. A character's clothes, textures, hair and eye look, and color are conceptualized before we touch the computer. Once we approve the concepts, we start to design in 3-D.

A lot of the initial questions we asked will also help set the parameters for the animator who has to go in and convey the message through physical action. For example, if a character is acrobatic, then the animator has to rig the character to be able to perform more dynamic animation. Sometimes, a character just has to sit in a chair and deliver dialogue. In that case, you don't need to rig the legs for animation, just the upper body and face. Answering these questions well can save a great deal of time.

The Role of Art Director

It is managing the art team to pull off the vision. It is managing the designers to pull off a consistent feel. It is managing the whole world. If you don't make these choices, they don't work. You have to refine the ideas so that they are visually appropriate to everything else that's been asked of us but also doable. I do a lot of the design by refining loose ideas that then can fit into the big picture and then create a cohesive vision.

Most Important Element of Game Design

Playing the game as soon as possible. A game that looks brilliant and is no fun is still no

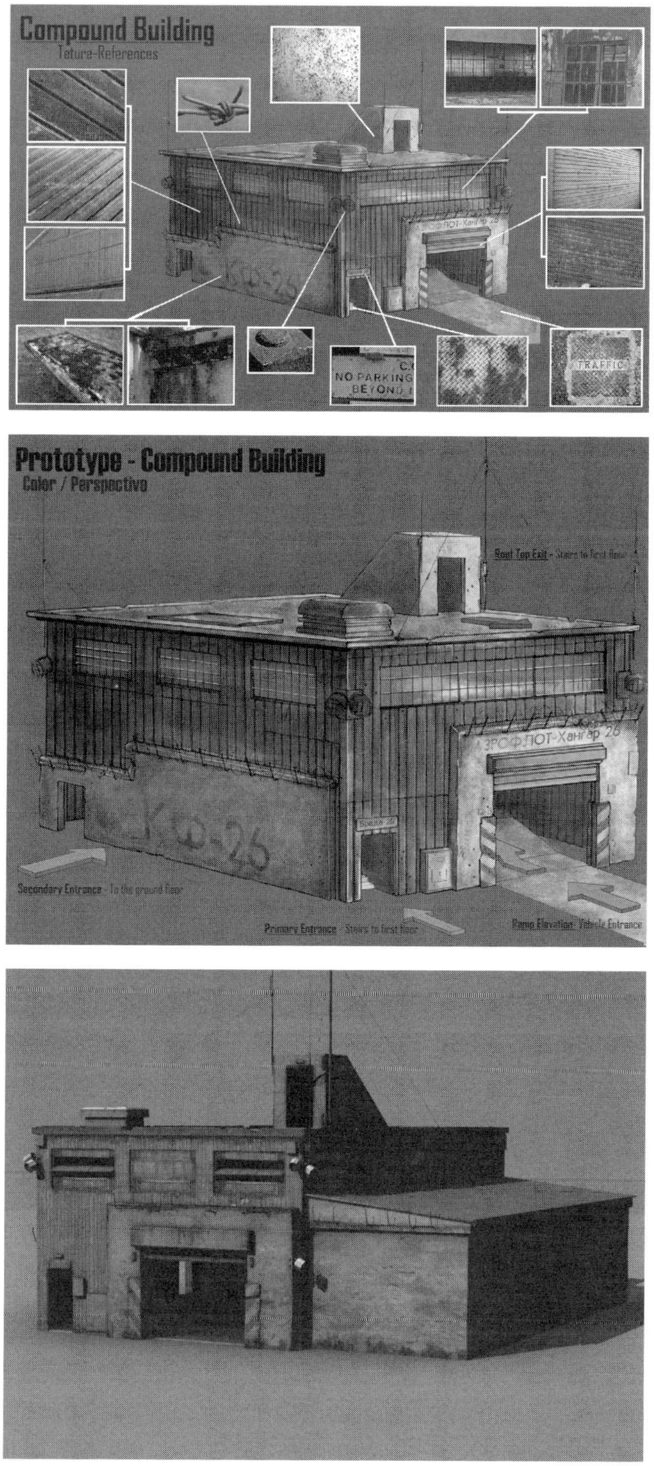

By Luis Cataldi

figure | 11-5 |

Illustrations, diagrams, and renderings as developed throughout the design process.

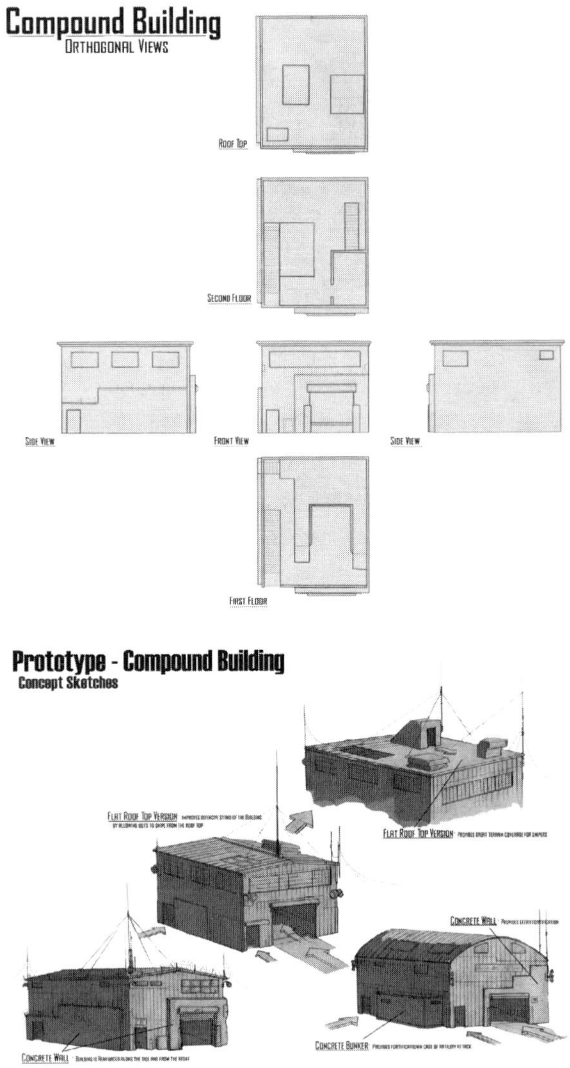

figure 11-5 (continued)

fun. If you block it out and put all of the elements in, you already can play it and prove that it's going to be fun. If you're not playing your game as soon as possible, your game will probably suck. You play, and you hire a professional group of quality assurance specialists who play the game and make sure you've thought of everything.

Influence of Audience Expectations on Design

There are a lot of games being made. You can measure your audience's response to a published title by looking on websites like metacritic.com. Metacritic.com takes all of the reviews written about a particular game worldwide and gives you an average of every review. It will tell you how many people loved it, why they loved it, and gives an idea of what we would have to do to make one that's similar. You can scale your production in a similar way and hope your team can come up with a formula. Publishers who put up money are not willing to take many risks. They keep making the same things over and over again because they know they'll make money. There are some games that cost under a million dollars that make truckloads, so there is always someone trying to second-guess the formula.

What Is Good Game Design?

Making something that people want to keep doing. Making the game re-playable. If you make a repetitive task monotonous, then the audience is done, and they never get to the end.

Challenges of the Game World

In film you can really direct the audience down a very structured, guided path. They're being emotionally manipulated in a well-crafted way. It is very difficult to emotionally affect someone in a game because you're giving them the option to take it on.

There is a lot of fun and emotional satisfaction from the freedom to choose, yet it's very difficult to figure out how much freedom to give our audience and how to get them involved in the game and on board emotionally. That's why there are a lot of high-action, fun, edge-of-your-seat games, because it's not that hard to get that kind of emotional response. But try to scare someone or make someone cry. That's very hard. That is the greatest design challenge—to bring that emotional range into this medium and make it something that isn't just fun, fun, fun.

The Future of Game Design

The game industry is a wonderful place for designers. It is one of the youngest mediums of new designers. It encompasses so many interests, and there are so many things being built into tomorrow's games. It requires areas of expertise that you wouldn't think of, and almost everything that we've learned has been learned by playing a game. Gaming is going from something that is fun to a way in which employers teach employees to work.

Game designers are asking, "How do I keep the CD of my game in the tray so that the players don't swap it out for another game?" They don't want you to pay once for a game in the future. They want you to keep paying. You'll get immersed, so that they'll charge your credit card extra. The idea is that as you play the game, you buy more and more into the game and make micro-transactions. You'll have to pay if you want to drive a certain vehicle. Or you'll have to pay every time you want to go a different place in the game.

And the effect of paying as you go? Now we'll have to bait the audience and make the game something that's appealing. The first part will have to be so much fun that the second part is worth buying. For example, with a driving game, if you want a much faster car and a bigger track, you'll have to buy it. What makes you want to buy that will have to be designed into the game. ◄

| VIDEO GAMES AS LEARNING TOOLS |

Studies as early as 1984 have shown the positive impact of computers and computer games on the learning outcomes of children. Students who were exposed to computers were more confident with computers and viewed them in a more positive light than did students who were not exposed to them.[2] Various experiments conducted throughout the 1990s showed that interactive media was able to hold students' attention longer, thus engaging them more in the subject matter, and that there was a positive correlation between working with developmentally appropriate computer programs and students' knowledge, nonverbal skills, memory, and manual dexterity (Din and Caleo 6, 7).

Additionally, a 1998 study showed that after six months of playing a Super Nintendo video game featuring two elephants at a summer camp for children with diabetes, children were more likely to discuss their health condition with their parents, had greater knowledge about the disease, and were more likely to form healthier habits than children who were assigned to play a pinball video game.[3] And in an experiment with two groups

2 Feng Din and Josephine Caleo, *Playing Computer Games versus Better Learning.* Paper presented at the Annual Conference of the Eastern Educational Research Association (Feb. 2000).

3 Debra Lieberman, *Health Education Video Games for Children and Adolescents: Theory, Design, and Research Findings.* Paper presented at International Communication Association, Jerusalem, 1998.

of kindergarten students, Feng Din and Josephine Caleo found that the experimental group, which incorporated the Sony PlayStation Lightspan educational game into their curriculum, made greater progress in verbal skills like spelling than the control group, which did not incorporate the video game into the curriculum (Din and Caleo 11).

Finally, Michael Posner, a psychologist at the University of Oregon, conducted a 2005 study that showed increased brain activity in children after playing his specially designed computer game. His belief is that when games are constructed to create a conflict, they can stimulate pathways in children's brains that help them focus and acquire reading and mathematical concepts. Though his study is not conclusive regarding the long-term effects of the games, he hypothesizes that children would want to keep playing the game, and the more they play, the more likely there would be positive long-term benefits.[4]

While the evidence for the value of video games is clear in school-aged children, some parents and toy manufacturers have taken this evidence to mean that exposing babies and preschoolers to these electronic games will make them smarter and more academically adept. However, according to the Kaiser Report, released in the winter of 2005, the jury is still out on what kind of effect, if any, these interactive toys have on young children. In fact, having looked at many products on the market such as Leapster and the Baby Einstein video series, the writers of the report found no evidence that these toys improved children's intellectual abilities. Moreover, the idea of exposing children to these devices goes against the advice of the American Academy of Pediatricians, which recommends no screen time at all for children under the age of two.

Ironically, while manufacturers profit from parents who run out to spend money on these games to stimulate their young children's brains, incorporating learning games into the classroom, where there have been proven benefits, has been more difficult. Money has caused the delay. Video game publishers spend anywhere from $10 to $30 million developing a game and fear that educational games do not sell as well as traditional video games.

In November 2005 educators and game developers met to discuss how to bring educational games into the classroom. Among the economic concerns was the fact that further studies needed to be conducted on the games in order for them to be ready for classroom use and that the federal budget was about to be cut.[5] Educators and game designers alike can see that, given the amount of time children and teens spend playing video games, educational games are a teaching tool of the future. Studies from the past two decades reinforce that fact, but, alas, the final hurdle is a financial one. If educators, game designers, and game developers can find a way to surmount this problem, they will be successful in enlisting technology in strengthening the way students perform in the classroom.

4 Lauren Barack, "Computer Games May Foster Learning," *School Library Journal* 51, no. 11 (Nov. 2005).

5 Andrew Trotter, "Despite Allure, Using Digital Games for Learning Seen as No Easy Task," *Education Week* 25, no. 10 (Nov. 2005).

▷ Professional Profile ◁

| *Prithvi Virasinghe* |

Background

Years as a Designer: 5

Education: BA in Marketing/Management/Finance, MFA in Design & Technology

The Draw to Design

My banking job was boring and not as cool as I thought it would be. Being a very low-level analyst performing very "important" number crunching probably had something to do with this. . . . I wanted something more creative and got a job as a marketing assistant.

First Design Before Becoming a Professional

I used to design maps for role-playing games and fantasy novels that I would start writing, but ended up doing mostly maps. I was thirteen at the time so of course I had every ambition of writing the next *Lord of the Rings* (although I had not read *Lord of the Rings* at that time, I had read the *Belgariad*, which was just as good).

First Professional Design Job

I created a 3" × 4" black and white ad for my boss because she was too busy with other stuff. That eventually got me promoted.

Design Process

Collaboration

It depends on the project. The scope of the project will almost entirely determine how many designers are involved: with the lead designer setting the creative tone to the production level designers putting parts of the project together to the assistant designers churning out bits and pieces of artwork that will eventually be composited together. As a game designer, the design process works a lot like this because there are so many small assets that have to come together to make a single frame/level/scene in a game.

Audience Considerations for Game Design

As a game designer, the design process has to revolve around your audience. Ideally, you place game play from the player's perspective first, usability as a close second, and then put the burden on your programmers to miraculously make everything possible. In all seriousness, it's an iterative process, oftentimes you put in a design requirement that you would like to see, programmers tell you it's impossible, you change it to accommodate them and try to make the best solution to

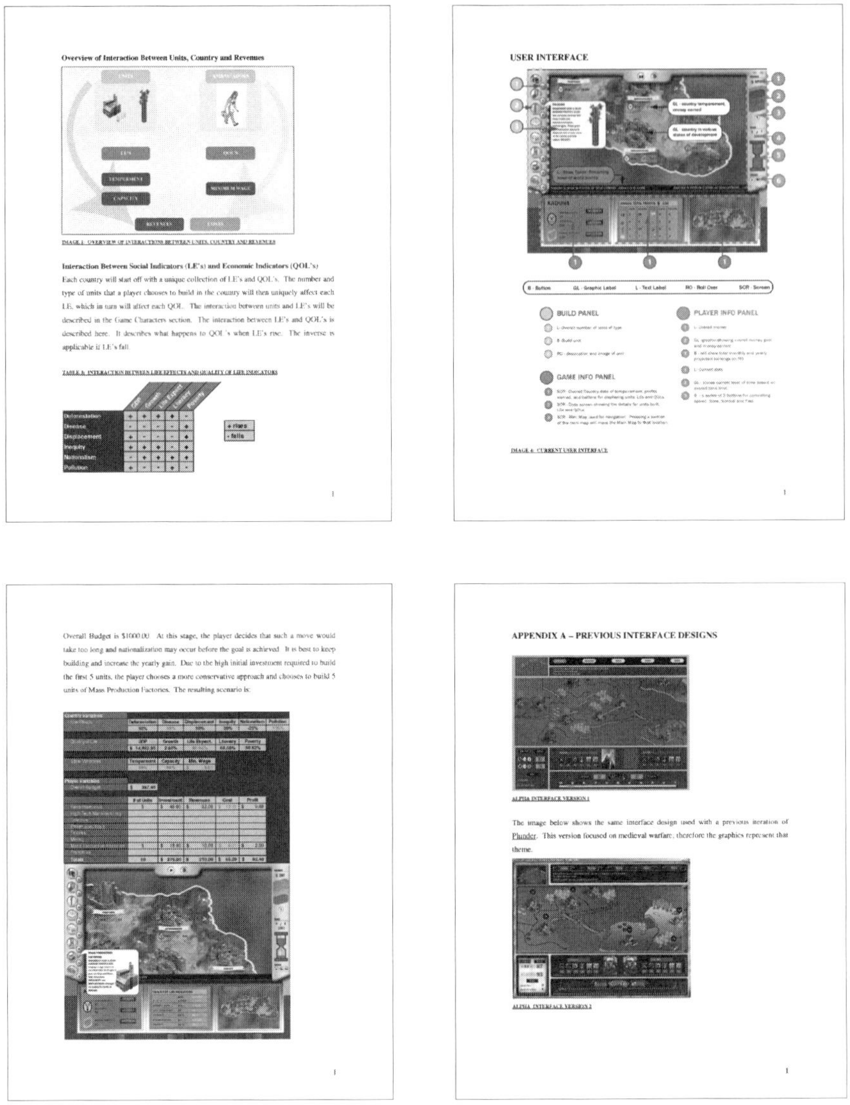

By Prithvi Virasinghe

figure | 11-6 |

Pages from a fifty-plus page design document that details game specifics and theoretical areas of exploration; all of which was developed from a collaborative process.

the problems. Many times as a designer you can design creative game mechanics, the programmers can perform miracles in their physics logic, and when you test the game you find that the player has no idea what's happening. So you have to be prepared to start from scratch. . . . This is why it's very crucial to have constant game testing throughout the design process.

How Technology Has Affected Game Design

The most noticeable thing is that technology has advanced to a level that a single person can create a sophisticated game in one application. It is possible for the single developer to create memorable gaming experiences without needing an entire graphics/programming/sound team. The flip side, of course, is that the technology has gotten so advanced that when you think of larger AAA (console level) games, you need a small army of developers to make it happen. Everyone is so specialized now, you can't just have a programmer, you need a graphics programmer, a network programmer, an AI programmer, et cetera. Same thing with 3-D; you need a modeler, a lighter, a texturer. . . .

Most Important Element of Game Design

Make it FUN!

The Effect of Interactivity of Design

The basic element behind any game is that it's interactive, otherwise you just have a slideshow. Interactivity has to be looked at purely from the user's side, in terms of the game's core mechanic (the constant activity that the player is asked to do throughout the game) and usability (the way in which the player navigates through the options offered in the game). So I would say that planning the interactivity is the most influential aspect of design.

Adapting Design Skills for Different Media

When you have to work with so many different people across many disciplines it helps to be able to understand their language. The more personal experience you have with various media, the better you can communicate with the people that use them. As a games producer I need to understand design and technical constraints. If my developer tells me they cannot do something on a particular platform, I need to have the knowledge to either tell them it's possible or suggest a new avenue. But first and foremost, I need to understand what the heck he/she is talking about.

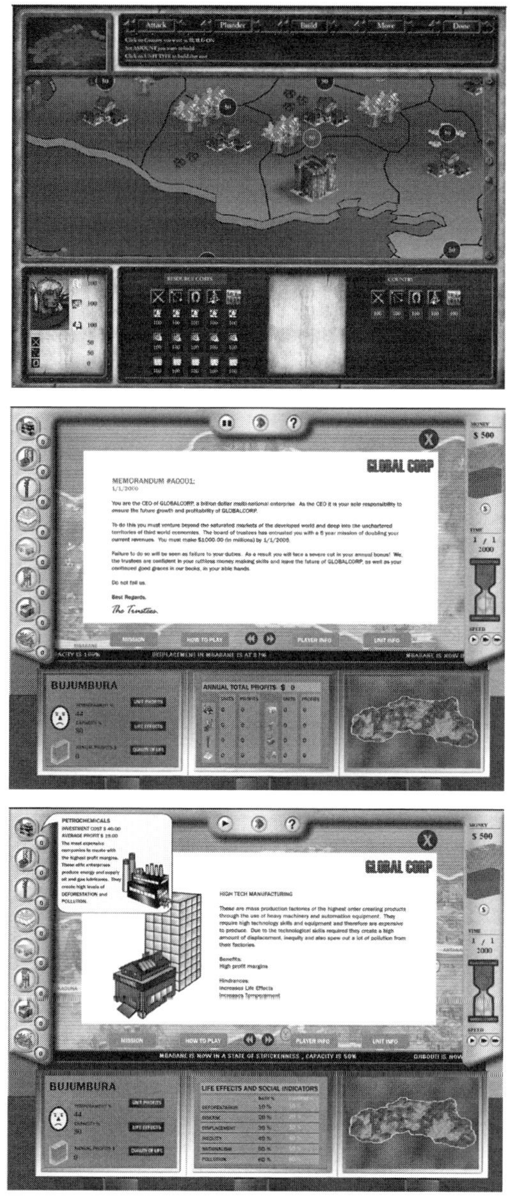

By Prithvi Virasinghe

figure |11-7|

The initial design of *Plunder* (above) eventually developed into a real-time strategy game that explores globalization issues.

Most Challenging Project

I'd say that would have to be my Master's Thesis. I designed a real-time strategy game but did not have the benefit of having a development team behind me to flesh out all my ideas. As a single developer it's hard when you have to let go of a great idea because you don't have the resources/knowledge/funding to get it done. How did I design my way through it? Lots of coffee and cigarettes.

Future of Video Game Design

The general description of a gamer is no longer cut-and-dry. It used to be teenage boys, but now they are only a portion of the gamer market. Gamers range from kindergarten kids to eighty-year-old grandparents that like to play Grand Theft Auto. So the market is really going to start segmenting and you will see a lot of games come out that cater to different levels of gamers. That being said, I think immersive games that work across multiple platforms on multiple devices is the way things are going. Imagine an MMORPG (massively multiplayer online role-playing game) that I can play at home, on my phone, on my commute, and I can play with my controller, keyboard, cell phone, 3-D glasses, and a whole host of physical interactive devices that are being thought of as we speak. I think games will integrate themselves more tightly into other mediums/platforms that we are not accustomed to seeing them in. They will be more ubiquitous. ◁

SUMMARY

Video games are an American pastime. First invented in the late 1950s, they have evolved to become sophisticated forms of virtual entertainment, available on computers, portable consoles, and other digital devices. *Pong* (1970) was the first video game released for home use, and with the invention of Atari, video games became widely popular in many American homes during the 1980s. Video game designers must factor in their audience's expectations in creating an environment where users will want to play. Character and story development can be as sophisticated as the technical means to create the games. Maya and 3ds Max are the prevailing software of game design and allow designers to use motion graphics that engage and excite users to play the games over and over again.

in review

1. What was the first video game and when was it invented?
2. What was the impact of Atari?
3. What kind of software do video game designers use?
4. What are wireframes?
5. What are some of the challenges of video game design?

exercises

Exercise

Design an updated version of a retro video game from the 1980s.

Design and Research

In developing your video game concept, consider the following questions:

- What elements will you keep?
- What game elements originally made the game successful?
- How will you update those elements so that today's audience will appreciate them?
- How are today's audience expectations different from those of the 1980s?
- What technical elements must you include for your game to be successful?
- What story elements are required to engage your audience?

Inspiration

Central to the design of video game is the premise, because all other elements of the game hinge upon it.

- What is the player's goal?
- How does the player reach the goal?
- What are the obstacles that make the goal a challenge?

The characters and the environment stem from the premise.

- Who are the characters?
- What are their skills? Weaknesses?
- What is the function of each character in the game?
- What do the characters look like?
- What is the environment of the world in which the game takes place?
- How does the environment aid the player in attaining the objective?
- How does the environment challenge the player in attaining the objective?

Once you have developed the concept, conduct research to estimate the budget required to complete the project.

Method

1. Sketch out your ideas for your video game characters, paying special attention to the character representing your player and the villains.

2. Sketch out the world where your video game takes place. Create at least five different environments to represent five levels of play.

3. Create detailed colored designs of your characters and your different levels.

4. Write a proposal outlining your premise, characters, and environment.

5. Select clips from movies, videos, and video games that are similar to your game.

6. Using your sketches and the selected clips, pitch your proposal to your class.

Is this a video game that your classmates would be interested in playing?

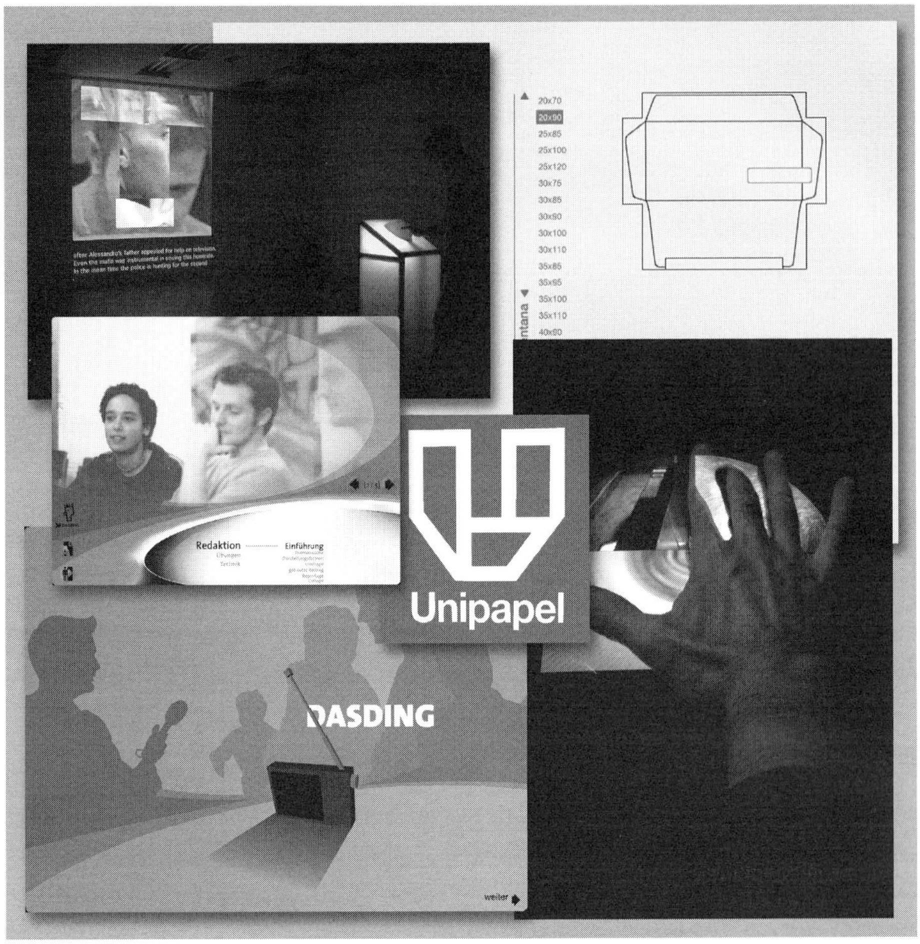

CHAPTER 12

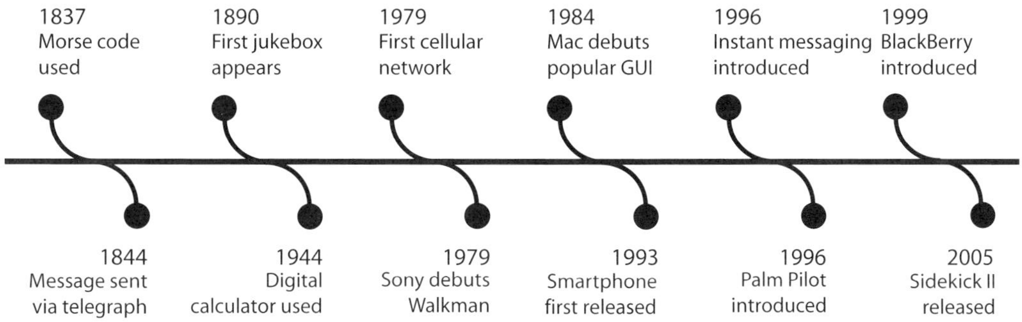

Chapter Objectives

Recognize the growing importance of interactive devices

Understand the audience and technical considerations for interface design

Learn to apply design principles to the rapidly expanding field of interactive design

Explore the growing possibilities available in the field of interactive design

Introduction

Interactive designers are required to look at all designs from the perspective of the technology, or machine, and also from the user's perspective. How the machine is programmed determines how the user can interact, and how the interface is designed determines how the user will want to interact.

In this world of instant results we have become entirely dependent on mobile interactive devices that connect us with others. We interact with computers and other devices on multiple occasions every day. In some instances we interact for practical purposes to withdraw money from the ATM, make a phone call on our cell phones, or heat up a TV dinner in our microwaves. In other instances, we interact purely for entertainment—when we surf the web, read the news on a PDA, or play a video game on a handheld player. Handheld devices are an integral part of our culture, and the vast majority of us own a cell phone, PDA, or personal gaming device. These devices, in conjunction with the modern technological delivery systems, enable us to carry information with us wherever we go, accessible at the touch of a button. Advancements with wireless systems allow us to also retrieve new information just as easily.

ANALOG VERSUS DIGITAL

Since the dawn of the industrial revolution, we have interacted with mechanical devices created and developed with the intent of automating many processes; the ultimate goal being to bring society into the modern age and make daily tasks easier. There have long been limitations on the usage and capabilities of mechanical designs. For example, typewriters were developed in a manner that compensated for the physical constraints of the device. The typewriter keys could not move quickly enough to handle very fast typing—the keys would hit each other as they moved up and down causing a malfunction. To compensate for this, the keys were laid out in such a way that frequently used letters were spaced to cause the typist to slow down. This QWERTY system (named for the first six keys from left to right on the top row of the keyboard) is what we still use today on all keyboards.

As we entered the digital age, such mechanical constraints were no longer the major drawback, but then we faced new problems. Digital issues became the concern, such as bandwidth, file size, and cross-platform compatibility. With mechanical devices there was typically only one way to interact with them, in a very linear fashion. When you pushed the key on a typewriter, the corresponding metal letter popped up, struck the inked ribbon, and the ink was transferred from the ribbon to the paper. Today's interactive devices offer many more choices, but unlike the manual functioning of the typewriter, users cannot always see how these additional options work. These options occur within the virtual world of the device and are therefore more conceptual. Users can often be confused or overwhelmed by choices in the nonlinear, multi-choice environment of interactive design. Interactive designers, and all motion graphics designers, must consider these drawbacks and compensate for them when appropriate.

DIGITAL CONVERGENCE

"McLuhan is out. The medium is no longer the message. . . . Today it's the mashup (mixed media devices) that is the message," declared Saul Hansell in his January 2006 *New York Times* article on digital **convergence**. Digital convergence is the current movement in which technological devices are becoming more versatile, serving several purposes and dealing with various media at once. As a result content for these devices may encounter a more varied audience as it is repurposed from one digital device to another.

Once upon a time every device served a specific purpose, not multiple tasks; moreover, it was the only device of its kind that could do its job. Television was once the only way to watch broadcasts, although at one point it appeared that Web TV might merge the Internet and the experience of television. Videos and DVDs were the medium of movies, viewable only in a theater, on TV, or in a home or portable player—the result of traditional media distribution. When computers originally entered people's homes, before the age of the Internet, they were simply devices for word processing and not seen as a means to communicate with others. But while each digital device once served a specific purpose, digital convergence is changing this idea. PDAs and cell phones are merged into one unit, allowing us to communicate via voice or Internet, while also updating our busy schedules and address books. Cell phones, digital cameras, and MP3 players have come together, allowing us to talk, listen to music, and even download broadcasts. Gaming, music, and video have

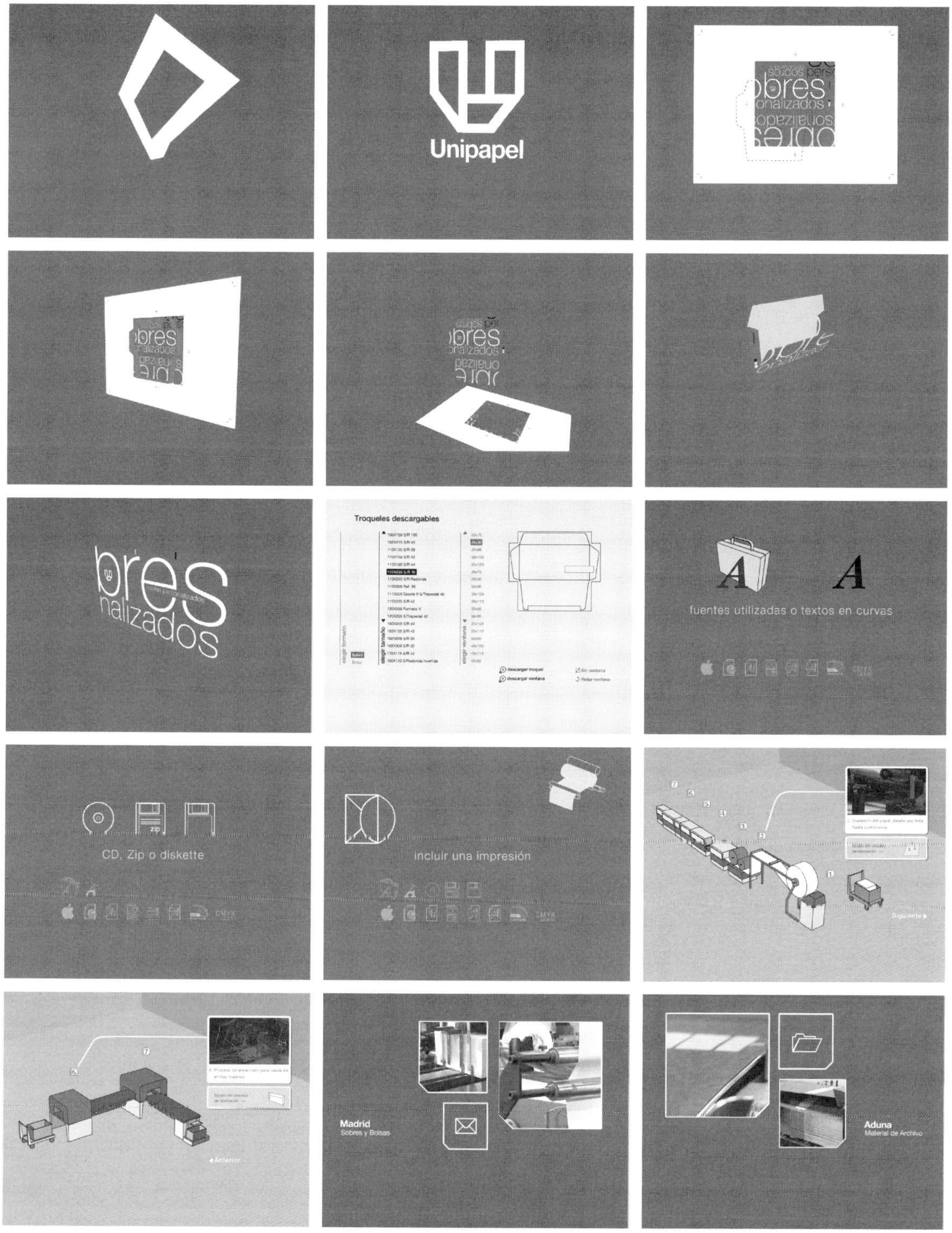

By Jan Mathias Steinforth (mateuniverse)

figure |12-1|

The interface for this CD-ROM for paper manufacturer Unipapel is intuitive and easy to follow. The goal was to design an interactive CD-ROM to show clients its line of high-tech envelopes. Animations help the viewer to visualize the product.

recently come to a single device with the introduction of PSP, produced by Sony, and the newer versions of Apple's iPod.

In much the same way that conglomeration in the 1980s and 1990s provided new sources of film content and new outlets for marketing and selling film products in Hollywood, digital convergence is revolutionizing the technology and entertainment industries because it creates new distribution outlets for large entertainment companies and independent artists alike. The merging of media entities with technology companies such as The Walt Disney Company with Apple allows a natural symbiotic relationship to take place: the entertainment company can supply content to be viewed on the technology company's device.

Music distributors can increase their audience by partnering with music downloading services, such as iTunes, to allow listeners to play their songs on their computers, cell phones, or other portable music devices. And the doors have opened to independent musicians and filmmakers, who no longer have to go through established studios or record labels for distribution but can market themselves through Internet websites. Even television networks are taking advantage of the Internet. They are using it as an outlet for surplus product or programming that they do not have space for on their regular channels. MTV announced during the summer of 2005 that the network would no longer include music videos in its regular programming—never mind the fact that MTV put itself on the map by being the first music channel, featuring music videos twenty-four hours a day. Realizing that their produced series, both reality and scripted, were what their audience and sponsors wanted, they opted to move music videos to airing in the wee hours of the morning and on the Internet. Similarly, NBC/Universal took its Trio Network off the air and placed it on the Internet. The Internet has become a veritable outlet mall where the networks can unload their surplus products and still make money. With so much digital media available from traditional and nontraditional sources, convergence will only continue to dominate the evolution of digital technology.

Not to be overlooked in their contribution to the convergence trend are technological accomplishments such as improved Internet access. With broadband technology and its increased speed and capacity for handling large bits of information, it is far more pleasurable to view videos on the Internet than it once was. As a result, more people use the Internet as a viable source for viewing news and movie clips as well as movies and music videos. The added benefit to using the Internet is the convenience of viewing what one wants, when one wants, and with the portability of the entertainment, where one wants. Increased availability of wireless accounts in airports, cafés, and other public spaces has also made it easier for audiences to take advantage of the content offered through wireless services on laptops.

Convergence does, however, offer some challenges. Entertainment companies that make their shows available for download on digital devices risk diminishing their traditional viewing audience by giving them the option to download their products instead of watching them on television or in the theater.[1] At the same time the technology moguls face competition from the latest device and from each other. Currently, cell phone manufacturers are courting the same audience as handheld manufacturers, because they both offer the option of downloading music, videos, and games. In order to triumph over the competition, each manufacturer will have to add a new function to its device that is not available on the competitions'.

But while consumers are happy to take advantage of the ability to download music or to snap photographs with their cell phones, they are less likely to take advantage of the full menu of services offered on what are known as the 3G (third generation) cell phones. The fact is that while the devices combine several features—camera, video monitor, music player, cell phone, game console, e-mail browser—the cost of the services to activate these features is too expensive, and consumers are not willing to pay for the added conveniences.[2] The challenge then becomes balancing the advantage of convenience with the cost of convenience. Only when the cost of using the services becomes more reasonable to the average consumer will the true value of convergence appeal to a larger section of the general public and thus fuel the profits of the technology moguls.

Finally, we must not forget about the digital designers who are also faced with a new challenge. In this world in which media can now be played on various devices and in which designers must design for a larger, more diverse audience, we have to think about how convergence will affect the future of design. The number of design considerations increases when creating for more than one medium at a time as it does

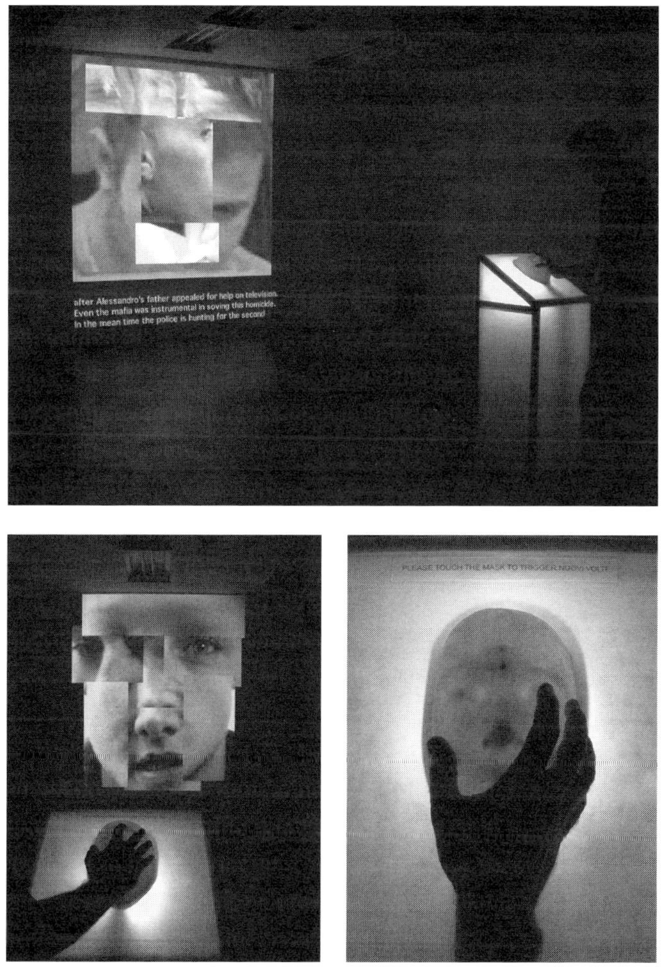

By Roberto Bocci

figure |12-2|

When creating this piece, *Nuovi Volti*, the artist considered how an audience would interact with it in a large physical space and then at home on DVD (seen in Chapter 10). *Nuovi Volti* is a multimedia piece that combines tangible, sculptural elements and digital technologies such as sound, video, and interactive software.

1 Saul Hansell, "As Gadgets Get It Together, Media Makers Fall Behind," *New York Times*, 25 Jan. 2006.

2 Ken Belson, "It Rings, Sings, Downloads, Uploads. But Can You Stand It?" *New York Times*, 20 Feb. 2006, C1.

when trying to appeal to a broader audience. The digital designer of the future must know how to apply traditional design theory while innovating for newer technologies.

MOTION GRAPHIC DESIGN FOR INTERACTIVE DEVICES

Interactive design is a newer and ever-growing field in the larger field of design. Interactive designers are responsible for not only the overall look of the finished design piece but also need to anticipate typical user interaction with the device. Interactive design is nonlinear with the viewer controlling the experience. A strong interactive design will be intuitive to the user. We are accustomed to following certain conventions in the process of interacting. First and foremost, we expect a reaction. When a user inputs information, she expects a response that is directly related to her action. The button on the ATM interface that says "withdraw cash" should produce the result of cash coming out of the machine.

As more media merge into one device, the interactive designer will be ever more challenged to design for multiple audiences with a wide variety of aesthetic interests. The technological capabilities that allow for better designing for the digital interface have grown exponentially over the past few years. Technology has opened the doors to more freedom for designers; more color choices, typeface choices, and smoother animation to name a few.

Having said this, though, an interactive designer must always consider the medium in which the design will be viewed. When designing for a cell phone, PDA, or other small portable device, the choice of typeface will differ greatly from the choice for a design that will be viewed on a digital kiosk. Above all else, when choosing a typeface for a portable device, select one that is legible. Legibility is especially important when reading text on a small screen. Often, the more stylized a typeface is, the more physical space it will take up on the screen, which will force the viewer to scroll through more text for the same information. A sans serif, narrow typeface may often be the optimal choice. It is also best not to use **anti-aliased** typefaces. Anti-aliasing is used to smooth the edges of a font to reduce the appearance of jagged edges of each letter. The effect of this on a small screen is soft or slightly blurry letters, making it difficult to read. **Aliased** typefaces have jagged edges, which increase legibility in a small space.

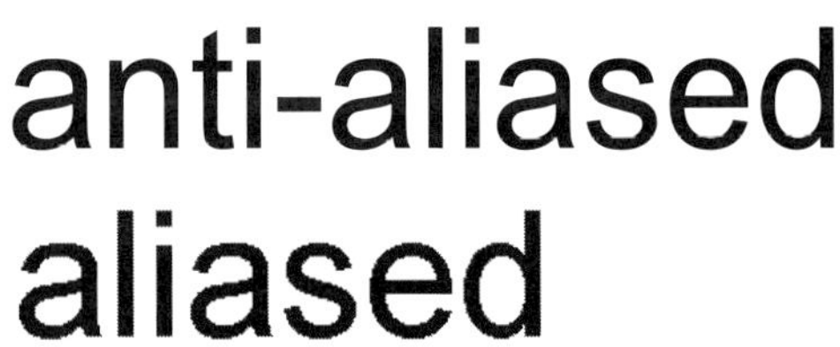

figure |12-3|

The jagged edges are visible on the aliased fonts, making it easier to read on a small screen.

Interactive designers have a solid foothold in the world of design, and work produced for the medium of digital devices is now being recognized. In November 2005, The National Academy of Television Arts & Sciences announced a new Emmy Award category for "original programming created specifically for non-traditional viewing platforms, including computers, mobile phones, PDAs and similar devices." With ever more programming being produced for digital devices, new avenues are opening for interactive designers. New ways of interacting with the traditional media of movies, television shows, and other broadcasts could be on the horizon.

Now more than ever, the digital designer for interactive media must find innovative ways of communicating with a large and varied audience through newer and sometimes complicated technologies. Robert Hall and Jung Yi Sin, design professionals, discuss how their creativity meet the challenges of designing for interactive interfaces.

▷ Professional Profile ◁

| *Robert Hall* |

Background

Years as a Designer/Developer: I have worked thirteen years professionally, but have done artwork all my life, and have been involved with computers since the age of twelve, back in the early 1980s.

Education: I graduated high school from Westminster Academy in Fort Lauderdale, Florida, and attended Broward Community College in Fort Lauderdale, Florida, off and on in the early nineties. I was working toward a Fine Arts degree, but I kept landing too much work and ended up getting so experienced in the field that I was unable to dedicate enough time to college to complete my degree. All of my computer and programming skills are self-taught, and I hope someday to go back and get a degree in computer science and human-computer interaction.

The Draw of Interface design

It is more of an evolution than a direct draw. Being able to apply my skills in new areas and constantly expanding and challenging myself seems to bring me to unique destinations throughout not only my career but my life. Interface design is just one stop among many that I've bumped into along this journey.

First Design Before Becoming a Professional

I'm not sure if it was the first or not, but the most memorable was a tribal-style tattoo logo for a T-shirt that I had designed for a local surf store, B.C. Surf and Sport. I knew the owner of the shop, Bruce Cromarty, a really great guy, and had been on their skateboard team, and hung out there all the time when I was younger. I delivered what I thought was a pretty good design, overcharged for it by a mile because of my lack of experience and youthful hubris. I'm not sure that it was ever even used. I later realized Bruce was just trying to help me out and get me some experience, which I really appreciated.

As for development, the first real application I built was a delivery tracking application for my father in QBasic—I wrote the application to allow my father to print out a list every morning for his delivery drivers at his business. It would sort the routes by Zip code so that the drivers were as efficient as possible. I also added a small amount of code so that when it printed a list for me, as I would often make deliveries during the summer for my father, the Zip codes would alternate between cross-town trips so that I could stay in the air-conditioned truck making deliveries out of the hot south Florida sun, instead of hurrying back to the garage to do menial tasks like taking out the garbage or cleaning the garage.

First Design Job

My first professional job was working for a local copy and print shop chain in Fort Lauderdale, CopyRight Centers of America. At the time it was like a really upscale Kinko's with their own pressroom, darkroom, computers, and more. It was a great job for me; looking back it was one of the most fun places I have ever worked. I worked the late shift when I first started. I came in at 3 p.m. and worked until 10 p.m., then I often stayed all night just experimenting and learning how to use all the equipment that was there. I started out as a basic designer and typesetter doing the simplest jobs, but eventually worked my way up the chain and reported directly to the owner and presidents of the company. Before I left I was in charge of pretty much all the technology departments and related decisions, training, you name it. This is when I first started to bring my focus to the web, in 1995, and programming again instead of pure design and artwork.

Process

Determining the Audience

To me, the main driver of how a UI [user-interface] or interface layer should be designed is dictated by the deployment method or device that the user will be interacting with. For a kiosk with a large touch-screen, this might lend itself to a certain style or requirement; if the touch-screen was outdoors and publicly accessible, you would need to consider lighting, ADA requirements, the age level of people using the device, et cetera. All these items and more come into play in determining the best way to design the interface. In this case bright, high-contrast iconic elements, which provide the user discrete commands rather than options, generally tend to work the best.

Recently with mobile device applications, the traditional notions of drop-down style menus and other familiar desktop user-interface paradigms has begun to evolve into a much more intuitive, contextually sensitive design. For example, creating a user-interface for a Flash Lite application on a Nokia mobile handset requires a different approach. Instead of using a traditional menu-based system to navigate, where a user makes a choice from a drop-down menu, you may now opt to use

| TIP |

The goal of interface design is to try to make things accessible in terms of the relationship of the content to the viewer or end user.

| NOTE |

Flash Lite, formerly owned by Macromedia and recently bought by Adobe, is technology specifically developed for mobile phones and other electronic devices. It is widely used in Japan and other parts of Asia to develop content-rich media and customized user-interfaces.

the five-way directional control. An even more effective, compelling, and intuitive method would be to provide direct access to additional content by allowing the display and content itself to become navigational elements.

The idea is to allow the content to help guide the user by providing contextual hints, rather than outright navigational elements such as a desktop application might employ. This method provides a more organic and natural feel to working with a device.

Every type of device and even its purpose can bring various elements into play, so a lot of planning and thought can, and should, go into any interface design. Everything you can think of, and then some things you won't think of until you have another set of eyes to look at or interact with it, will be important.

| TIP |

Focus groups and usability labs are great ways to determine where things are working and where they are not on a particular audience.

| THE INTERACTIVE DESIGN FOR DASDING KLASSEDING REPORTER |

DASDING Klasseding Reporter CD-ROM, designed by Jan Mathias Steinforth of mateuniverse, features over two hundred pictures, animation, and over three hours of audio material. This interactive CD-ROM was developed for teachers and students who want to learn to produce professional-quality sound bites for the radio. The specific needs and desires of this audience were considered before producing the final product. The CD-ROM offers explanations of the process, in-depth technical instructions, exercises that allow users to test their newfound knowledge, and an encyclopedia. Knowing who the audience is allows for a clear definition of content and presentation.

The audience further defines how the material is to be laid out, what style of graphics to use, and how complex the interactions should be. The material for DASDING is sensibly divided into easily digestible chunks of information, with a visually engaging interface. The graphics are compelling and aid in guiding the user through the screens within each section. Graphic buttons are visible in the same place on every page, creating a consistent interface with solid usability. Each button is an easy-to-decipher symbol, indicating a specific action: go home, print page, or exit presentation. It is vital that the user experience the desired reaction when interacting with the device.

By Jan Mathias Steinforth (mateuniverse)

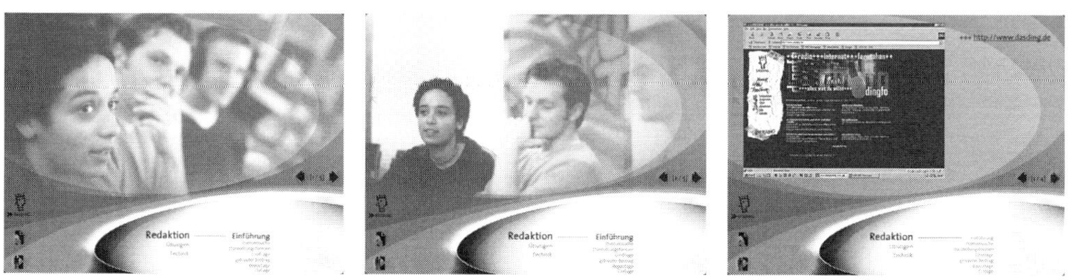

figure | 12-4 |

DASDING.

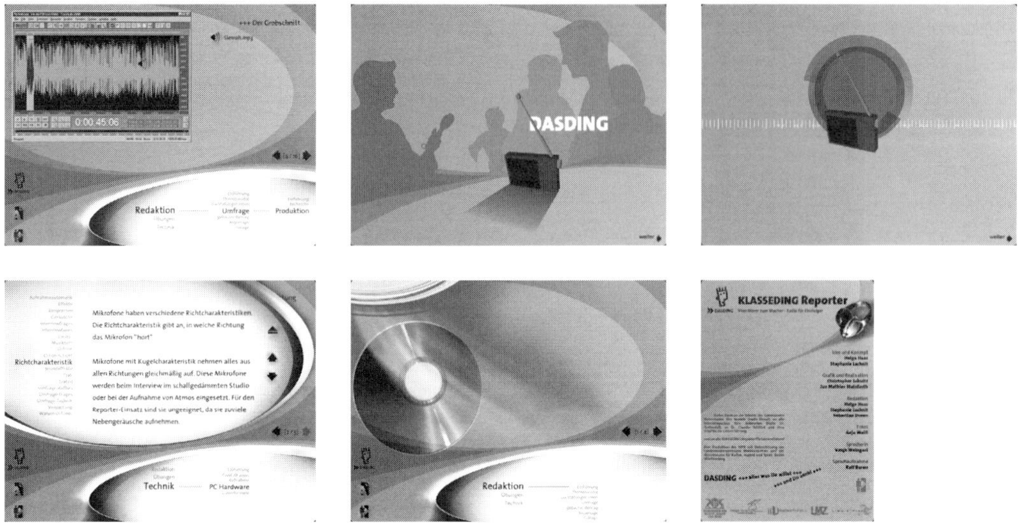

figure | 12-4 | (continued)

What Makes a Strong Interface Designer?

I feel a strong designer is someone who can convey the core ideas and elements of an interface and its purpose in the simplest and most elegant visual terms. There are a lot of designers who can make "Rube Goldberg" style, incredibly complex, dynamic and interesting interactive interfaces, and I certainly have a great deal of respect for that type of talent. However, for me, I think it's harder to reduce things to their barest, most simple forms and still provide an engaging and interesting interface. I agree that "less is more" is a good virtue to strive for, but it's not always what is best for the design.

As for developers writing code, there is always a balancing game you play with budgets, time, and client requirements, which always seem to be at odds with each other. I'd love to say that the ideal developer is someone who writes up nice UML diagrams, stubs out all their classes and functions, writes perfect code, perfectly commented, using all the best practices and industry recommendations, and using a source-code repository following an agile-development manifesto, but at the end of the day, that might not fit in with a budget or a time constraint. For me this is tough. I love it when I have a client or when working on projects where these are not luxuries, but requirements, and the right amount of time has been provided to do things properly. In my experience, that is hardly the norm, though, so a strong developer in my mind is someone who is knowledgeable, knows how to get answers to their questions in a timely fashion, is motivated, and can remain flexible at all points in a given process.

| TIP |

Flexibility is key in order to help maintain that constant balancing act between time, budget, and requirements.

Collaboration and Design

My process when working on something for myself is entirely different; it's really difficult to nail any one thing down. I gave up years ago on trying to come up with a logo for myself simply because I have too much freedom, I'll play with every typeface known to man, and come up with thousands of permutations. It is just the amount of freedom I give myself that is the key problem. I've tried working on that by setting simple goals and narrowing them down over time, which helps a great deal.

For projects for clients, I simply work backward from their detailed requirements. Typically, I'll sit down and really try to get a strong understanding of what the end product or application is in the mind of the client; from there everything is outlined, and each pass back through, you try to add another layer until you can't go any deeper. This again is tempered with budgets and timetables. Coming from a printing/prepress background is really helpful. In that business, if you don't capture every detail of what the client wants and expects, the first time you go to press you won't have the opportunity to fix it without potentially losing thousands of dollars. You have to get it right the first time. Software development really goes against this idea, as it can be such an iterative process if you don't have all the details and requirements nailed down initially.

When I'm working on something in a group or collaborating on a project, communications are the key piece of the puzzle. Having everyone on the same page, in regards to materials, requirements, deadlines, budgets, even the smallest details available to all team members, in my opinion makes things go much smoother. Not everyone has to react or act on all items at all levels, but having everyone familiar with all aspects of a project always lends itself to a better result in my personal experience. Working specifically with software development, a centralized source-code repository system like Subversion or other similar systems are great tools to facilitate collaboration in a development environment.

| TIP |

Communications tools are key in collaboration—the phone and e-mail are your friends.

Challenges and Overcoming Them

I feel that the biggest challenge that comes in interface design and development is having to compromise. Compromises on functionality, compromises on usability, compromises on budgets, compromises on design. Each project has its own set of challenges, but having to juggle the compromises that have to be made to deliver something that is balanced, intuitive, and functional can often be a source of frustration. I have found that designers and developers who are passionate about their work often have a hard time taking criticism and making compromises in order to meet client expectations, budgets, or simple changes based on personal preferences or opinions. Some of the best designers and developers I have worked with actually look at having to make compromises and re-designs as challenges they want to tackle, rather than challenges that impede them or prevent them from expressing their creativity. The ability to remain as flexible as possible allows the creativity to continue to flow and lends itself toward surmounting compromises that have to be made.

User Expectations

I can't really answer this for a hypothetical group, but I personally gravitate toward clean, simple designs that are intuitive and easy to use without a great deal of explanation. The more complex an application becomes, the more difficult it is to retain a clean, consistent flow from state to state. I love designs that challenge a user's notion of what is normal, as long as it is intuitive. Some controls on newer consumer devices provide some really compelling experiences. Nearly everyone is familiar with Apple's iPod clickwheel interface; it's easy to use, functional, and intuitive. Iriver has an MP3 player, the U10, which has video, Flash Lite, and other advanced features. They chose an even simpler navigation system, a four-way control simply by pressing on each side of the device; it's simple and effective. Combined with the navigation style they designed into the interface, four directional clicks seems like it wouldn't be enough, but in reality it's more than enough as long as proper thought and planning are put into coming up with the user experience. I loathe every remote control in my house for my stereo, TV, VCR, DVD, even my Xbox controller. They are covered in dozens of buttons, and I hate it. I want five buttons, one for each direction and a selection button. If you have an onscreen control system, that is all you really need. I think Apple believes in this tenet, as shown by their recent iMac with Remote to control their new Front Row application.

Signature Components

I don't really feel I have yet developed a signature style that would visually differentiate my application development and design work from others in any significant way. However, I feel that perhaps over time I think that it's possible something will emerge. I feel that is primarily the result of doing work for clients, and committing to bring their visions to life as opposed to being a pure visual artist catering to sharing my own personal ideas, whims, and expressions. If I were to show you some of my personal artwork, it would be much easier to discern my external influences than looking at an application or design for a client.

Future of Interface Design

I have a lot of hopes for Macromedia Flash and Flash Lite. They really understand the potential for utilizing Flash for UIs in other areas than the desktop. From consumer devices like digital cameras, MP3 players, PDAs, to cell phones, to car navigation systems, and the list goes on. Licensing the Flash player to third parties to implement into their control systems is going to be a big source of revenue for Macromedia/Adobe, and I am betting my career on following them down this road. More and more device manufacturers are taking notice and realizing the potential as well.

A perfect example is Kodak's EasyShare-One camera. It's a 4-megapixel camera, not that much by today's standards, but what it lacks in megapixels and resolution, it makes up for in usability and other features. It is one of the first cameras on the market to feature built in WiFi connectivity via an SDIO WiFi card. This allows you to e-mail and send photos directly from the camera to an online gallery or your friends via e-mail. You can even crop your images interactively on the screen before you send them. Additionally, the camera can even connect and browse your online gallery directly from the camera. It also features a large three-inch touchscreen and an included stylus to make navigation much simpler. Kodak chose to license the Flash player from Macromedia, as they realized it was a perfect solution to their needs. By adding all these rich features, they knew that they needed to provide a very intuitive, easy-to-navigate device and control user experience. I simply can't imagine any other way that they could have effectively implemented this set of features in the time frame they were allotted to bring the product to market.

I think over time as devices become increasingly complex simply due to the richness of their features and capabilities, that the key challenge will be determining how to provide an effective and intuitive user experience. Reinventing the wheel for each new device UI is going to be counterproductive; this is where Flash really shines, it provides seamless programming capabilities and rich visual, auditor, and interactive experiences that can be moved relatively painlessly from the desktop to a plethora of devices. I'm really counting on the widespread adoption of Flash for user experiences on a variety of upcoming devices. ◁

▷ Professional Profile ◁

| *Jung Yi Sin* |

Background

Years as a Designer: 8

Education: BFA from William Paterson University, with a major in Communication Design and minor in Art History; MFA in Design and Technology from Parsons School of Design

The Draw of Design

Coming from the fine arts training, the idea of making my art digital seemed sexy. I thought it was "cool" to create things, which people will buy and see. Also, by designing I thought I was becoming a trendsetter. I was only eighteen and naïve, and had no idea what design was "really" about.

Deriving from the fine arts training, the idea of making my art digital and commercial seemed appealing. Although the way to express my artistic aesthetics was more commercially driven, I liked the idea of influencing the industry with my aesthetic philosophy. I thought I was becoming a part of the trendsetting and that idea seemed important.

First Design Before Becoming a Professional

Growing up in a house of tailors there were always fabrics and sewing materials lying around. I once used scraps of fabric, strings, chiffon, and a button to make a chick carrier: It was made to be worn around the neck. I loved animals, but living in the city, dogs and cats were too much work so I was only allowed to have chicks every spring. I wanted to carry my chick around, like the way people took their dogs for a walk. Since you can't put a chick on a leash, I decided to make a carrier. The materials were made of wool, because the chicks caught colds very easily and often died from it. The carrier had the flap with a button to secure the chick in case it tried to break out. There was also a hole that allowed the chick to expose its head, and a white chiffon to deflect the sun in case it was too bright or too hot. I knew that my design failed when I carried the chick out in the carrier on a hot sunny day and it had a nosebleed. The materials must've been too hot and the chiffon did not reflect the sun enough. I felt really bad. I was about nine at the time.

First Professional Design Job

My first job was at a foreclosure real estate magazine as a designer.

Design Process

How Do You Determine the Design for an Audience?

It depends. Every design project has a different audience, so I think about the cultural and social behavior of that particular audience. I think about the kind of design they may be exposed to and try to introduce something that is different but within the parameters of what they may be used to and what they know. So I may integrate design elements that are out of the targeted audience realm to intensify the engagement with my design, or I may integrate several familiar design icons or elements to allure a bigger audience.

What Makes a Strong Interface Designer?

I believe a strong interface designer is a well-informed individual who can integrate function and form fluidly. Designers must study the audience. They must think intuitively, like the audience, but still be able to introduce their vision thus achieving their intent with the design. Being well informed about the scope of the project and knowing all the detailed components that make up the project is essential.

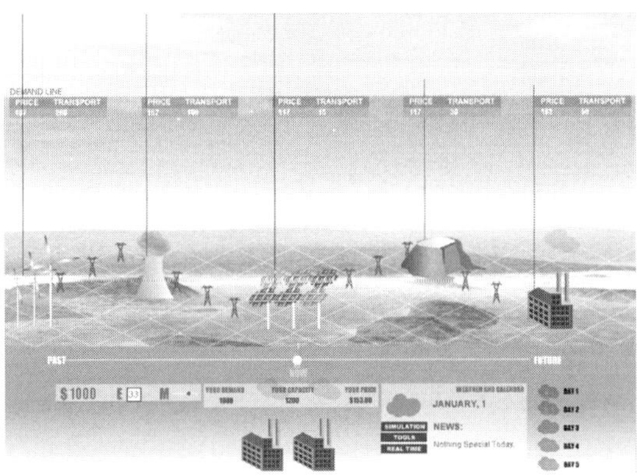

By Jung Yi Sin

figure |12-5|

Interactive interface on the web platform.

To measure the success of an interface design is to see how well the audience can use the design; there should be no difficulties. Hence, not only must the designer consider the logistics between the user and the interface, she must cater to the user's needs. A good interface designer will allow users to walk away thinking that they achieved their goal within the fluidity of the design. If this happens, the users actually walked away with the designer achieving her goal. I believe the content/concept design along with great visual aesthetics draws the users to partake in the process of the design, as if the users agree to the process of the design iteration because they see themselves during the process. A good interface designer will allure the audience with simplicity—user's fundamental behavior of interaction—then leading them to achieve actions and understandings of the designer's concept. Designers must always try the "happy" innovation and medium approach. What I mean by "happy" is that users want to feel satisfied, fulfilled, accomplished, or enjoying the moments of viewing or interacting with any design, print, or interactive.

Is There a Different Process for Designing for Self versus Designing for a Client?

Not really. When I design for myself, I become the user so I analyze myself in hope that my design piece will be functional to my needs when I see it or use it.

Collaboration

When I'm collaborating with other designers, I try to observe the strong points of other designers and try to adjust my strong points. Although I may be better at designing the interface, if there is another designer who I think fits the job better, I will find my next strong point in hope to satisfy the need of the group and the project.

Challenges of Interface Design

Assumptions. Because interface design relies on interactivity with an audience, even with all the research, logistics, and concept theory, if people don't get it then your design fails. I can't just assume that because the design makes sense to me, it will make sense to others. I have to user test, design more, and then test it again. It does sometimes discourage you and slow your design process because of the time lapse between initial concept and fruition of the final product.

User Expectations and the Introduction of New Ideas

First, users expect to see something they are familiar with. Depending on the project, the idea of familiarity may vary in content or elements. For my "haptic glove" interface, I used the concept of sharing through the actions of contact. Socially, when we come in contact with others in any shape or form, we expand our personal space. It's like giving an approval to share our space with others. Universally, we shake hands when we introduce ourselves; it's almost like an approval to open ourselves to others. Deriving from this fundamental understanding of touch/contact, I've designed an interface that allows the users to mix and create music by touching each other's hand. Each person has a circuit that plays a sound that is different from the others. Each person also wears a glove, which when in contact with other gloves combines the sound of the touched gloves.

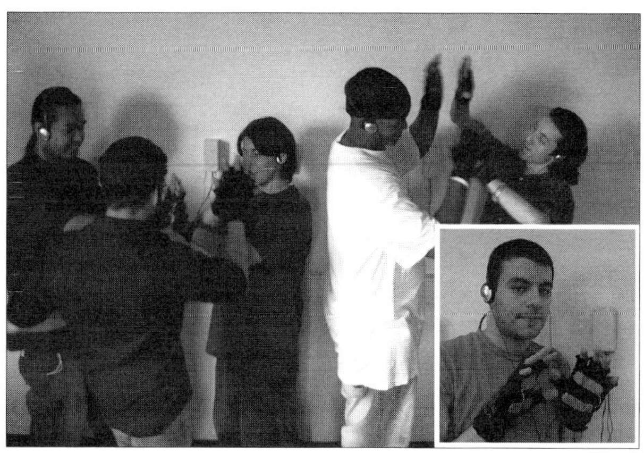

By Jung Yi Sin

figure 12-6

Sometimes with the introduction of a new style of interaction, the viewer needs to be educated as to how to correctly use it for optimal results.

I transfer something of the familiar to the unfamiliar or integrate one familiar with another familiar, which when combined together does not really exist in our physical/real environment. This is what I do with the abstract or virtual, but it can also be applied to the physical form, and I can use the same formula. For example, a telephone made out of shoes would integrate two familiars, the shoe and the telephone, into a new unfamiliar that did not previously exist. Integrating two familiar concepts into one context alters the original meaning of both. Basically, this is how I bring humor to altered design ideas. Nothing is ever really new.

Signature Design Style

I follow the rules of design 80 percent of the time, doing all that you are supposed to, according to design books, but then I add 20 percent of what I think people will disagree with. This makes it more interesting, to give more identity to the design. My formula is 40 percent function, 40 percent aesthetics, 20 percent purely me, my quirky personality.

Future of Interface Design

In the future everything will be wireless and location based, and people will be more mobile because information will be mobile. The structure of how we integrate ourselves to the digital world will change, and the digital world will follow our natural structure of living. Information will also change based on location, not just on the idea of supply and demand. How we present information, form, and visual design will depend on our physical environment because we've lived through the era of the virtual world. The idea of virtual will live amongst our physical world.

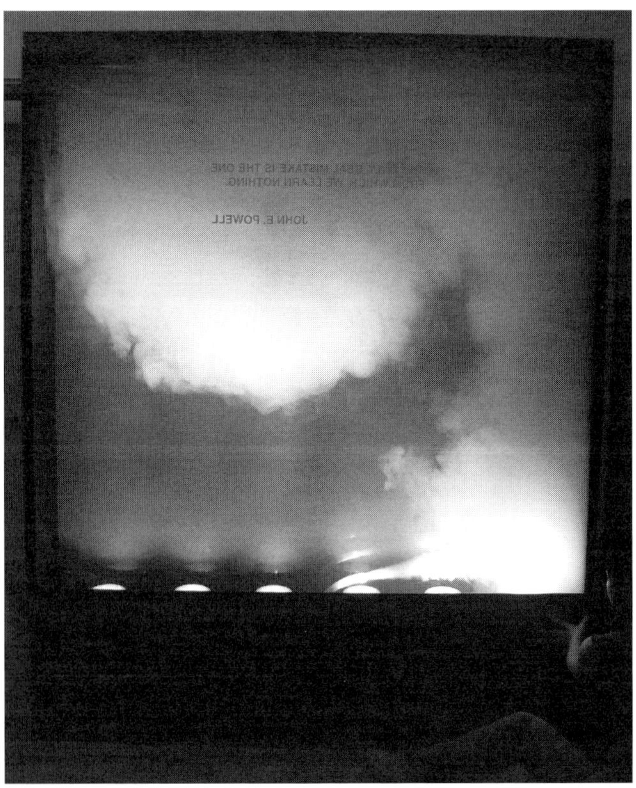

By Jung Yi Sin

figure |12-7|

Physical interface.

I think the next big change for designers is taking the idea of websites and making it accessible in the physical environment. The web interface has conditioned our process of information sorting. As interfaces begin to appear in buildings and public spaces, future designers should be able to interpret the same information sorting process as an interactive, three-dimensional information interface.

How we want to communicate will determine the kind of material. Today, much information is processed digitally, and many may assume that the use of paper is fading. I disagree. I believe that the concept of paper is changing but not disappearing. Much like designing an interface to conjure specific feelings and nuances, the paper itself has a specific functionality: it is a tactile interface. One's writing on a paper conveys emotions like no current design can ever produce. The paper—mobile and with no interactive features like the web—displays the intimacy of one's handwriting or doodling, hence the experience of reading a letter becomes special and personal. The tactile process of opening, unfolding, and seeing the details of human touch will convey emotions and it will always co-exist with the future information display products. Paper will be an ancient novelty and timeless. It will only take on different cultural meaning as we humans constantly redesign different ways to communicate.

| AUDIENCE RESPONSE TO DIGITAL DESIGNS |

Artists have long explored how an audience interacts with their work. The artist creates an environment in which the viewer becomes immersed, completely enveloped in the piece. Often the viewer is able to interact with the piece without any intrusive and unintended noise or interference. The artist controls the viewer's interaction with the work. The space in which the piece is presented is controlled, so the viewer's physical interaction is dictated. With interactive, or installation, art, viewers make a conscious decision to participate with the work and therefore offer more of their undivided attention to the piece.

This differs greatly from the amount of control motion graphics designers have over their viewers and the amount of attention one is willing or able to give. Viewers maintain the majority of control with any interactive design and expect that at any time during the interaction they can skip to the desired destination in the piece, or if unable to do that, exit the presentation, either to start over and try again, or simply end the interaction.

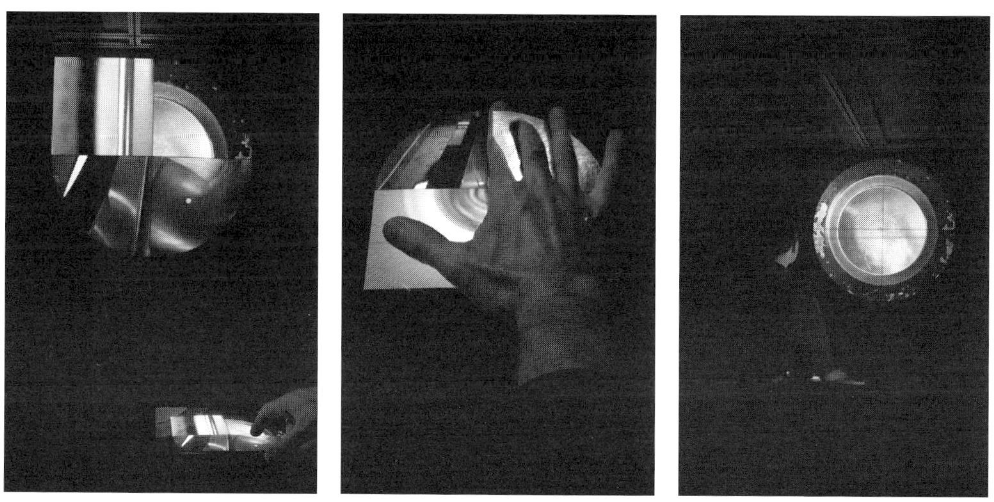

By Roberto Bocci

figure |12-8|

Cycles of Confusion is an interactive multimedia installation that uses digital technologies and programming to combine sound, video, and interactive design. The viewer is surrounded by images and sounds and interacts with the piece in a large space.

By Anne Holst, Jean-Marc Matos, and Antoine Schmitt (K. Danse Company)

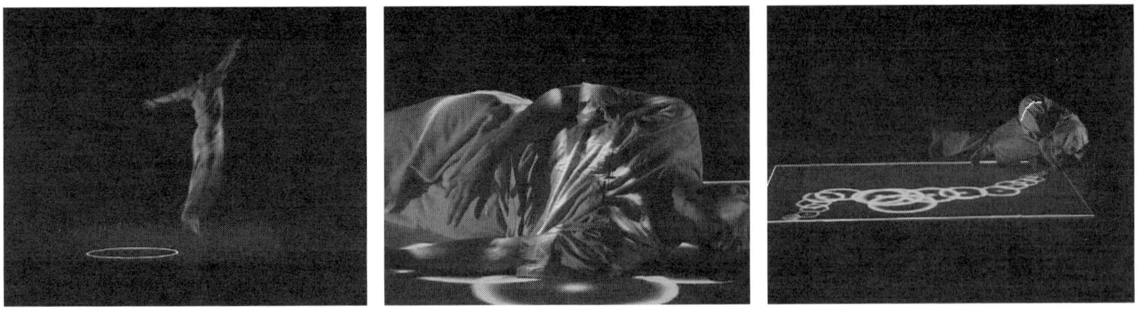

figure |12-9|

Game Play is an encounter between dance and programmed art. In a choreographic show, a dancer is confronted with a visual and sonic semi-autonomous environment that is sensitive to his presence.

SUMMARY

We use interactive devices on a daily basis. Because the mechanisms that make a digital device work are internal, the user cannot always see and understand the numerous choices available. This is why interface designers must strongly consider the user in their designs. Once the interactive piece is released to the user, designers no longer have control over the interaction. The device needs to be clear and intuitive, with an easy-to-use interface and engaging design. As other media like music, television, and the Internet continue to merge, design for digital devices continues to evolve, thus presenting designers with new challenges and new venues for their design.

in review

1. What is the difference in the way analog and digital devices work?
2. How does the user influence the design of a digital interface?
3. In what ways are digital media merging, and how does that affect the field of interface design?

exercises

Exercise

Design an interface for a national park. The interface should be able to be used on a multitude of platforms: an interactive kiosk housed at the park, the website, and downloads of information and trail maps to the user's cell phone or PDA.

Process and Research

Choose a national park and gather information about it.

- What kinds of services does the park offer?
- What kinds of information will your visitors need? Lodging? Activities? Food services?
- Information about wildlife?
- Information about the area's geology?
- What is the best possible way to present all of this information?

Inspiration

Because of the amount of information these kiosks, websites, and downloads will provide, information architecture will be a key part of your design. Group your information in a logical and digestible manner to facilitate ease of use. For example, your main menu may contain the following information:

- Park Services
- Lodging and Food Services
- Park History
- Nature Education

Upon selecting "Park Services," the next menu might read:

- Emergency Guest Services
- Guided Hikes and Nature Walks
- Ranger-led Activities
- Children's Programs
- Animal Exhibits

Selecting the "Guided Hikes and Nature Walks" menu could then lead you to yet another menu that would offer a list and description of the hikes and tours along with their times. What is important is that the information is broken down into manageable groups.

Although you are designing an interface for three different media, your mission for each is the same—to present information in as clear and as interesting a manner as possible. At the same time, each interface must also be easy to navigate. While the technical considerations for each medium may require that you change some elements of your design from medium to medium, you can still use a consistent motif that flows throughout all of them.

- Colors could be a unifying factor. Does the national park have special park colors? If not, you may choose colors found in nature such as greens, browns, yellows, and blues.
- Type style and graphics can also be a running motif. Choose one that is both communicative and works within the composition of the page. Because the screen of a kiosk or a computer is bigger than that of a PDA, you will have to choose fonts that read well on a small screen as well as a larger screen. Whereas you may have chosen a font with serifs for a webpage, one without serifs is easier to read on the small screen of a cell phone or PDA.
- What is the park's logo? How can you include it in your design?
- Composition may also be affected by the screen size of the medium. Less information can be displayed at a time. This may require alternative grouping of information. When planning composition, design for each individual medium. If there is variation, that is okay because the colors, fonts, and graphics will be similar across the different media.
- How will you incorporate sound for each medium? While visitors may take kindly to a talking kiosk that walks them through the menu, Internet users may see talking as an imposition. Think about what sounds would be effective for a website. A PDA may not be equipped to run sound. Even if that is the case, the visual design should be strong enough to communicate on its own without the use of sound.

Method

1. Sketch out a template for a menu design for a website, and think about composition and presentation of information.

2. Sketch out a template menu design for a kiosk.

3. Sketch out a template menu design for a PDA.

4. Once you are satisfied with the presentation of information and the type style for each of your menus, do mock-ups of each page of each menu. Aim for consistency in color and graphics across the three media.

5. Execute your designs for each medium. You can do your kiosk and PDA information in Flash and your website in Dreamweaver.

6. Run your kiosk from Flash. Does the sound work when it is supposed to? Do all of the links take you to the correct menus?

7. Upload your website. Do your links work? Check the website in different browsers (Explorer, Safari) to see that it runs and looks as you designed it.

8. Download your menus to your PDA. Can you read and follow the information?

9. Show all three interfaces to an audience and have it interact with each.

How did your audience respond to your designs? Did it find them easy to navigate? Did your viewers get all of the information they wanted? What did you learn from the process?

glossary

A

achromatic—Absence of color; a color scheme using only white, gray, and black.

action safe—The designated area in which an image will be displayed when viewed on television or other video screen.

additive color system—Used for screen views; red, green, and blue are the primary colors.

aliased—The appearance of jagged edges around images or letters.

analogous—Colors directly next to each other on the color wheel.

anti-aliased—The appearance of smooth edges around images and letters.

apparent motion—Illusion of seeing movement in continuous single frames due to the fact that the image in each successive frame has changed position slightly.

artificial intelligence—Refers to the way in which video game characters are programmed to respond to a player's actions during a game.

ascenders—Strokes of a letter that rise above the meanline.

avatar—Graphic used in electronic communication that serves as a personal identifier.

B

baseline—Invisible line that text sits on.

Bauhaus—German school of design, started in 1919, which espoused the principles of form working together with function.

bitmap—See *raster*.

blinkies—See *avatar*.

bug—Station logo placed in the lower quadrant of the television screen.

C

cel—A clear sheet of celluloid used in traditional animation. Due to the cel's transparency, when animators draw on it, they are able to composite images from different cels to create one complete picture.

chunking—Grouping like elements together.

color—All hues, including all levels of saturation and value.

clash—A color scheme using one color plus the color directly to the left or right of its complement.

closure—Tendency to perceive a set of individual elements as one recognizable pattern.

collage—An experimental film technique that entails gathering different textures, images, and drawings and placing them together to create a single picture.

color bars—Appear at the beginning of video to match color from device to device and ensure broadcast quality.

color wheel—A visual aid for showing primary, secondary, and tertiary colors in any color system.

common fate—Objects moving in the same direction are perceived as being related whether or not they are.

communication model—Different scenarios for conversation or interaction that include a sender, a receiver, and a message.

complementary—Colors directly across each other on the color wheel.

compositing—Layering images from different sources to create a single image.

computer animation—Using a computer to achieve either 2-D, 3-D, or experimental animation.

content real estate—Division of images, text, navigation, and other elements on the screen.

convergence—A trend in which single digital devices are able to perform multiple functions and play different types of media.

cool colors—Greens, blues, and purples.

cut—Instantaneous transition from one source to the next.

cut scenes—Scenes that play at set points during a video game and are therefore not under the influence of the game's player.

D

desaturated—Low levels of pure hue.

descenders—Strokes of a letter that fall below the baseline.

direct-on-film—A method of experimental filmmaking in which the filmmaker draws, paints, scratches, or burns images directly onto celluloid.

dispersion—Elements all scattered about the frame.

dissolve—Transparency levels of two overlapping sources that are altered during transition.

E

emoticons—Graphics used in electronic communication that represent an emotion.

exclusion—All elements but one are grouped together in the frame.

F

flicker fusion—The phenomenon that causes the eye to perceive separate static images as one constant image when the images occur at a certain speed per second. In the case of film, the eye perceives a constant image at twenty-four frames per second. With video it is thirty frames per second.

frame—Smallest component of film or video. Twenty-four frames make up a single second of film. Thirty frames make up a single second of video.

frame rate—The rate at which single frames appear on screen to compose a single second of screen time.

G

gathering—Elements all grouped together in one quadrant of the frame.

Gestalt principles of perception—Explains how we perceive the graphic elements we see.

golden ratio—Ratio elements within a form; specifically width to height.

grid—Set of imaginary lines that equally divide the design space.

H

hue—A visible color on the color spectrum.

I

icon—Most closely resembles the sign with recognizable features; an example is a photograph.

ideograph—Simple drawing that represents an idea or abstract thought.

index—An action that is understood universally and is the physical manifestation of the sign in semiotics.

K

kerning—Adjusting the space between two characters.

kinetoscope—Invented by Thomas Edison and his assistant, W. K. L. Dickson, in 1891, it played back films shot with the kinetograph camera. Individual viewers could watch films through a peephole at the top.

L

leading—Refers to the amount of space between lines of copy.

legibility—Measures the ability to successfully read words as they are placed in the overall design.

M

meanline—Invisible line that sits atop lowercase letters.

mise-en-scene—Literally, *put on the stage*; everything that appears on screen that helps the audience understand the story.

monochromatic—A color scheme using one hue with the shades or tints of that hue.

N

noise—Any type of interference that hinders communication.

O

off-center—An element positioned to the left or right on screen.

optical center—Natural center of the frame, based on our perception, not actual measurements.

P

persistence of vision—Theory formerly used to explain how motion was perceived in film. It was believed that when the human eye retained a memory of an image a moment after it had disappeared, the various still images merged on the retina to become a moving image.

pictograph—Simple drawing that represents a specific object.

pigment color system—Defined by non-digital colors, such as paint. The primary colors are red, yellow, and blue.

pinboard—An experimental form of animation created by pushing or pulling pins on a screen, thus creating images by the variation of shadows, grays, blacks, and whites.

pinscreen—See *pinboard*.

pixel—Picture element; the smallest component of a raster graphic, a single dot.

pixilation—See *stop-motion animation*.

polygon—Simplest component of a video game character; when manipulated and combined with other polygons the character's form is created.

pre-production—The planning process that precedes production and usually entails brainstorming, sketching roughs, storyboarding, and getting client approvals.

primary colors—The three main colors from which all other color is created in any color system.

push—One source is pushed out of the frame by another source during transition.

R

raster—Any graphic made up of pixels.

readability—Measures the ability to decipher the shapes of the letters that form a word.

rotoscoping—Filming live-action footage and then hand-drawing over each frame in order to create realistic movement in animation.

rule of thirds—The imaginary division of a grid into horizontal and vertical thirds; designers use the intersect points as guides for dynamic placement of elements within the design frame.

S

sand animation—Experimental animation technique that animates different shades of sand using the stop-motion technique.

sans serif—The lack of a finishing stroke off of the main stroke of a letter.

saturation—Intensity or amount of pure hue.

secondary colors—The three colors made from combinations of the primary colors in any color system.

semiotics—Study of signs and their relationship to the actual object they represent.

serif—The finishing stroke that emerges from the main stroke of a letter.

shades—Darker values of a hue.

sign—In semiotics, the written word or actual object.

signified—In semiotics, the concept or idea elicited from signifier.

signifier—In semiotics, the spoken word that refers to a concept.

slide—One source enters the frame covering the other static source.

snype—Mini advertisement for upcoming show that appears in the lower quadrant of the television screen.

spectral band—Shows all colors we are able to see with the naked eye.

split complementary—Three colors on the color wheel: one plus colors from both sides of its complement.

station ID—Identifier of logo of the television station, shown during commercial breaks.

stop-motion animation—A technique used to animate objects by stopping the camera, adjusting the position of an object in the frame, and shooting one frame at a time; also referred to as *pixilation*.

stop-motion camera—A technique used to make objects appear or disappear on screen by stopping the camera and adjusting the position of an object in the frame.

storyboard—Sketches used to aid in the initial development of a design.

subtractive color system—Used for printed materials; cyan, magenta, and yellow are the primary colors.

symbol—Represents the idea or concept of the sign without any recognizable features of the sign itself.

T

tertiary colors—The colors made from combinations of primary and secondary colors in any color system.

tint—Lighter values of a hue.

title cards—Placards with text used to convey information about the storyline or production of the film to the audience.

title safe—The designated area in which type will be displayed without risk of distortion when viewed on television or other video screen.

tracking—Equally adjusting the space between letters in a word, sentence, or paragraph.

traditional color system—See *pigment color system*.

V

value—Overall darkness or lightness of the hue.

vector—Graphic made up of computer code, composed of 0s and 1s.

visual hierarchy—Laying out graphic elements in a manner that confers different levels of visual importance to each element.

W

warm colors—Oranges, yellows, and reds.

webbing—A form of brainstorming that entails making connections between words associated with a particular concept.

weight—How thin or thick the stroke of a letter is.

width—How narrow or wide an individual letter is.

wipe—Typically, a graphic shape that reveals or hides one source during transition to the next source.

word association—A form of brainstorming that entails making a list of words that are connected to a particular concept.

appendix

Bill Byrne
sirwildbill@rocketmail.com
http://www.billbyrne.net

Luis Cataldi
luiscataldi@hotmail.com

Dorian J. Compo
dorian@rekonstrukt.com
http://www.rekonstrukt.com

Mark Ezovski
mark@diabolicalbrain.com
http://www.diabolicalbrain.com

Henry Ferrini
henry.ferrini@verizon.com
http://www.ferriniproductions.com

Danny Glix
d@dannyglix.com
http://www.dannyglix.com

Robert M. Hall
rhall@impossibilities.com
http://www.impossibilities.com

Carlos Lema
carlos.lema@carlos-lema.com
http://carlos-lema.com

Carlos Pisco
carlospisco@eyepop.com
http://www.eyepop.com

Jung Yi Sin
jungyisin@jungyisin.com
http://jungyisin.com

Jeffrey Sproul
mcphloo@yahoo.com
http://www.jeffsproul.net

Jan Mathias Steinforth
info@mateuniverse.com
http://www.mateuniverse.com

T2 (TakeTwo)
Nick Balda
nbalda@t2.tv
http://www.t2.tv

T2 (TakeTwo)
Linda Buchner, Director of Marketing
lbuchner@t2.tv
http://www.t2.tv

T2 (TakeTwo)
Darton Simons
dsimons@t2.tv
http://www.t2.tv

Prithvi Virasinghe
virasinghe@gmail.com
http://virasinghe.com

Roger White
whitelied_2000@yahoo.com
http://www.rogerwhite.com

index

INDEX

D

E

F

G

H

T